MW01036842

Immortal Memories

Immortal Memories

A Compilation of Toasts
To the Immortal Memory
of
ROBERT BURNS
as delivered at Burns Suppers
around the world
together with other orations,
verses and addresses
1801 - 2001

Selected and Edited
with an introduction and commentary by
JOHN CAIRNEY

Luath Press Limited
EDINBURGH
www.luath.co.uk

First Published 2003

The paper used in this book is recyclable. It is made from low-chlorine pulp produced in a low-energy, low-emission manner from renewable forests.

Typeset in 10 point Sabon by S. Crozier, Nantes.

Printed and bound by
Creative Print and Design, Ebbw Vale

To Dr Alan M. Marchbank
and our fellow members
of the Nine

Contents

Acknowledgements

First of all, I must gratefully acknowledge all the contributors for their Memories and to all those hundreds of people around the world who took the time to reply to my letters, e-mails, faxes and phone calls. Their response and continued co-operation made a seemingly impossible job possible.

This is the kind of book that could not have been written at all had it not been for so many others. Since, however, it was based on Burns, I had first call on that high table of Burns doctors – Jim Mackay, Maurice Lindsay, Tom Crawford, Ken Simpson, Marshall Walker and the work of the late Donald Low in Stirling. Without help such as this it is impossible to embark on Burnsiana of any kind.

There is also the assistance received from Margaret Craig at the Burns Federation in Kilmarnock, Donald Nelson at the Mitchell Library in Glasgow and Christopher Neale at the Murison Collection in Dunfermline. They must all have played a part in every book written about Burns over the last decade. Thanks to their assistance I was able to plunder the pages of almost every *Burns Chronicle* that ever was and any Burns book printed and if information was required locally here in New Zealand, then Janet Copsey and her staff at the Auckland University Library came to the rescue.

Thanks must also go to His Grace, the Earl of Elgin for his introduction to the minutes of the Dunfermline United Burns Club and, for their material help, similar appreciation must be accorded to Dr Alan Riach at Glasgow University, Dr Jim and Elma Connor of London, Ontario (who sent me their book on Canadian Burns Memories), James Skinner OBE of the Paisley Burns Club for invaluable information and Ian Blair of the Channel Islands who told me of the Burns Club of St Louis and their printed collection of Speeches and loaned me his own copy of Ross's Burns Addresses. In like manner, I must thank Norrie Paton of Campbeltown for his tapes, Colin Hunter McQueen in Glasgow for his general Burns enthusiasm, Frank Ryan in Dumfries for local contacts, Mrs Nancy Norman of Masterton, New Zealand for material and my old friend and fellow-actor, David McKail, in Kent who offered his usual help and encouragement.

Finally I must give my gratitude and total admiration to young Jean Lim of Auckland who transcribed all the material that came in on to disc so that I might work on it on my computer at a near degree of leisure. I am in awe of the speed and accuracy she showed in dealing with several bales of typing.

The Editor is happy to acknowledge the following for use of excerpts and material:

The Burns Federation for use of Burns Chronicle articles in issues up to 2001;

The Burns Club of St Louis, Missouri for use of quotes from speeches in period 1955-64;

The United Burns Club of Dunfermline for use of archive material;

The Paisley Burns Club for programme and brochure material;

Mrs Sheona Low for use of the works of Dr Donald Low;

Mrs Deirdre Grieve and the MacDiarmid Trust for use of quotes from the works of Hugh MacDiarmid;

and those many others who contributed their memories to this collection without reservation.

Preface

Hear, Land o Cakes, and brither Scots
Frae Maidenkirk tae Johnie Groat's,
If there's a hole in a' your coats,
I rede ye tent it;
A chield's amang ye takin' notes,
And faith he'll prent it...

(On the Late Captain Grose's
Peregrinations thro Scotland)

This is not the first collection of Immortal Memories, but it is certainly the most comprehensive, in that it covers the two hundred years from the very first Burns Supper in Alloway in 1801 to the Millennium Burns Suppers of 2001. Full recourse has been made to the only other collections of speeches available at the time of writing – *The Chronicle of the Hundredth Birthday of Robert Burns* edited by James Ballantyne in 1859, *Printed Orations, Immortal Memories and other Burns Speeches from around the World* (undated) edited by Edward Atkinson, *Brief Addresses commemorating the genius of Scotland's Illustrious Bard* of 1899, editor John D Ross, *There Was a Lad*, a collection published by the Burns Club of St Louis, Missouri, USA in 1965. and the *Chronicle of the 200th Commemoration of the Death of Robert Burns* compiled by Dr Jim Connor of London, Ontario.

The purpose of this present book has been to gather into one volume the best speeches from these volumes as well as those gathered from modern Burns writing and from my own researches to date so as to offer a wide and updated view of Burns to the contemporary reader.

The 'Immortal Memory' is the chief toast and centrepiece of the traditional Burns Supper and is offered all over the world to the memory of the poet and songsmith, Robert Burns. To be asked to deliver this oration in honour of Scotland's National Bard is recognised as a privilege in itself. It is not, therefore, a project that can be taken lightly, but, despite this, the speaker should not be overwhelmed by its solemnity. If it concerns Burns at all, it should have an element of fun. It is, after all, a joyful social occasion – or should be. Its central theme is not that Robert Burns has been dead for two hundred years but that he lives on yet in his poetry and song.

It is inevitable in such a compilations that no matter the ingenuity of selection of theme or the variety of individual attitude shown in all these different speeches there is unavoidable repetition and duplication. This has been adjusted as far as possible but the essential quality of what has been said is allowed to speak for itself. The contributor's views are their own and if, in some cases, their facts vary from accepted Burns scholarship, I am sure it is unwittting and does little harm to the case they offer. The calibre of material generally is high and if it is variable it is this gives the volume its diversity.

These voices deserve to be heard, for they give a broad, informed, illuminating, and, above all, heartfelt view of the poet via the spoken word. Some of the speakers are poets themselves, not so much that they speak in verse, but that they do so with a simplicity born of directness and sincerity. In this area, some written pieces are inserted because they add to the general tone of the chapter in which they appear and offset the speeches selected. I have tried, as far as possible, to obtain permission for all printed extracts used, but where this has been omitted, I should be glad to hear from the source or sources involved so that I might make proper acknowledgement in any future edition.

Accounts of the 1844 Burns Festival in Ayr and the subsequent festivals there from 1975 have been included as well as a chronological account of the development of the Burns Clubs and the Burns Federation based on the official history by Dr James Mackay. Regular annual events like the West Sound Burns Suppers in Glasgow and the Burns Federation's annual conferences also yield valuable material but it is the contribution of ordinary Burnsians from all over the world that makes this particular publication of interest to the general reader. In telling their story of Burns they are telling their own story, singing their own song. They make a unique choir of voices in a tribute to the written word through the spoken word and the results are now recorded here for all to study, compare, and, hopefully, enjoy.

This book is not a wholly original work. As editor, I have felt free to comment and to develop the theme historically so that it provides, as a corollary, a parallel history of the Burns Movement in the broadest sense. It is intended first as a compilation, an anthology, a storehouse of different Burns fruits as gathered by many different kind labourers in the field. It has been my job to get this rich harvest into the one barn, as it were.

I trust that the resulting volume will have the comprehensiveness and quality its subject deserves. Robert Burns can take our scrutiny, and anyway, he is big enough to survive whatever anybody says of him.

John Cairney
Mt Eden, Auckland, New Zealand
November 2002

Introduction

It becomes a man of sense to think for himself.
(Letter to Mr Muir)

The annual Burns Supper, held on or around his birthday, January 25, has become something of a cult in virtually every country in the world where 'Scottish' is spoken – and even where it is not. This is an occasion when people gather around a dinner table to give tribute to a Scottish poet who died more than two hundred years ago. It really is an extraordinary phenomenon. That the dead author of a small book of dialect verse, who lived a short life in an obscure corner of a tiny country, should be so remembered by so many is unique to say the least. It is a signal honour for any writer, and one not given to Shakespeare or Tolstoy or Mark Twain or Charles Dickens. Ironically, the least surprised by all this would be Burns himself. Not long before he died, at only 37, he told his wife, Jean, 'Don't be afraid. I'll be mair respeckit a hundred years after I'm dead, than I am at present.' He underestimated himself.

Two hundred years after, he is even more respected for what he was – a formidable wordsmith, remarkable poet and a lyricist of genius – but it is the man we are drawn to. In his person, and in his own time, he won the hearts of the ordinary people and at the same time, drew the admiration of the aristocracy and what he termed, somewhat dryly, the 'polite and learned'. For a brief time at the end of what is called the Age of Enlightenment, that is between 1750 and 1800, he united Scotland, and almost every aspect of it, in himself. William Pitt, the Prime Minister of Great Britain and Ireland, and exactly the same age as Burns, was a known admirer, although Burns didn't always admire him. (Oddly enough, Robert Louis Stevenson was to have the same relationship with Gladstone.) In 1786, however, it was surely extraordinary that a self-educated Scottish farm-boy's goose-quill scratching in rural Ayrshire should reverberate as far as Westminster.

Even English critics and men of letters like W.E. Henley have been drawn to the works of Burns, and that eminent Victorian edited (with T.F.Henderson) the controversial four-volume Centenary edition of 1896. Henley considered that Burns's first importance in literature was that he represented the final flowering of a great Scottish vernacular tradition before it succumbed to the 18th-century fashion for Englishness among the Scots *literati*, yet the irony is that Burns's grounding in letters was, with only a few exceptions, almost entirely English, as the list of his boyhood reading shows. Professor Tom Crawford of St Andrews properly asserts that Burns imbibed as much of an English literary tradition as he did Scottish and this is what makes him unique among writers of that age. He straddled both schools. This is why he was able to speak in a larger voice than that of a mere provincial rhymer. This fact is at the root of his international standing despite the fact that the vast bulk of his work was in his native tongue.

To my mind, this classlessness and timelessness is most apparent in his songs, which are now considered more and more as his main contribution to letters because of the flawless art works they are. Not all of them of course, but there may be as many as a hundred in the nearly four hundred he wrote, re-wrote or discovered as fragments, that can be held to a perfect blending of words and music, indicating a rare mastery of two distinctly disparate arts, and a hitherto little recognised industry on his part as a musicologist and song collector. Given his care and concern in this area, why can't we then learn the correct words of *Auld Lang Syne*? And why do the ladies insist on singing *Sweet Afton* when the penultimate line says – 'My Mary's asleep by the murmuring stream…' and the tenors and baritones go on to complain about how 'my fause lover staw my rose – but ah! he left the thorn wi' me' in *The Banks o Doon*? Even in our free age, such lines de-genderised are ambiguous to say the least. These lyric pearls don't deserve to be sold as imitations. They tell of feelings, true feelings between men and women in any age. And *at* any age. See *John Anderson, My Jo*.

The deeper one digs in nationalism of any kind, the more international it seems to become. Universality is a truth that will out if it is there in the first place. Commonality is a human condition that far outweighs narrow chauvinism. My country right or wrong hardly applies when the work of that country reaches beyond its borders and touches everyone. All great art goes global, because the kind of response it elicits knows no frontiers. We are indeed all Jock Tamson's bairns.

Which brings to mind, the late and learned Secretary of the Burns Federation, Jock Thomson, once pointed out to me that, while there were only two or three authentic portraits for which Burns sat, everyone seems to have their own idea of what Burns looked like. The only thing all agree upon is that there must have been something essentially *likable* about the man for his impression to have fixed itself for so long upon a whole nation. Charm is normally evanescent, people grow out of their attractiveness, but he appears to have grown into the very real affection of an entire people.

His personality was such that stories abound about him. Many of these stories are quite untrue but they are good stories for a' that, and they pass from one generation to another, gathering further apocryphal moss as they go, and so is a legend made. His readiness to seem all things to all men makes him a natural for dramatic representation and impersonation. He has fascinated performers to this very day, myself included. There have been plays about him, films made of his life and loves and countless radio programmes and recordings on every aspect of his works. All of which testifies to the genuine and continuing magnetism in the man. He really must have had something.

From the time he 'wore the only tied hair in the parish' and wrapped his *fillemot* plaid about his shoulders in his distinctive way, he was rehearsing for his role as a player on a larger stage than that offered by Mauchline belles and Tarbolton bachelors. Every spoken word so carefully considered, every written line even more carefully contrived, even every moment of youthful excess away from the grinding farm, was a plank in the bridge he built to cross the divide of prejudice and custom that kept him and his fellow-peasants immured in their rural station. For him, every hand-written page of verse was to him a further step on the way out and up.

He did so first through a local fame as a rhymer, then national fame as a bard and posthumously an international fame as a poet, which even now shows little prospect of diminishing. His public life was no more than a decade, his travels hardly took him further than a few day's riding from his birthplace, yet Robert Burns must be seriously considered today as the best-known son of Scotland. After all, was he not declared by the Scots themselves in a public poll the Scot of the Millennium?

It all began with one slim book of rhymes – *Poems, Chiefly in the Scottish Dialect* – published at Kilmarnock on 31 July 1786, one volume octavo, price stitched, three shillings. It caused an immediate sensation in Ayrshire and sold out by subscription in little over a week. The ripples were picked up very soon in Edinburgh and not long after, in far-away London. He burst upon the literary world like a meteor, and just like a meteor, fell to earth, burnt-out and spent. Yet all he had intended in that first printing was to make enough money to emigrate to the West Indies in order to avoid a writ of maintenance from the irate father of a local beauty whom Burns had made pregnant with twins, not once, but twice. At this distance, and bearing in mind all his other protestations around the same time, it is hard to know how much Burns loved Jean Armour, but it is very certain that she loved him.

From their first meeting at a penny-fee dance during Mauchline race week in 1785, till she gave birth to their ninth child on the day of his funeral in 1796, Jean Armour regarded Robert Burns as the only man in her life. Hers was the very object-lesson in female loyalty and forbearance within a relationship and it is telling that her only comment on her husband's sexual lapses, was – 'Oor Robin should hae had twa wives.' That, of course, was her comment for the world. Who knows, however, what she said to him behind closed doors? Poor Jean, she must have suffered greatly in the years they were together but she never ceased to love and care for her man, and in the end I think he must have loved her for it. But by then it was too late.

Burns was the very stuff of which romantic poets are made – handsome, witty, daring and different. And best of all he died young. While he lived, he needed to love in order to write his poetry and inspire his songs. Perhaps Jean, in her womanly wisdom understood this, hence her remarkable tolerance. At any rate, she stood by him and survived Mary Campbell, Nancy McLehose, Maria Riddell, Lesley Baillie, Peggy Chalmers, Anna Park, Jessie Lewars and those countless other women in his life including the nameless 'very pretty girl, a Lothian farmer's daughter.' It is to her, as much as to the rest of his amours (proper and otherwise) that we owe the great legacy of love songs. *Songs like Afton Water*, *Ae Fond Kiss*, *Wee Thing*, *Banks o Doon*, *Comin' Thro the Rye*, *Mary Morison*, *The Rigs o Barley*,

Green Grow the Rashes O, *Ca' the Yowes*, *A Red, Red Rose* and so many others. Songs the whole world knows.

There is also his wonderful collection of racy, witty adaptations of old Scots songs, and I don't mean the bawdry, but those robust lyrics like *Last Night a Braw Wooer*, which he realised, even as he penned them, might never be sung in every withdrawing room. They are still, nonetheless, part of his great opus and demand to be remembered. Taking all in all, surely this an artistic output worth a few kisses here and there, and only three births on the wrong side of the blanket? Without the girls we would not have had the songs.

> Then out into the world, my course I did determine.
> Though to be rich was not my wish,
> Yet to be great was charming...

The 1787-88 Edinburgh experience was both the making and the breaking of him. He entered on the capital with nothing to lose and in the end he got more than he bargained for. Ironically, it was not rakery or drink or any kind of debauchery that brought him to an early end, it was celebrity – or the effects of it. From the time he was lionised in Edinburgh and took his 'leisurely progress through Caledonia' with the proceeds of his second edition until he arrived in Dumfries, as arguably the most famous man in Scotland at the time, he was a changed man. It was not that he was indolent, but he never wrote again with the same fervour. He remained as charming and well-liked as ever by both men and women but he appeared to crave fame for fame's sake in a way that he had never done before. He unashamedly used contacts and well-placed friends whenever he had to, all in the pretext of gaining time to write, but it looked suspiciously like place-serving with more than a hint of sycophancy in many of those well-phrased letters. But who can blame him?

He always had to win his way out of some awkward situation, for the most part of his own making, but not always so. Like so many before him, and since, he found that his novelty in society soon wore off (as he said it would). In the end, he was left with little but his wits to help him survive. In desperation, he had often to take, by his standards, desperate measures. He had only pretended to be the 'heaven-sent ploughman'. He knew only too well the work that had gone into making him a writer. He never however, pretended that he was other than the self-taught peasant he was. He was too honest to claim otherwise.

Unfortunately, his natural aristocracy of mind made him ready enemies from the start among the gentry and they waited their time, knowing it was on their side, not his. They knew better than he, that for all his dazzling talk and dashing airs, he was not one of them. No matter how superbly equipped, mentally and physically, he still did not belong, and he was made very aware of this. Notwithstanding, he had taken on the Establishment but they had taken him in only to spit him out when they had tasted him sufficiently. There was no doubt that for a time, he strode Scotland like a colossus, but in the end he was brought down to size – ordinary size. Thus reduced to appropriate provincial obscurity, he was allowed to slip, virtually unnoticed, into Parnassus.

If Burns was a man's man he was a thinking man. When he had first come to Edinburgh in November 1786, it was to seek for a second edition of his poems but it was also to look for a new, and more amenable way of life that would allow him time to write. This is why he responded to the idea of entering the Excise Service, but he was looking for a sinecure not a punishing daily regimen on the road. He might as well have emigrated to the Indies as he had first intended. After all, wasn't that what the book was to pay for in the first place? All he knew was that he didn't want to farm. He had seen enough of farming since he was seven years old.

He would aim for a safe job and write in his spare time. As it happened, he got his safe job but it was one that would near-kill him by its physical demands – like forcing him to ride two hundred miles a week in all weathers. He did try another farm but it was just as unlucky for him as the others had been for his father, and he walked away from it, ostensibly, a ruined man. In all this time, he had kept writing although he only managed one piece of completed verse, but since that was *Tam o Shanter* in 1790, his acknowledged masterpiece, it was perhaps worth its exclusivity. From then on till his death six years later, he gave himself almost entirely to songs. But then, what songs they were.

It would be left to a more understanding posterity to restore his stature as a man, and generations of critical analysis to affirm his world status as a literary giant, recognised universally – if only as the author of *Auld Lang Syne*. But Robert Burns is more than that to all Scots – he is also a national hero, an icon, a legend and as a result, the man himself has been obscured by what can only be called a genuine Scotch myth. In the meantime, 'facts are chields that winna ding' and the most important fact about Robert Burns was the publication of the Kilmarnock Edition in 1786. It was the watershed in his life. Everything led up to this one event and everything thereafter undeniably led away from it.

Whatever his supposed moral and social defects, and no matter any weaknesses of temperament, he must be seen a unique man by any standards and an extraordinary figure in his time. Almost single-handedly, even as he was dying, he rescued a whole body of Scottish song and, in the best of his poetry, bursting out in a flood as it did between 1785 and 1786, he gave voice to an old Scotland that was rapidly disappearing in the then fashionable Anglophilia. Burns's life-span was was almost exactly that of the Scottish Enlightenment but his Scotland was not yet the North Britain that Stevenson so rightly deplored. *The Dying Words of Old Mailie*, as the young Burns phrased them, were also the epitaph for an ancient tradition that stretched back to Dunbar and Henryson and the other Makars. He was, as Henley rightly put it – *ultimus Scotorum*, the last expression of the old Scots world.

He had an uncanny instinct for what was right in the older tradition, especially in its minstrelsy, and he preserved it. He had the true poet's instinct for what was apt. This allowed him to keep the best of what had been begun by older, often anonymous writers and by adding to it his own lyric genius, he virtually created new songs which still live today as his own. He was, at root level, the 'satirist and singer of the parish' telling of ordinary things in unordinary ways so that a mouse, a daisy, a louse become metaphors for a larger world and offer a unique insight remarkable in such a young man. This is the first thing about his genius that is remarkable; he did his finest work so young. Yet he could speak with all the wisdom of the ages, with shrewd insight into men and their manners, and above all with encompassing compassion for every living thing, albeit with a country man's realistic attitude to animals and all growing things. It was rather that these themes also served his poetic purpos.

In a way, one is almost glad he received no greater patronage or came under any fashionable pressures. He would have lost his special voice. Had he written entirely in English to ingratiate himself with possible patrons, he would have been quite forgotten today. Thankfully, he held to his own muse, which was anything but untutored, and so he survives. Like all geniuses, he knew he was good. He needed that certainty to do what he had to do. This is what gave him the legs to walk straight off the rigs, as it were, and stride across a carpet. He had something to say and he was going to say it.

In a sense, he was a watershed in himself – on the one hand, the culminating expression of the past, and on the other, a pointer towards the new romanticism and the ideas of personal freedom and equality. This Janus-like quality of being able to look forward and backward at the same time is what typifies the artistic greats. They can find the universal in the particular, the timeless in the ephemeral, the meaningful in the absurd and Burns showed this in almost every line he wrote. Which is why we still need the genius of all poets as seers and chroniclers of our human situation. As mere mortals, we are in constant need of reassurance. Some mortals, such as Robert Burns, have been able, in some measure, by their works, to provide this from generation to generation. It is this keeps them in our memory and thus makes them immortal.

And for more than Scots. The first Russian translation was less than a decade after his death but the Frenchman, Auguste Angellier, with his *Etude sur la Vie et les Oeuvres de Robert Burns* in 1893 was the first substantial foreign appreciation. This growing interest beyond Scotland was underlined by the publication in Glasgow of *Burns in Other Tongues* by William Jacks in 1896. Out-of-Scotland interest has been maintained in our own day by two Canadians, Professors Ross Roy and Robert Carnie, working out of universities in South Carolina and Calgary respectively. North Americans would know better than anyone that everybody has his or her fifteen minutes of fame or hour in the sun, or whatever. Some even survive to become a nine-day wonder, but only a special few outlive their lifetimes, and Burns has certainly done that – as he himself foresaw.

However, it is what he has left us in the works that really matters. Only what he set down counts in the end. What he said in his writing is the stuff that lasts not the anecdotes or apocrypha that abound about what he said in his time, although he did this strikingly enough. He has continuing relevance. This is yet another reason why he is so vividly remembered, and it is this on-going vivacity that makes his memory immortal to most Scots.

To understand this, and measure the true proportions of the Burns presence in the world today one must first appreciate the impact of the original book, *Poems, Chiefly in the Scottish Dialect*. As has been mentioned, the first edition sold out in weeks across the country. People scrambled for copies in the way that teenagers today would clamour for the latest pop record. Robert Heron, a contemporary, and the first to write about Burns, said about the publication:

> With his poems, old and young, grave and gay, learned and ignorant, were alike transported. I was at that time resident in Galloway, and I can well remember how even plough-boys and maid-servants would have gladly bestowed the wages they earned the most hardly... if they might procure the works of Burns.

This was testimony indeed, for in 1786, it would have taken a maidservant a week to earn the price of the book. The Edinburgh edition in the following year was even more successful, and it put money in the poet's pocket as well. Enough to allow him to travel around Scotland like a gentleman, taking his applause like an actor, but the experience unsettled him completely for the ten years he had left of his life. He had, by his own efforts, risen from local rhymer to national Bard of Scotland, duly proclaimed and sanctioned. From then on it was only a matter of the rest of the world.

Since the first nine guests assembled for the very first 'Burns Supper' in 1801, there have been countless 'Immortal Memories' of Scotland's Bard delivered by every kind of speaker to all sorts of audiences in most of the English-speaking world – and even where English is not spoken. The guid Scots tongue is by no means mandatory and Burns is still Burns even if it is rendered in Japanese, Urdu or in Esperanto. What may be lost in translation gains, one hopes, in immediacy. Over the years, the original intimate, informal suppers have become veritable banquets at some centres and many more than the original nine often struggle to obtain expensive tickets. The cottage industry has become a factory process and now has attained mass production proportions.

However, this hasn't prevented some great minds saying splendid things about our man at such functions. Nor has it stopped the laughter genuinely raised from the matter in hand and not from the mere recitation of a stock joke. Good Immortal Memories are performances, and the best are great ones, trenchant, moving and telling us something about Burns we hadn't known or thought of until then. We have all been privileged at some time to be present when a first-rate speaker has developed a pertinent theme, cogently and winningly, so that we are given yet another light on a many-sided genius.

What is also astonishing is that so many people have such different ideas about Burns, and hold these views passionately. This is what makes him so fascinating – that he is so many men in one young man. He is, in his own words, 'formed of various parts, the various man'. Any good Immortal Memory should try to catch at least a facet of this prismatic Burns in the Toast. Unfortunately not every speaker is a Cicero. Toasts can vary, not only in standard of oration but in content and where two or more views are gathered together, there you have dissension and controversy. But you can also have interest and the value of the alternative point of view. Such compensation also serves to fill out the subject, taking in all the extremes and contradictions that make up any mortal's frame. But we are dealing with an Immortal here, and it is this aspect of him that we observe in our Memory each year.

Hopefully, we are also entertained in the process, and edified by hearing a good thought well put. This is the Immortal Memory as it should be, and it was to make a record of such memorable orations that I undertook to oversee this compilation of Immortal Memories from all sources. It also nicely marks the two hundred years since the first speech at Alloway. Gathered here are some of the best, and even, some might say, some of the more eccentric, Immortal Memories ever delivered, in a survey of speeches never before attempted in print, at least on this scale. In selecting the various insights and attitudes to Burns revealed in such utterances and packaging them in such a manner, these thoughts will now be available to all Burns lovers, in this and future generations.

It is interesting to note that because the inaugural Memory was given in verse, speakers at early suppers throughout much of the

19th-century did likewise and consequently were referred to as 'laureates'. We have several laureates in this collection. because theirs was once a very special place in club proceedings. At Burns Suppers, for instance, their contribution was the *only* spoken part of the evening. Would that were so today. We are now offered such a proliferation of toasts at the modern supper, that the Immortal Memory, which is, after all, the keynote address and the main reason for the gathering, is often lost in the welter of often irrelevant words surrounding it. The real wood can't be seen for the trivial trees.

Essentially, the Burns Supper should consist of a good meal among friends culminating in the toast drunk to our absent friend, Robert Burns. Time should be given for someone to propose this soberly and seriously, but not dully or at undue length. The speaker should be introduced and thanked, which is only polite after all, and after that there should be recitation if required (and not always *Holy Willie's Prayer* or *Tam o Shanter* either) followed by general singing of Burns songs by the whole company concluding with *Auld Lang Syne* before dispersal. It is a very simple format. It always was and should be allowed to be so again. It should not be reduced to the level of a variety bill by extraneous toasts that turn out to be no more than that – mere 'turns'.

At the core of the Supper is the Immortal Memory, all else is extra. Burns is at the heart of the whole evening and his work serves him better than any 'act', however expertly presented. I stress the importance of the central toast because that's what I want to highlight in this book, and by using as examples the Immortal Memories found from all available records, historical accounts, published reports and anecdotal reference, the Memory itself is brought sharply into deserved focus as the highlight of the whole proceedings. My hope is that this volume will not be just another book about Burns to be added to the three thousand or so already written but that it might give a special international acknowledgement to our national poet of Scotland in that what it says comes from every kind of voice and every kind of country.

Yet it is to Scotland that he is inextricably bound as it is to him. This point was underscored by Hans Hecht in his study of Burns, simply entitled *Robert Burns*. This German Burns scholar, speaking of Burns the poet, said that he

> reached out to the universal. By combining the finite with the infinite, he left behind him a legacy of unequalled magnificence...

Incidentally, this book, translated into English by Jane Lymburn in 1936, was the first book about Burns I ever owned, only because it was given to me as a Christmas present in 1959. I bought the next one, Maurice Lindsay's Burns Encyclopedia, with my own money and on these twin piers, my own bridge to Burns was built. Despite the seemingly forlorn circumstances of Burns's early end, Herr Hecht concluded

> He has been granted the happiest lot that can fall to any poet: he is enshrined forever in the hearts of his countrymen, and has become such a part of their spiritual possessions that it is impossible to imagine Scotland without Robert Burns. He has remained a living force in the nation. The sun that rose over the grave by the churchyard wall in Dumfries was the sun of immortality.

Which is why the speakers featured here, whether at a simple supper or sumptuous banquet, whether from the past and present, or from far and wide, and no matter their language or oratorical skills, are all saying the same thing in the end as they raise a glass in the famous toast – 'To the Immortal Memory of Robert Burns.'

A Burns Chronology

1750 William Burnes (1721-84), of Kincardineshire in the North-East of Scotland, moves south to Edinburgh to work on the Meadows project before moving west to Alloway to become a gardener on the estate of Provost Fergusson.

1757 15 December – Marries Agnes Broun (1732-1820) of Maybole, also in Ayrshire. They set up home in the two rooms of the clay cottage he builds with his own hands.

1759 25 January – Robert Burnes born at Alloway.
26 January – Baptised as Presbyterian by the Reverend William Dalrymple of Ayr.
William Burnes begins his own *Manual of Religious Belief*. (completed circa 1764).

1760 28 September – Gilbert Burnes born. (m. Jean Breckenridge. d. Haddington 1827).

1762 30 September – Agnes Burnes born. (m. William Gault. d. Dundalk, N. Ireland 1834).

1764 14 September – Annabella Burnes born. (Dies unmarried, Haddington, 1832).

1765 January – Robert and Gilbert attend William Campbell's school at Alloway Mill.
March – Campbell closes his school. William Burnes engages a tutor, John Murdoch (1747-1824) to teach his sons and some neighbouring children for a three-year period.

1766 April – William Burnes takes over 70-acre Mount Oliphant farm near Alloway on 12-year lease from Provost Fergusson at forty pounds per annum. Leases his cottage.

1767 30 July – William Burns born. (Dies unmarried, London, 1790).

1768 John Murdoch leaves Alloway. William Burnes teaches his sons himself.

1769 10 July – John Burnes born. (Dies unmarried, Mossgiel, 1785).

1771 27 July – Isobel Burne.s born. (m. John Begg. Dies Bridge House, Alloway, 1858).

1772 The Burnes boys take turns to attend Dalrymple School, week about, during the summer.

1773 John Murdoch returns to Ayr. Robert joins him for a month to study French, Latin and English poetry.

1774 Hard times at Mount Oliphant but Robert falls in love for the first time – with 14-year old Nellie Kilpatrick in the harvest field. He writes his first song for her – *My Handsome Nell.*

1775 Summer term at Hugh Rodger's school at Kirkoswald to study mensuration and surveying. Makes friends with Willie Niven. Falls in love with Peggy Thompson. Writes *O Tibbie, I hae seen the day, I Dream'd I lay where Flowers were Springing.*

1776 Provost Fergusson dies. Affairs put into thc hands of a factor. Annual rent increased. Writes *The Ruined Farmer.*

1777 Whitsun – the family moves to Lochlie Farm, near Tarbolton. 130 acres at 130 pounds per annum. The land is wet and William and his sons work hard and long to improve drainage. Robert's reading increases. Attends dancing class at Dalrymple.
William Burnes fails to break lease. His health deteriorates.

1778 Burns meets Agnes Fleming and Annie Rankine, the first of his many heroines in song. Writes *The Tarbolton Lasses.*

1779 Makes friends with such as James Smith (b 1765) and James Candlish (1769-1806). Becomes increasingly skilled as 'blackfoot' and letter-writer on behalf of local suitors.
Writes *Montgomerie's Peggy.*

1780 29 July and 3 November – Writes first published letter to

William Niven from 'Lochlee'. 11 November – Founds the Bachelors' Club in Tarbolton in the company of Gilbert, Hugh Reid, Alexander Brown, Thomas Wright, Willam McGavin and Walter Mitchell. Later members included Davie Sillar (1760-1830).
Writes *The Ronalds of the Bennals*, *The Lass of Cessnock Banks*, *Mary Morrison*.

1781 Courts Alison Begbie. Courts Elizabeth Gebbie. Writes *Winter: A Dirge*. Dispute between William Burnes and his landlord, David Maclure, about improvements. Robert sent to Irvine to learn flax-dressing. Writes *A Prayer under Pressure of Violent Anguish*. 4 July – inducted into St David's Lodge, No 174, Tarbolton. Passed 1 October. Meets Richard Brown (1753- 1833) at Irvine. First idea of publishing verses. November – Falls ill in Irvine, visited by father.
Writes *A Prayer in the Prospect of Death*.

1782 1 January – Fire at heckling-shop in the Glasgow Vennel, Irvine. Burns returns home.
24 September – Maclure dispute referred to arbiters.
Burns's poetry increases. Writes *No Churchman am I*, *My Father Was a Farmer*, *John Barleycorn*.

1783 16 January – Awarded three pounds prize for 'linseed saved in growing'.
April – begins First Commonplace Book 1783-85 – ('Observations, Hints, Songs, Scraps of Poetry etc., by Robt. Burness.'). Includes *My Bonny Nanie-O*, *Green Grow the Rashes*, *The Rigs o Barley*, *Now Breezy Winds*, *The Death & Dying Words of Poor Mailie*. It also includes the first of two verse letters to John Lapraik.
17 May – William Burnes receives Writ of Sequestration. Appeals.
18 August – The 'Oversman' reports in favour of William.
25 August – He makes further appeal to the Court of Session in Edinburgh.
Autumn – Robert and Gilbert make secret arrangement with Gavin Hamilton (1751-1805) to rent Mossgiel Farm in the parish of Mauchline – 118 acres at ninety pounds per annum – 'as an asylum for the family in case of the worst'.

1784 27 January – The Court of Session in Edinburgh finds in favour of William Burnes.
13 February – He dies at Lochlie. Robert's affair with Bess Paton, a serving girl in the house. He and Gilbert move the Burnes family to Mossgiel.
27 July – Elected Depute-Master of St James Lodge Kilwinning, Tarbolton.
Writes The Poet's Welcome to His Bastard Wean, Man Was Made to Mourn and The Twa Herds; or the Holy Tulzie.

1785 His *annus mirabilis*.
He writes *Holy Willie's Prayer*, *Death and Doctor Hornbook*, *Rantin Rovin Robin*, *To a Mouse*, *The Jolly Beggars*, *The Cotter's Saturday Night*, *Address to the Deil*.
April – Meets Jean Armour at a dance during Mauchline Race Week.

22 May – Bess Paton gives birth to Elizabeth Paton Burns (d. 1817) – his first child.
Courts Jean Armour. Suffers first fainting fits, headaches, irregularities of the heart.
September – Writes *The Belles of Mauchline* – first mention of Jean Armour in verse.
Jean pregnant – and 'every day arising more and more to view'. He writes an Attestation of Marriage to mollify Armours but his mind in a whirl of love and verses.
September – Writes *Love and Liberty* (or *The Jolly Beggars*) after night with John Richmond at Poosie Nancie's Inn in Mauchline. He is on a creative high surge.
October – Finishes his first Commonplace Book in the middle of a line.
November – Writes *To A Mouse*. Poems, Epistles and Epitaphs pour from him.
In the *Epistle to William Simpson* (1785) he signs himself 'Burns' to match the rhyme required for the line – 'While Terra Firma, on her axis, / Diurnal turns;'

1786 March – James Armour scornfully cuts out his daughter's name from 'marriage' paper.
3 April – Subscription proposals for printing his poems sent to John Wilson, Kilmarnock. Robert and Gilbert officially arrange with Postal Service to change their surname to Burns.

14 April – Wilson sends out proposals.

23 April – James Armour repudiates Burns as son-in-law. Jean is packed off to Paisley to be reconciled with Andrew Wilson. Burns immediately tries to forget her in – 'all kinds of dissipation and riot – Mason-meetings, drinking matches... and now for the grand cure: the Ship is on her way home that is to take me out to Jamaica.' Meantime, he takes up with Mary Campbell (1763-86), a Highland dairymaid at Coilsfield House.

14 May – Burns and Mary Campbell exchange Bibles and 'matrimonial vows' at Failford prior to her departure for Greenock where she would await him and together they would set sail for the West Indies. He writes two songs for her – *The Highland Lassie -O* and *Will Ye Go to the Indies, my Mary?* He also writes in this year *The Auld Farmer's New Year Salutation*, *The Twa Dogs*, *Address to the Unco Guid*, *To A Louse*, *The Holy Fair*, *To A Mountain Daisy*, *The Brigs o Ayr*, *Tam Samson's Elegy*, *Address to A Haggis*.

June – Burns sends copy to Wilson for printing.

10 June – Jean confesses by letter to the Kirk Session that Burns has made her pregnant.

15 June – Burns makes the first of three consecutive Sunday penitential appearances before the Reverend William Auld (1709-91) and the congregation of Mauchline Kirk.

9 July – James Armour issues writ against Burns – 'for an enormous sum'. He goes into hiding – 'wandering from one friend's house to another'.

22 July – Transfers his share of Mossgiel to Gilbert.

31 July – *Poems, Chiefly in the Scottish Dialect by Robert Burns* – The Kilmarnock Edition – 618 copies at three shillings a copy published to immediate acclaim and is sold out within a week. Burns emerges from hiding to find himself famous throughout Ayrshire. Armour withdraws his writ. Burns as Ayrshire's Bard.

6 August – He makes his final appearance at Mauchline Kirk and is thereby granted his Certificate of Bachelorhood by 'Daddy' Auld. He is a free man again.

1 September – First postponement of the West Indies voyage on the *Bell* out of Greenock on 20th. Still hoping for a second edition from Wilson at Kilmarnock.

3 September – Jean gives birth to twins – Robert (d.1857) and Jean (d.1787).

27 September – 'The feelings of a father' prompt Burns to cancel the second sailing in the *Roselle* under Captain Richard Brown.
October – Mary Campbell dies at Greenock, possibly of premature childbirth induced by typhoid fever. Burns abandons all ideas of emigration. Considers idea of Excise. Jean returns to Mauchline. Meets secretly with Burns. Second edition rejected by Wilson. Dr Blacklock recommends that Burns try for a second Edition in Edinburgh while he goes forward with plans for the Excise.
15 November – Begins correspondence with Mrs Dunlop of Dunlop.
27 November – Sets out for Edinburgh on a hired pony.
29 November – Arrives Edinburgh. Lodges with John Richmond at Mrs Carfrae's.
Meets May Cameron, a serving-girl.
1 December – Bess Paton accepts settlement of her claim on Burns.
9 December – Henry Mackenzie reviews the Kilmarnock Edition in *The Lounger*.

1787 7 January – Meets 'a very pretty girl, a Lothian farmer's daughter, whom I have almost persuaded to accompany me to the West Country'.
13 January – The Grand Lodge of Scotland toasts Burns as 'Caledonia's Bard'.
14 January – Patrick Miller of Dalswinton offers lease of Ellisland Farm in Nithsdale.
6 February – Writes to Bailies of the Canongate regarding memorial to poet, Robert Ferguson (1750-74) – 'my elder brother in misfortune'.
22 March – Completes proof-reading of Edinburgh Edition at William Smellie's Print Shop.
9 April – Begins Second Commonplace Book but calling himself 'Burness'.
Sits for portrait to Alexander Nasmyth (1758-1840).
17 April – William Creech publishes first Edinburgh Edition.
23 April – Burns sells his copyright to Creech for one hundred guineas.
5 May (to 1 June) – Tours the Borders with Robert Ainslie.
22 May – First volume of *Scots Musical Museum* published by James Johnson.

26 May – May Cameron gives birth to a boy and claims Burns as the father.
2 June – Burns asks Ainslie, a lawyer, to 'send for the wench and give her ten or twelve shillings... and advise her out to some country friends'.
4 June – Made an Honorary Burgess of Dumfries. Given Freedom of Lochmaben.
8 June – Returns triumphant to Mauchline. James Armour changes his mind. Burns meets Jean again. Continuing his 'leisurely progress through Caledonia', he tours the West Highlands to Arrochar and Inveraray.
2 August – From Mauchline, writes long autobiographical letter to Dr John Moore.
8 August – Returns to Edinburgh.
15 August – Freed from May Cameron's writ *in meditatione fugae*.
25 August – Begins Highland Tour with schoolmaster, William Nicol.
16 September – Returns to Edinburgh via Queensferry.
4 October – Tours Stirlingshire with Dr Adair.
20 October – Returns to Edinburgh. Takes up residence with William Cruickshanks and family at St James Square. Jean Burns dies in infancy. First London edition.
November – Collaborates with James Johnson on *The Scots Musical Museum*. Goes to Dalswinton to discuss lease of Ellisland Farm with Patrick Miller.
4 December – Meets Mrs Agnes MacLehose (1759-1841) at Miss Mirren's tea-party.
7 December – Dislocates knee in carriage fall with actor William Woods (1751-1802).
28 December – Begins correspondence with Nancy McLehose.

1788 4 January – Visits Clarinda at home.
7 January – Seeks patronage for Excise from Graham of Fintry.
14 February – Second volume of *Scots Musical Museum* published.
Writing four letters a day to Nancy/Clarinda. Involved with her maid, Jenny Clow.
18 February – Leaves Edinburgh. Returns to Jean.
23 February – Sets up house in Mauchline with Jean. Buys her a mahogany bed, thus making public acknowledgement of her as wife. Continues to write to Nancy.

27 February – Re-visits Ellisland with John Tennant of Glenconner.
3 March – Jean gives birth to twin girls who die on 10th and 22nd.
13 March – Burns returns to Edinburgh.
18 March – Signs lease of Ellisland at rent of fifty pounds per annum.
20 March – Leaves Edinburgh.
April– May – Receives instruction in the Excise at Tarbolton and Mauchline.
Enters 'marriage' arrangement with Jean. Writes notice giving her 'legal entitlement to the best blood in my body; and so, farewell Rakery!'
11 June – Burns settles at Ellisland. Begins on second great creative period (until 1791). Writes *Of a the Airts*, *Auld Lang Syne*, *The Wounded Hare*, *Tam Glen*, *Go fetch to me a pint o wine*, *John Anderson, my jo*, *Ca the Yowes*, *To Mary in Heaven*, *Tam o Shanter*, *The Banks o Doon*, *Bonie Wee Thing*, *Sweet Afton* and *A Scots Prologue*.
14 July – Excise Commission issued to Burns.
5 August – Burns/Armour marriage recognised by Mauchline Kirk Session.
Friendship begun between Burns and Riddells of Friar's Carse.
September – Commutes between Nithsdale and Mauchline.
November – Jenny Clow bears Burns' son in Edinburgh.
December – Jean joins Burns in rented accommodation at the Isle, Nithsdale.

1789 16 February – In Edinburgh to settle matters with Creech the Publisher and to deal with paternity writ issued by Jenny Clow.
27 February – Settles with Jenny Clow. Returns next day to Ellisland.
April – Burns orders books on behalf of Monkland Friendly Society in Dunscore.
May – Waits for an Excise appointment.
June – Meets Captain Francis Grose, an English antiquary.
18 August – Francis Wallace Burns (d.1803) born to Jean.
7 September – Commences as Excise Officer in Upper Nothsdale at 50 pounds p.a.
November – Ill with 'malignant squinancy and low fever'.
December – Influenced by reading of Shakespeare, has 'some thoughts of the drama'.

1790 January – Overworked as farmer and exciseman, complains of 'an incessant headache, depression of spirits, and all the truly miserable consequences of a deranged nervous system', but nevertheless listed for promotion to Examiner or Supervisor on 27th.

February – Third volume of *Scots Musical Museum* published.

18 February – Inaugural meeting of subscribers towards a new theatre in Dumfries.

July – Transferred to Third Division of Excise, Dumfries. Meets Anna Park at Globe Tavern. Francis Grose asks for story to go with drawing of Alloway Kirk.

November – Writes *Tam o Shanter* at Ellisland.

1 December – Sends manuscript to Francis Grose.

1791 January – Burns injured by fall 'not from my horse, but with my horse'.

30 January – Death of patron, the Earl of Glencairn, at Falmouth on return from Portugal.

31 March – Birth of Elizabeth Park Burns (d.1873) by Anna Park at Dumfries.

9 April – Birth of William Nicol Burns (d.1872) to Jean at Ellisland.

March – *Tam o Shanter* printed in *Edinburgh Magazine* and *Edinburgh News*.

April – *Tam o Shanter* published in the Grose's *Antiquities of Scotland*.

27 April – Glenriddel Manuscript formed.

19 June – Attends Gilbert's wedding in Mauchline.

25 August – Auction of crops at Ellisland. Thirty people engage in three hours of fighting – 'such a scene of drunkenness was hardly ever seen in this country'.

August – Sends an account of the Monkland Friendly Society to Sir John Sinclair for inclusion in the *Statistical Account*.

10 September – Formal renunciation of Ellisland lease.

11 November – Burns moves his family to three rooms above John Syme's solicitor's office in the Wee Vennel (now Bank Street) in Dumfries.

6 December – In Edinburgh. Parts from Nancy McLehose.

27 December – Sends *Ae Fond Kiss* from Sanquhar to Nancy as parting gift.

1792 February – Promoted to Dumfries Port Division at seventy pounds per annum with extra in perquisites – 'worth twenty pounds a year more than any other Division, besides as much rum and brandy as will easily supply an ordinary family'.
Writes *Duncan Gray*.
29 February – Capture of the French brig *Rosamond* at Gretna.
10 April – Elected an Honorary Member of the Royal Company of Archers.
16 April – Offers Creech 'about fifty pages of new material' for a new edition.
19 April – Sale of French carronades at Dumfries. Burns tries to buy them in order to return them to the French revolutionaries.
August – Fourth volume of *Scots Musical Museum* contains sixty songs by Burns.
September – Visits Ayrshire.
16 September – Contributes to George Thomson's *Select Collection of Scottish Airs*.
29 September – Theatre Royal opens in Shakespeare Street in Dumfries.
October – Contributes to fifth volume of *Scots Musical Museum*.
13 November – Subscribes to Edinburgh *Gazetteer*.
21 November – Birth of Elizabeth Riddell Burns (d.1795).
December – Four-day visit to Mrs Dunlop at Dunlop House with Dr Adair.
Friends of the People formed in Edinburgh. Political unrest in Dumfries.
31 December – Collector Mitchell ordered to investigate Officer Burns's political conduct – 'as a person disaffected to the Government'.

1793 5 January – Defends himself before Robert Graham of Fintry, Excise Commissioner.
18 February – Second Edinburgh edition of *Poems* published by Creech.
March – Burns asks for Burgess privileges for the education of his sons in Dumfries.
19 May – Burns family moves to Millbrae Vennel (now Burns Street).

May – First set of Thomson's *Select Collection of Scottish Airs* published.
30 July (to 2 August) – Tours Galloway with John Syme. Writes *Scots Wha Hae*, *O Whistle and I'll Come to Ye, my Lad*, also epigrams, addresses and prologues.
1 August – Meets Pietro Urbani at Lord Selkirks's, St Mary's Isle.
30 August – Sends *Scots Wha Hae* to George Thomson
October – Meets Nathaniel Gow, fiddler son of the famous Niel Gow.
9 December – Attends Isabella Burns's marriage at Mossgiel.

1794 7 January – Proposes reorganisation of the Dumfries Excise service.
12 January – Maria Riddell breaks with Burns.
20 April – Robert Riddell dies at Friar's Carse.
1 May – Declines post with London *Morning Chronicle*.
25 June (till 28th) – Second Galloway tour with John Syme.
12 August – Birth of James Glencairn Burns (d.1865).
22 December – Begins work on *Select Collection of Scottish Airs* for Thomson.
Writes Wilt Thou be My Dearie?, *My Love is like a Red, Red Rose*, *Charlie, he's my Darling*, *My Nanie's Awa*, *For the Sake of Somebody*.

1795 January – Income reduced – 'These accursed times, by stopping up Importation, have for this year at least, lopt off a full third of my income.'
12 January – Estranged from Mrs Dunlop.
31 January – Joins Dumfries Volunteer Militia as founder-member. Buys uniform.
February – Reconciled with Maria Riddell.
March – Supports Patrick Heron's candidacy for the Stewartry Election.
April – Sits for miniature portrait by Alexander Reid of Kirkennan (1747-1843) - 'who has hit the most remarkable likeness of what I am at this moment.'
24 June – Death of William Smellie, printer, in Edinburgh.
September – Death of Elizabeth Riddell Burns – 'Autumn robbed me of my daughter.'
December – Ill with rheumatic fever.

Writes *A Man's A Man, I'll Ay Ca in by Yon Toon, Last May a Braw Wooer.*

1796 31 January – Recovering slowly – 'beginning to crawl across my room'.
March – Famine in Dumfries – Bread riots in the streets – 'money cannot purchase it'.
June – Final letter to James Johnson. Writes *O Lay thy Loof in mine, lass, Here's a Health to ane I love dear, O wert thou in the cauld blast*, and his very last song – *Fairest Maid on Devon's Banks.*
3 July (till 16th) – At Brow Well. Meets Maria Riddell for the last time.
12 July – Final letter to George Thomson – 'Do, for God's sake, send me five pounds...'
18 July – Final letter to James Armour asking for Mrs Armour to come to Jean.
21 July – Dies at five o'clock in the morning.
25 July – Funeral to St Michael's Kirkyard in Dumfries. Gilbert attends.
Jean gives birth to Maxwell Burns (d.1799).
John Syme and Alan Cunningham raise subscriptions for Jean and the children.
The response is poor due to the bad press received by Burns in the national obituaries.
Jean refuses to leave Dumfries to return to Ayrshire. She lives on in the same house for another thirty-seven years – her late husband's exact lifetime.

1800 Dr James Currie (1756-1805) chosen as first biographer. The resulting four volumes go into nine editions, damaging Burns's reputation for more than a century.

1801 The first Burns Dinner at the King's Arms Hotel, Alloway
The first Immortal Memory by Rev Hamilton Paul.
The Burns Movement had started, the Burns Industry was about to get under way and the Burns Supper may now be served...

I

The First Supper

> The person to whom I allude is Robert Burns, an Ayrshire ploughman, whose poems were some time ago published in a country town in the West of Scotland, with no other ambition, it would seem, than to circulate among the inhabitants of the country where he was born, and to obtain a little fame from those who have heard of his talents. I hope I shall not be thought to assume too much if I endeavour to place him in a higher point of view, to call for a verdict of his country on the merit of his works, and to claim for him those honours which their excellence appears to deserve..
>
> (Henry Mackenzie in *The Lounger*, 9 December 1786)

The first step on the journey toward this wider, international recognition of Robert Burns was taken in the very place where he himself had been born – Alloway – when, in the summer of 1801, a company of nine gentlemen met at the King's Arms Inn in that little village a few miles outside Ayr, on the invitation of the Reverend Hamilton Paul. They had convened to remember the young man some of them had known very well as it had only been five years since he had been laid in his grave. This intimate, informal gathering is now accepted as being the first of what was to become known as the 'Burns Supper'. The *Burns Chronicle and Club Directory* of January 1983 gives the following account:

> In the summer of 1801... friends of Burns proposed to dine at the cottage in which he was born, and to offer a tribute to the memory of departed genius. The party was small but select and formed a most interesting group from the circumstances of nearly one half of the company having their names associated with some of the most gratifying particulars in the poet's history... Two gentlemen of distinguished philanthropy

> and taste waited on the author of the following Odes, and requested him to produce a short poem on the occasion. The author never saw Burns, but was an early and enthusiastic admirer of his writings. The party was such as Burns himself would have joined in with satisfaction.

The author mentioned, the Rev Paul, had the typical reaction of the clergyman to Burns, in that he expressed himself an admirer of the works rather than the man. Yet his admiration was genuine and showed itself in his continued concern for the poet's name and fame after his death. Paul was to produce a readable life of Burns in 1819. A lifelong bachelor, Mr Paul is said to have been 'a member of every literary circle, connected with every club, chaplain to every society, a speaker at every meeting, the poet of every curious occurrence, and the welcome guest at every table.' Now, here he was at the very first Burns Supper, a very 'curious occurrence' in 1801, rising as the Laureate of this first impromptu Alloway Burns club and already to hand with his rhymes about it. When he rose to deliver that particular Ode to that particular group it is certain that the reverend gentleman had no idea what he was starting. Regrettably, we have no idea what he said because no record was kept, or if it was, it has been long lost, but he was to repeat the service annually for the next decade, and on his ninth, and last occasion, he recited the following *Farewell to the Allowa' Club*. It is added here because it might give us something of the flavour of his earlier verse to the poet. This kind of well-meant rhyming was to become a tradition at Burns Suppers and set a trend that would last down through the years.

> Nine times the annual lyre I've strung
> Nine times the Poet's praises sung;
> Thus have the Muses all, by turns,
> Paid homage to the shade of Burns.
> While you, the patrons of the Nine
> Delighted, charm'd, enraptur'd, fir'd
> By love of poesy and wine
> Politely listen'd and admir'd:
> But should my day be overcast
> And this effusion prove my last,
> In words that oft have met your ear,
> This last request permit me here:
> When yearly, ye assemble a'

> One round, I ask it with a tear,
> To him, the Bard, that's far awa'.

Thus, the good man imprinted himself in the very first pages of the Robert Burns story as far as it has been told by Burns Suppers. Mr Paul had organised the original event on behalf of the 'two gentlemen of philanthropy and taste', John Ballantyne, the Provost of Ayr, and the lawyer, Robert Aiken, (listed as 'Aitken'). Both men had been good friends to Burns. Burns acknowledged this in dedicating *The Twa Brigs o Ayr* to Ballantyne and *The Cotter's Saturday Night* to Aiken. 'Orator Bob' had been a most zealous enthusiast for the Kilmarnock edition. Burns himself attested that Aiken sold the book single-handedly throughout Ayrshire by reciting the poems in it at every opportunity. This was word-of-mouth plus.

The others attending on that auspicious evening were William Crawford of Doonside, whose father had engaged Burns's father as a gardener at Alloway; Patrick Douglas of Garallan, who was to have helped Burns obtain a post in Jamaica in 1786; Primrose Kennedy of Drumellan; Hew Fergusson, Barrackmaster at Ayr: David Scott, like Ballantyne, a banker at Ayr and Thomas Jackson, then Rector of the Air [sic] Academy and later Professor of Natural Philosophy at St Andrews. They all deserve to be remembered, for the Burns Movement, as such, may be said to have begun with their initial action. The Burns Chronicle account goes on:

> These nine sat down to a comfortable dinner, of which sheep's head and haggis formed an interesting part. *The Address to the Haggis* was read and every toast was drank [sic] by three times three, i.e., by nine...

This reference to the toast is only one of the links to Freemasonry in the Burns connection. It cannot be overstressed how important to Burns this connection was. The present Lord Elgin, to whom the present writer is much indebted for historic Burns material, is himself a Past Grand Master Mason of Scotland. During the Symposium on 'Aspects of Burns' at the 1976 Burns Festival in Ayr, he had this comment to make on why Burns was drawn to become a Freemason at Tarbolton in 1781.

> It is no secret that for a society of men to prosper successfully in so small a country as Scotland and inhibited by the fullest

> freedom of travel other than by horse or foot, this meant *all* men living in a particular area. This growth of the thoughtful, or speculative, lodges of Freemasons was one of the most important elements in the building up of the character of Scotland. Membership meant the observance of discipline and the acceptance of responsibility, but the rewards were many. A wider understanding in all walks of life, and a greater encouragement to be articulate and at ease among his fellow men, were among the opportunities which opened to Burns.

One can see why he would have jumped at such opportunities and why the social possibilities would also be seized with enthusiasm. The Masons repaid his fervour by underwriting the original Kilmarnock edition in 1786 and subsidising the Edinburgh edition in the following year. When they proclaimed him 'Brother Burns – Caledonia's Bard' before all the Grand Lodges of Scotland gathered in Edinburgh at that time, it was a matter of national as much as Masonic importance. If Burns had not been a Mason he would not have been a published poet. It is as simple as that.

The same applies to the rites and traditions of the Burns Supper. The original nine were likely to be all Masons, hence the toasts drunk 'three-by-three'. The tradition of delivering the Toast to the Lassies with the proposer standing on a chair with one foot on the table also has its roots in Masonic practice. One notes that Burns's *Address to the Haggis* featured at this first gathering but it would be unfair to blame the Masons for its inclusion in the menu. Interest in the haggis still obtains to this day, and it an amazing that such a prosaic dish should excite such curiosity and levity, especially among non-Scots, for whom 'haggis' has become a virtual synonym for Scottishness.

Yet the dish itself, made from the maw of a sheep and minced in a bag with its lungs, hearts and liver, is actually Scandinavian in origin, although in France it was known from the late Middle Ages as *le pain benite de l'Ecosse*. It is not necessarilly confined to the sheep's intestines either, it can be made from chicken, or pig and there is even a camel haggis. The Greeks, too, had a word for it and the Romans ate something they called *cum intestinis omnibus*. The stuffed bladder was for centuries the comic jester's prop which may account for the fact that the haggis is rarely taken seriously – except at modern Burns Suppers where the address to it is recited portentously and gravely as if it were Holy Writ, which to the Haggis Addresser it often is.

For Burns himself, it was little more than a jocular improvisation, a piece of fun with a satirical mock-heroic seriousness which, unfortunately, over the years has become etched in stone. He might even have seen its first appearance in a cookery book, when Mrs McIver printed her version in 1787. It achieved further culinary fame when Meg Dodds published her recipe in *The Cook and Housewife's Manual* in 1826. Meg's Cleikum Club haggis won first prize at the famous Haggis Club Competition held at Mrs Ferguson's in the High St. Incidentally, the second prize went to 'Christopher North' who was actually John Wilson, Professor of Moral Philosophy at Edinburgh University, who is featured in the pages of this book as one of the first great Burns orators. It is perhaps unfortunate that the Burns Supper, and therefore Burns himself, should be so linked with haggis, but it would appear that the association has been there from the beginning. The *Burns Chronicle* account of the 1801 dinner concluded:

> Before breaking up, the company unanimously resolved that the Anniversary of Burns should be regularly celebrated in praise of the Bard of Coila and that the meeting should take place on 29th January, the supposed birthday of the poet...

The nine got it wrong because Dr Currie, the first official biographer got it it wrong, yet Burns had written of his own birth in *Rantin Rovin Robin*:

> Our monarch's hindmost year but ane
> Was *five-and-twenty days* begun
> Twas then a blast o' Janwar wind
> Blew hansel in on Robin.

Perhaps the good doctor confused the christening with the birthday, but for whatever reason the Alloway nine met on the 29th in 1801 and again in 1802 and persisted in meeting on the nearest Saturday to this date until 1805. In point of fact, it wasn't until 1818 that the correct date was confirmed when R.A. Smith, a music-teacher and a founder-member of the Paisley Burns Club, took the trouble to look up the Ayr Parish Records and see for himself that the 25th January was the real birth-date. Why had no one done that in the first place?

For some reason, the Alloway Nine, now increased to twenty, switched to a summer date. Sadly, the club did not flourish in the sun, and slowly wilted not to be revived until 1908. However, its ground-breaking, pioneering example was not lost on other Ayrshire men, especially those then resident in the port of Greenock just to the north. In that same year of 1801 gentlemen of the Greenock Ayrshire Society met over a meal at the Tontine Hotel to commemorate their fellow-countyman on 21 July, his death date, and in the following year, they did likewise on his birthdate.

Those present at that first meeting included such names from the Robert Burns story as Captain Richard Brown, whom he had met in Irvine, and fellow-Exciseman, James Findlay, who had married Jean Markland, one of the Mauchline Belles ('Miss Markland is fine...'). Burns, in fact, had introduced them. Adam Patrick, the son of Burns's herd-boy at Mossgiel, also took part. Members of Mary (or Margaret) Campbell's family, like Archibald Campbell, then an old man 'well stricken in years,' were also involved in proceedings, deciding that their kinswoman gained more in fame than shame from her brief affair with Burns. It was their involvement with the Greenock Burns Club that led to her grave's becoming a place of pilgrimage at the Old West Churchyard. In 1842, the Club erected a monument to her on the site

The Greenock club met at the early years in the Henry Bell Tavern, which was managed by a Mrs Cottar. Their meetings soon became known as 'Cottar's Saturday Night'. One of their first Presidents around this time was the redoubtable Colin Rae-Brown, who will feature in these pages as one of the founding fathers of the Burns Movement. He is only one of the great names associated with this club. Greenock has gone on to win high prestige in the matter of her roll-call of honorary presidents which includes such as Lord Tennyson, Oliver Wendall Holmes, Sir Henry Irving and Hamish McCunn, the composer, himself a Greenock man. Thus was begun what came to be called the Mother of all Burns clubs and, happily, she was to have many children in the years to come, including a Daughter from Paisley who felt she had just grounds to be a Sister.

The still-surviving Minute Book (lodged in a Paisley bank vault) shows that the Paisley Burns Club was inaugurated at the Star Inn, Paisley, on 29th January 1805. The idea was put forward by Paisley's own poet and Burns admirer, Robert Tannahill, and, following his efforts as the Club's first Secretary, a company of more than seventy sat down to dinner. On this occasion, the first President, William McLaren, proposed a toast – 'To the Memory of Our Immortal Bard, Robert Burns'. In 1806, the same toast must have been delivered by the next President, William Gemmill, for in February 1807, Tannahill wrote to James Clark, Bandmaster of the Argyle Militia, then stationed in Edinburgh:

> I hope the meeting succeeded your wishes. Ours went on gloriously. Eighty-four sat at supper; after which, Mr Blaikie addressed us in a neat speech calculated for the occasion, concluding with a toast – To the Memory of Robert Burns.

This 'calculated' speech by Andrew Blaikie has become what is now known as The Immortal Memory and what was, from this time on, to become the pivot of all Burns functions. What is less known, however, is that a Paisley weaver, William McLaren, has good claim to the first deliverer of an Immortal Memory and that the Paisley Club by the same token has substantiated grounds to be considered as the first *official* Burns Club. I am indebted to Paisley's present Secretary, James Skinner, for this information and for pointing me towards the considerable detective work done by the late Clark Hunter, himself a respected Burns author, in uncovering the complicated facts surrounding the question of the first-ever Burns Club and the long-standing rivalry between Paisley and Greenock on this delicate matter.

This is not the place to rake over those old ashes. Sparks still fly in this debate, but my own view is the facts are clear – Greenock came first historically and Paisley came first officially. There is anecdotal evidence to support the former as being active between 1801 and 1805 and there is concrete proof that the latter was instituted in 1805. Tradition nods towards Greenock and it is a tradition that still holds despite the fact that Paisley have been protesting strongly since 1892. According to Clark Hunter the Club would appear to have a good case, but it would seem even more that it is a long-standing and unending feud between Mother and Daughter. But then that sort of thing happens in families.

It is difficult to believe that men of the calibre of Rae-Brown would consent to a deliberate fraud or even the extenuation of an error by default. In the end it comes down to book-keeping and, unfortunately, Greenock didn't keep theirs and, memory being the frail thing it is, things were mis-remembered or mis-applied and one thing led to another as the years went by. The fact remains that two sterling Burns Clubs emerged around the same time, both having the distinction of having been formed out of a genuine, disinterested and impersonal regard for their subject-patron and inspiration. Perhaps they should celebrate all that they have in common rather than maintain a squabble about what keeps them apart. Kilmarnock Burns Club, instituted in 1808, had something of the same problem with regard to seniority over London and this was solved by naming Kilmarnock as Number 0 and London as Number 1. These niceties seem to matter in the Burns world.

In 1810 the Argyle Militia returned to Ayr Barracks and the *Glasgow Courier* reported:

> A number of non-commissioned officers and privates of the Argyle Militia went out from Ayr to visit the cottage (at Alloway) attended by the band of the Regiment, who played a number of appropriate airs.

These were the first notes of what was to become a world-wide anthem to Burns.The chorus was taken up all over Scotland, but not every note was approving. There were a few dissonant chords heard in the land. Burns, when living, had presented a proud, stubborn face to the world, even at his lowest, and this attitude was wholly consistent with his character and personality.

> Our poet was rather below the usual standard, but was neatly formed and active in his habits. He had a ruddy complexion, the index of his uniformly temperate habits and good health – a piercing eye and an animated countenance; a somewhat irritable temper, the characteristic of the poetical temperament...

That was written by Alexander Ross, a schoolmaster at Lochlee, who had at least known and seen Burns in real life, which was more than could be said about those who were now to follow in having their say about this most complicated man. Ross was as entitled to his opinion as any and no doubt that was how Burns alive looked to him. Burns dead, however, seemed to take on a thousand faces, each more resembling the describer more than the described, but with his death, the Burns Industry, as it has come to be called, was born.

The funeral in 1796, on a typical Scottish summer's day, a wet Monday in July, had passed almost in silence as a huge street crowd of many thousands peered beyond the bayonets of the soldiers facing them to watch the cortege go by as if it carried the remains of a gnarled general who had lived too long rather than what was left of a poet who had not lived long enough. It was almost laughable in its incongruity. There had never been a funeral like it in Scotland nor was there ever to be again. Not even Sir Walter Scott was so honoured in death. A good friend of Burns, William Grierson, who had travelled down from Glasgow to attend, noted in his diary that night – 'in respect to the memory of such a genius as Mr Burns his funeral was uncommonly splendid...'

In addition to the Dumfries Volunteers, two regular army units were detailed to attend – The Angus-shire Fencibles and the Cinque Ports Cavalry – the latter under the command of Robert Banks Jenkinson, later to become Lord Liverpool and a future Prime Minister of Great Britain. They assembled at the Court House and escorted the cortege to St Michael's Kirkyard. Gilbert was the only family member present among the party of dignitaries who walked slowly behind the muffled drums of the Cinque Ports Cavalry band. At the same time, every bell in every church in Dumfries tolled. Their tolling and the beating of the army drums were the only sounds to be heard.

But once the body was in the ground and the martial parade had marched away with its bands and bayonets, it was as if other weapons came out. Rather than Mr Handel's Dead March from *Saul* one feels the band ought to have played 'Fats' Waller's *I'll be glad when you're dead, you rascal, you*. Never mind, his person was now beyond all harm, but his reputation, still wet with his last exertions on the songs for George Thomson, was hanging up like a shirt waiting drying in the wind. It was hardly pegged before it was cut to shreds by another kind of army, each armed with their own particular grudge-knife. Figuratively speaking, they took possession of the empty hearse, determined to get to Parnassus on his broad back rather than on their own feet. Most would never make the foothills of Fame even if they crawled on their hands and knees, but that didn't stop the barrage of printed words that opened up then and has been rumbling away on paper ever since.

Fortunately, we are concerned in these particular pages with the spoken word as it relates to Burns but it is impossible to ignore the noise that rose up around his name after that numbing, enormous, and largely silent funeral. One of the first to cast a stone was the Reverend William Peebles, who saw an opportunity for revenge for the poet's satirical barbs against the clergy when he pricked Peebles nicely in *The Holy Fair*:

For Peebles, frae the water-fit,
Ascends the holy rostrum.
See, up he's got the word o God,
An meek and mim has viewed it...

By 1811, the meek had inherited a certain reservoir of spleen and it was directed towards Burns in something Peebles called *Burns Renowned* in which the good Doctor, showing nothing of Christian charity, and without the least intention of turning the other cheek, lambasted Burns and the Burnsians. The following is merely an excerpt:

And do you grudge the ploughman's praise,
The Bard of Scotland's far-famed lays;
The man of humour, wit and fun,
Rewards confer'd, and honours won;
Whom Caledonia's Hunt of Squires,
Ev'n first nobility, admires,
By fairest ladies brought in view,
By clergymen and poets too...
Nor is this all: from age to age,
As for a monarch, hero, sage,
Let anniversaries repeat
His glories, celebrate a feat
Imbibe his spirit, sing his songs,
Extol his name, lament his wrongs,
His death deplore, excuse his fate,
And raise him far above the great.
What call you this? Is it Insania?
I'll coin a word, 'ts Burnsomania...'

Luckily, Burnsomania wasn't contagious, although it has never been completely eradicated even to our own day, but traces of it can be found in most non-Scottish comments about Burns, that is when they are not being fatuously patronising. But their day had not yet come, though it must be noted that Oxford University was early in the field with a Burns Dinner in 1806, which was hosted by John Wilson of Magadalen College and featured 'a poetical address' by Mr McCormick of Balliol. It was only in Scotland that the gatherings could be considered, as the Edinburgh Evening Courant put it – 'as the indication of a general national feeling'. The country was still getting used to having a literary hero.

The Dunfermine United Burns Club was the next to be formed. Mr J. Johnstone, the original secretary, writing from the New Inn on 25 January 1812, explains further:

> Met according to agreement and having spent the day in a manner highly satisfactory to all present, resolved to perpetuate the institution by the name of *The Haggis Club*... Ordered, that office-bearers do meet on the evening of Auld Hansel Monday AD 1813 in McLellan's Inn to arrange the business of the Club preparatory to the annual meeting on 25th of January.

And on 25 January 1814:

> This day the Haggis Club met in terms of the regulations and dined together in commemoration of the birthday of Burns. Mr Stenhouse, younger, being President, and failing to appear, or to rend a sufficient excuse for his absence, was fined ten shillings sterling. Mr Bowes was also fined five shillings for having mislaid the Minute Book of the Club. Ordered that these fines be applied to the purchase of a portrait of Burns to be hung in the clubroom.

The importance of the Laureate at the Club was underlined by the following entry:

> At this sederunt, the Haggis Club elected, and hereby do elect, Mr Andrew Mercer, commonly called Aldie, to be Laureate at the Club *ad vitam aut culpam*; and ordained, and hereby do ordain, that at every meeting of the Haggis Club, the

> aforesaid Laureate, as the sole emoluments of his office, shall be entitled to a Canister of Black Toffees; *quantam sufficit*; of Scotch Fare and Scotch Drink *ad libitum…*'

Aldie duly obliged. The following example, from his *Lamentation* of 1814, is typical of the bardic effusions of the day.

Auld Scotia ay mourns now
The birth day of Burns now
Ay when it returns now
Since Burns is awa.

The auld town of Ayr now
Needna haud her Fair now
There's nae lilting there now
Since Burns is awa.

There's nae Hallowe'en now
There's nae April Queen now
We've blear'd a' our e'en now
Since Burns is awa.

There's naething but gloom now
On the braes o' bonny Doon now
The flowers never bloom now
Since Burns is awa.

Scotia's harp is unstrung now
Her praise never sung now
She's lost her very tongue now
Since Burns is awa.

That was surely worth a cannister of black toffees.

If the Battle of Waterloo in 1815 marked the end of Napoleon, it also indicated the temporary eclipse of that known Burns admirer, William Pitt the Younger. It would appear that sometime after the death of Burns, Pitt was at Lord Liverpool's table and was heard to remark that 'since the time of Shakespeare poetry has never come so sweetly from the hand of Nature as in his rhyme.' The admiration was not mutual. At a dinner in Dumfries, a toast to Pitt was proposed. Burns refused to drink it and instead, countered with 'I will give you a better man – George Washington.' Since the American

War of Independence was of recent memory and Washington was president of a revolutionary country, this was not only foolhardy, but dangerous. Instead, Burns's local and national fame protected his indiscretion and he was merely shouted down. But incidents like this, and there were many, probably cost him a Civil List pension.

One hundred years later, he was even more famous, and in little need of a pension. Those shouted down now were those who dared to impugn his memory in any degree. The dinners now had their air of canonical, rather than masonic rites as speaker after speaker tried to make a miserable saint out of a happy sinner. However, some voices rang true and none more so than when a grand assembly met in Edinburgh to celebrate Burns's birth in the presence of his brother Gilbert and with another old play-mate and travelling companion, Robert Ainslie, in the chair. 'At a late hour', no less than James Hogg, the Ettrick Shepherd, gave the toast from the Burns Bowl of whisky punch and no doubt favoured the company with a song. Echoes of this must have been picked in the following year, for the Edinburgh *Evening Courant* of 27 January 1816 reported:

> The meeting was held on Thursday last at MacEwan's Tavern, in the Royal Exchange, where an extremely good dinner, and plenty of good wine, was given to the guests for a guinea a head. The company exceeded one hundred in number, and comprised a respectable proportion of rank and fashion, and a high display of literary talent...'

Walter Scott was one of the stewards, and John Wilson ('Christopher North') attended as did George Thomson, the publisher of Burns's songs. Also there was Lieutenant-Colonel Wilson – 'late from the field of Waterloo'. The company sat down at 6 o'clock and after 'a fine canon' and some songs, they got down to the main business of the evening which was the long lists of toasts in descending order, starting with the King, the Prince Regent and then Robert Burns.

> The Memory of Burns' in solemn silence was drank [sic] by the company standing; after which some beautiful verses, the composition of Mr [Alexander] Boswell, were recited. These were followed by the Glee, 'Come, Shepherds, we'll follow the Hearse'.

The next toast was 'The Widow and Children of the Poet' followed by 'The Friends of Burns'. Those named included Dr Blacklock, Mrs Dunlop, the Earl of Glencairn and Dr Currie. Succeeding this was the toast 'The Admirers of Burns' which, by inference, included everyone there, and after another glee, the toasts continued via the poets of Scotland mentioning Thomson, Ramsay and Fergusson, then the poets of England from Chaucer to Byron, then *Ye Mariners of England* (written by a Scot, Thomas Campbell). Next came the Duke of Wellington coupled with *The Heroes of Waterloo*, when, no doubt, Colonel Wilson took a bow.

The lengthy toast list was officially closed with the name of Joanna Baillie, 'a Scotswoman who yields the palm of poetical excellence to neither sex, and to no country'. This put Robert Burns firmly in his place. Not that it mattered. By eleven o'clock, the Chairman had departed, indisposed, and it was two o'clock the next morning before the last of the informal toasts was drunk and company dispersed, the object of their gathering, the Poet Burns, quite forgotten. Regrettably, this set a pattern for such events that has been assiduously copied ever since, even if their company did not boast a hero from the battle of Waterloo.

In the meantime, John Syme, Burns's good friend in Dumfries was trying to raise some kind of memorial to Burns in that town where Jean Burns still lived with her three sons, but Dumfries was apathetic. An appeal was launched nationally and the sum of 1200 pounds was raised on behalf of the widow Burns and her five surviving children. Dr Currie's book on Burns brought in another 1400 pounds so it could said that Jean and the bairns were provided for. It was not until 1823 that she was offered a Government pension of less than a pound a week, which she proudly turned down as being insulting to her late husband's name. Her two sons in the East India Company made her an annuity instead.

Discussions went on through 1814 about a possible Burns monument in St Michael's Kirkyard but it took till the following year to raise the necessary 2000 pounds for it. Eventually his remains were moved to an imposing marble mausoleum in its south-east corner, but one feels it was as result of the efforts of the few rather than the will of the many as far as Dumfries was concerned. Burns was dead and, according to some in the town, both he and Dumfries were the better for it. Critic, William Hazlitt, who gave a public lecture *On Burns and the Old English Ballads* commented on this very point of public apathy by certain people in his Table Talk published in 1821:

> When a man is dead, they put money in his coffin, erect monuments to his memory, and celebrate the memory of his birthday in set speeches. Would they take any notice of him if he were living? No! I was complaining of this to a Scotchman who had been attending a dinner and a subscription to raise a monument to Burns. He replied, he would sooner subscribe twenty pounds to his monument than have given it him while living; so that if the poet were to come to life again, he would treat him just as he was treated in fact. This was an honest Scotchman. What *he* said, the rest would do.

Sadly, this might be the case. The dead can be safely dealt with, but the living can be awkward and embarrassing.

No less so was the meagre donation of His Royal Highness King George IV of 50 guineas towards the cost of the Burns Mausoleum, considering that His Majesty's father gave 500 guineas to the messenger who brought him the news of his son's birth. It is hard to think that this utterly useless Royal appendage was held to be ten times the value of our poet. It is questionable, however, that Burns, had he been alive, given his Republican sympathies, would have taken a penny from a Hanoverian booby, although there was nothing he would have liked more at the end than a wealthy patron or even that wished-for sinecure with the Excise. But it was all too late. Now public subscription from all sides saw his dead body given marble housing at a cost that would have kept the Dumfries poor for a year. Instead, the same poor folk, who had truly loved and admired the poet, were kept from his funeral by bayonets.

By this time, clubs were sprouting in every main city and almost all towns and even the smallest villages. In 1820, Dumfries finally capitulated to the trend and the Dumfries Burns Club, destined to be one of the finest in the movement, was founded at the Globe Inn, the poet's own 'local'. Around the same time, David Sillar, the 'Dainty Davie' of Burns's youth, was involved in the setting-up of the Irvine Club and before long there were as many as a hundred Burns clubs in existence. The Burns Supper became part of the fabric of Scottish social life, both at home and abroad, and by the end of the 19th-century, as we shall see, it had expanded to such a degree as a symbol of Scottish identity, as to become a virtual Burns festival in itself.

It had not yet degenerated into the corporate, kilted Burns bonanza of modern times. Burns never wore a kilt in his life, nor did he know anyone who did, yet it seems to have become required dress at the Burns Supper today. I suppose it lends a Scottish distinctiveness to what, after all, is a Scottish occasion, but it is more a bow to sartorial fashion than a gesture towards the Lowlander at the centre of their festivities. He was a proud Scot but he was strictly a breeches man.

As I have said elsewhere, the Burns Supper of today, despite the top speakers, the best singers, the finest fiddlers, and the army of waitresses hired for the occasion, has only a nominal association with the Bard. In many cases it is nothing more than a sham ritual masquerading as a rite. This is Burns as entertainment. Which is why we have personalities as comperes and comedians for the Toast to the Lassies. If, as they all say, his 'sweetest hours were spent among the lassies' there is a singular lack of sweetness in most of the modern toasts which are nothing more than unsubtle innuendo and schoolboy smut. It also occurs to me that the simple message of Burns that 'man to man the warld o'er should brothers be' is rather contradicted by the presence of a top table. All Burns Suppers should be in the round.

All the spontaneous gaiety of the man, not to mention his manly dignity, is lost in a welter of onerous introductions, boring speeches, and what is even worse, hackneyed singing of the great songs and incomprehensible or lugubrious recitations. And all this under a Niagara of drink. This surely does scant honour to a man who loved the social occasion, but not one run riot in the lesser interests of a good night out with the boys. They prefer Rabbie with his breeches down, a glass in his hand and a girl in his arms. You can be sure that few of these fellows had given a thought to Burns since the previous year and won't until the next. Fewer still had read him, but then Burns has always been more praised than read, but just enough of him is read to keep the flame alive.

Meantime, the ubiquitous Nasmyth reproduction has looked down on a kind of Burnsian bacchanalia. Normally sober and hard-working citizens seem to consider that a ticket for a Burns Supper is a passport for any kind of licence. Of course there are the serious students and the genuine Burns lovers who attend such nights and know and respect the works and the man, but they are in a large minority, if you see what I mean. Their voice is little heard above the noise of unsteady feet going and to and from the men's room.

Yet all over the world, there are quiet gatherings where the essence of Burns is still evident, where people have taken the time to think about the man and be grateful for him, but the Burns industry has no place for such specialism. It needs the numbers, and the bigger the better in most cases, but these over-blown occasions with their empty charades and offensive cabaret acts do Burns, and the real Burnsians, more harm than good. It must be admitted, however, that people do enjoy their annual blast of Janwar hot air, and Burns, despite them, does get the odd look in, but it's generally very odd. I suppose, like the poor, the present format, with James Thomson's outdated lyrics for *The Star o Robbie Burns* being lustily sung out, in the chorus at least, will always be with us, as long as there are secretaries who see that it's done as it's always been done, and that the piper gets his dram.

In 1823 work was begun on a Greek Temple on top of the Calton Hill in Edinburgh to commemorate Burns and a statue by Flaxman was inserted into it. The statue came free but the building cost over three thousand pounds. The committee organising it was headed by General Dunlop, the son of Mrs Dunlop of Dunlop. Generals, and statues and lords and ladies, mausoleums and cenotaphs, Princes of the realm and all the names of the day. Whatever can be said of it all, the Burns image had come a long way from that first simple supper for nine friends in 1801.

Jean Armour Burns died in 1834, a little-known wife who had dwindled into a celebrity widow, but she remained the same Jean Armour despite her spread of years. She was buried beside her husband, leaving three grown sons out of the nine births she had known with the poet. The toast was 'Three-times-three' to the name of Burns, but the Burns children the world was to know better were the offspring of his wit and imagination, born out of zeal for his country and love of its men and women – in other words, his poems and songs. His natural children, that is the three sons and two daughters out of wedlock, made their own lives, as we shall see, well away from celebrity spotlight of their father. The boys were educated, two of them at Christ's Hospital in London, and the girls found marriages. Jean stayed on in the house, despite many invitations to return to Ayrshire and was content to remain single although still under forty and still a fine-looking woman. I think, after a volatile life with Robert Burns, she was glad of the rest.

When she died, the house was bought by Dr Maxwell, and then, in 1851, purchased by her son, William, who, seven years later, signed a Disposition, giving it over to the Dumfries Education Society to maintain in return for a small annuity to the family. It was not until 1934 that the Burns House was taken over by the Dumfries and Galloway Infirmary as the trustees of the property, who in turn leased it to the Town Council. The house was completely renovated and restored to the state of Burns's time. The finished work was formally opened to the public in a ceremony broadcast nationally by the BBC by Jean Armour Burns Brown, a grand-daughter of the second Robert Burns – on the wrong side of the blanket. This fact was not broadcast, yet somehow, it seemed fitting.

Ninety years earlier, the last of the family showed a much greater reluctance to go public with their private link to the poet, but his youngest sister and two of the three surviving sons were to feature as guests of honour at the next posthumous Burns milestone – the Ayr Festival of 1844. *Punch* in London commented at the time: 'Scotland is tremendously earnest in all that relates to Burns; earnest alike in her gratitude and her penance.' But then London is a long way from Ayr in every sense. Scots knew the importance of being earnest about Burns and on Tuesday 6 August they flocked to the south-west from all parts of the country for the event. Some reports say that as many as 80,000 men, women and children men assembled on the Braes o Doon that day. Whatever the actual number, it was certainly a crowd of football stadium proportions and it was just as enthusiastic. It was the first-ever Burns Festival, it was summer time and, as usual, it was raining.

Notwithstanding, in the specially-built pavilion before a specially-favoured 2,000 persons, the speeches went on throughout the day, and none was brief. Under the Presidency of the Earl of Eglinton and with Professor John Wilson as croupier, the vast audience endured hour after hour of damp oratory sustained only by fervour for their young poet and their Scottish sense of duty and proper respect for the dead. One wonders, given the size of the crowd and their informal spread over the area involved, how many of them actually *heard* what was being said, but there is no record of anybody's leaving before darkness fell.

As mentioned, the principal guests were Burns's two sons, the oldest Robert, and the youngest Major James Glencairn Burns. Also attending with the poet's only surviving sister, Isabella (Mrs John Begg) was Jessie Lewars (Mrs John Thomson) who attended Burns in his last illness. The Earl of Glencairn's was a lengthy introduction and he apologised for having gone on so long. Cries of 'No! No! No!' came from those assembled but through them could be heard the applause of agreement. The noble lord hurried to his conclusion by asking those present to join with him in 'raising one overflowing bumper, and in joining to it, every expression of enthusiasm you can, to The Memory of Burns.' At this there was 'rapturous applause' and Robert Burns Junior then rose to reply for the family:

> My Lord, Ladies and Gentlemen. Of course it cannot be expected at such a meeting such as the present, that the sons of Burns should expatriate on the merits and genius of their deceased father. Around them are an immense number of admirers, who, by their presence here this day, bear a sufficient testimony to the opinion in which they hold his memory and the high esteem in which they hold his genius. In the language of the late Sir Christopher Wren, though very differently applied, the sons of Burns can say, that to obtain a living testimony to their father's genius, they only have to look around them. I beg in the name of my aunt, brothers and myself to return our heartfelt and grateful thanks for the honour that this day been paid to my father's memory.

Professor Wilson's was an even lengthier oration, but then everybody was out to make a day of it despite the rain. This is a short extract.

> I fear I am trespassing on your time too much, but I would fain keep your attention for a very short time longer, while I say that there is a voice heard above and below and round about – the voice of mere admiration, as it has been expressed by men of taste and criticism. There is a voice which those who listen to it can hear – a voice which has pronounced its judgment on the character of Burns – a

judgment which cannot on earth be carried to a higher tribunal, and which never will be reversed. It was heard of old, and struck terror into the hearts of tyrants, who quaked and quailed and fled for fear from this land before the unconquered Caledonian spear. It is a voice they were pleased to hear; it was like the sound of distant waterfalls, the murmurs of the summer woods, or the voice of the mighty sea which ever rolls even on. I mean the voice of the people of Scotland, of her peasantry and trades, of all who earn their bread by the sweat of their brow – the voice of the working men.

I shall not pretend to draw their character; this I may say of them now, and boldly, that they do not choose to be dictated to as to the choice of those who with them shall be a household word. They are men from whose hands easier would it be to wrench the weapon than ever to wrench their worship from their hearts. They are men who loved truth, sincerity, integrity, resolution, and independence – an open front and a bold eye that fears not to look on the face of clay. They do not demand in one and the same person inconsistent virtues; they are no lovers of perfection or of perfectibility; they know that there are fainter and darker shadows in the character of every man; and they seem, as we look back on their history, to have loved most those who have been subject most, within and without, to strong and severe temptations. Whether in triumph or in valour, they have shown at least, by the complexion of character of their souls, that they loved their country, and had no other passion so strong as the defence of the people.

Ay! They too, unless I am mistaken, loved those who had struggled with adversity; they loved those who have had their trials, their griefs, their sorrows; and, most of all, they loved those who were not ashamed of confessing that they were so, and who threw themselves on the common feelings and forgiveness here below, and trusted for forgiveness on other principles and feelings altogether to that source from which alone it can come. The love of the people of Scotland for those whom they have loved has not been exclusive: it has been comprehensive. They left the appearance of their different characters, and honoured them for every advance they made, provided they saw the strength of character, moral and intellectual. Such a people as this, possessing such feelings,

> could not but look upon Robert Burns, and while they admired him they also loved him with the truest affection, as well for the virtues as for the sorrows and the griefs of that great, but in some respects unfortunate, man.

This Wilson was the same man who, as 'Christopher North', had written of Burns in 1818, in an article pithily entitled 'Some Observations on the Agricultural and that of the Pastoral District of Scotland, illustrated by a Comparative View of the genius of Burns and the Ettrick Shepherd':

> There is a pathetic moral in the imperfect character of Burns, both as a poet and a man; nor ought they who delight both in him and his works, and rightly hold the anniversary of his birth to be a day sacred in the calendar of genius – to forget, that it was often the consciousness of his own frailties that made him so true a painter of human passions.

Wilson had much to answer for in the ensuing century when the matter of Burns's 'frailties' seems to obsess every speaker on every Burns occasion. At the Ayr Festival, however he had to speak as himself, and after several hours, he concluded,

> Was he worthy of their love? Taking it for granted, and we are entitled to do so, then why did they love him? They loved him because he loved his own order, nor ever desired for a single hour to quit it. They loved him because he loved the very humblest condition of humanity so much, that by his connection he saw more truly and became more distinctly acquainted with what was truly good, and imbued with a spirit of love in the soul of a man. They loved him for that which he had sometimes been most absurdly questioned for – his independence. They loved him for bringing sunshine into dark places; not for representing the poor hard-working man as an object of pity, but for showing that there was something more than is dreamed of in the world's philosophy among the tillers of the soil and the humblest children of the land.

This speech brought what was called the 'Demonstration' at last to a close, and, once again, Robert Burns rose to reply – briefly:

> My Lord, Ladies and Gentlemen. You may be assured that the sons of Burns feel all that they ought to feel on an occasion so

> peculiarly gratifying to them, and on account of so nobly generous a welcome to the Banks of Doon. In whatever land they have wandered – wherever they have gone – they have invariably found a kind reception prepared for them by the genius and fame of their father; and under the providence of Almighty God, they owe to the admirers of his genius all that they have, and what competencies they now enjoy. We have no claim to attention individually, we are all aware that genius, and more particularly poetic genius, is not hereditary, and in this case the mantle of Elijah has not desended upon Elisha. The sons of Burns have grateful hearts, and will remember, so long as they live, the honour which has this day been conferred upon them by the noble and illustrious of our own land – and many generous and kind spirits from other lands – some from the far West, a country composed of the great and the free, and altogether a kindred people. We beg to return our heartfelt thanks to this numerous and highly respectable company for the honour which has been done us this day.

The second Robert Burns was something of a lost figure in the Burns saga. Of great promise as a boy and with high intellect, much was expected of him, especially in mathematics, but after winning prizes at Glasgow University, he drifted into the Stamp Office at Somerset House in London, a dull post offered to him by the Prime Minister in 1832. He 'retired' within a year and lived out the rest of his life in Dumfries on a small pension given him because of 'the great literary talents of his father'. He found it hard to be the famous son of a famous father and took solace in the bottle and by taking pupils in the classics and his beloved mathematics. He had married young and he and Anne Sherwood had a daughter, Eliza. As soon as she was old enough, Eliza went out to India to join her Uncle James where she married a doctor and died in 1878. Her father never married again but he had two children by Emma Bland, another son and another Robert, and a daughter, Jane Emma.

Interestingly, this Robert Burns married a Mary Campbell, and they had yet another Robert, who died in Edinburgh in 1895. Jane Emma married a Thomas Brown and they had the daughter, Jean, who opened the Burns House as a museum, and from time to time gave genteel readings of her great-great uncle's more respectable poems, dressed in his costume, and looking uncannily like him. This performing ability was certainly not a trait inherited from her father. Essentially this Robert Burns was a loner. He died in 1857 having done nothing with the fine brain he was born with.

James Glencairn Burns was one of the two Burns sons who prospered and both did so as far from Scotland as they could. Both James and William Nicol Burns received commissions in the East India Company and both retired as colonels, William, the elder, to Cheltenham and James to become a Judge and Collecter at Cahar, in India. When he finally retired, he joined his brother in Cheltenham. By this time both men were widowers. William was childless but James had two daughters by two wives and these ladies laid the basis of the highly respectable, if rather dull, lineage that saw the Burns stock move up the social scale and into blank, professional obscurity. James's first daughter, Sarah, had also married a doctor, and her son was the last direct male descendant of Robert Burns. He went to America and worked in a shipping office. It was a rather prosaic end to the line, but the fire had only flamed once and it had long burned itself out.

The Burns brothers skilfully avoided their father's limelight. They were no less proud of their giant of a father's reputation but had no wish to trade on it. They therefore limited their visits to Scotland as much as possible. However, after the huge success of the 1844 Festival at Ayr, the middle brother, William, was constrained to join James in a return in the following year, this time to follow their father's footsteps through the Highlands. The Inverness Courier carried a full report of the brothers' visit to that town.

> They were both extremely shy men and the last thing they wanted was publicity, but there were many ardent literati in Inverness in those days, and they straightaway decided to pay all the honour in their power to the two pilgrims. A public banquet was spedily arranged, but that was not considered to be sufficient, and the Town Council were prevailed upon to confer the Freedom of the Burgh on the visitors. The two functions were combined, and on the 6th August an enthusiastic gathering assembled in the Caledonian Hotel, Provost Sutherland occupying the chair, and Colonel Mackintosh of Farr being croupier. Both the visitors were officers in the army, the elder then being Lieut. Colonel

> William Nicol Burns and the younger Major (subsequently Lieut. Colonel) James Glencairn Burns. Colonel Mackintosh of Farr had served with the latter in India, and during the dinner referred to their youthful acquaintanceship. As was usual in those days, the speches were many and eloquent, but the guests, as we have remarked, were shy men, and when the ceremony of conferring the Freedom of the Burgh was reached, only one of them could be prevailed upon to reply, the elder brother, Colonel Burns, returning thanks for both. But the company were determined to have a speech from Major Burns, especially as his brother, in the course of his remarks, had disclosed the interesting fact that the Major was proficient in Gaelic, the study of which he had commenced in his college days, and had continued ever since. But how could a speech be extracted from the reticent Major? Somebody hit on a brilliant idea. He remembered that Major Burns was the proud father of several daughters, and straightway their health was proposed, and pledged with the real Highland fervour. Whereupon there was no course open to the blushing guest but to rise and reply. So the company got their speech, and something else as well; for the Major, after returning his thanks, said he was no speaker, but that if they would permit him, he would sing one of his father's songs to them instead, a proposition which, needless to say, was received with the greatest enthusiasm. So he sang 'O' a the airts the wind can blaw' to the great delight of the company. Thus did the Major repay the courtesy of the toast by giving an Inverness gathering the privilege of hearing one of Burns' own songs sung by one of Burns' own sons.'

Strangely enough, it was Burns' singing that Aunt Isabella remembered of him best. Bella was the baby of the Burns family, and perhaps she got the best of her big brother. As time went on the youngest child became the oldest survivor. She was constantly sought out by celebrities, information-seekers and scholars for direct information about Robert as she remembered him. Her comments as an old woman, and the mother of nine children, tended to vary according to her whim, but her callers had to bear in mind that here was a voice that had all the sounds of old Ayrshire in it, and one which Burns had heard intimately when both were young.

Mrs Begg considered her brother 'no great efficient in music'. This despite the fact that he could read music and notate from singing. His own singing voice, she thought, was just like his fiddle playing – 'rude and rough, but croonin' tae a body's sel' does weel enough.' Apparently, Burns used to play the fiddle in the fields in the summer when they sheltered from the rain, and in the winter:

> He used to rise early and chop the gathering coal, then play for the amusement of thae that were in bed. It could not be borne forever and speedily came to an end.

It is amusing to think of the Burns siblings shouting down Scotland's greatest songwriter before breakfast, but where better to learn his trade than at his own fireside?

Isabella Begg died in 1858 at Bridge House in Alloway, not far from the cottage from where William Burnes had started out just over a hundred years earlier. She was the final link with the original family and now that she was gone there were fewer left, outside the family, who could say that they knew the living Burns.

But the dead Burns continued to fascinate, as edition after edition of the complete works followed in succession all round the world. The centenary of his birth was approaching and that same world, or at least its Scottish segment, geared itself for what was to amount to one huge, year-long Burns Supper in what was to be called 'The Universal Burns Centenary Celebrations of 1859'. It was a year that was to be marked memorably.

> With melting heart and brimful eye
> I'll mind you still, tho far awa.
> (The Farewell)

2

The Centenary Celebrations

1859

> Through busiest street and lonliest glen are felt the flashes of his pen…
> Deep in the general heart of men his power survives.
>
> (William Wordsworth)

In the early summer of 1858, workers at the Glasgow *Daily Bulletin* (the first Penny newspaper in Great Britain) were given a day's outing by their employers to the Brig o' Doon Hotel in Ayrshire. The proprietor of the paper, Colin Rae-Brown, as croupier for the dinner that evening, was given the duty of proposing a toast to 'The Memory of Burns'. While walking over the old brig to the hotel, he was puzzling over what he might say about the poet that was not hackneyed and had not been said before, when he realised that the following January would be exactly a hundred years from Burns's birth. And with that thought, came his great idea and the theme for his speech a few hours later. As he said, he would call for 'a *national* celebration of the glorious twenty-fifth in 1859 throughout the kingdom – and even beyond – wherever Scotsmen are congregated, throughout the world'.

The idea was taken up with enthusiasm at the *Bulletin* dinner and before long a committee was set up in Glasgow and Rae-Brown was appointed Honorary Secretary, authorised to circularise from his office at 119 St Vincent Street news of the proposed Memorial Celebration. The Circular sent out stated:

> To Scotsmen and Scotswomen everywhere – and to their posterity in the generations to come – this Centenary will, if universal, prove not only a source of the greatest delight, but a lasting bond of union between the inhabitants of Caledonia, and those of every country and clime who sincerely adopt as their creed – A MAN'S A MAN FOR A' THAT.

The reaction, not only nation-wide, but world-wide, was astonishing. Rae-Brown's idea had touched a nerve and Scots people everywhere were energised to immediate action. The extent of the celebrations can be seen in a glance at the statistics. According to James Ballantine of Edinburgh, there were 676 recorded Burns events in Scotland, 76 in England, 61 in the United States, 48 in what was then termed 'the Colonies', 10 in Ireland and a solitary dinner in Copenhagen.

These figures say much for the state of our poet's name and fame a hundred years after his birth but they hardly convey the passion that caused every kind of Scotland that existed in the world to suddenly assert itself in the name of Burns. In all sorts of situation, in every range of climate, fur-coated or sun-hatted, men convened in small groups, modest dinners and in spontaneous gatherings to remember Robert Burns. In short, wherever two or more hands could be found to cross in a chorus of *Auld Lang Syne*, there was the spirit of Burns in the midst of them.

There had been a similar sort of commemoration for a poet before when the Stratford Jubilee of 1769 honoured the memory of Shakespeare but it turned out to be more of homage to the actor, David Garrick, than to the English Bard. In any case, it was strictly confined to Stratford but in 1859 Burns went international. Not that England did not do its bit for the centenary, and once again an actor was involved. Samuel Phelps was a famous Shakespearean in his day and he was chosen to recite the winning entry in a country-wide poetry competition organised by the *National Magazine* in conjunction with the directors of the Crystal Palace to celebrate a hundred years of Robert Burns. There were 621 entries and the winner of the prize of fifty guineas was a Miss Isa Craig who submitted three poems. Her prizewinner was declaimed by Mr Phelps 'in that grave and weighty style for which he is notorious', as The Times put it, before fifteen thousand people who had paid as much as half-a-crown a head to hear him. The opening lines were:

> A Poet peasant born
> Who more of Fame's immortal dower
> Unto her country brings
> Than all the Kings...

Punch described the event in its own idiosyncratic style:

Truly, as writers remark, whose lines are well guerdoned by pennies,
The scene which arrested the eye was little way short of imposing.
Full in the midst was a bust which the vulgar described as a buster;
Burns, with a gold wreath on his brow, size the colossal, by Marshall.
Round him, but smaller, the bards of the soul-stirring days when he flourished.
Near him, was drawn, like a bow, a shrine of tasteful description,
Wherein, secured by plate-glass, (for collectors are thundering priggers)
Lay, in their niches, Burns relics, autographs, snuff-boxes, letters,
Hair of the poet himself, hair of his loved Highland Mary,
The portrait by Nasmyth, undoubted, likewise the portrait by Taylor
Which folks have accepted as Robert but which I believe to be Gilbert;
There too, the worm-eaten desk on which was composed Tam O'Shanter,
Brown as the limbs of the hags who danced in that Scotch Walpurgis...

At St Martin's Hall, *A Nicht Wi' Burns* was held in which Mr Arthur Young appeared as Shakespeare and recited from The Merchant of Venice. At Liverpool they danced till six in the morning and in Edinburgh, the shops were closed and Mr Walter Glover, who once had been given a drink by Burns, was led to the platform to recite *Tam o Shanter. The Times* reported all these and the many other various events over seven columns although it thundered against the Crystal Palace Burns Festival:

> In what way the centenary celebrations of the Scottish poet's birth could possibly concern the Crystal Palace, and why Englishman, who had never thought of celebrating Shakespeare or Milton with similar pomp, should suddenly get up an extraordinary display in honour of Burns, or would possibly have been thought the questions worth considering...

What it goes on to consider very pointedly was that fifteen thousand people paid half-a-crown a head on the day. Even Charles Dickens was moved to protest. In an article entitled 'Burns as a Hat-Peg', he saw a great poet reduced to a hat-peg on which promoters of all kinds could hang their hats, and where even the children of Elizabeth Thompson of Pollokshaws (his daughter by Anna Park), were among the exhibits in the Glasgow Exhibition.

Ballantine devoted no less than 606 closely typed pages to his account of the year. Each event, complete with comprehensive guest list, no doubt in strict pecking order, offered complete texts without comment and the sheer weight of words in itself was praiseworthy, if daunting. Victorian speakers, in that age of the public lecturer, would never use one word where ten would do, and their peroration went to the very limit of their hearer's indulgence. Length was measure of importance to them. The gentry, of course, were out in force. Everybody loves a lord, and no one better than the man trying to arrange a public dinner. Lords abounded in Burns's name during 1859, especially in the capital, Edinburgh.

> Edina! Scotia's darling seat! All hail your palaces and towers...

Lord Ardmillan, for instance, himself an Ayrshire man, presided at the banquet held in the Music Hall, Edinburgh, for which 'tables were laid for seven hundred persons'. Great interest was shown in the event, and on the day, shopkeepers began to close their shutters from early in the afternoon. Despite a snell wind, crowds began to gather in George St to watch the notables arrive in their cabs and carriages, much as they do today for the Oscars in Hollywood. The difference here was that the star of the evening was dead. Of course, *The Star o Robbie Burns* would never lose its gleam, and this lends a particular poignancy to Lord Ardmillan's reference in the 'hearty, manly eloquence' of his toast to the Immortal Memory, to the new-fangled phenomenon of electric light. At the conclusion of his speech, which reports say was delivered 'with great power and fervour', his Lordship said:

> Let us rather deal with the power of Burns' name as science has dealt with the electric element. Science has not stood afar off, scared by each flash, mourning each shivered tower; science has caught and purified the power, and chained it to the car of commerce and the chariot of beneficence, and applied it to the noble purpose of consolidating humanity – uniting all the world by the interchange of thought and feeling. On this day Burns is to us, not the memory of a departed, but the presence of a living power – (enthusiastic cheering) – the electric chain which knits the hearts of Scotchmen in every part of the world, stirring us not only to admiration of the poet's genius, but to the love of country, of liberty, and of home, and of all things beautiful and good. Therefore, I call on you to pledge me, not to solemn silence, but with our heartiest honours to 'The Immortal Robert Burns'.

The Music Hall celebrations went on for another four hours then the whole company, standing, hand in hand, sang *Auld Langsyne* [sic] and departed in the early hours in their cabs and carriages, but this time with no gaping crowd to watch them go.

There were four other Burns Banquets that night in four of the largest halls in Edinburgh, and at the Corn Exchange, the event was hosted by the Total Abstinence Society. One wonders how Burns himself would have enjoyed this one, even though report had it that it had 'come off with great *eclat*'. The Chairman, in his extended remarks, made reference to their more sober approach to the occasion, acknowledging in his opening remarks that they were gathered to do honour to a man who 'was not an immaculate character'.

> No doubt, ladies and gentlemen, many things could be pointed out which are deserving of severe criticism; but, when we consider the character of the man, we must consider it in reference to the times in which he lived. We must not measure a man like Burns by the gauge of the customs and sentiments of the present day alone. For example, if in the days of Burns, some great meeting had been called to celebrate the heroes whom he idolized and almost worshipped – I mean Wallace and Bruce – had a meeting been called for such a purpose when Burns lived and was in the zenith of his fame, I ask you, would it have been possible to have called 2,500 persons together in a hall like this, where they had nothing stronger to drink than tea and water?

Despite this tepid approval, one can be sure that 'frae Maidenkirk to Johnie Groats' that night a stronger beverage was preferred in other places. The Trades Delegates offered a fruit soiree in the Queen Street Hall, beginning at six o'clock, and Professor George Wilson, who held the Chair of Industrial Science, nevertheless claimed that:

> We are all poets in some degree. The child who thinks it can climb the rainbow, who believes that the moon can be clipped into stars, or who looks into its pillow, and sees wondrous things there, is a poet; every child who reads the Arabian Nights, who believes in Aladdin's lamp, or who goes to a pantomime, is a poet. And in later years we are all poets – love makes us poets. Every man lover is a poet; every gentle sweetheart is a poet; every mother bending over her suckling

> child is a poet; every son comforting his old mother is a poet. There is a poetry in all our lives, if we can feel it; and if we cannot, no Burns or any one can teach us it. But we want some one to sing it for us, and this Burns did; and how did he do it? He so sang that we not only enter intensely and sympathisingly into all his feelings, but he sang in the very way that we ourselves would have sung had we had the power. Think of this – that he has sung our native land into greater glory in the earth because it is the birth-land of Burns. There is not anywhere over the civilized world where men are able to appreciate genius, or worth, or reality, a nation which does not say that Scotland, in producing a ploughman like Burns, who did not pretend to speak more than the feelings of his own countrymen, but spoke them with the poet's power, must be a grand land. And he sang our Scottish tongue into a repute that it never had before, and secured for it a longevity that otherwise it never would have had, so that he would be a bold man who would predict the time when that mother speech will die, since Englishmen learn it for nothing but to read the songs of Burns. Such is his power over the language of our hearts and the language of our country, Scotsmen scattered over every part of the world are on this day assembled as we are now; and I have just learned that, at this very moment, my dear brother will be presiding at a meeting like this in far-distant Toronto.

A Mr Gorrie, speaking at the same meeting, must have spoken for many when he said, 'I feel as if I were trying to speak where a thousand voices already filled the air.' How true. And no doubt, a thousand different Robert Burns rose from their lips. All they would have in common was an uncomfortable mid-Victorian public attitude to his sex life and his reputed drinking, but at the 'Working Man's Festival' at the Dunedin Hall, emphasis was placed on his egalitarianism. Donald Ronald Macgregor presided and took the chance to recount an anecdote. It seems that Burns was walking in Leith Walk with a modish friend when they came upon a disreputable character, poorly dressed, whom Burns recognised as an old friend from Ayrshire. Burns immediately stopped and greeted the man warmly. When he had finished his crack and continued on his way, the Edinburgh dandy wondered why he had acknowledged such a shabby fellow. 'Sir', replied Burns, 'do you think it was the man's coat I was talking to? Or his hat or waistcoat? I was talking to the man within the clothes. A man, I may say, of more sense and worth that many of my fine, city friends.' The speaker also wished that some of these 'fine, city friends' might have helped Burns more than they did. Especially at the end of his short life, a time when the poet needed friends of any kind. It is ironic that most of the men gracing these public platforms in 1859 in Edinburgh could still be described as 'fine, city friends' to Burns.

Yet James Burn at the Globe Hotel in Hill Place made the point that 'no man in the present day, with anything like Burns's talents, could long go unrewarded; and we have good proof of what his countrymen would have done for him, if they had known the living man as well as they have known the poet.' I wonder. Burns had the knack of discomfiting many of his influential acquaintances just as much as he intrigued them. Or maybe he just frightened people off by his very intensity? Like many gifted people he was often his own worst enemy. His weak points were just as much a part of him as his strong. One must take the whole man or nothing. And the man they were all considering was not an Edinburgh man:

> Of a' the airts the wind can blaw, I dearly like the west...

In Glasgow, the capital city of the West, Sir Archibald Alison neatly dealt with the fact of Burns's frailties by quoting Bolinbroke's retort when reminded of the faults of his great political antagonist, Marlborough: 'Yes, I know he had faults; but he was so great a man I have forgot what they were.' He also added, to cheers, 'Let him that is without sin among you, throw the first stone.' Sir Archibald was speaking in the City Hall where the Immortal Memory was given 'with all the honours' rather than in the solemn silence that attends a toast to the dead, given that, as the speaker said, 'the Burns spirit lives on and will never die'. There were further great cheers at this. The toast was drunk with the whole company standing, with both the gentlemen and the ladies waving their handkerchiefs and 'making every demonstration of enthusiasm'.

The next to rise was no less than Colonel James Glencairn Burns, the fourth son of the poet. Colonel Burns, then aged 65, was no orator, and did not speak long. But who else, however spell-binding, could have made the effect this reserved man made when he said,

> As a leal and true Scot, and a warm admirer of the genius of the Bard, I have joined in doing honour to his memory. As his son, permit me to return to you my most sincere thanks for the same.

No one could follow that except an Englishman, and it was as such that the author of *Memories of Many Scenes*, Mr Monkton Milnes was introduced and received with great applause by the Glaswegians. He won them over at once by identifying the Scots as a people 'who read by turns, the Songs of David and the Poems by Burns'. While striving as a man, Burns had stirred the heart of a nation and '... something of a sacred halo now surrounds him.' Toasts started to come from right and left and on almost any heading. Colonel Burns found himself unexpectedly on his feet again when he had to reply to 'The Existing Relatives of the Poet'. The risk of being at the top table is that one must be ready to rise at any moment. As the night goes on, this becomes more difficult. However, the good colonel was again received with great applause.

> I have to thank my friend Trotter very heartily for the way in which he has introduced the toast, and you for the hearty manner in which you have responded to the toast of 'The Sons and Relatives of the Bard'. I may as well here enumerate them, as far as my knowledge extends. There is my brother William Nichol and myself; my two daughters, Mrs Hutchinson, with her two children, in Australia, and Annie Burns, now in Edinburgh; and my late brother Robert's daughter, Mrs Everett, with her daughter, in Belfast. These are the direct descendants. My uncle Gilbert left a large family, of whom survive one daughter (Ann) and three sons (William, Thomas and Gilbert). The three brothers have many olive branches. For the survivors of my late dear aunt, Mrs Begg, I leave my cousin Robert to thank you himself. (*Applause)*

Mr Robert Burns Begg, nephew of the poet, also responded to the toast, and said:

> I did not expect to be called upon to speak just now. I am unaccustomed to public speaking, and I cannot let my voice reach this immense assembly. All I can say is, that I have met with many kindnesses in the world, and I believe they are all owing to my connection with Burns. I owe the honour of

being here as a guest tonight solely to that, and I believe to an acquaintance many years ago with the late Sheriff Steele. I may, however, be allowed to say that I should like very much to live another hundred years to see such a sight as this... I thank you kindly.

Mr William Burns, no relation, was not nearly so complimentary or placatory.

When, not long ago, a few humble admirers of the poet and lovers of the man, met together for the express purpose of concerting a festival celebration in Glasgow on the occasion of the centenary of Burns, I must confess they had no conception of the result that was to follow from the labours. They were ignorant at that time of the deep fountain that was to be opened in the heart of the public. Their idea on the subject was that a great meeting might be held in Glasgow, as convenient locality, as had been done some years before on the banks of the Doon, towards which the worshippers of the poet – men eminent in literature both in Scotland, Ireland, and elsewhere, might congregate. Under the impression, they proposed to give the celebration in the City Hall, Glasgow, the designation of national, a designation which, it may be observed, it still retains. Probably that designation is not now absolutely correct. Still, it may not be thought altogether inappropriate, considering the magnitude of the meeting itself, and keeping in view that, whether national or not, it has been the mother of such a large project. Strange as it may appear now, when we see the dimensions to which this movement has attained, it was stated that the people of Edinburgh would look on the movement with a certain degree of disfavour.

(Signs of impatience)

But these speculations were dissolved by a process over which no individuals or set of individuals had any control, because a chord had been struck in the heart of the people which very soon vibrated, not only throughout Scotland, but through England and Ireland, and far away over the ocean, wherever the name or songs of Burns were known.

(Renewed interruptions)

Very soon, in place of the people of Edinburgh meeting the

> movement with opposition, they entered into it with the utmost enthusiasm.
> *(Continued signs of impatience)*
> Their example was followed by every town and village in the country. *(Interruptions and hisses)*
> I may mention one circumstance which has been made known to me since I entered the hall, and it is that the idea of a centenary celebration was first ventilated and brought under notice on the very spot where the poet himself was born.
> *(More signs of impatience)*
> I shall at once propose the toast, which I am glad to see you are all so anxious to drink.
> *(The toast was drunk with enthusiasm)*

This element of discord provoked by the mention of Edinburgh would come as no surprise to a Glasgow man, nor would it surprise him if a fight broke out. After all we were in Glasgow. Nevertheless, however noisily they were received, the toasts went on, column by column, page by page, hour by hour. So did the cat-calls and the cheers, the boos and the hisses, the hurrahs and the 'Hear-Hears', not to mention all the songs between. This went on until nearly midnight when people began to leave. Those who remained were, in the words of the press report, 'rather confused in their jollity'. No wonder. They had been there since five o'clock in the afternoon.

Things were calmer in the Merchants' Hall and Mr Thomas N. Brown was given the best of order when he rose to speak. He began by quoting a Burns letter:

> For my own affairs, I am in a fair way of becoming as eminent as Thomas a Kempis or John Bunyan; and you may expect henceforth to see my birthday inserted among the wonderful events in the Poor Robin's and Aberdeen Almanacs along with the black Monday and the Battle of Bothwell Bridge…

John Bunyan and Thomas a Kempis are indeed great names in their respective fields but do they really compare in terms of world recognition to the Ayrshire ploughman? And when was the Battle of Bothwell Bridge last commemorated? 1679? Even the almanacs he mentioned have long gone, but Burns's own eminence continues. This point, or something corresponding to it, was further taken up by Mr Brown.

> To single out from among the mass of men all living for their generation, and all destined to die with their generation, the one man of whom it may be truthfully predicted this man is not for an age, but for all time, is a task to which few are equal. The heart knoweth its own bitterness, and often genius alone knoweth its own greatness. In that seemingly random selection of names by which to illustrate his future celebrity, Burns very exactly foreshadowed the character of his renown. Thomas a Kempis and John Bunyan, the mystic of the middle ages and the marvellous dreamer of Elstow, are found alike in the mansion of the noble and the shielding of the peasant, but as the people's prophets are they specially honoured. The songs of Burns resound in castle and in hall, but as the poet of the people the memory of the bard is encircled with a wreath that shall be green forever... Fame so universal can receive but little expansion. Indeed all now left to even the most enthusiastic admirers of our national bard is simply to cast a few insignificant pebbles on the mighty cairn already towering to his glory from out the rock of humanity. But though the memory of the poet cannot possibly profit, we may profit much by this centenary. If the homage this night offered to his shade were not a hollow mockery, it is impossible it should fail to exert at once a potent and salutary influence upon modern society. The sincerity of that homage will be best discovered by interrogating ourselves whether it is simply a fashionable idol we follow the multitude to honour, or Robert Burns as he lived, laboured, loved, sung and suffered, to whom the incense of our admiration spontaneously arises...

He then took the opportunity to mention a contemporary Burns controversy.

> During the last few weeks some things have been said and some things have been written of our national bard which indicated that malice with its mask, and venom with its dart, are not yet wearied with assailing his reputation. The tirade of one of the most self-complacent of the clergy of the Scottish metropolis – a report of which I presume most of those I am now speaking to have seen in the newspapers – is worthy of no serious answer. It would be doing the Church of Scotland the grossest injustice to suppose that reverend gentleman any

> representative of her sentiments respecting this centenary. What motive prompted his outburst of impotent spleen, it would be difficult to determine. But in presence of such an ebullition of rage these words of the wise man flow to our lips, and commend themselves to our judgement, 'Answer not a fool according to his folly.'
> *(Cheers)*
> What superlative fascination lies in Burns, that honours Milton, Dante, Goethe had never received, are so profusely lavished on his memory? A genial English litterateur shall answer. The philosophy of the universal love of Burns is thus beautifully expounded by Leigh Hunt in this week's Spectator. 'What' he asks, 'is the reason of this difference between the fond love of the memory of such a man as Burns and the no love at all for those other great men, Shakespeare himself not excepted? For personal regard mixes little with our astonishment at Shakespeare genius – perhaps because of the very amount of the astonishment, and because we know little personally about him. The reason is, that Burns we do know; that we are astonished at him, but not enough to be oppressed with the astonishment; and that he fulfils all the other conditions necessary to universal regard. He is allied to the greatest minds by his genius, to the gravest by his grave thoughts, to the gayest by his gay ones, to the manliest by his independence, to the frail by his frailties, to the conscientious by his regrets, to the humblest ranks by his birth, to the poorest among them by his struggles with necessity; above all, to the social by his companionship, and to the whole world by his being emphatically a human creature, 'Relishing all sharply, passioned as they'.

Mr Brown concluded:

> Give praise to the man! a nation stood
> Beside his coffin with wet eyes,
> Her brave, her beautiful, her good,
> As when a loved one dies

There was great cheering as the speaker resumed his seat. George Troup of the *Glasgow Bulletin* had the unenviable job of following, but after spreading the Burns net internationally, and a timely mention of Burns's father, he ended with the obvious.

> I shall never speak again at a centenary of Robert Burns' birth. WE can never meet more for the purpose we have met tonight. It will be celebrated next time by our grandchildren and our great grandchildren, and we shall all be forgotten on the earth. But we can go out now again to our several duties in the world, with a warmer love to the land he loved dearly; and, in our hearts, a warmer wish for its prosperity and its social improvement and progress. On our different ways we can have no better guide than the poet's prayer:
>
> 'Stranger, go, Heaven be thy guide,
> Quo' the bedesman of Nithside.'

At the Royal Hotel, some forty or fifty gentlemen sat down to a sumptuous Scotch dinner at the end of which, James Hedderwick, editor of the *Glasgow Citizen*, and no mean writer himself, made a more material approach to the Bard's memory, but one which would have a greater relevance as time went by. This was the first foretaste of Burnsomania.

> Ten thousand people thronged to his funeral. Every scrap of his burly handwriting became a treasure. The public sorrow took visible shape in stone and marble. Not in favourite haunt of his but became immediately and forever classic. Why, the very stool on which he had sat while correcting his proof sheets in Edinburgh was elevated into an object of respect! I suppose it has long since been broken up into snuff boxes...
>
> When, in the doom which overtakes all things human, his household good came to be scattered, how marvellously had their value risen! An old fender on which he had been accustomed to toast his toes, while crooning, it might be, his immortal 'Vision' in the flickering hearthlight, brought twentyfold its original cost. The top of a superannuated shower bath, which had been employed to drench away a poetic rheumatism, was run up to a fabulous sum. A dilapidated coffee pot, a pair of bellows sorely afflicted with asthma, and other such lumber, commanded prices which, had there only been more of them – and they might easily have been multiplied – might have supplied funds sufficient to pension all his relations for life.
>
> But perhaps the piece of household furniture which excited most attention was an eight day clock. As that article was

> neither made in London nor in Paris, I should not like myself to put a price upon it... Perhaps a liberal valuator might have been inclined to appraise it at say thirty shillings. But that clock had been often would up by the hand which penned *The Jolly Beggars*, *Tam O'Shanter*, *The Cottar's Saturday Night*, *Scots wha hae wi' Wallace bled!*, *My Nannie O*, and *Auld Lang Syne*. I will not say, too, that it had not many a queer story to tell about 'The wee short hour ayont the twal!' At all events, it was ultimately knocked down, not at thirty shillings, but at thirty five pounds, the purchaser considering himself fortunate, as the limit he had fixed was sixty! From that time to this the Burns furore has certainly not abated.

And certainly not in Burns's home town.

> Auld Ayr, whom ne'er a toon surpasses...

Flags were flying from early morning and the bands were playing around the town from noon. Several hundred of the brethren of the 'mystic tie' assembled in Academy Square and marched in colourful procession up the High St to the Old Church where Brother Francis Rae of Wallacetown Church led the service. After which, they re-formed to process to the Monument via the Cottage – 'uncovering as they passed'. In the Monument grounds, they stood 'uncovered' for a long address on Burns by the Rev William Buchanan. That afternoon, most of the same men met for a banquet at the County Hall, where the chair was taken by Sir James Fergusson of Kilkerran, supported by Professor Aytoun as Croupier, to whom Sir James might have been referring when he said:

> I know that I speak in the presence of the living poet of Scotland – whose glorious lines cause every cheek to glow with pride and pleasure of him who has drunk deep at the fountain whence Burns derived his inspiration who has restored to us so many of those noble old Scottish lays from the perusal of which Burns imbibed no little of his genius. I speak also to many upon whose ears must linger the burning words of the panegyrics of Eglinton, of Wilson, and of Aytoun, delivered on the banks of the Doon at the first great celebration in honour of the poet's memory, and whose hearts must have been struck in their tenderest chord by the written praises of Wilson, of Jeffrey, of Carlyle, of Wordsworth, and

> of Montgomery. I know, however, that the memory of Burns is not the property of poets or of men of literature alone, his name is a heritage of all the natives of the country which gave him birth. Uncultivated as I am in the study of poetry, and coming here simply as a country gentleman, to join in the celebration in which my countrymen take so much interest, I know that the few sentences plain and prosaic perhaps, yet sincere and earnest, in which I shall mark our grateful task of today, will find a response which they have not excited, because it will be the offspring of that undying gratitude which is laid up for the name of Burns to all generations.

At the Assembly Rooms, men of the cloth met under the chairmanship of Rev William Buchanan. The evening was unusual in that the Rev Robert Pollock, who had travelled down from Kingston Church in Glasgow, remembered certain Burns characters from his youth, like Holy Willie Fisher and Jean Armour. He said of Jean:

> I have seen and conversed with Mrs Burns, formerly Jean Armour, when on a visit to her relations in Mauchline. I have talked and 'blethered' with the noisy polemic Jamie Humphrey, I have discussed religion and politics and joked with Adam Armour, Jean's brother, and I have seen the man reputed to be Holy Willie, and I attached no importance to these incidents at the time. They were merely the passing events of my thoughtless youth; but now, when every scrap of an old letter that has any connexion with Burns or his posterity is printed and circulated through the wide world, I am beginning to feel myself a man of some importance; important to you and important in the eyes of a kind Providence who has connected such events with my early history. I think as far as my memory serves me it would be in the summer of the year 1817, Mrs Burns was on a visit to Mauchline and called at Haughholm, where I was residing then. She was then a stoutish, gausie woman, of darkish complexion, affable and easy in manners and although Burns' fertile and enamoured fancy has arrayed her in all the charms of the singular beauties of the West, it did not appear that she would ever have had such charms for me...

The soiree of the Ayr Working Men's Reform Association took place in the Theatre, with Colonel Shaw, of the Queen's Indian Army, in the chair. In beginning his address, the Chairman requested the audience to note the fact that his name appeared upon the bills as the 'President of the Ayr Reform Association.'

> This circumstance gives you the point and pith of this commemorative effort; it is as the Reformers of Ayr that we have met together tonight. We have not come together for the purpose of doing homage to Burns' private character, no, nor even to his genius; we have assembled for the purpose of doing justice to the reformer who, more than seventy years ago, went for 'manhood suffrage' – singing 'a mans' a man for a' that.' Permit me, at the hazard of seeming somewhat tedious, yet, in justice to myself and to the noble-minded, virtuous, and honourable working men with whom I stand associated, to be distinctly clear and very unmistakable upon this point. I say, was Burns a Mormon, or was he an angel of purity? We have nothing to do with these questions. Was he a sybarite of intemperance, or was he a model of sobriety? We have nothing to do with these questions. Did he abase – not to say profane – his God-given genius, or were his poems, every one of them, the effusions of a seraph? I repeat it, we have nothing earthly to do with these questions; we are commemorating the great Reformer who, more than seventy years ago, went for 'manhood suffrage' – singing 'a man's a man for a' that'.
>
> In Burns' day the times were dismally dark. Social, politically, and morally speaking, our country was at that time in a low and very melancholy condition. Why, it was then thought the only real and right hospitality to make a guest dead-drunk; and no one with the least pretension to the name of gentlemen ever went to bed sober. The song of the poet – inexpressibly sweet and beautiful when, like the bird in the morning, it soared towards heaven – became steeped in the predominant rage. But we may not enter on this topic; I repeat it once more; we are assembled to do justice to the mighty genius who, in so dark an age, sang the glorious song, *A man's a man for a' that*; and as it will now be sung. The whole of the proceedings were of a character to show that, if others are offering an idolatrous homage to the shade of departed genius, the sons of toil are able to enter upon the subject in a spirit of high moral discrimination. There is no danger to any country where-in such is the case.

It must be said that this was a minority view, especially in the town that Burns last knew. One remembers the Bread Riots there and the bayonets at his funeral.

However, Dumfries on this great day declared a public holiday. There were the usual procession of bands and town dignitaries, tradesmen and children waving flags, and in addition a body of carters attended on horseback. The difference here was that they all marched through arches made by Mr Mein, the local joiner, which led them from the Academy to Burns's House in Bank St, as the street was then called. The tea-time banquet took place in the Assembly Rooms, and it has to be noted that they followed the example of the very first Burns Supper at Alloway by having haggis and sheep's head on the menu. On this occasion Colonel William Burns replied briefly 'under much emotion' to the Immortal Memory proposed by Dr W.A.F.Browne, one of Her Majesty's Commissioners in Lunacy for Scotland. He then left to join a deputation to a similar meeting at the Nithsdale Mills. Colonel Burns was being made to work for his many suppers. He left with the Chairman's injunction ringing in his ears – 'May you and your brother live to see another centenary!'

Arriving at the Mills, Colonel Burns made his usual short response, still 'full of emotion' but this time he found a formula to serve by saying that 'he could only utter a few words of thanks, his heart being too full to permit him to say anything more'. It was certainly one way out. Incidentally, it was in Dumfries that one of the last links to the living Burns was severed. In May 1875, John Brodie died, who remembered as a boy 'running messages for the poet Burns'.

Well, that Burns message was ringing out all through 1859, for in Ballantine's meticulously *verbatim* record of the year in Scotland, there were reports of gatherings from Aberdeen to Wigtown but neither space nor time allows this present writer to follow in Mr Ballantine's painstaking footsteps. Instead, notice will only be taken of those events which took place in locations already familiar to readers of the Robert Burns Story – Mauchline, Greenock, Paisley, Montrose, and, of course, Kilmarnock, where one might say his story really started.

This was the first place to refer to him officially as a poet in 1786 and one would have thought this title sufficient to deflect them from the need in 1859 to comment on his sex life and drinking habits. But

Archibald Finnie of Springfield, who was in the chair at the Burns Dinner in the George Hall would not be deterred.

> We are not here to contend that his conduct was at all times worthy of himself, or that his character should go down to posterity as more than mortal. We are, on the contrary, free to admit that his faults and failings were great; but had they been otherwise they could not have been Burns'! All about him was great, and so were his failings. When the atmosphere of that mighty mind became disturbed by the intensity of its own mysterious workings, the thunder and the lightning were of no ordinary character; but the clouds cleared away, there stood revealed the native majesty and serenity of his soul, and there broke forth those brilliant beams which shall irradiate and gladden the great heart of humanity till the end of time. *(Cheering)*
>
> But, gentlemen, where is that name on the long scroll of fame against which nothing unworthy was ever made known? And are a hundred years not to suffice to have buried in eternal oblivion all that was mortal of that noble spirit, whose breathings shall ever brood over the hills and the valleys of our dear native land? The glorious sun has his spots, and the silver moon her exhausted volcanoes; but are these always to be remembered when we enjoy the splendours of the one, or the melancholy radiance of the other?
>
> The verdict of posterity is before you – and this day the name and genius of Ayrshire's Bard are being celebrated as far as waters roll, or winds can waft them. And, gentlemen, well does it become Auld Kilmarnock to rejoice on this great occasion. He was one of ourselves- he looked down our fertile valley from the heights of Mossgiel – he attended our fairs and our markets – he brightened the society of many kindred spirits in the days of our forefathers, whose names and characters he has justly honoured; and our printing press had the privilege of first giving forth those heart-stirring strains, which now encircle the globe. All honour then "To the Immortal memory of Robert Burns" '
>
> *(The toast was drunk mid thundering and prolonged cheers)*

Messrs Bicket's, Barclay's and Paxton's employees met in their respective workplaces in the evening to enjoy a Burns Dinner and Entertainment provided by their employers. All three events were accounted a great success and each adjourned happily 'some wee, short hour ayont the twal'. This kind of happening would surely have been to Burns's own taste. Ordinary, plain men enjoying ordinary, plain fare and making a night of it. The Abstainers' Union had a Social Tea in Robertson's Coffee-house. Several 'negro songs' were sung and the meeting broke up at a seasonable hour. The Shoemakers and the Bonnet-Makers also celebrated the Centenary although the latter made a point of breaking up at an *early* hour.

A great crowd of people assembled at the Cross of Mauchline at 2 o'clock in the afternoon and began the walk up to Mossgiel, much in the way the poet himself might have done as a young man, except that he didn't walk behind a rustic cart decorated with a bust of himself surrounded by laurels. The Mauchline Belles of 1859 came next behind their flag, which was the silk scarf Jean Armour had worn when she had last visited Mauchline. Andrew Smith addressed some 2,000 people as they gathered in the courtyard at Mossgiel and all around the famous farm. When he had finished speaking he handed over the bust to be left at Mossgiel with the injunction that the wreath of holly which had been added by Miss Agnes Smith be not removed for another hundred years – when it should be replaced by a new one. Was it, one wonders?

The unique aspect of the Mauchline celebrations was the presence in the town of five men who had actually *seen* Burns. Matthew Lerrie was a serving boy at Gavin Hamilton's when Burns used to call there to see Mary Campbell. James Hamilton, as a boy, once delivered a letter from Burns to Jean Armour. William Patrick had been a servant at Mossgiel in Burns's time there and had many stories to tell of him. Unfortunately, he told none at the dinner in The Institution. The two other Burns contemporaries, George Patrick and John Lambie, were too frail to attend. What stories *they* might have been able to tell. Among the inanimate relics on display were a candlestick owned by the poet and a knife and fork set said to have been used at his christening. And, of course, Jean's scarf. After all, she was a Mauchline girl.

It was appropriate that the then President of the first Burns Club, Mr James MacFarlan should be chosen to propose the Immortal Memory at the port of Greenock. He was nothing if not direct.

> To call Burns a peasant poet is absurd. Great as was Lord Byron he was not so noble. Burns was a ploughman and an exciseman, but even in this respect he was a teacher, as every true poet is, and must be. He showed us that the discharge of ordinary homely duties does not detract from a man's dignity, or from the greatness of his mind. He is not a great man who neglects the most ordinary duties that come to his door as it were to be discharged. Through hard trials he never cringed; he took care of his own house, did not deny the faith, and battled like the most ordinarily endowed man – this I take to be a grand feature in his character.
>
> In writing to his friend, Mr Dalrymple, he used this strange and pointed simile – I don't pretend to give the words but merely the expression as illustrative of how he battled in the discharge of his ordinary duties, and to show how much he valued the proper discharge of these; He said 'I can't say I am altogether at my ease when I see anywhere in my path that meagre, squalid, famine-faced, spectre poverty, attended, as he always is, by iron-fisted oppression and leering contempt, but I have sturdily withstood his buffeting many a hard laboured day already, and till my motto is I dare.' This was the man, gentlemen, who, born in a cottage, felt and acted throughout life as if he had been born in a castle. That was an accident that happens frequently, for great Scotchmen are as often born in cottages as in castles.

Paisley, the little town 'where Cart rins rowing to the sea', celebrated in the Exchange Rooms. A hundred ladies came in to occupy the gallery at the conclusion of the dinner enjoyed by the hundred husbands, fathers and brothers of the St Mirren and the Renfrew County Kilwinning Lodges. The chairman, Robert Brown, Provost of Paisley, actually knew Alexander Wark, now dead, who told him that he (Wark) had been looking out of his window in Paisley when he saw a man whom he thought looked like the portrait of Burns riding by in the street below. Hurrying out, he chased after the rider and asked him if he were indeed the poet Burns? Burns laughed and said that he was. Alexander then asked if he might shake his hand. Burns offered it at once and rode on. Alexander Wark was left standing in the street looking at the hand that shook the hand of Robert Burns.

The bells rang in Montrose, where Burns had family ties, and the ships in the harbour showed their colours to mark the day. Two horses dragging a plough held by a man in Burns's costume led the procession from the Links, and the shops all being closed, the people gathered in the streets determined to enjoy the holiday in the clear and dry weather. Arriving at the Town Buildings, the crowd was addressed by Adam Burnes. They then gave three cheers in memory of the National Bard before dispersing. The same Burnes, who shared the same family name as William Burnes, the poet's father, and his cousins, the Montrose writers and lawyers, also addressed the company that afternoon in the Guild Hall, and, in the course of his remarks, said.

> Burns taught, in fact, that to be a man was the grand distinction, and that all other distinctions were but the clothes that wrap the figure, while the figure itself was the real thing. That without the man these were nothing, had no value, could have no existence. That without that solid, central, and sentient monarch, man, titles are but as air; gay clothes but the furniture of a Jew's shop; great houses but empty, useless shelves; carriages no better than wheelbarrows. This Burns held to be the grand principle.
>
> 'The poor Indian whose untutored mind
> Sees God in clouds, and hears him in the wind,'
>
> might imagine some superiority attached to his feathered chief; but it was well to impress on the world that an enlightened people should look upon rank and title in its true aspect. It was well to let the noble understand that they were not to presume, and to let the masses understand that their feet were set on the firm rock of eternal truth. The man who breathes the soul rational dignity into the minds of the people is the greatest of public patriots, and the words – 'A mans' a man for a' that' engraved in your hearts in letters more enduring than adamant – while they ring in our own age, will reverberate for ages to come, at each period shaking from its foundation the insolence of tyranny and oppression, and putting to the blush the meanness of subserviency. It has been said that every man of genius feels within himself a consciousness of his great ability and of the influence he possesses over the minds of his fellow men; and a remarkable prediction by Burns himself appears in one of his own letters, sufficient to startle us now. When warned to act and not to think, he said – 'Burns was a poor

> man from birth, but the sterling of his honest worth no poverty could debase...'
> *(The toast was rapturously received and was drunk with great enthusiasm)*

This enthusiasm was lifted and carried from town to town throughout the land and it drifted through much of the route Burns himself had travelled in his Highland and West Highland tours and through the same Border country, where in 1787, he touched a toe into England. He never got further than Newcastle in the North-east of England and Carlisle in its North-west and seventy-two years later, his name was being remembered in both centres.

When Burns was in the latter town he had his horse, Jenny Geddes, impounded for grazing it on the mayor's land. It would be the equivalent of a parking fine today, but in 1859 the Carlisle mayor was one Robert Ferguson, a scholar and poet himself, so possibly he might have been more lenient. His brother, also a poet, John Clarke Ferguson, presided over the Burns function at the Coffee-House Assembly Room which was 'numerously attended'. There is no record of any poetical effusion from either brother to mark the occasion. However, Philip Henry Howard of Corby Castle, 'than whom no man, from his refined taste and literary research, is more capable of appreciating the lives and works of great men', was Chairman and proposed the toast to Burns at the Lion and the Lamb Tavern. While doing so, he took the opportunity to take up a collection on behalf of Mrs Isabella Burns Begg's daughters who had been left in straitened circumstances after their mother's death only a month before. Mr Howard concluded:

> One great peculiarity of Burns's writings is their intense nationality; and no wonder for Scotland can boast almost solely of being the only country that did not bow the neck to foreign invasion. When the southern portion of the country was overrun successively by Romans, Danes, Saxons, and others, all that even the conquering Romans could attempt was to bar them out by that gigantic wall which has been contemplated with wonder by both countries for centuries, and which in July will no doubt be the occasion of great interest both to us and many strangers from a distance. Now, gentlemen, I may safely leave the toast in your hands, to honour it as it deserves, but before resuming my seat I may

> mention that I have received from Mr Walter Buchanan, of Ayr, a recommendation that you will not forget the nieces of the poet – the daughters of Mrs Begg, who paid the debt of nature only in December last. I hope that some time, at an hour better adapted to business than just now, your names will be put down for contributions that will show that you wish to render a living and lasting tribute to the memory of the great poet...
>
> Gentlemen, I now call upon you to drink to the Memory of Burns, and I feel sure that at another time you will not forget the necessities of his nieces who survive him.

It might be said to be 'Ladies Night' at the Lion and the Lamb, for the next toast of the evening was 'To the Poet's Wife, Jean Armour' which was gallantly proposed by the Vice-Chairman, Mr Robert Dixon. It was good to see Jean given her place.

The Carlisle report ended:

> There were other minor festivities which are noticed elsewhere. Altogether the Border city has no reason to be ashamed of the effort made to commemorate the birth of the greatest genius the sister country has ever produced.

Newcastle had equal reason to be proud, as the centenary of Robert Burns was celebrated there 'with extraordinary enthusiasm'. The Town Hall Festival began at 5 o'clock before a company of 400 gentlemen. After dinner, the ladies were invited to the gallery. The cloth having been withdrawn, the Chairman (Sir John Fife) rose to make the main toast, which, after a lively exposition on Burns and Highlanders, felicitously linked his listeners to similar gatherings elsewhere:

> While I feel in my own heart that brotherhood towards the admirers of Burns, let me wish a happy evening to those other societies under different roofs in this town who are now with us celebrating his memory, and let us, with your consent and that of the ladies, send at this moment a telegraph to Edinburgh, to Lord Ardmillan, who is the chairman of the Burns's festival there, and let us assure him, as we assure our townsmen under different roofs, that we fraternise with them most sincerely – that we join with them most heartily in the

> large hearted, liberal spirit which Burns himself possessed, in celebrating this great day... I give you, ladies and gentlemen, 'To the Immortal Memory of the poet Burns'.

It is fitting that all these hundreds of Tuesday evenings in 1859 (in Europe at least) should return us to that honest man from Ayr, Lord Ardmillan, and keep the focus fixed on Ayrshire and its epicentre at Alloway. The reverberations from that 1759 event were felt on every atoll or mountainside, forest clearing or city street – wherever the Caledonian diaspora had extended. The speeches here were all very much of the same thing as in Britain, only more so. It would appear that the further a Scotsman is from Scotland, the more Scottish he becomes – and therefore, the more Burnsian. But it was not only the Scots who responded. The native speakers, in whatever country, rose up in all their rhetorical splendour before their respective expatriates. In the United States, for instance, the Reverend Henry Ward Beecher, in a lengthy but eloquent address enthralled 3,000 listeners at the Cooper Institute in New York:

> The nation which read Burns in the nursery could never have tyrants in the Parliament House. The men who drink at Burns's spring will be too sturdy for oppression, too contagious for power to tamper with, and with too much self-respect for blandishment and bribes.

Yet didn't Burns say:

> What force or guile could not subdue through many warlike ages
> Is wrought now by a coward few for hireling traitor's wages.
> For English steel we could disdain secure in valour's station;
> But English gold has been our bane-
> Such a parcel of rogues in a nation.'

And the rogues he referred to were Scots themselves who proved very bribable.

The Rev Beecher went on:

> Burns had pre-eminently this love for man in all his moods, weaknesses, sorrows, joys, hopes, and fears for life, and for eternal life. He is universal in his sympathy. He loves the very shoe-latches of the poor Scotch peasant. He loves the very daisy his shoe trod upon. Terrible often with rage that sounds

> as thunder in the mountains, yet it is love both personal and general that marks the poems of Burns, and that gives them their wondrous vitality, and will never let them die so long as a soul yearns, or hearts desire to be tenderly cheered.
>
> Finally, tonight let us give to the memory of Burns something of that food of love and praise which his own should hungered for his life long, and never had. If he has faults, let us, like them of old, walking backward with reverence and affection, cast a mantle upon them. If every man within these twenty-four hours the world around who shall speak the name of Burns with fond admiration were registered as his subjects, no king on earth would have such a realm.

At Boston there was a posse of poets out to capture Burns. One who did was Ralph Waldo Emerson, who called himself 'the worst Scotchman of all' but rose to give a wonderful speech, which has been deservedly much-printed since.

> Not Latimer, not Luther, struck more telling blows against false theology than did this brave singer. The 'Confession of Augsburg', 'The Declaration of Independence', 'The Rights of Man', The French 'La Marseillaise' are not more weighty documents in the history of freedom than the songs of Burns. His satire has lost none of its edge. His musical arrows yet sing through the air. He is so substantially a reformer that I find his grand plain sense in close chain with the greatest masters – Rabelais, Shakespeare in comedy, Cervantes, Butler and Burns.

Despite the surprising inclusion of Samuel Butler among the 'greatest masters', this is the real perspective on Burns and it takes the self-confessed 'worst Scotchman of all' to see it.

> He is an exceptional genius. The people who care nothing for literature and poetry care for Burns. It was indifferent – they thought who saw him – whether he wrote a verse or not: he could have done anything else as well. Yet how true a poet he is! And the poet, too, of poor men, of gray hodden and the Guernsey coat and the blouse. He has given voice to all the experiences of common life; he has endeared the farmhouse and cottage, patches and poverty, beans and barley; ale, the poor man's wine; hardship; the fear of debt; the dear society

> of weans and wife, of brothers and sisters, proud of each other, knowing so few and finding amends for want and obscurity in books and thoughts. What a love of Nature, and, shall I say it? Of middle class Nature. Not like Goethe, in the stars, or like Byron, in the ocean, or Moore, in the luxurious East, but in the homely landscape which the poor see around them, – bleak leagues of pasture and stubble, ice and sleet and rain and snow-choked brooks; birds, hares, field mice, thistles and heather, which he daily knew. How many 'Bonny Doons' and 'John Anderson my jo's' and 'Auld Lang Synes' all around the earth have his verses been applied to! And his love songs still woo and melt the youths and maids; the farmworkers, the country holiday, the fishing cobble are still his debtors today.

And this poet concluded on a poet:

> And as he was thus the poet of the poor, anxious, cheerful, working humanity, so had he the language of low life. He grew up in a rural district, speaking a patois unintelligible to all but natives, and he has made the Lowland Scotch a Doric dialect of fame. It is the only example in history of a language made classic by the genius of a single man. But more than this. He had that secret of genius to draw from the bottom of society the strength of its speech, and astonish the ears of the polite with these artless words, better than art, and filtered of all offence through his beauty. It seemed odious to Luther that the devil should have all the best tunes; he would bring them into the churches; and Burns knew how to take from friars and gypsies, blacksmiths and drovers, the speech of the market and street, and clothe it with melody... The memory of Burns, every man's, every boy's and girl's head carried snatches of his songs, and they say them by heart, and, what is strangest of all, never learned them from a book, but from mouth to mouth. The wind whispers them, the birds whistle them, the corn, barley, and bulrushes hoarsely rustle them, nay, the music boxes at Geneva are framed and toothed to play them; the hand organs of the Savoyard in all cities repeat them, and the chimes of bells ring them is the spires. They are the property and the solace of mankind.

Thus it was, through places as contrasting as the mansion of Nowrozjee Arrdaseer Davur in Bombay and the Commercial Hotel,

Dunedin, New Zealand, the ribbon of words wreathed its way around the world as *emigre* Scots came 'from every airt and pairt' to listen, laugh, drink and sing about their Poet and share, if only for the night, a jovial commonality. Dunedin stoutly continues its Scottish connection to this day.

Considering that Burns's own nephew Thomas Burns settled there as a clergyman before the middle of 19th-century, it's hardly surprising that the Burns connection there is also sound. The Burns Club is one of the most active organisations in the town and celebrated its centenary in February 1991. Their principal guest on that occasion was the tenor, Kenneth McKeller, who delivered a pawky Immortal Memory to a rather senior audience, who, one feels, would rather have had him sing. The lady who hosted the garden party next day was one of the Rev Burns's descendants, but Ken still didn't sing. Needless to say, his concerts that night and the following night were both sold out, and a great time was had by all.

Which was more than could be said for the final item in this review of that other centenary in 1859. This was the solitary celebration in Copenhagen, where, on the evening of 25th January, a few expatriates plus some Scandinavians and Icelanders met at the University and paid one shilling each to hear Professor Stephens read 450 lines of his own poem – *The Rescue of Robert Burns, February 1759*. The proceeds were given towards the building of an English Episcopal Church in the city.

Then each took off his several way
Resolved to meet some ither day.
(The Twa Dogs)

3

The Burns Federation

1885

> The object of the Federation will be to strengthen and consolidate the band of friendship existing among the members of Burns Clubs, by universal affiliation; its motto being – 'A man's a man for a' that'

Before beginning this chapter, I must declare a conflict of interests. I once was a Burns Club myself. For a few years in Edinburgh from 1978, the John Cairney Burns Club, Number 947 in the official roll of federated clubs, existed from my office in Colinton Road, reluctantly supervised by my then manager, Colin Harvey Wright, who said he had enough to do without involving himself with Burns Clubs – and anyway, as he pointed out in his quiet way, 'You're never here.' He was quite right. We were both away too much (on my solo tours as Burns) to attend any of the meetings. The club had been started informally by a group of Edinburgh friends at the behest of an old actor, and sometime colleague, Elliot Williams, (*The Last of the Barn-Stormers*) who thought it would be a good idea to mark the end of my playing career in the Burns one-man-show by starting a Cairney Burns Club. I didn't know I was to play him in the theatre until 1981 and after that as an after-dinner solo until the time of writing this book.

However, the John Cairney Burns Club did not prove to have the same durability and with Elliot's death in 1983, it fell into abeyance and died a natural death.As so often with Burns Clubs, or any kind of club for that matter, it is often the energy of one person who makes things happen and keeps them happening. Colin Rae-Brown, Duncan McNaught and Jock Thomson were all examples of this in the Burns world, solo dynamos that kept the engines turning. I am sure it is still the same in the 350 Burns Clubs extant in the world today. They will each boast a pivotal member round whom everything turns, and as long as he – or she – is there the club will survive and even flourish.

What is ironical, in view of their historical place, is the role that women play in the contemporary Burns movement. Not being eligible for membership of the then existing Burns clubs, they formed their own, starting with The Bingry Jolly Beggars in 1924, followed by the Glencraig Bonnie Jean and the Newton Jean Armour in 1925, and so on until the Hawick Conference of 1931 when six all-ladies clubs took part as affiliated members. The first thing the ladies proposed was a memorial to Jean Armour. This was rejected, 'the present not being an opportune time for entering upon such an undertaking'. The grey heads of the Executive still held the purse-strings, but 1931 was, after all, at the very height, or depths, of the Depression.

But the women were not to be denied. Jean did eventually get her Memorial Homes in Mauchline, and the first woman President of the Federation was the translator of Hans Hecht, Jane Lymburn (Mrs Burgoyne). In 1937 the highest honour that could be given by the Federation, the Honorary Presidency, went to Dr Annie Dunlop of Kilmarnock. Considering that the very first such presidency had been awarded to Lord Rosebery and less than thirty had been given since then, it was a significant gesture. Since that time, women now comprise more than half the membership of mixed clubs. Indeed, since that time, a rare triple was achieved when Mrs Mary Thomson of the Mary Campbell Club in Cambuslang, her daughter, Mrs Molly Rennie, and *her* daughter, Mrs Moira Dunsmore, all became Presidents or Vice-Presidents of the Burns Federation in their respective generations. The ladies had made their point

However, in the beginning it was strictly 'men only'. Such had been the impact of the world-wide centenary celebrations that it was natural that there would be a reaction, and a falling-off in Burns interest was felt for a time. In this pause for breath, as it were, opportunity was given for more considered, and less overt propagation of the poet and his work. The time was right for a scholarly and classical approach, which was perhaps why, speaking in Newcastle in 1859, Sir John Fyffe, resorted to a Latin tag to make a point in his Centenary address – 'Homo sum et nihil humanum mihi alienum puto.' And he went on:

> That sentiment ran through the world. It exercised its influence wherever civilisation existed, and greatly advanced the progress of mankind; Burns, without knowing that motto, said as much in five words, 'A man's a man for a' that.' And this glorious principle, which is constantly breathing through his works and through his character, even in his least prosperous days, seems to have exalted into a brotherhood all those who are his admirers...

Few of whom, it must be said, would have been classically trained, yet in 1862 his works were being translated into Latin. Alexander Leighton was the first to attempt the conversion and 'up in the morning's no for me, up in the morning early' came out as 'Surgere mane, mordet me, surger lectulo mane'. *MacPherson's Farewell*'s 'And there's no a man in all Scotland, but I'll brave him at a word' appeared as 'Et vir nullus in Scotia quin verbo obstringam'. Further editions were issued in 1892 and 1899 so someone must have been reading them.

Nor did it stop there. By 1896, William Jacks had, as has been mentioned before, compiled a whole book, *Burns in Other Tongues*, which recorded the various foreign translations Burns had undergone until that date with the exception of Hebrew and Polish. Both these versions had to wait until 1956 for translation. In his Introduction, Jacks made no pretence to know all the languages included in his volume. As he said:

> It would be hypocritical pedantry to leave it to be assumed that I knew all the various languages which appear here, sufficiently well to enable me to criticise those translations as I have done; indeed some of them I do not know at all. In such cases I had each translated literally into a language which I did understand, and the retranslation was sent to a native of the particular country for confirmation and comment, and in this way I was able to make my remarks.

That such translations can work, both for itself and for the original work, is shown by the style of Bartsch's fluent re-working of *My Heart's in the Highlands*:

Mein Herz ist im Hochland, mein Herz ist nicht hier
Mein Herz ist im Hochland und jagt in Revier;
Da jagd es den Hirsch und das fluchtige Reh
Mein Herz ist im Hochland, wo immer ich geh.

What one can see, linguistically speaking, is how close a second-cousin the German tongue is to Scots, nearer in many ways than English. In fact, some selected poems were turned into English by William Corbett and published by subscription in 1892. Interestingly, *Holy Willie's Prayer* survives almost word for word as does *An Epistle to Davie*. More recently, in 1954, William Kean Seymour also turned Burns into English but somehow, to a Scot at any rate, *Tam o Shanter* doesn't sound quite the same.

When pedlars pack and leave the street
And thirsty neighbours neighbours meet,
As market days are wearing late
And folk begin to quicken gait;
While we sit drinking pot on pot
With tipsy pleasure in our lot...

In 1909, a Swede, Gustav Froding, did a complete translation, and Samuil Marshak in Russia, who had been studying his Burns since around that time, produced *Roberta Burnsa* in 1954 which sold in Moscow as if it were a best-seller. Marshak was not the first to translate Burns into Russian. As early as 1800, his *Address to the Shade of Thomson* had appeared and in 1820, Ivan Kozlov had given versions of *The Cotter's Saturday Night* and *To A Mountain Daisy* but undeniably, Marshak is the doyen as far as a Russian view of Burns is concerned. He was not only a good translator but was a good writer himself. That helped. So that the familiar opening lines of *Tam o Shanter* could still live poetically in Russian as:

When on the town lie shadows, and ends the market day...

Compare that with the feel of Seymour's 'English' translation above. Marshak also ended the poem stylishly:

Just remember the night with rain and snow – and the old
mare Meg!

There is no mere *verbatim* here of giving word for word. or line for line. A poet was rendering another poet. It takes one to know one.

The first language outside the mainstream of Burns translation must surely have been the 1892 adaptation into Bohemian but since that time he has been re-worked into every possible language, including the nearer-home Gaelic by Charles MacPhater of Glasgow in 1910 – *Dain, is Luinneagan – Eader – Theangaichte Do'n – Ghaidhlig, Albannach*. Given Burns's stated aversion to the Highlands and Highlanders, Mr MacPhater's work has a missionary significance. The same might be said of Hans Hecht's famous *Life*, entitled simply *Robert Burns*, originally published in Heidelberg in 1919, and re-published in the Lynburn translation of 1936. This has since become a classic of Burns literature.

An Icelandic translation appeared in 1922 but a huge step forward in Burns colonisation was made when C.M Butler converted him into Esperanto for the British Esperanto Association in 1926. This is dealt with more fully in Chapter Five. A Japanese edition had appeared in 1934 and since then a Japanese academic, Ishebashi Magoichiro, has added to the sum of Burns knowledge throughout the world with his study of Burns in 1952. Toshio Namba was another well-known Japanese Burnsian a decade later. The Bard emerged into Hebrew in 1956 and in 1976, Pierluigi Simonini dealt with Burns in Italy. Today, at the very time of writing, Channon Singh, at present living and working in Coventry, is still at work in translating Burns into Punjabi for students at Guru Nanak University in the Punjab. All that needs to happen now is for Robert to be contracted into tchspk for use in cell phones.

Despite this universal cover, it would seem that the English as a whole prefer their Burns in anything but Scots. Even Robert Louis Stevenson turned to his lawyer's Latin when he came to write his essay on Burns in 1879. 'Teres atque rotundus – a burly figure in literature', which, roughly translated, meant that he was seeing Burns in the round. Stevenson, like other Victorians, while paying lip service to the bust of gold (as seen by Carlyle) seemed to be obsessed by the feet of clay (as seen by Professor Shairp), forgetting that the heart of the man lies somewhere in between. Stevenson considered Burns as one of the Four Great Scotsmen he intended writing about as early as 1874, the others being John Knox, David Hume and Walter Scott. As it was, he only completed two, Knox and Burns, both in the following year, but the Burns article was turned down by the *Encyclopaedia Britannica* (although he was paid his five guineas for it) and it was 1879 before he saw a revision of it published as *Some Aspects of Robert Burns*.

It was hardly worth waiting for. Although Stevenson could never be dull in anything he wrote, and had a generous understanding of the more robust side of Burns, this was a pedestrian trek through the familiar thicket of bastard weans and buckets of wine and the sharp decline as a consequence. Like so many at the time, Stevenson couldn't see the real wood of Burns because of the biographical trees in the way. He was to be asked again to give his thoughts on Burns in the preface for a Burns Exhibition Catalogue being arranged in Glasgow by the Burns collector, W.Crabie Angus, in 1891, and, although RLS was excited by the idea and looked forward to receiving the catalogue details, nothing more was heard of his involvement. It might have been interesting to see if his opinion had changed any. After all, he had said in the Burns piece:

> If you are so sensibly pained by the misconduct of your subject, and so paternally delighted with his virtues, you will also be an excellent gentleman, but a somewhat questionable biographer.

And also:

> There is, indeed, only one merit in considering a man of letters – that he should write well; and only one damning fault – that he should write ill.

Quite. And would that the 'memorisers' from that day to this would remember that.

In this same year of 1879, an event took place in Scotland, that would have considerable repercussions within Burns circles in the years to come, and even yet resounds at Burns Suppers when its stirring chorus often starts proceedings. I refer, of course to that other Scottish anthem – *The Star o Robbie Burns*. This song owes its genesis to a Burns gathering in Hawick where the president of the Burns Club at the time was a certain James Thomson, who was also a well-known local rhymer and song-writer. Born at Bowden in the Scottish Borders in 1827, he was the son of Henrietta Wilkie, now Mrs Robert Thomson, and an enthusiastic literary enthusiast. Her brother, Dr Wilkie of Innerleithen, was a familiar of James Hogg, the

Ettrick Shepherd, and Sir Walter Scott, no less, so young James grew up in a writing environment and quite soon showed some skill in verse-making.poetry. However, as a Border callant, his first job was herding sheep on the Eildon Hills. At 16, he was apprenticed to a Selkirk cabinet maker and wood turner and as soon as he became a tradesman himself, he moved to Hawick where he spent the rest of his life. He had continued to write, songs mostly, and many of these are clearly inspired by his adopted Border town, so much so that he became known as the Hawick Poet. Two of his songs, *Up Wi' the Banner* and *The Border Queen*, are still sung at the annual Border Common-Riding Festival.

At the Literate Dinner held in the Tower Hotel sometime late in 1878, he met the musical accompanist who was also the composer of the famous Scots song *Scotland Yet* and he turned out to be an Englishman. James Booth was born in Congleton in the North of England in 1850. As a boy he studied the organ and piano with a Mr George Barlow, a local, but sound, teacher. Young Booth got his first job travelling with an opera company and soon developed his skill as an accompanist. This led to concert work and a constant demand from travelling singers, especially throughout Scotland. It was this experience that turned him to compositions of the Scottish songs that were to become so popular in their day. *They're Far, Far Awa*, *My Own, My Native Land*, *On Comrades, On* were others to which he set original music, but the one for which he was remembered is undoubtedly *The Star o' Robbie Burns*.

The Burns Centenary of 1859 had proved a memorable occasion for Hawick, where some four hundred people attended a gathering in the Commercial Hotel (now a Roman Catholic hall). Among the speakers were well-known townsmen like James A H Murray of Denholm, a schoolmaster, later to be knighted for his work in the compilation of the *New Oxford English Dictionary*. Twenty years later, at that year's Burns Supper. the local blacksmith, Thomas Strathairn, got up to sing a new song especially written for the Burns occasion by the Hawick rhymer and the Congleton travelling accompanist. It was an immediate success. The 29-year old composer supplied a splendid tune with a rousing chorus, both of which flattered Thomson's stiff lyrics. They were, of course, of their time and no doubt fitted the taste of those first hearers but the words creak a little today. Few kings have lately arisen and all the courtiers have fallen. However, the tune is lively and the surging chorus is irresistible. It is a march triumphant and I defy any set of feet to resist it.

Let kings and courtiers rise an' fa'
This world has many turns
But brightly beams abune them them a'
The star o' Robbie Burns.

It has two verses only.

There is a star whose beaming ray
Is shed on ev'ry clime.
It shines by night, it shines by day,
And ne'er grows dim wi' time.
It rose upon the banks o' Ayr,
It shone on Doon's clear stream.
A hundred years are gone an' mair
Yet brighter grows the beam-

Tho' he was but a ploughman lad
And wore the hodden grey,
Auld Scotland's sweetest bard was bred
Beneath a roof o' strae.
To sweep the strings o' Scotia's lyre,
It needs nae classic lore,
It's mother-wit an' native fire
That warms the bosom's core.

The first verse is tolerable – just – but the second has an earnest, 'ploughman' tread and has nothing of the 'mother wit and native fire' it sings about, but just when it reaches 'the bosom's core' in the last line the rousing chorus comes to the rescue. The tune is the main reason that the song has survived for nearly 120 years. It occurs to this writer, however, that a modern re-write of this lyric is urgently called for.

However, Thomson is to be congratulated on meeting the needs of his day. The song fully served its purpose in adding to the lustre that surrounded Burns then. Victorians wanted to think of him as the 'Heaven-inspired genius' sprung up from peasant soil as if a by a miracle and then laid low by cruel fortune and his own misdeeds. They did not want to think of him as a man with a mind and a radical point of view who belonged more to the 18th than the 19th century. But by 1800, he might be said to have been 'Curried'. It has taken Burns almost the whole two hundred years since to be seen, as Stevenson tried to see him, 'in the round'.

James Thomson eventually became the respected Bard of Lodge St James 424 in Hawick, and for the occasion of the unveiling of the Burns Statue in Dumfries in by Prime Minister Balfour in 1882, he penned the following:

> I see noblest of the earth
> Bend low to him of humble birth.
> I see a vast, enraptured throng
> Pay homage to the chief of song
> And place a garland round his brow
> And kiss the hands that held the plough.

Encouraged by the success of *The Star* at Hawick, the 47-year old Thomson decided to release his *Doric Lays and Lyrics* in 1884. This was the first publication of *The Star* and it brought the song to the notice of that great Scots tenor of the time, J.M.Hamilton, who made it his own and gave it much of his celebrity. Thomson died at the end of 1888, a justified singer at last, but nothing is known of the end of James Booth. Possibly he just went on travelling. If he didn't, his song did – right round the world and his sturdy tune goes marching on to its own kind of immortality in being published by Mozart Allen in Glasgow and sung by such as Robert Wilson and later, Kenneth McKellar. It is still being lustily sung at the Suppers. Well, the Chorus is.

I doubt if it were given, however, at the gathering met to unveil a statue if Burns in Central Park, New York on 2nd October 1880. The speaker was a certain George William Curtis, an American and an inveterate name-dropper:

> The year 1759 was a proud year for Great Britain. Lord Chatham had restored to his country the sceptre of the seas, and covered her name with glory of continuous victory... It was the year of Minden, where the French army was routed; of Quiberon, where the French fleet was destroyed; of the heights of Abraham in Canada, where Wolfe died happy, and the dream of French supremacy upon the American continent

vanished forever. The triumphant thunder of British guns was heard all around the world. Robert Clive was founding British dominion in India; Boscawen and his fellow admirals were sweeping France form the ocean; and in America Colonel George Washington had planted the British flag on the field of Braddock's defeat. 'We are forced to ask every morning what victory there is,' said Horace Walpole, 'for fear of missing one!'

But not only in politics and war was the genius of Great Britain illustrious. James Watt was testing the force of steam; Hargreaves was inventing the spinning-jenny, which ten years later Arkwright would complete; and Wedgwood was making household ware beautiful, Fielding's *Tom Jones* had been ten years in print, and Gray's *Elegy* nine years; Dr Johnson had lately published his *Dictionary*; and Edmund Burke his essay on the *Sublime and Beautiful*. In the year 1759 Garrick was the first of actors, and Sir Joshua Reynolds of painters; Gibbon dated in this year the preface of his first work; Hume published the third and fourth volumes of his *History of England*; Robertson his *History of Scotland*; and Sterne came to London to find a publisher for *Tristram Shandy*; Oliver Goldsmith, 'unfriended, solitary,' was toiling for the booksellers in his garret over Fleet ditch, but four years later, with Burke and Reynolds and Garrick and Johnson, he would found the most famous of literary clubs, and sell the *Vicar of Wakefield* to save himself from jail. It was a year of events decisive of the course of history, and of men whose fame is an illustrious national possession. But among those events none is more memorable than the birth of a son in the poorest of Scotch homes; and of all that renowned and resplendent throng of statesmen, soldiers, and seamen, of philosophers, poets, and inventors, whose fame filled the world with acclamation, not one is more gratefully and fondly remembered than the Ayrshire ploughman, Robert Burns.

It cannot be said of Burns that he 'burst his birth's invidious bar.' He was born poor, he lived poor, he died poor, and he always felt his poverty to be a curse. He was fully conscious of himself, and of his intellectual superiority. He disdained and resented the condescension of the great, and he defiantly asserted his independence. Perhaps, as Carlyle suggests, he should have divided his hours between poetry and virtuous industry. We only know that he did not. Like an untamable eagle he dashed against the bars he could not break, and his life was a restless alternation of low and lofty moods, of pure and exalted feeling, of mad revel and of impotent regret.

Distracted by poetry and poverty and passion, and brought to public shame, he determined to leave the country, and in 1786, when he was twenty seven years old, Burns published his poems by subscription to get the money to pay his passage to America. Ah! Could that poor, desperate ploughman of Mossgiel have foreseen this day, could he have known that because of those poems, an abiding part of literature familiar to every people, sung and repeated in American homes from sea to sea, his genius would be honoured and his name blessed, and his statues raised with grateful pride to keep his memory in America green for ever, perhaps the amazing vision might have nerved him to make his life as noble as his genius...

Burns's sudden fame stayed him, and brought him to Edinburgh and its brilliant literary society. Hume was gone, but Adam Smith remained; Robertson was there, and Dugald Stewart. There, also, were Blacklock and Hugh Blair and Alison; Fraser, Tytler, and Adam Ferguson and Henry Erskine. There, too, were the beautiful Duchess of Gordon, and the truly noble Lord Glencairn. They welcomed Burns as a prodigy, but he would not be patronised. Glad of his fame, but proudly and aggressively independent, he wanders through the stately city, taking off his hat before the house of Allan Ramsay, and reverently kissing Robert Fergusson's grave, 'his elder brother in misfortune,' as Burns called him. He goes to the great houses, and although they did not know it, he was the greatest guest they had ever entertained, the greatest poet that then or ever walked the streets of Edinburgh. His famous hosts were all Scotsmen, but he was the only Scotchman among them who had written in the dialect of his country, and who had become famous without ceasing to be Scotch.

The dazzling Edinburgh days were a glaring social contrast to the rest of his life. The brilliant society flattered him, but his brilliancy outshone its own. He was wiser than the learned, wittier than the gayest, and more courteous than the courtliest. His genius flashed and blazed like a torch among the tapers, and the well-ordered company, enthralled by the surprising guest, winced and wondered. If the host was condescending, the guest was never obsequious. But Burns did not love a lord, and he chafed indignantly at the subtle but invincible lines of social distinction, feeling too surely that the realm of leisure and ease, a sphere in which he knew himself to be naturally master, must always float beyond, beyond – the alluring glimmer of a mirage...

Five years of letting his life 'wear only way it would hang,' and Burns's life was ended in 1796, in his thirty seventh year. There was an outburst of universal sorrow. A great multitude crowded the little town at his burial. Memorials, monuments, biographies of every kind followed. Poets ever since have sung him as of no other poet. The theme is always fresh and always captivating, and within the year our own American poet, beloved and honoured in his beautiful and unwasted age, sings of Burns as he sees him in vision, as the world shall forever see him, an immortal youth cheerily singing at his toil in the bright spring morning. The young man who would gild his dissipation with the celestial glamour of Burns's name snatches the glory of a star to light him to destruction... 'Except for grace,' said Bunyan, 'I should have been yonder sinner.'

But we unveil today, and set here for perpetual contemplation, not the monument of the citizen at whom respectable Dumfries looked askance, but the statue of a great poet... Great poets before and after Burns have been honoured by their countries and by the world; but is there any great poet of any time or country who has so taken the heart of what our Abraham Lincoln, himself one of them, called the plain people that as was lately seen in Edinburgh, when he had been dead nearly a hundred years, workmen going home from work begged to look upon this statue for the love and honour they bore to Robert Burns? They love him for their land's sake, and they are better Scotchmen because of him...

But the power thus to depict national life and character, and thus to kindle an imperishable patriotism, cannot be limited by any nationality or country. Burns died at the same age as Raphael; and Mozart, who was his contemporary died only four years before him. Raphael and Mozart are the two men of lyrical genius in kindred arts who impress us as most exquisitely refined by careful cultivation; and although Burns was of all great poets the most unschooled, he belongs in

> poetry with Raphael in paining, and Mozart in music. An indescribable richness and flower like quality, a melodious grace and completeness and delicacy belong to them all.

A proposer of the Immortal Memory from this era was much nearer home, indeed, he had stayed in Burns's own home in Dumfries for a time although not much is known about him at all. He is on record as 'an anonymous speaker '(probably a clergyman, by his tone) who, in February 1881, opened his address by explaining his singular link with the Dumfries Burns.

> Having passed the greater portion of my life in the house in which Burns lived and died and taking an intense delight in everything relating to him, I have become somewhat familiar with the records of his life. I thought it would not be uninteresting if I brought some of the more prominent features of his career and writing before your notice, and trust that unworthy though they may be, they may throw some little light in the life of this remarkable man.
>
> To render the incidents of the humble story of Robert Burns generally intelligible, it seems to me advisable to prefix some observations on the character of the order to which he belonged, a class of men distinguished by many peculiarities. By this means we shall form a more correct idea of the advantages with which he started and of the obstacles which he surmounted. A slight acquaintance with the peasantry of Scotland will serve to convince an unprejudiced observer that they possess a degree of intelligence not generally found among the same class of men in the other countries of Europe. In the very humblest condition of Scottish peasants everyone can read, and most persons are more or less skilled in writing and arithmetic, and under the disguise of their uncouth appearance, and of their peculiar manner and dialect, a stranger will discover that they posses a curiosity and have obtained a degree of information corresponding to these acquirements. These advantages they owe to an Act of Parliament made in 1646 for an establishment of a school in every parish throughout the country, for the express purpose of educating the poor but which has been superseded some years ago by the 'Compulsory Education Act'. I may mention here, that the reading was chiefly taught from the Bible, as other books were too expensive at that time...

Robert received the greatest portion of the education from his father, and by borrowing books he made rapid progress. When about 13 or 14, his father sent him and his brother Gilbert 'week about' to a Parish school at Dalrymple 2 or 3 miles from their home. The good man not being able to pay two fees, and while one was at school the other helped their father at the work on the farm. At this time Robert was a dexterous ploughman. When he was at the age of sixteen the family removed from the vicinity of Ayr to Lochlea in the Parish of Tarbolton in Ayrshire. At this place Robert began to write poetry for the first time. He says in one of his letters 'I never had the least thought or inclination of turning poet till I got once heartily in love and then rhyme and song were in a manner the spontaneous language of my heart.'

It was here where he met a bewitching creature a year younger than himself and whom he described as a 'bonnie, sweet, sonsie lass' and upon whom he composed his first production:

> Oh once I loved a bonnie lass
> Ay and I love her still
> And whilst that honour warms my breast
> I'll love my handsome Nell.

Robert and Gilbert were employed by their father as regular farm servants, he allowing them seven pounds of wages each per annum, from which sum, however, all the clothes they received was deducted...

[W]hen his father died he succeeded him in the farm of Lochlea but here again he failed... and after learning Lochlea he resided at a farm his brother Gilbert had taken named Mossgiel, [at Mauchline] for four years, the most important part of his life...

> In Mauchline there dwells six proper young belles
> The pride of the place and its neighbourhood a'
> Their carriage and dress a stranger would guess
> In London or Paris they'd gotten it' a'.
> Miss Miller is fine, Miss Markland divine
> Miss Smith she has wit and Miss Betty is braw
> There's beauty and fortune to get wi Miss Morton
> But Armour's the jewel for me o' them a'.

But not being equal to the maintenance of a wife he was on the eve of departing for Jamaica where he hoped to find better fortunes. However a Mr Hamilton advised him not to go, but encouraged him to publish some of his poems, he therefore went to Edinburgh where he succeeded fairly well in disposing of his words and was introduced to society. [W]ith the money he had saved in Edinburgh he gave farming another trial, and took the farm of Ellisland in the country of Dumfries [and] married 'the jewel' Jean Armour in 1788.

At Ellisland he got on remarkably will for a few years but towards the close of 1791 he finally despaired of his farm owing to bad crops, & he moved to Dumfries where he became an Exciseman...

His conduct as an Excise officer met with uniform approbation and he cherished warm hopes of being promoted by devoting himself altogether to the service, but death intervened and cut him off on July 21st 1796 at the early age of 38. [sic] The chief persons of the town and neighbourhood flooded together to attend his remains to their last resting place with military honours, the chief mourner being Lord Hawkesbury once Duke of Liverpool. During the funeral solemnity Mrs Burns gave birth to a posthumous son who shortly afterwards followed his father to the grave in St Michael's churchyard...

With all Robert Burns's faults no Scotchman has done more to develop that kindliness of heart and that fraternity of feeling which ought to prevail amongst us, and which only requires to be purified by the Spirit of God to give us 'peace on earth and goodwill among us' and to make our homes below as much as possible like our homes above. It is not possible however to speak of Burns in relation to religion without offending two classes of people. On the one hand, those who, because of what was bad in Burns refuse to acknowledge what was good, on the other hand those who make the good that was in Burns a reason for condoning what was bad. It is not about poor Burns himself that I am now going to speak but I speak of Robert Burns as a living and active power as one who by the force of his genius has made his life, his songs and his poetry, a mightier and more permanent influence in the world, more potent both for good and for evil than that of ten millions of men who are living and working around us.

One noble service he has rendered to humanity and therefore to a live Christianity is the bringing out of the dignity and worth of man as man apart from name, rank or fortune. Christ taught the same truth, it was the *man* he looked to, not the rank, not the robe. By His word, by His conduct, Christ taught the worth and nobleness of man. Burns sang it:

What tho' on homely face we dine
Wear hodden gray an a' that
Gie fools their silks, and knaves their wine
A mans' a man for a' that.
For a' that and a' that
Their tinsel shows and a' that
The honest man tho e'er sae poor
Is king o' men for a' that.
For a that an a' that,
Our toils obscure and a' that
The rank is but the guinea stamp
The man's the gowd for a' that.

By the bringing out of this great truth Burns helped the labouring poor to a spirit of contentment and self respect. He taught them to look for, and find enjoyment in life, in home, in friendship whatever their rank or station might be. He helped them to feel the wonder and the loveliness of nature. The green fields, the sounding shore, the storm, the sky, the little flower, the mavis' song, the music of the 'burnie trilling doon the glen'. The 'wee, modest, crimson- tipped daisy' looking out from amongst the green grass, was for them as well as for the rich, was even near to them because there was less of worldly pomp to separate man from nature…

He let the whole world see that in all circumstances, high or low, man is the same being, that everything that nature has bestowed upon us is found amongst the poor as well as among the rich. Burns taught Scotchmen to love and adore their native country, the true patriotism of which any of you can gather by reading *Scots wha hae*. It is a call to the defence of liberties, which the world needs defended as well as we. Nowhere does this comes and more clearly than when in *The Cottars Saturday Night* (which I would advise you all to peruse), before the bard pours out his prayer to Heaven for Scotland's defence and prosperity he pictures the Scottish life and Scottish character which he deems it worth defending:

Oh Scotia my dear my native soil
For whom my warmest wish to heaven is sent
Long may thy hardy sons of rustic toil

Be blest with health and peace and sweet content
And oh, may heaven their simple lives present
From luxury's contagion weak & vile
Then howe'er crowns and coronets be rent
A virtuous populace may rise the while
And stand a wall of fire around their much lov'd isle.

Such patriotism is, I think, not a menace but a strength to the world's liberty and progress. It is a patriotism rooted in virtue and purity and kindly love – a love of Scotland that helps instead of hindering the wider love of all. And who is there amongst Scotchmen, aye, Englishmen too, who has joined hands round the festive table at home, or with fellow countrymen in distant lands, and sung of *Auld Lang Syne* but has felt his heart not only glowing with fresh love to country but warming with a wider love for all mankind...

The fame of Burns is remarkable for its rapid development and constant extension. It has grown, is growing, and will continue to grow, it is more than local, more even than nationals, it is well nigh world wide, not only on the banks of the ditch but throughout the length and breath of the United Kingdom and in the backwoods of Canada, in the bush of Australia, east and west to the very antipodes wherever on Earth's wide surface the sons and daughters of Scotland may go, the name of Burns is a pledge of unity a passport to brotherly communion.

Of course Burns had his sins. In some form or another we all have sinned. Even those whose lives have been more wisely governed than that of Burns. Abraham told a lie, David committed treachery, and Peter on one occasion cursed and swore, but as well might men seek to honour Abraham by telling lies and David by committing treachery and Peter by profane swearing as seen to honour Burns by indulging in the drink that was his curse and perpetuating the customs that seduced him into sin and brought him to an early grave.

But, gentlemen, I call upon you to withhold your judgement as to Burns's inner life, and responsibility and sin and judge of the influence of his actual word and conduct, and while Burns is dead and gone with no longer the power even to attempt to recall or to check the influence for evil which he had set in motion, this cannot be said of those who are living in presence of that influence and under it. The responsibility is shifted now from Burns to his admirers. They can and they are bound

> to distinguish between what is great and beautiful and good in Burns that they may rejoice in it and help to let it have free course and be glorified. And what is bad in Burns that they may war against it for his sake, for their own sake and for the sake of humanity – Like other poets Burns reaps the benefit of the good he bestowed upon the world, when he is no more and when he cannot know or enjoy it. More money has been lavished in Scotland and America on statues to his memory than was ever given to his troubled life. But his works, and his life, and his death have endeared him to his countrymen. They are not merely proud of his fame which is worldwide, they keep his memory with affection…

Here the transcript is marked 'Finis', and presumably the toast was drunk – in tea, no doubt, as temperance was a Victorian obsession pursued by the good with as much intensity as alcohol was by the bad. Similarly, the totally erroneous picture of Burns eking out his last year in squalor and abject poverty was to this attitude assisted by several hysterical letters of his at the end caused more by his illness than by his actual situation. However, we must bear in mind that this was the age of Dickens and Little Nell, plumed horses and caparisoned hearses, professional mourners and an almost romantic view of death, especially of those who die young. If not quite thanatopsis, it was a fascination with death and every aspect of it.

It helped towards that Victorian sense of smug complacency, especially among the new emerging middle classes. They liked to be seen to be helping the poor and sympathising with the unfortunate. To them, Burns was both. They quite ignored the fact of his working stamina which upheld him almost to the last and preferred to think of him as the poor young man wasting away in neglect and disgrace. They felt comfortable with that picture of a romantic, poetic end. It suited the taste of the times and just as discreetly they forgot the Burns that was the social rebel, the political firebrand, the theatre-lover, the folk-philosopher, the man who looked out into a whole world wider than Dumfries High Street. This sentimental strain ran through all the songs and odes and most of the speeches in the 1859 celebrations and an element of the same attitude persisted to the end of the century. It has not been completely eradicated to this very day.

Yet there was no denying that the speech given in Dumfries by this patently good man, who had lived in domestic surroundings that Burns himself would have known, had a real love for the poet and his works, no matter his distaste for 'the drink', as he terms it. There would be better orators, more gifted speakers, finer minds and more original themes put forward in future Burns Suppers, but none would surpass the unknown proposer in heart, and, in the Burns sense, that is the vital and ultimate ingredient. As Burns said in his *Epistle to Davie*:

> Nae treasures nor pleasures could make us happy lang,
> The heart ay's the part ay that maks us right or wrang.

Towards the end of the 19th-century, the Burns Movement was growing almost too fast and its organisation was becoming cumbersome and difficult to control. It was in danger of trying to go in different, and often contradictory, directions at once. Was it to develop as a populist movement on a social basis or become a literary society with an elitist bias? The ideal would be a combination of both. The time was right for a pause for thought if only to further define their common purpose, which was the propagation of Burns's works and to rationalise their activities to this end. It was important at some point to get the clubs together andthrash it all out.

It was in this kind of climate that a couple of visiting Scots took a walk in London. Provost David Mackay was secretary of the Kilmarnock Burns Club and Captain David Sneddon was its past-president. In the summer of 1884 they were there to discuss the placing of a statue of Burns which was planned for the following spring. To understand their status at this time, it is necessary to realise that in the early years of the Burns Movement the Kilmarnock Burns Club (the future Club No 0, a token of its unique status) *was* the movement and these two men, Mackay and Sneddon, were virtually the Kilmarnock Burns Club.

Now they were searching London for a site for the new statue. While walking along the Embankment looking for a suitable spot, the two men were joined by Colin Rae-Brown, the man behind the 1859 Centenary Year and now founder-president of the London Burns Club. It is almost impossible to overestimate the contribution made to the Burns Movement by this man. As has been already mentioned, he was from Greenock, born there in 1821. After training as a journalist, he joined a publishing house in Glasgow where he also contributed both prose and poetry to its various publications. As he rose in the newspaper world, he adopted the views of such as Cobden, Bright and Cassell in advocating a popular press for the masses at an affordable price, so the idea of a people's newspaper was born.

In 1855, he helped to promote the *Daily Bulletin* in Glasgow as a penny paper. He also established two weekly journals, the *Scottish Banner* and the *Workman*. The latter title gives some idea of his political sympathies so it was no surprise that he was drawn early to Burns. He was honorary secretary of the Greenock Burns Club and it is safe to say that he was behind almost every event that honoured Burns in Britain from his first such involvement with Professor James Wilson ('Christopher North') in the 1844 Festival at Ayr to his last in 1897 with Lord Rosebery for the unveiling of the statue to Highland Mary Campbell at Dunoon. Between these times, he was the mainspring of the hugely successful Burns Centenary Festival of 1859, which was, of course, his original idea.

He became a good friend of James Glencairn Burns, the poet's youngest son, and despite his many professional and Burnsian activities, was recognised as a minor poet himself. He continued to publish, despite failing health, until his death in London at the age of 76. By 1862, he had moved to London to further his newspaper interests and in 1868 he founded, with artist George Cruickshank and Irish writer Samuel Lover, the first Burns Club in London. This club is still extant, proudly bearing the title No 1, which in itself is a further tribute to the zeal and energy of its founder. Already a proved winner with centenaries, this was the man who met with Messrs Mackay and Sneddon, in that afternoon walk along London's Embankment. Rae-Brown now mentioned the forthcoming centenary of the Kilmarnock Edition in 1886 and the possibility of a Burns 'demonstration' in that town at that time. He saw this as an ideal opportunity to sound out the attending clubs on the idea of federation.

The trio decided that a secluded spot near to Cleopatra's Needle was the spot for the statue. At the same time, it was also agreed that Rae-Brown's idea for a Federation was a good one and that there ought to be some kind of covering of all of the clubs in Scotland.

'Why not England as well?' asked Rae-Brown.

'Why not the world?' asked Captain Sneddon.

'Why not?' agreed Mackay.

And so the idea of a world Federation of Burns Clubs was set in motion by three Scotsman walking together along the sides of the Thames. All in all, it had been a good day's work for Burns.

Both projects, the statue and the federation of clubs, were put in hand almost at once. John Gordon Crawford, a Glasgow merchant, agreed to pay for the sculptor, Sir John Steell, to create a likeness out of Peterhead granite based on the Nasmyth portrait. It was ready in time for Lord Rosebery (who else?) to unveil it officially 'in the presence of a large gathering of ladies and gentlemen' on 26 July 1884. No doubt the gathering included Messrs Rae-Brown, Mackay and Sneddon and further discussions would have taken place regarding federation. These talks culminated in a preliminary meeting at Kilmarnock in February 1885, and the matter was moved forward.

In the following month the trio were together in London again. On 7 March 1885, the ubiquitous Lord Rosebery unveiled a bust of Burns set three feet to the right of Shakespeare in Poet's Corner, Westminster Abbey. The ploughboy and the butcher's apprentice had both obviously come a long way. But then so had the two friends from Killie. A few months later, on 17 July, 1885, at a meeting in the George Hotel, Kilmarnock, under the auspices of the Kilmarnock Burns Club, the Burns Federation was officially proposed.Inevitably, the leading name on the list of the seventeen present that night was Colin Rae-Brown and the last was David Mackay. Between them was the exciseman and part-time soldier, Captain David Sneddon, flanked by the printer, James McKie, who had taken over the business from John Wilson, who had printed Burns's first book, and that splendid reciter of *Tam o Shanter*, John Law, who attended from Springburn, Glasgow.

Also featured on the list was the Provost of Kilmarnock, the coalmaster and future MP for Kilmarnock, Peter Sturrock, who was to be elected the Federation's first president. Richard Armstrong was there too. He was a hatter and hosier in the town until his health broke down and he was to leave Scotland in 1900 to settle first in South Africa, then Australia and finally, in Wellington, New

Zealand, where he died in 1936, the last surviving member of that body of Victorians which founded the Burns Federation. Its object was, as Rae-Brown had directed, formally adopted and stated:

> to strengthen and consolidate the band of friendship existing among the members of Burns Clubs, by universal affiliation...

It should be noted that they also added 'its motto being *A man's a man' for a' that.*' It was a principle that was to supply the underlying ethos in all the Federation's doings and it is to their credit that the seventeen good men of Killie did not propose it in Sir John Fyffe's university Latin.

At that famous meeting the entry fee for clubs was set at a guinea. Its headquarters were to be established at Kilmarnock as that was the place where the first edition had been printed, and action towards federation was to be begun at once. All Rae-Brown's professionalism was brought to bear on the project. A circular was sent out at once to all the known Burns clubs following this meeting but the initial response was not encouraging. Many of the older clubs, in a typical Scottish way, resented Kilmarnock's taking such a daring initiative and held aloof from the new federation. Especially when the idea had emanated from London, albeit via three Scots. Gradually, however, sense prevailed, and, one by one, they all affiliated – Greenock in 1886, Paisley in 1891 but Dumfries did not join until 1913 and Ayr not until 1920.

All these clubs took part in the First Edition Celebrations in Kilmarnock on Saturday 7 August 1886, when they all processed from Barbadoes Green to the Burns Monument in Kay Park, where Dr Stoddart delivered the oration to a large crowd prior to a music festival followed by a banquet at the Corn Exchange. It was the annual holiday in the district but the turnout, according to reports of the time, was 'spectacular'. This event did much to confirm the Federation, with ten members (two outside Scotland) as an established fact in the Burns world.

Meantime, in the United States, they were putting up more statues. This time at Albany, New York, where the Rev Robert H Collyer's address was delivered on 30th August 1888:

> I will begin by asking you to turn with me for a moment to the first year in this century, and to the old churchyard of St

Michael's at Dumfries in Scotland, where we find one grave covered all over the Scotch thistles, and to notice, as we easily may, how they have not been left to grow there by a worthless sexton, but have been planted there and tended as if they were so many slips from the Rose of Sharon. That was the grave of Robert Burns when the century came in. They had laid him to rest there not very long before, in what should have been his fair, full prime, to the music of the Dead March in *Saul*. And as the music went sobbing into his home it would meet the wail of a babe just entering the world its father had left.

Englishmen, and Scotsmen too, in those times were voting incredible sums in salaries and pensions to no end of people because they were the offspring of the bastards of Charles II, and for equally delectable reasons; and that royal blackguard, George IV, was drawing more than half a million dollars a year for being a great deal meaner and more stupid than his father, George III, of blessed memory. Well, they made Burns a gauger on a salary of about £50 a year, with £20 more if he had good luck among those who got on the shady side of the revenue, and for this he had often to travel 200 miles a week in all sorts of weather, and Scotch weather at that... And when they had laid Burns under the greensward they did not think it worth their while to mark the spot with a stone. Those thistles were the only token and sign to tell you where he lay. How natural it would be for a good many of those who had once held him in esteem to conclude it was best that he should be speedily forgotten in the grave.

So they would imagine, but the truth they missed was this: that there was still a Robert Burns they could not bury any more than they could bury all the sunshine or all the daisies or all the birds that sing in the blue arches of heaven. Ploughmen and shepherds, and men at the bench and loom, were reading the poems he had written, and hiding them away, as an old Scotchman told me once, from the ministers and elders of the Kirk, for fear of what would happen if it was known they had the book. Then Burns began to be heard of far and wide. He went there the Bible went, and so at last, at the end of that hundred years, we gathered in his name hundreds of thousands strong all round the world...

By this time, another seminal Burns figure had emerged. Duncan

McNaught, a schoolmaster from Kilmaurs, was to become a very important figure indeed and a leading Burns authority over the next forty years or so. With Sneddon and Mackay, he formed the formidable triumvirate which became known as 'The Old Guard'. It was these three who held the fledgling federation together in its first tentative decades. 'Doing all the work and all the paying' as McNaught was to recall in 1925.

Thanks to Provost Sturrock's connections, James Dick, a Glaswegian factory-owner, but Kilmarnock-born, gave the town the building which became the Dick Institute, and for many, many years the headquarters of the Burns Federation. On Friday 4 September 1891 the Executive Council of the Burns Federation met there and on the motion of the ex-newspaper man, Colin Rae-Brown, it was agreed that an annual Burns Chronicle and Directory would be published from Kilmarnock starting in 1892. Captain Sneddon proposed John Muir of Glasgow as acting editor. Mr Muir was editor for the inaugural issue only, after which the indefatigable Duncan McNaught took over for what was to be his life's work. According to McNaught:

> The No.1 Chronicle was a dead failure in every respect, and I was hustled (much against my will) into the Editorial chair with something like a debt of one hundred pounds to wipe off.

Presumably his attitude changed, for Dr McNaught was to remain editor until his death from a heart attack in 1925. Few men have served Burns better. Or the Burns Federation. His heart was in all that he did for the Federation and if his heart eventually gave out, what he had built up in the *Chronicle* through 34 volumes stood as his lasting memorial. It was decided that this compilation should be known as the First Series in his honour and a new editor was sought to bring in the Second Series. If anything, James Ewing was of even greater calibre than McNaught in that he was the better all-round intellectual, and under his aegis the *Burns Chronicle* became a considerable platform for literary discussion that did not confine itself to Burns alone. It branched out into every aspect of the Scottish language and its cultural expression. It is really quite astonishing that a publication devoted to one man's life and work should now have been going for more than a hundred years without repeating itself. It would seem that Burns was sufficient to engage, engross, and entertain generation after generation of Scottish minds and inspire them to lift their pens and fill the more than a hundred pages of each issue with lively debate and original comment.

If it is rare in publishing it is also quite unique in scholarship. Whole theses were propounded between the updated covers and the *Chronicle* was carried forward on its own momentum at a rate it would maintain until the Second World War when it would celebrate its Golden Jubilee against a background of air raid sirens and the noise of German bombs. In a Burns sense, it is salutary to think that before that war was over it would be British bombs over Berlin that would kill Hans Hecht, the first German Burnsian.

In 1891, however, stentorian Victorian voices were still rolling around the supposedly civilised world making sonorous sound waves in praise of Burns (for the most part) and to the delight of their perfervid listeners (for the most part). First, was the Honourable Wallace Bruce – who, with such a name could be described as a belt and braces Scot – but his voice was more London Club than Burns Club. Notwithstanding, the gentlemen of Ayr gave him the best of order on 25th January 1891. He reminded them of the last time he had visited their town.

> Just before I came here in 1870 I was in Paris. I left that city three or four days before the gates were closed. While I was there the Marseillaise hymn burst forth form the heart of that people. It had been closed by an edict, but it had been locked up in the French heart, and then when the emperor was captured at Sedan every one in France sang the Marseillaise. In the hotel in which I was, a man stepped up to the piano and played the heart-stirring song. From the further end of the room came a Scotsman, and he sat down by the piano, and, filled with the same flush of patriotism, he played *Scots Wha Hae*. There I saw those two grand songs put in contrast with each other, and I don't think I was prejudiced in thinking that there was more stirring strains in *Scots Wha Hae* than even in the great rush of the Marseillaise hymn.
>
> E'en then a wish – I mind its pow'r –
> A wish that to my latest hour
> Should strongly stir my breast

> That I, for puir auld Scotland's sake,
> Some usefu' plan or beuk could make,
> Or sing a sang at least.
>
> And he did do it. He sang the song, and he made the book.
>
> Robert Burns taught the world the great principle of reciprocity. He was the only man that ever built a greater bridge than Sir William Arrol, Robert Burns has swung his choral bridge of poetry across the Atlantic, the Pacific, and the Indian oceans, so that the world today is bound together by the cords of one man, the genius of your town of Ayr. Could he have had a vision as he lay upon his dying bed, that before one hundred years had gone by the city of New York should be the centre of three millions of people, and he could see that, although the world had grown, it had not outgrown his songs? Did not the vision pass before him, for he was conscious of the power that slumbered in him? And now, tonight, all over the world, we come together to give the memory of Burns, and I ask you to pledge it in solemn silence.

Which they did.

In the following year, Mr Andrew Lang, one of the best Scottish minds of the time, and a still undervalued writer, spoke to the Edinburgh Burns Club. Regrettably, space allows only an extract from his address. In it, he refers to himself as a Cockney, despite the fact that he was born at Selkirk in 1844.

> I admit that Burns has written better things than
>
> My Mary, dear departed shade!
> Where is thy place of blissful rest?
> See'st thou thy lover lowly laid?
> Hear'st thou the groans that rend his breast?
>
> This song is under the disadvantage of being written in English. As far as I remember, Burns made no other song under the influence of grief for the dead. It is possible that what Scott says about other poets applies to Burns. 'The language of passion is almost always pure, as well as vehement; and it is no uncommon thing to hear a Scotsman, when overwhelmed by a countryman with a tone of better and fluent upbraiding, reply, by way of taunt to his adversary, *You have gotten to your English*.' Burns, then, uses English here under the stress of this unwonted passion; as he also does in rare movements of religious exaltation. Now, it is certain that in English verse he is never at his best.

Nobody in his senses will maintain that all Burns's poems, or all of anybody's poems, are always on the same level of excellence. But, perhaps, we may say that Burns is at least as often equal to himself as any other great poet; he has not the ups and downs of Wordsworth or of Byron. In this country, at least, the depressing critics are scarce. We are more plagued by a frantic enthusiasm which makes every Scot who writes regard Burns as his own private property, his special fetish, whom nobody else can speak of rightly, whom nobody else can with propriety praise.

For my sins, I lately published a book – a selection from Burns's poetry. No such selection can ever be satisfactory; in truth, as a counsel of perfection, we should advise people never to make selections at all. Indeed, I don't think that I satisfied anybody but a genial critic in Bonnie Dundee, who, on this occasion only, overlooked my sins as a Cockney – a native of the city that hears the music of Bow Bells. Well, these are personal matters, and not of cosmic importance; but is it not a fact that whatever we say of Burns irritates one Scot or another, and makes him take up his confounded testimony against us? If you hint that Burns was 'a liberal shepherd' in parts of his private conduct, you are 'unco guid.' If you say nothing about it, you leave a great element in his life and poetry out of sight. If you gloss over these things as seeming 'genial, venial faults,' you make allowances for Burns which you would not make for anyone else, and which are not of the best example. Well, it is easiest and most pleasant to drop a hackneyed theme, which has been made the topic of poems and preachings; the world is weary of it.

Verily, we are not a people of one lonely poet, though in one nature combined many of the voices of the past, much of the music of the future, in the good, the generous, the tender, the kindly, the homely, the impassioned Burns, the brightest of our lyrists, the most human of our satirists, the most perfervid of the perfervid Scots.

Had Burns been living today, would the world that lay around him have been so fit to inspire him with song? The mirth, the sport, the tradition are *a' wede awa'*. London would inevitably have sucked him into its dingy and disastrous Corrievreckan. He would have battered at the door of the theatre, he might have scribbled articles for the press and drunk in Fleet Street, and contributed verses to the

> magazines. His magnificent genius would have been frittered away in the struggle for life. He was not happy; no man with his passionate nature could be happy; few men of genius, indeed, have been happy, 'even as mortals count happiness.' They may not be more miserable than others, but we hear more of it. Whoever represents humanity, as Burns represents it, whoever is to utter its voice, as Burns utters it, must know its sufferings in his own heart, and endure them in his own life.
>
> In the Scottish phrase, we are not here as 'doon-heartit loons' to 'make a poor mouth' over Burns, nor greatly to blame the world for its treatment of him. He has received what he would have valued more than wealth, or ease, or an inglorious life; he has added renown to the country he loved, and for himself has gained that immortal garland, which is not to be run for without dust and sweat.

Mr Lang retired to St Andrews to take up the golf and walk on the links after a distinguished life in letters at Oxford and London. Meanwhile, across the Atlantic, Colonel Robert G Ingersoll addressed the Chicago Caledonian Society on 23rd January 1893. Colonel Ingersoll was an army man with a most un-military eloquence.

> We are here tonight, to honour a poet, and it may be well enough to inquire in the first place what a poet is? What is poetry? Every one has some idea of a poet, and this idea is born of his experience, of his impressions, of his education, and depends largely on whether his soul has burst into blossom. There have been more nations than poets. Many people imagine that poetry is a kind of art, depending upon certain rules, and that is only necessary to find out the rules; and if that were all, possibly it would be impossible to find out the rule. These rules have never been found, and yet the great poet follows them unconsciously, and the great poet is as unconscious as Nature, and the product of the highest art seems always to be felt instead of thought. The finest definition perhaps that has been given is this – 'As Nature unconsciously produces that which appears to be the result of conscience, so the greatest artist conscientiously produces that which appears to have been an unconscious result.' Poetry, after all, must rest on the experience of men. It must sit by the fireside of the heart. It must have to do with this world, with the place in which we live, with the men and women we

know, with our loves, with our hopes, with our fears, and with our joys.

I was taught that Milton was a wonderful poet, and above all others sublime. I have read Milton once. Few people ever read him twice. We have been taught also that Dante was a wonderful poet. He describes with infinite minuteness the pangs and agonies endured by the damned in the torture dungeons of God. But there was one good thing about Dante – and for that one good thing I have forgiven him many faults. He had the religious democracy in his heart, and the courage to see a Pope in hell. That is something to be thankful for. Poetry cannot be written by rule. It is not a trade. It is not a profession. Let the critics lay down the laws of poetry, and the true poet will violate them all. By the rule such as the critics make, you can construct skeletons, but you cannot clothe them with flesh; you cannot put sight in their eyes and passion in their hearts.

In the olden time in Scotland most of the so-called poetry was written by pedagogues and parsons – gentlemen who found out what little they knew about the living world by reading the dead languages, by studying epitaphs in the cemeteries of literature. They knew nothing of any living thing that they themselves thought poetic. The men then living were not worth writing about; the women then alive were not beautiful enough to attract their scholarly attention. They bestowed their praise on the dead, on dust, on skeletons, on phantoms – phantoms that, if they did not live here, were supposed to live somewhere else. In those days they made poetry about geography. The critics then always looked for mistakes, not beauties, not for perfection of expression and feeling, but for syntax, grammar. These gentlemen would object to the clouds, because they are not square. And at one time it was thought the scenery, the grand and beautiful in Nature, made the poet. Let me tell you tonight – it is the poet who makes the scenery; the scenery never made a poet, and never made an artist in the world. The poet makes the scenery. Holland has produced far more genius than the Alps. There is not much scenery in Holland.

Where Nature is prodigal, where the crags kiss the clouds, man is overawed, overpowered, and becomes small. In England and Scotland the hills are low; nothing in the scenery is calculated to arouse poetic life, and yet those countries have produced the greatest and the most magnificent of all poets of all time. The truth is, the poets make the scenery. The place where man has died for man is grander than any snow-crowned summit in the world; the place where man has loved and suffered.

A poem itself is something like scenery; and let me say right here, that there is greater scenery in this world than the physical. There are mental seas and continents, and ranges of mountains and constellations of the imagination greater than the eye has ever yet beheld. A poem is something like a mountain stream that ripples into light and then is lost in shadow, ripples along with a kind of wild joy under overhanging boughs, and then leaps and hurls its spray on high over some cascade; then running peacefully along over pebbly bottoms, balling of joy, murmuring delight, and then sweeping along to its old mother, the sea. A mountain stream is a poem in itself.

Thousands and millions of men live poems, but do not write them; but every great poem that was ever written has been lived by the man who wrote it. I say tonight that every good and self-denying man, every man who lives and labours for those he loves, for wife and child, is living a poem. The loving mother rocking the cradle, singing the slumber song, is living a poem; the man who bares his breast through shot and shell for the right has lived a poem; the poor woman in the tenement, sewing and looking with her poor blurred eyes upon her work, for the love of her child, is living a perfect poem; all the pioneers, and all the builders of home, and all the brave men of the world, and all the brave and loving women have been poets in action, whether they have ever written one word or not.

But tonight we are going to talk about a poet; one who poured out his soul in the music of song. How does a country become great? By producing great folks. Why is it that Scotland, when the roll of nations is called, can stand up and proudly cry 'Here'? It is because Robert Burns has lived. It is Robert Burns that puts your well-loved Scotland in the front rank of nations. Robert Burns was a child of the people. I am glad of it. Robert Burns was a peasant, a ploughman, and yet a poet.

And why is it that millions and millions of men and women love this man? Why is it? He was a Scotchman, and all the tendrils of his heart struck deep in Scottish soil. He voiced the ideals of the best and greatest of his race, and of his blood. He was patriotic to the last fibre, and yet he is as dear to the citizens of the great Republic as to Scotia's sons and daughters. And why? We, of course, admit that all great poetry has a national flavour. It tastes of the soil. No matter how great it is, how wide, how universal, the flavour of locality is never lost. We love Burns because he made common life beautiful, because he idealised sun-burned girls who worked in the field, because he put honest labour above titled idleness, because he made the cottage far more poetic than the palace, because he painted the simple joys and ecstasies and raptures of sincere love, and because he put native common sense above the culture of students. We love him because he was independent, sturdy, self-poised, social, generous; thrilled by a look, by a touch, full of pity, carrying the sorrows of others in his heart, those even of enemies; hating to see anybody suffer, lamenting.

Burns had another art – the art of stopping; the art of stopping at the right place. Nothing is more difficult than this. It is very hard to end a play. It is very hard to get the right kind of roof on a house. There is not one storyteller in a thousand that knows just the place where the rocket ought to explode. They go on talking after the stick has come down. Burns wrote short poems, and why? All poems are short. There cannot be a long poem any more than there can be a long joke. Burns knew when to stop. I believe the best example of an ending perfectly accomplished you will find in his *Vision*. There comes into his house, into that auld clay biggin', his muse, the spirit of a beautiful woman, and tells him what he can do, and what he can't do, as a poet. He conversed with her; he has a long talk with her, and now the thing is how to get her out of the house. You may think that is an easy thing. It is easy enough to get yourself into difficulty, but not to get out. But I was struck with the beautiful manner in which Burns got that angel out of the house. 'And like a passing thought she fled, in light away.' That is the way he got her out of the house.

A little while ago one of the greatest poets died, and I was reading one of his volumes, and at the same time during the same period reading a little from Robert Burns, and the difference between these two men struck me so forcibly that I concluded to say something about it tonight. Tennyson was a piece of rare china decorated by the highest art. Burns was made of honest human clay moulded by sympathy and love. Tennyson dwelt in his fancy for the most part with kings and queens, with lords and ladies, and with counts and nobles. Burns lingered by the firesides of the poor and humble, in the thatched cottage of the peasant. He loved men and women, and without regard to the outlook. Tennyson was touched by place and birth, and by the insignia given by birth and chance of fortune. As he grew old he grew narrower, and less in touch with the world around him. Tennyson was ingenious, Burns ingenious. Tennyson had intellectual taste, Burns's brain was the servant of his heart. One was exclusive, and the other pressed the world against his breast. Burns was touched by wrongs and injustice. Tennyson touched art on many sides, writing no doubt of lordly things, dealing with the vast poesies of his brain, and he satisfied the taste of cultured men. Tennyson is always self-possessed. He possesses in abundance poetic sympathy, but lacks the fire and the flame. Burns dwells on simple things, on things that touch the heart and arouse the highest sympathies of men. The religion of Burns was great enough to include everything. Tennyson's imagination lived in a palace. The imagination of Burns dwelt lower down, among the people; his heart went out to them, and he recorded the poems of their simple life in imperishable verse. His songs were sweet harmonies drawn from the breast of Nature.

Both men were great poets. Tennyson appealed to the intellectual in his readers, Burns to the tenderest feelings of the soul. Men admire Tennyson: men love Robert Burns. How that man rose above all his fellows in death! Do you know, there is something wonderful in death. What a repose! What a piece of sculpture! The common man dead looks royal, a genius dead, sublime.

When a few years ago I visited all the places where Burns had been, from the little house with one room where he now sleeps, I thought of this. Yes, I visited them all; all the places made immortal by his genius: the field where love first touched his heart; the field where he ploughed up the home of the mouse. I saw the cottage where Robert and Jean first lived as man and wife and walked on 'the banks and braes of bonnie Doon,' and all the other places rendered immortal by his genius, and when I stood by his grave I said: This man was a great man.

The name of Robert Burns can never die. He is enrolled among the immortals and will live forever. This man left a legacy of riches untold, not only to Scotland, but to the whole world. And when I was at his birthplace, I wrote these lines:

Though Scotland boasts a thousand names
Of patriot, king, and peer,
Was loved and cradled here.
Here lived the gentle peasant prince,
The loving cotter king,
Compared with whom the greatest prince
Is but a titled thing.
'Tis but a cot roofed in with straw,
A hovel made of clay;
One door shuts out the snow and storm,
One window greets the day;
And yet I stand within this room,
And hold all thrones in scorn;
For here beneath this lowly roof
Love's sweetest bard was born.
Within this hallowed hut I feel
Like one who clasps a shrine,
When the glad lips at last have touched
The something deemed divine.
And here the world, through all the years,
As long as day returns,
The tribute of its love and tears'
Will pay to Robert Burns.

Which seems a suitable place to pause.

Come, friend, we'll pree the barley bree
To his braid fame that's noo awa'.

4

The Centenary Commemoration

1896

Lord Rosebery to his Lady said, 'My, hinnie, and my succour,
Shall we dae the thing,' he said, 'Or shall we have our supper?'
Wi' bonie face, sae fu' o'grace, replied the bonie leddie,
'My noble Lord, may dae as he please, but supper isna ready!'

The Centenary was to become a virtual Rosebery celebration, but as top of the bill, he was not due till later. The supporting cast had still to perform in the lead-up to the main attraction. For instance, on the night before Burns Night, 1893, Mr Lewis McIver spoke to the South Edinburgh Burns Club. He did so as a patriotic Scot but with some reservations.

> Mr Chairman, when I began I warned this goodly company of what they might expect; but, until I was fairly embarked, I had no notion how portentously dull I could be. And herein is a double crime; for gloom is most inopportune at a convivial gathering, and dullness – always inexcusable – is an outrage in connection with a prince of good fellows, the father of so much mirth in the past, in the present, and in the ages yet to come. That is the side of the
>
> Sad, glad poet,
> Whose soul was a white dove lost in the whirling snow,
>
> Which is meetest for tonight; and, after all, to invert the words of Marc Antony, I come to praise, not to bury Burns. On the occasion of a genuine 'nicht wi' Burns' there is no need of an invocation to Euphrosyne. And one has but to pull out the mirthful stop in that magnificent instrument in order to flood this room with sunshine. That done, the scalpel of criticism is out of place. None of us want to dissect a nightingale.
>
> The gladsomeness of Burns lives for ever in his songs; and even as they are his most enduring monument, so his mirth and joyousness, which they embalm, are our indestructible

possession. He has been above all things a benefactor of humanity, and especially of his own countrymen as a songster, and a glad songster:

God sent His singers upon earth
With songs of sadness and of mirth,
That they might touch the hearts of men,
And bring them back to heaven again.

If with firm and confident finger he struck many noble and lofty chords in the national harp that no musician before or since has found, and which still vibrate, and will continue to vibrate while the heart of Scotland beats, he has also given echoing expression to the gayest and gladdest impulses of our nature. He discovered a rich mine of joyousness under the rough rock surface of our national character. He brought its gems to light from the depths. He cut and polished them, and he left them to us an imperishable inheritance, a perennial source of brightness and good fellowship; and we can best perpetuate our gratitude and his glorious name by keeping foremost that brightest aspect of his achievement, and by being glad to think of him as he would have chosen we should. What though

His regal vestments soil'd,
His crown of half its jewels spoil'd,
He is a king for all.

Edinburgh invited the Rev Wallace Williamson in 1895 and he spoke to the Burns Club on 26 January in the presence of Edinburgh's Lord Provost. On his own admission, the Rev Williamson did not say anything new, but he said it modestly but cogently enough.

Mr Chairman, my Lord Provost, croupiers and gentlemen, – in rising to propose the toast of the evening, I must say at once you will not be wise if you expect anything new. For ninety-nine years the poet, whose memory we are met to honour, has been numbered with the dead. During that long period I know not how many speeches have been delivered on similar occasions, and I am appalled to think that I am about to add another to the number. My only defence in speaking, and your only satisfaction in listening, must be that, however often and however admirably the thing has been done before, another anniversary has come round.

The genius of Burns had shed a lustre over our native land. The unforced beauty of his song has found a place in every

Scottish heart. We instinctively feel that our national life – that is to say, the life of the people – in all its many-sidedness, in every mood of joy and grief, in the strenuousness of its daily toil as well as the abandonment of hours snatched from care, has found expression through him as it never did before; and we know that from that fuller and freer development which he has helped to give it can never return. This is true as a general fact; but not merely so, for it comes home to the heart of every individual Scotsman. There is a certain subtle element which unites the personality and work of Burns in the imagination of his countrymen in a manner quite unique.

Between the poet and us language seems to melt into actual thought and feeling. He requires no interpreter. He speaks the language of the human heart, and the human heart infallibly responds. And behind the beauty of his work, behind the splendid gifts of his genius, there is also the pathos of a career which, with all its failings, claims for itself, and secures for itself, a sympathetic and abiding place in the memory of his countrymen. For this reason it seems to me the language of apology which has sometimes pervaded the utterances at such gatherings as this is entirely out of place. We need no apology for remembering the greatest genius our country has produced. I say the greatest genius. I do not say the greatest man.

The personal failings of Burns have been the theme of the moralist for a hundred years. For once we will let them alone. It is not his faults we are here to speak of. Another judge will deal with these and with ours. It is his genius.

There is hardly a side of human life which he does not touch, and in touching has not adorned. Is it the weird borderland on which the human should delights to hover? You have it in *Tam o Shanter*. Is it the wild abandonment of roving, rugged penury? You have it in *The Cotter's Saturday Night*. Is it the scorn of hypocrisy? You have it in *Holy Willie's Prayer*. Is it the pathos of separation and love? You have it in *To Mary in Heaven* and *My Nannie's Awa'*. Is it the 'comic humour' of the country courtship? You have it in *Duncan Gray*. Is it the warm grasp of human friendship? You have it in *Auld Lang Syne*.

In closing, gentlemen, I shall merely say I regard Robert Burns as the brightest gift of genius God ever gave to our native land. We do well to cherish that noble heritage of poetry and song he has bequeathed to us. He has deepened

> and strengthened our love of country. He has purified the springs of our emotional life. He has sweetened the world of toil for careworn men, and knit closer the ties of human brotherhood...

A year later, to hansel in the Centennial Year, Mr Robert Fergie 'memorised' his piece before the South Edinburgh Burns Club.

> The toast I have the honour to propose – The Memory of Burns – is one that, as year succeeds year and brings round the natal day of the bard, appears ever increasingly honoured in this country, and, indeed, all over the world. Men eminent in statecraft, in literature, and in arts, as well as lesser notables – honoured in the hamlet, the village, or the burgh, most worthy men not infrequently – are ever coming forward lauding the poet, descanting and enlarging upon his words and acts, and doing their best to keep his memory green. Keeping this in view, one is apt to think the subject would long ere this be pretty well exhausted; yet somehow, while each year or decade develops new ideas and aspirations, with new problems to solve, new difficulties to overcome, and new duties to face, the life and works of Burns, interpreted and read in the light of recent events, or of those assuming the ghost-like, shadowy forms of the future ere they take the realities of the present, will ever afford valuable guidance and awaken fresh interest when considering what is best to be done in emergencies or trials. At any rate, it is well, once in a way, to ponder over the treasures our fathers prized and test their worth, even at the risk of a little wearisome repetition.
>
> But, I would here, with your kind permission, like to say a word or two upon his attitude towards religion, or the religious forms and opinions of his fellow-countrymen. No church, no organisation, and no man in this world is altogether good or perfect, and abuses will creep in even to the holy of holies, so that unless, like a tree which must be lopped or pruned to be maintained in perfect health and vigour, the pruning knife be applied to abuses and foul fungus sure in time to develop, the organisation or church is bound ere long to lose its strength or sap, and ultimately rot or decay. Burns, to some extent at least, acted the part of the skilful gardener in respect to the Presbyterian Church. His *Holy Fair* virtually put an end to the great scandals which had

sprung up side by side with the celebration of its most sacred ordinance; and his *Holy Willie's Prayer* dealt one of the hardest blows ever struck against canting religious hypocrites, with the exception, perhaps, of some passages in the Bible record.

And yet one of Burns's latest biographers, the late Principal Shairp, accords faint praise to the one, and expresses his regret that *Holy Willie's Prayer*, *The Ordination*, and some other verses of a like nature were ever penned. Perhaps, for super-refined minds like Professor Shairp's, this may be so; but for ordinary mortals who prefer plain, easily understood, though it may be unpalatable, truth to fine sophistries, the contrary view unquestionably prevails. The latter would, on no account, wish to see the poems blotted out; they do not regret they were ever written. For myself, I would sooner see the doctrine of election plainly stated as it is in the first stanza of *Holy Willie's Prayer* than wade through the confused and bewildering questions and answers and proofs of the Westminster Catechism, to arrive at a similar conclusion.

To change the theme, I would have liked to have spoken at length on his plea for the dignity of labour and manhood and independent though, and noted how his concentrated scorn and contempt oft break out upon these who can but will not assist their poorer brethren. We may almost fancy we see his brilliant eyes glowing with indignation as we read the lines:

See yonder poor, o'erlabour'd wight,
So abject, mean, and vile,
Who begs a brother of the earth
To give him leave to toil;
And see his lordly fellow-worm
The poor petition spurn,
Unmindful, tho' a weeping wife
And helpless offspring mourn.

If I'm design'd yon lordling's slave –
By Nature's law design'd –
Why was an independent wish
E'er planted in my mind?
If not, why am I subject to
His cruelty or scorn?
Or why has man the will and pow'r
To make his fellow mourn?

Why, indeed has often been asked, but remains, like the religious questions previously referred to, unanswered; and, perhaps will ever remain so.

Before concluding, however, let me refer to just one other of his poems – perhaps his greatest – because it shows so well how in life the happiest and most blissful moments may be shrouded, interwoven, or intermingled with gravest and saddest thought. These thoughts unbidden come; how they do come at such times will probably never be explained. Now, listen how artistically and naturally the lines I am going to quote depict this sensation, which all at times must have felt; how they dovetail into each other, though as opposite as may be, just like, as I have said, sad thoughts coursing over the mind of the gay dancer. Few poets, indeed, could have written such lines, and in the whole range of literature within the same compass I know of none so apt:

As bees flee hame wi' lades o'treasure,
The minutes wing'd their way wi' pleasure;
Kings may be blest, but Tam was glorious,
O'er a' the ills o' life victorious!
But pleasures are like poppies spread,
You seize the flow'r, its bloom is shed!
Or like the snowfall in the river,
A moment white – then melts for ever!
Or like the borealis race,
That flit ere you can point their place;
Or like the rainbow's lovely form,
Evanishing amid the storm.

The July of 1796 found Burns on his dying bed, haunted by the fear that he might be arrested and carried off to jail for debt; his Bonnie Jean lying ill and just about to be confined, but both well tended and nursed by a kindly neighbour, Jessy Lewars, in praise of whom his last song is written. And yet, undaunted amidst all this pain and misery, he can still bear up. He had previously written to an old Edinburgh friend these notable words, which must oft have recurred to him during this trying period: – 'There are two great pillars that bear us up amid the wreck of misfortune and misery. The one is composed of a certain noble, stubborn something in man, known by the names of Courage, Fortitude, Magnanimity. The other is made up of those feelings and sentiments which, however the sceptic may deny them, or the enthusiast may disfigure them, are yet, I am convinced, original and component parts of the human soul, those senses of the mind – if I may be allowed the expression – which connect us with, and link us to, those awful obscure realities – an all powerful and equally beneficent God, and a world to come beyond death and the grave. The first gives the nerve of combat, while a ray of hope beams on the field; the last pours the balm of comfort into the wounds which time can never cure.'

Thus amidst poverty and suffering he passed away, his greatness unrealised till his death, his fame obscured and hidden and besmirched by the little nobodies who surrounded him, till ultimately it burst through all trammels, and since then has ever been extending and increasing. We in Scotland, above all others, have reason to be proud of him. The fame, even the name, of Scotsmen had fallen lower – owing mainly to the crushing out of the Rebellion of '45 – than at any other time, if we except that short period in her history of English domination immediately before the appearance of Wallace. He, like a second Wallace, aroused her from her depression and degradation. He inspired her sons with fresh courage. He gloried in his nationality. He showed what could be done, and has been done, even though, to use his own words, there was 'a parcel of rogues in the nation.' We honour ourselves by honouring his memory.

Gentlemen, I give you the toast, 'The Immortal Memory of Robert Burns.'

The 'Hat-Peg' that Dickens had referred to in 1859 was even larger in 1896, for even more hats were thrown into the ring. Even the respectable topper of the Poet-Laureate, Mr Alfred Austin, who, as Cyril Pearl points out, was known more for his moustache than his poetry, found a place on the peg. He had not seen fit to compose an ode for the earlier occasion, merely confining himself to a brief comment:

> It is perfectly idle to suppose that you (he was addressing the Scots) will give up loving this man (Burns) because, as no one can deny, he was as weak as water in the presence of your natural beverage and your natural beauties. He loved them overmuch and he loved them very much in the wrong sort of way.

A remark that illustrates not only his Englishness, but his ignorance of Burns and reveals his own level as a putative poet. One can only be grateful that he never attempted an ode. In 1896, he relented sufficiently to come north to Irvine to speak at the unveiling of the Burns statue in the town. If he was not a poet, he was certainly no orator either, but he made appropriate Laureate noises and took his moustache home again as soon as he could and left the stage clear for the 'star of Robbie Burns' himself – Lord Rosebery.

Archibald Philip Primrose, the 5th Earl of Rosebery was the great-great grandson of Henry Primrose who, in 1695 supported William and Mary against the rightful James VII of Scotland, and was rewarded with the Earldom of Rosebery, near Edinburgh. He was likely to be the Rosebery mentioned at the head of the chapter. The Rosebery we are concerned with here inherited in 1868, and although a conventional Eton and Oxford aristocrat, he regarded himself as completely Scottish and with a genuine concern for 19th-century Scotland which he saw as 'mumbling the dry bones of political neglect'. He worked hard at the Home Office towards the creation of a Scottish Office, although it wasn't to happen for another 40 years. Meantime, all his considerable energies (he was a widower and an insomniac) were given to his house, the Durdans, near Epsom, horse paintings by Stubbs and to his hobbies, which were various, but included Burns and Burns-related events.

This was to be later acknowledged in his being made the first Honorary President of the Burns Federation and having the Rosebery Burns Club named for him in Glasgow. Lord Rosebery might have been a great man had he applied himself wholly to any one thing but his whole was never quite as good as any of his many parts. What matters here is that he put his gifted tongue at the disposal of the early Burns movement and was tireless on its behalf. He unveiled statues, begged for money for monuments, attended dinners for every kind of good Burns cause, and generally spent his wit and wisdom in furthering the understanding of a man who could not have been more different to himself in every way. And when the Prime Minister of the day, Arthur Balfour (more related to Stevenson than to Burns) begged to be excused what he called – 'the demonstration in honour of our National Poet' – at Dumfries for health reasons, and because of Parliamentary demands in the House, who should take his place but Lord Rosebery

This is perfectly appropriate for a man who was to be Prime Minister of Great Britain himself in 1894-95. He also found time to own three Derby winners), become patron of the Scottish Football Association, (the Scotland team wore his racing colours, primrose and pink, in a 1900 international against England), and a published author of biographies on Napoleon and the two William Pitts. Most of all, he became a public orator and wit. His was a genuine admiration for Burns, and this showed in all his speeches. So much did he dominate the commemorations of the death of Burns in 1896 that they were thought of by Burnsians of the time as the Rosebery Celebrations.

This main event of this Centenary year took place on the actual anniversary of Burns's death – 21 July 1896, and Dumfries made quite a day of it. Once again, the weather was not entirely propitious. It could more be described as precipitous. As soon as the very large procession got underway from Whitesands on its way to St Michael's Kirkyard, the rain came down in torrents. The Freemasons, bellhangers, stockingmakers, fleshers and vanmen all got uniformly soaked along with their respective bands and the huge turn-out of Burns Club members from Britain, America and the Colonies. The gentry and those and such-as-those came, of course in their carriages between lines of wet King's Own Scottish Borderers, the Earl of Rosebery travelling with Sir Robert and Lady Reid. Their arrival at the mausoleum was greeted with loud cheers and the noble earl dutifully laid his 'magnificent wreath of choice exotics' upon Burns's grave.

That afternoon, after the public lunch, he gave the main oration in the Drill Hall, New Hall Terrace, and the place was fill to its 4,500 capacity. After apologies were read from the Prime Minister (he was to be made a Burgess of the town in the following year) Rosebery rose to prolonged cheering.

> Ladies and gentlemen, I come here as a loyal burgess of Dumfries to do honour to the greatest burgess of Dumfries... but you impose on your youngest burgess an honour that might well break anybody's back – that of attempting to do justice in any shape or fashion to the hero of today's ceremony... We are surrounded by the choicest and the most sacred haunts of the Poet. You have in this town the house in

which he died, the 'Globe,' where we could have wished that some phonograph had then existed which could have communicated to us some of his wise and witty wayward talk. You have the street commemorated in McCulloch's tragic anecdote when Burns was shunned by his former friends, and you have the paths by the Nith which are associated with some of his greatest work. You have near you the room in which the whistle was contended for, and in which, if mere legend is to be trusted, the immortal Dr Gregory was summoned to administer his first powders to the survivors of the memorable feast...

You have near you the walk by the river, where, in his transport, he passed his wife and children without seeing them, 'his brow flushed and his eyes shining' with the lustre of *Tam o Shanter*. 'I wish you had but seen him,' said his wife 'he was in such ecstasy that the tears were happing down his cheeks.' That is why we are in Dumfries today... But it is not in Dumfries alone that he is commemorated today; for all Scotland will pay her tribute. And this, surely, is but right. Mankind owes him a general debt. But the debt of Scotland is special. For Burns exalted our race, he hallowed Scotland and the Scottish tongue. Before his time we had for a long period been scarcely recognised, we had been falling out of the recollection of the world. From the time of the union of the crowns, and still more from the time of the legislative union, Scotland had lapsed into obscurity. Except for an occasional riot or a Jacobite rising her existence was almost forgotten. She had, indeed, her Robertsons and her Humes writing history to general admiration, but no trace of Scottish authorship was discoverable in their works; indeed, every flavour of national idiom was carefully excluded. The Scottish dialect, as Burns called it, was in danger of perishing. Burns seemed at this juncture to start to his feet and reassert Scotland's claim to national existence; his Scottish notes rang through the world, he preserved the Scottish language forever; for mankind will never allow to die that idiom in which his songs and poems are enshrined. That is a part of Scotland's debt to Burns.

But this is much more than a Scottish demonstration; it is a collection of representatives from all quarters of the globe to own a common allegiance and a common faith. It is not only Scotsmen honouring the greatest of Scotsmen – we stretch far beyond a kingdom or a race – we are rather poetical Mohammedans gathered at a poetical Mecca, and yet we are assembled in our high enthusiasm under circumstances which are somewhat paradoxical. For with all the appearance of joy we celebrate, not a festival but a tragedy. It is not the sunrise but the sunset that we commemorate. It is not the birth of a new power into the world, but the subtle germ of a fame that is to survive and inspire the generations of men; but it is perhaps more fitting that we celebrate the end and not the beginning. For the coming of these figures is silent; it is their passing that we know. At this instant that I speak there may be born into the world the equal of a Newton or a Caesar, but half of us would be dead before he had revealed himself. Their death is different. It may be gloomy and disastrous; it may come at a moment of shame or neglect; but by that time the man has carved his name somewhere on the Temple of Fame…

This day a century ago, in poverty, delirium, and distress, there was passing the soul of Robert Burns. To him death comes in clouds and darkness, the end of a long agony of body and soul; he is harassed with debt, his bodily constitution is ruined, his spirit is broken, his wife is daily expecting her confinement. He has lost almost all that rendered his life happy, much of friendship, credit and esteem. Some score years before one of the most charming of English writers, as he lay dying, was asked if his mind was at ease, and with his last breath Oliver Goldsmith owned that it was not. So it was with Robert Burns. His delirium dwelt on the horrors of a jail; he uttered curses on the tradesman who was pursuing him for debt. 'What business,' said he to his physician in a moment of consciousness, 'what business has a physician to waste his time upon me; I am a poor pigeon not worth plucking. Alas! I have not feathers enough to carry me to my grave'. For a year or more his health had been failing. He had a poet's body as well as a poet's mind; nervous, feverish, impressionable; and his constitution, which, if nursed and regulated, might have carried him to the limit of life, was unequal to the storm and stress of dissipation and a preying mind…

In his last April he wrote to his friend Thomson, 'By Babel's streams I've sate and wept almost ever since I saw you last. I have only known existence by the pressure of the heavy hand of sickness, and have counted time by the repercussions of pain. Rheumatism, cold, and fever have formed to me a terrible combination. I close my eyes in misery, and open them without hope.' It was sought to revive him by sea bathing, and he went to stay at Brow. There he remained three weeks, but was under no delusion as to his state. 'Well, madam,' he said to Mrs Riddell on arriving, 'have you any commands for the other world?' He sat that evening with his old friend, and spoke manfully of his approaching death, of the fate of his children, and his farm, sometimes indulging in bitter-sweet pleasantry, but never losing the consciousness of his condition. In three weeks he wearied of the fruitless hunt for health, and he returned home to die. He was only just in time. When he re-entered his home on the 18th he could no longer stand. He was soon delirious... 'On the fourth day,' we are told, 'when his attendant held a cordial to his lips, he swallowed it eagerly, rose almost wholly up, spread out his hands, sprang forward nigh the whole length of the bed, fell on his face, and expired.'

I suppose there are many who can read the account of these last months with composure. They are more fortunate than I am. There is nothing much more melancholy in all biography. The brilliant Poet, the delight of all society, from the highest to the lowest, sits brooding in silence over the drama of his spent life – the early innocent home, the plough and the savour of fresh turned earth, the silent communion with nature and his own heart, the brief hour of splendour, the dark hour of neglect, the mad struggle for forgetfulness, the bitterness of vanished homage, the gnawing doubt of fame, the distressful future of his wife and children – an endless witch-dance of thought without clue or remedy, all perplexing, all soon to end while he is yet young, as men reckon youth, though none know so well as he that his youth is gone, his race is run, his message is delivered. His death revived the flagging interest and pride that had been felt for him. As usual, men began to realise what they had lost when it was too late. When it was known that he was dying the townspeople had shown anxiety and distress. They recalled his splendour, and forgot his fall. One man was heard to ask, with a touch of quaint simplicity, 'Who do you think will be our poet now?' The district set itself to prepare a public funeral for the Poet who died almost penniless among them.

A vast concourse followed him to his grave. The awkward squad, as he had foreseen and deprecated, fired volleys over his coffin. The streets were lined with soldiers, among them one who, within sixteen years, was to be Prime Minister.

And while the procession wended its gloomy way, as if no element of tragedy were to be wanting, his widow's hour of travail arrived, and she gave birth to the hapless child that had caused the father so much misgiving. In this place, and on this day, it all seems present to us – the house of anguish, the thronged churchyard, the weeping neighbours. WE feel ourselves part of the mourning crowd. We hear those dropping volleys and that muffled drum; we bow our heads as the coffin passes, and acknowledge with tears the inevitable doom. Pass, heavy hearse, with thy weary freight of shattered hopes and exhausted frame; pass, with thy simple pomp of fatherless bairns and sad moralising friends; pass, with the sting of death to the victory of the grave; pass, with the perishable, and leave us the eternal. It is rare to be fortunate in life; it is infinitely rarer to be fortunate in death. 'Happy in the occasion of his death,' as Tacitus said of Agricola, is not a common epitaph. It is comparatively easy to know how to live, but it is beyond all option and choice to compass the more difficult art of knowing when and how to die. We can generally, by looking back, choose a moment in a man's life when he had been fortunate had he dropped down dead. And so the question arises naturally today, was Burns fortunate in his death – that death which we commemorate? There can, I fancy, be only one answer; it was well that he died when he did; it might even have been better for himself had he died a little earlier. The terrible letters that he wrote two years before to Mrs Riddell and Mr Cunningham betoken a spirit mortally wounded. In those last two years the cloud settles, never to be lifted. 'My constitution and frame were aborigine blasted with a deep incurable taint of hypochondria which poisons my existence.' He found, perhaps, some pleasure in the composition of his songs, some occasional relief in the society of boon companions; but the world was fading before him.

There is an awful expression in Scotland which one never hears without a pain 'So and so is done,' meaning that he is physically worn out. Burns was 'done'. He was struggling on like a wounded deer to his death. He had often faced the end, and not unwillingly. 'Can it be possible,' he once wrote to Mrs

Dunlop, 'That when I resign this frail, feverish being I shall still find myself in conscious existence? When the last gasp of agony has announced that I am no more to those who know me and the few who loved me; when the cold, unconscious course is resigned to the earth to be the prey of reptiles, and become a trodden clod, shall I be yet warm in life, enjoying or enjoyed?' Surely that reads as if he foresaw this day, and would fain be with us, as indeed, he may be. Twelve years before he had faced death in a less morbid spirit:

Why am I loth to leave this earthly scene?
Have I so found it full of pleasing charms?
Some days of joy, with draughts of ill between,
Some gleams of sunshine, mid renewing storms.

He had perhaps never enjoyed life so much as is supposed, though he had turned it a brave, cheerful, unflinching face, and the last years had been years of misery. 'God have mercy on me,' he wrote years before the end, 'a poor, damned, incautious, duped, unfortunate fool! The sport, the miserable victim of rebellious pride, hypochondriac imagination, agonising sensibility, and bedlam passions.' There was truth in this outburst. At any rate his most devoted friends – and to be admirer of Burns is to be his friend – may wish that he had not lived to write the letter to Mr Clark, piteously pleading that a harmless toast may not be visited hardly upon him; or that to Mrs Riddell, beginning 'I write you from the regions of hell and the horrors of the damned,' or to be harried by his official superiors as a political suspect, shunned by his fashionable friends for the same reason, wandering like a neglected ghost, in Dumfries, avoided and ignored. 'That's all over now, my young friend,' he said, speaking of his reign in society, 'and were'na my heart licht I wad dee.'

All this was in 1794. Had he died before then, it might have been happier for himself, and we should have lost some parts of his life which we would rather forget; but posterity could not have spared him; we could not have lost the exquisite songs which we owe to those years; but, above all, the supreme creed and comfort which he bequeathed to the world – 'A man's a man for a'that,' would have remained undelivered. One may, perhaps, go further and say that poets or those whom the gods love should die young. This is a hard saying, but it will not greatly affect the bills of mortality. And it applies only to poets of the first rank, while even here it has its exceptions, and illustrious exceptions they are. But surely the best poetry is produced before middle age, before the morning and its illusions have faded before the heaviness of noon and the baleful chill of evening. Few men too, can bear the strain of a poet's temperament through many years. At any rate, we may feel sure of this that Burns had produced his best, that he would never again have produced a *Tam o Shanter*, or a *Cotter's Saturday Night*, or a *Jolly Beggars*; and that long before his death, though he could still write lines affluent with tenderness and grace, 'the hand of pain and sorrow and care,' to use his own words, 'had lain heavy upon' him.

And this leads to another point. Today is not merely the melancholy anniversary of death, but the rich and incomparable fulfilment of prophecy. For this is the moment to which Burns looked when he said to his wife 'Don't be afraid; I'll be more respected a hundred years after I am dead than I am present!' Today the hundred years are completed, and we can judge the prediction. On that point we must be all unanimous. Burns had honour in his lifetime, but his fame has rolled like a snowball since his death, and it rolls on. There is, indeed, no parallel to it in the world; it sets the calculations of compound interest at defiance. He is not merely the watchword of a nation that carries and implants Burns worship all over the globe as birds carry seeds, but he has become the champion and patron saint of Democrats. He bears the banner of the essential equality of man. His birthday is celebrated – 137 years after its occurrence – more universally than that of any human being. He reigns over a greater dominion than any empire that the world has ever seen. Nor does the ardour of his devotees decrease. Ayr and Ellisland, Mauchline and Dumfries, are the shrines of countless pilgrims. Burns statues are hardy annuals. The production of Burns manuscripts was a lucrative branch of industry, until it was checked by untimely intervention. The editions of Burns are as the sands of the sea. No canonised name in the calendar excites so blind and enthusiastic a worship.

Whatever Burns may have contemplated in his prediction, whatever dream he may have fondled in the wildest moments of elation must have fallen utterly short of the reality. And it is all spontaneous. There is no puff, no advertisement, no manipulation. Intellectual cosmetics of that kind are frail a fugitive; they rarely survive their subject; they would not have availed here. Nor was there any glamour attached to the Poet; rather the reverse. He has stood by himself; he has grown by himself. It is himself, and no other, that we honour. But what had Burns in his mind when he made this prediction? It might be whimsically urged that he was conscious that the world had not yet seen his masterpiece, for the *Jolly Beggars* was not published till some time after his death. But that would not be sufficient, for he had probably forgotten its existence. Nor do I think he spoke at hazard.

What were, perhaps, present to his mind were the fickleness of his contemporaries towards him, his conviction of the essential splendour of his work, consciousness that the incidents of his later years had unjustly obscured him, and that his true figure would be perceived as these fell away into forgetfulness or were measured at their true value. If so, he was right in his judgement, for his true life began with his death: with the body passed all that was gross or impure – the clear spirit stood revealed, and soared at once to its accepted place amongst the fixed stars in the firmament of the rare immortals.

(*Loud and prolonged cheering*)

At the close of the meeting, Lord Rosebery was hurried to the railway station where a another kind of carriage awaited to take him to Glasgow where another audience awaited him in the St Andrew's Hall. The indefatigable Earl seemed to pick up where he had left off – without repeating a single word or phrase or quote. A truly astonishing feat of oratory by any standard but, it seemed, all in a day's work for him.

I cannot, perhaps, deny that the day has been a day of labour, but it has been a labour of love. It is, and it must be, a source of joy and pride to us to see our champion Scotsman receive the honour and admiration and affection of humanity; to see, as I have seen this morning, the long processions bringing homage and tribute to the conquering dead. But these have only been signs and symptoms of the worldwide passion of reverence and devotion. That generous and immortal soul pervades the universe today. In the humming city and in the crowd of man; in the backwood and in the swamp; where the sentinel paces the bleak frontier, and where the sailor smokes his evening pipe; and, above all, where the farmer and his men pursue their summer toil, whether under the Stars and Stripes or under the Union Jack the thought and sympathy of men are directed to Robert Burns.

I have sometimes asked myself, if a roll call of fame were read over at the beginning of every century, how many men of eminence would answer a second time to their names. But of our Poet there is no doubt or question. The 'adsum' of Burns rings out clear and unchallenged. There are few before him on the list, and we cannot now conceive a list without him. He towers high, and yet he lived in an age when the average was sublime. It sometimes seems to me as if the whole eighteenth century was a constant preparation for, a constant working up to, the great drama of the revolution which closed it. The scenery is all complete when the time arrives – the dark volcanic country; the hungry, desperate people; the firefly nobles; the concentrated splendour of the Court; in the midst, in her place as heroine, the dazzling Queen. And during long previous years brooding nature has been producing not merely the immediate actors, but figures worthy of the scene.

What a glittering procession it is! We can only mark some of the principal figures. Burke leads the way by seniority; then come Fox and Goethe, Nelson and Mozart, Schiller, Pitt, and Burns, Wellington and Napoleon. And among these Titans, Burns is a conspicuous figure; the figure which appeals most of all to the imagination and affection of mankind. Napoleon, perhaps, looms larger to the imagination, but on the affection he has no hold. It is in the combination of the two powers that Burns is supreme. What is his secret?...The secret, as it seems to me, lies in two words – inspiration and sympathy. But, if I wished to prove my contention, I should go on quoting from his poems all night, and his admirers would still declare that I had omitted the best passages. I know that profuse quotation is a familiar form of a Burns speech, but I am afraid to begin lest I should not end, and I am sure I should not satisfy. I must proceed, then, in a more summary way.

Now, ladies and gentlemen, there seem to me to be two great natural forces in British literature. I use the safe adjective of British. Your applause shows me that I was right to do so. I use it partly because hardly any of Burns's poetry is strictly English, because he hated, and was, perhaps, the first to protest against the use of the word English as including Scottish- well, I say, there are in that literature two great forces of which the power seems sheer inspiration and nothing else – I mean Shakespeare and Burns. This is not the place or the time to speak of that miracle called Shakespeare, but one must say a word of the miracle called Burns. Try and reconstruct Burns as he was. A peasant, born in a cottage that no sanitary inspector in these days would tolerate for a moment – struggling, with desperate effort, against pauperism, almost in vain, snatching at scraps of learning in the intervals of it, as it were with his teeth – a heavy, silent lad, proud of his ploughing. All of a sudden, without preface or warning, he breaks out into exquisite song, like a nightingale form the brushwood, and continues singing as sweetly – with nightingale pauses – till he dies. A nightingale sings because he cannot help it – he can only sing exquisitely, because he knows no other. So it was with Burns. What is this but inspiration? One can no more measure or reason about it than measure or reason about Niagara. And remember, ladies and gentlemen, the poetry is only a fragment of Burns. Amazing as it may seem, all contemporary testimony is unanimous that the man was far more wonderful than his works...

'No man's conversation ever carried me so completely off my feet,' said the Duches of Gordon – the friend of Pitt and of the London wits, the queen of Scottish society. Dugald Stewart says that 'all the faculties of Burns's mind were, so far as I could judge, equally vigorous, and his predilection for poetry was rather the result of his own enthusiastic and impassioned temper, than of a genius exclusively adapted to that species of composition. From his conversation I should have pronounced him to be fitted to excel in whatever walk of ambition he had chosen to exert his abilities.' And of his prose compositions the same severe judge speaks thus – 'Their great and varied excellences render some of them scarcely less objects of wonder than his poetical performance.'

The late Dr Robertson used to say that, 'considering his education, the former seemed to him the more remarkable of the two.' 'I think Burns,' said Principal Robertson to a friend, 'was one of the most extraordinary men I ever met with. His poetry surprised me very much, his prose surprised me still more, and his conversation surprised me more than both his poetry and prose.' We are told, too, that 'he felt a strong call towards oratory, and all who heard him speak – and some of them were excellent judges – admitted his wonderful quickness of apprehension and readiness of eloquence.' All this seems to me marvellous. It surely ratifies the claim of inspiration without the necessary of quoting a line of his poetry. I pass then to his sympathy.

If his talents were universal, his sympathy was not less so. His tenderness was not a mere selfish tenderness for his own family, for he loved all mankind except the cruel and the base. Nay, we may go further, and say that he placed all creation, especially the suffering and despised part of it, under his protection. The oppressor in every shape, even in the comparatively innocent embodiment of the factor and sportsman, he regarded with direct and personal hostility. But, above all, he saw the charm of the home; he recognised it as the basis of all society, he honoured it in its humblest form, for he knew, as few know, how unpretentiously, but how sincerely, the family in the cottage is welded by mutual love and esteem. 'I recollect once,' said Dugald Stewart, speaking of Burns, 'he told me, when I was admiring a distant prospect in one of our morning walks, that the sight of so many smoking cottages gave a pleasure of his mind which none could understand, who had not witnessed, like himself, the happiness and worth which they contained.' He dwells repeatedly on the primary sacredness of the home and the family, the responsibility of fatherhood and marriage. 'Have I not, ' he once wrote to Lord Mar, 'a more precious stake in my country's welfare than the richest dukedom in it? I have a large family of children, and the prospect of many more.' The lines in which he tells his faith are not less memorable than the stately stanzas in which Gray sings the 'short and simple annals of the poor.' I must quote them again, often quoted as they are

To mak' a happy fireside clime
To weans and wife,
That's the true pathos and sublime
Of human life.

His verses, then, go straight to the heart of every home; they appeal to every father and mother. But that is only the beginning, perhaps the foundation of his sympathy. There is something for everybody in Burns. He has a heart even for vermin; he has pity even for the arch enemy of mankind. And his universality makes his poems a treasure house in which all may find what they want. Every wayfarer in the journey of life may pluck strength and courage from it as he passes. The sore, the weary, the wounded, will all find something to heal and soothe. For this great master is the universal Samaritan. Where the priest and the Levite may have passed by in vain, this eternal heart will still afford a resource. But his is not only for the sick in spirit. The friend, the lover, the patriot, will all find their choicest refreshment in Burns. His touch is everywhere, and it is everywhere the touch of genius. Nothing comes amiss to him. What was said of the debating power of his eminent contemporary, Dundas, may be said of his poetry 'He went out in all weathers.' And it may be added that all weathers suited him; that he always brought back something precious, something we cherish, something that cannot die. He is, then, I think, the universal friend in an unique sense.

But he was, poetically speaking, the special friend of Scotland, in a sense which recalls a profound remark of another eminent Scotsman, I mean Fletcher of Saltoun. In an account of a conversation between Lord Cromarty, Sir Edward Seymour, and Sir Christopher Musgrave, Fletcher writes, 'I said I knew a very wise man, so much of Sir Christopher's sentiment, that he believed if a man were permitted to make all the ballads he need not care who should make the laws of a nation.' This may be rudely paraphrased, that it is more important to make the songs of a nation than to frame its laws, and this again may be interpreted that in former days, at any rate in the days of Fletcher, even to the days of Burns, it is the familiar songs of a people that mould their thoughts, their manners, and their morals. If this be true, can we exaggerate the debt that we Scotsmen owe to Burns? He has bequeathed to his country the most exquisite casket of songs in the world primarily to his country, but others cannot be denied their share. I will give only one example, but that is a signal one. From distant Roumania the Queen of that country wrote to Dumfries that she has no copy of Burns with her, but that she knows his songs by heart. We must remember that there is more than this to be said. Many of Burns's songs were already in existence in the lips and minds of people – rough and coarse and obscene. Our benefactor takes them, and with a touch of inspired alchemy transmutes them and leaves them pure gold. He loved the old catches and the old tunes, and into these gracious moulds he poured his exquisite gifts of thought and expression. But for him those ancient airs, often wedded to words which no decent man could recite, would have perished from that corruption if not from neglect. He rescued them for us by his songs, and, in doing so, he hallowed the life and sweetened the breath of Scotland.

I have also used the words patriot and lover. These draw me to different lines of thought. The word 'patriot' leads me to the political side of Burns. There is no doubt that he was suspected of being a politician and he is even said to have sometimes wished to enter Parliament. That was perhaps an excusable aberration, and my old friend Professor Mason has, I think, surmised that had he lived he might have been a great Liberal pressman. My frail thought shall not dally with such surmise, but it conducts us naturally to the subject of Burns's politics. From his sympathy for his own class, from his indignation against nobles like the Duke of Queensberry, and from the toast that cost him so dear, it might be considered easy to infer his political opinions. But Burns should not be claimed for any party. A poet, be it remembered, is never a politician, and a politician is never a poet that is to say, that a politician is never so fortunate as to be a poet, and a poet is so fortunate as never to be a politician.

I do not say that the line of demarcation is never passed a politician may have risen for a moment, or a poet may have descended – but, where there is any confusion between the two callings, it is generally because the poet thinks he discerns, or the politician thinks he needs, something higher than politics. Burns's politics were entirely governed by the imagination. He was at once a Jacobite and a Jacobin. He had the sad sympathy which most of us have felt for the hapless house of Stuart, without the least wish to be governed by it. He has much the same sort of abstract sympathy with the French Revolution, when it was setting all Europe to rights; but he was prepared to lay down his life to prevent its putting this island to rights. And then came his official superiors of the Excise, who, notwithstanding Mr Pitt's admiration of his poetry, snuffed out his politics without remorse. The name of Pitt leads me to add that Burns had some sort of relation with three Prime Ministers. Colonel Jenkinson, of the Cinque Ports Fencible Cavalry afterwards Minister for fifteen years under the title of Lord Liverpool was on duty at Burns's funeral, though, we are told the good man disapproved of the Poet, and declined to make his acquaintance. Pitt, again, passed on

Burns one of his rare and competent literary judgements, so eulogistic, indeed, that one wonders that a powerful Minister could have allowed one whom he admired so much to exist on an exciseman's pay when well, and an exciseman's half pay when dying. And from Addington, another Prime Minister, Burns elicited a sonnet, which, in the Academy of Lagado, would surely have been held a signal triumph of the art of extracting sunshine from cucumbers. So much for politics in the party sense. 'A man's a man for a' that' is not politics – it is the assertion of the rights of humanity in a sense far wider than politics. It erects all mankind, it is the charter of its self-respect. It binds, it heals, it revives, it invigorates; it sets the bruised and broken on their legs, it refreshes that stricken soul, it is the salve and tonic of character; it cannot be narrowed into politics. Burns's politics are indeed nothing but the occasional overflow of his human sympathy into past history and current events.

And now, having discussed the two trains of thought suggested by the words 'friend' and 'patriot', I come to the more dangerous word 'lover'. There is an eternal controversy which, it appears, no didactic oil will ever assuage, as to Burns's private life and morality. Some maintain that these have nothing to do with his poems; some maintain that his life must be read into his works, and here again some think that his life damns his poems, while others aver that his poems cannot be fully appreciated without his life. Another school thinks that his vices have been exaggerated, while their opponents scarcely think such exaggeration possible. It is impossible to avoid taking a side. I walk on the ashes, knowing the fire beneath, and unable to avoid them, for the topic is inevitable. I must confess myself, then, one of those who think that the life of Burns doubles the interest of his poems, and I doubt whether the failings of his life have been much exaggerated, for contemporary testimony on that point is strong, though a high and excellent authority, Mr Wallace, has recently taken the other side with much power and point.

But the life of Burns, which I love to read with his poems, does not consist in his vices; they lie outside it. It is a life of work, and truth, and tenderness. And though, like all lives, it has its light and shade, remember that we know it all, the worst as well as the best. His was a soul bathed in crystal; he hurried to avow everything. There was no reticence in him.

The only obscure passage in his life is the love passage with Highland Mary, and as to that he was silent, not from shame, but because it was a sealed and sacred episode. 'What a flattering idea,' he once wrote, 'is a world to come! There shall I with speechless agony of rapture again recognise my lost, my ever dear Mary! Whose bosom was fraught with truth, honour, constancy, and love.' He had, as the French say, the defects of his qualities. His imagination was a supreme and celestial gift. But his imagination often led him wrong, and never more than with women. The chivalry that made Don Quixote see the heroic in all the common events of life made Burns (as his brother tells us) see a goddess in every girl that he approached. Hence many love affairs, and some guilty ones; but even these must be judged with reference to time and circumstance. This much it is certain, had he been devoid of genius they would not have attracted attention. It is Burns's pedestal that affords a target. And why, one may ask, is not the same measure meted out to Burns as to others? The illegitimate children of great captains and statesmen and princes are treated as historical and ornamental incidents. They strut the scene of Shakespeare, and ruff it with the best. It is for the illegitimate children of Burns, though he and his wife cherished them as if born in wedlock, that the vials of wrath are reserved. Take two brilliant figures, both descended from Stuarts, who were alive during Burns's life. We occupy ourselves endlessly and severely with the offences of Burns. We heave an elegant sigh over the kindred lapses of Charles James Fox and Charles Edward Stuart. Again, it is quite clear that, though exceptionally sober in his earlier years, he drank too much in later life. But this, it must be remembered, was but an occasional condescendence to the vice and habit of the age. The gentry who pressed him to their houses, and who were all convivial, have much to answer for. His admirers who thronged to see him, and who could only conveniently sit with him in a tavern, are also responsible for this habit, so perilously attractive to men of genius. From the decorous Addison, and the brilliant Bolingbroke onward, the eighteenth century records hard drinking as the common incident of intellectual eminence.

To a man who had shone supreme in the most glowing society, and who was now an excisemen in a country town, with a home that cannot have been very exhilarating, and with a nervous system highly strung, the temptation of the warm tavern, and the admiring circle there, may well have been almost irresistible. Some attempt to say that his intemperance was exaggerated. I neither affirm nor deny. it was not as a sot he drank; that no one insinuated; if he succumbed it was to good fellowship. Remember, I do not seek to palliate or excuse, and, indeed, none will be turned to dissipation by Burns's example; he paid too dearly for it. But I will say this, that it all seems infinitely little, infinitely remote. Why do we strain, at this distance, to discern this dim spot on the Poet's mantle? Shakespeare and Ben Johnson took their cool tankard at the Mermaid; we cannot afford, in the strictest view of literary responsibility, to quarrel with them for that. When we consider Pitt and Goethe we do not concentrate our vision on Pitt's bottles of port or Goethe's bottles of Moselle. Then, why, we ask, is there such a chasm between the Mermaid and the Globe, and why are the vintages of Wimbledon and Weimar so much more innocent than the simple punch bowl of Inveraray marble and its contents?

I should like to go a step further, and affirm that we have something to be grateful for even in the weakness of men like Burns. Mankind is helped in its progress almost as much by the study of imperfections as by the contemplation of perfection. Had we nothing before us in our futile and halting lives but saints and the ideal, we might well fail altogether. We grope blindly along the catacombs of the world, we climb the dark ladder of life, we feel our way to futurity, but we can scarcely see an inch around or before us. We stumble and falter and fall, our hands and knees are bruised sore, and we look up for light and guidance. Could we see nothing but distant unapproachable impeccability, we might well sink prostrate in the hopelessness of emulation and the weariness of despair. Is it not then, when all seems blank and lifeless, when strength and courage flag, when perfection seems as remote as a star, is it not then that imperfection helps us?

When we see that the greatest and choicest images of God have had their weaknesses like ours, their temptations, their hour of darkness, their bloody sweat, are we not encouraged by their lapses and catastrophes to find energy for one more effort, one more struggle? Where they failed we feel it a less dishonour to fail; their errors and sorrows make, as it were, an easier ascent from finite imperfection to infinite perfection.

Man after all is not ripened by virtue alone. Were it so this world were a paradise of angels. No! like the growth of the earth, his is the fruit of all the seasons; the accident of a thousand accidents, a living mystery, moving through the seen to the unseen. He is sown in dishonour; he is matured under all the varieties of heat and cold; in mist and wrath, in snow and vapours, in the melancholy of autumn, in the torpor of winter, as well as in the rapture and fragrance of summer, or the balmy effluence of the spring – its breath, its sunshine, its dew. And at the end he is reaped – the product, not of one climate, but of all; not of good alone, but of evil; not of joy alone, but of sorrow – perhaps mellowed and ripened, perhaps stricken and withered and sour. How, then, shall we judge anyone? How, at any rate, shall we judge a giant – great in gifts and great in temptation; great in strength, and great in weakness? Let us glory in his strength, and be comforted in his weakness. And, when we thank heaven for the inestimable gift of Burns, we do not need to remember wherein he was imperfect; we cannot bring ourselves to regret that he was made of the same clay as ourselves.

...perhaps the honest man who had written a piece of rhyme or verse was remembered in a way that the chief in the government of his country at the time was not remembered. But in Burns there was something more than that. There was not only the admiration which attached to poets and prose writers, but there was a special love and special affection which was given to the very few. And to what kind of few? To those writers – poets and whatever they were – who had addressed not the head, not the intellect, of a nation, not even the imagination, not even the men who had produced delightful dreams and far away phantasies; these were not remembered and loved like the writers who had addressed the human heart...who had addressed the primal forces, the passions of human nature – love, hate, the family relations, and all those things which were not artificial, which did not belong to any one age or any one country, but which were universal and perennial. Those writers who had contrived somehow or other to grasp the human heart were those that were remembered with admiration and with love. Now Burns did that...

Burns, though he was a great poet, was a great poet in the finest place because he was a great man – because this swarthy

Scotsman had a brain co-equal with the best brains in his generation. It was the fortunate accident that this man with such powers took to poetry. But when he beginning a life of poetry it occurred to him tthat he might be at a disadvantage, and this he expressed in the address to himself. In the words of that poem they had the key to that great portal, to that great door through which the whole of British literature of the eighteenth swung us into the nineteenth century. Burns preceded and heralded Wordsworth, who acknowledged his inspiration. He showed Wordsworth the way to that great reform of which so much had been the consequence. In these things there was what they call a 'but' and a 'ben'. Now this influence of Burns on the literature of Great Britain, this influence of Burns on European literature, was shown by the fact that Germans, men of all nations, admired Burns, and had sent on this day expressions of their admiration. Still foreigners, the English people even, only got to the 'ben' of Burns. So when he said that Burns lasted, that he was remembered still, because he addressed not the head so much, or the imagination so much, as the human heart; he had to add this more specifically, that the heart he addressed was the Scottish heart.

Now, the Scottish heart had its peculiarities, and some of these peculiarities were hereditary and came from far back. The oldest of the sentiments that composed the Scottish heart was 600 years old –that was the love of this little land of the mountain and the flood – it was 600 years old at all events this love of liberty and freedom; almost the oldest thing in Scottish literature was Barbour's poem on liberty. But the Scottish heart was a variable thing. It had taken a great deal of various history and experience to make the Scottish heart what it had come to be. The Scottish heart, it might be said, divided itself into two views, two opposite views, the Mary Stuart and the Covenanting and Presbyterian views. He said that that very diversity had made the Scottish heart stronger today than it was even in the days of Burns. Burns grasped aright the Scottish heart because he had it in himself. He enlarged the Scottish heart. From his own looking round on Scottish society and Scottish manners he infused into the Scottish heart an addition of tenderness, of humour, of outspokenness, and especially a feeling of individual manhood and independence. Wherever the Scottish heart

> functioned at the present moment the Scottish heart functioned as the heart of Robert Burns.

The Reverend Donald McLeod rose to propose a vote of thanks and had the good sense, as his Lordship had a night train to catch, to be brief, but he made his points. For literary skill and beauty, the address was one of the finest he had ever listened to. Nay, more, he believed that if Lord Rosebery would only try it, he could give them two or three good Scottish songs. As Professor Masson had said, Burns had not spoken to them from the 'but' and not from the 'ben'. No man could understand Burns who was not a Scotsman. They could not get at the pith of the words, except that they had been brought up to speak the Scottish tongue. No foreigner could do it. It might be good work for the Burns Clubs to do something, in order to preserve what, he was afraid, was passing away, not from the peasantry, but from what were called the better classes – the knowledge of the Scottish language. Scots was not a dialect; it was a language, and they could not allow that language to die. Dr McLeod concluded by hoping that Lord Rosebery would be 'won away from the poor paltry way of politics in to those higher regions of literature, in which he had been born to shine.' The audience heartily responded to this – and so did Lord Rosebery – in his best English voice.

> Now my friends, Dr McLeod, has given me sound advice. He has advised me to give up politics for literature. Now, I want to ask him if he gives me that advice in the character of a politician or in the character of an editor?

His Lordship left the hall to loud cheering. Perhaps that night, as he lay awake listening to the click of the wheels on the line as he went south through the darkness, he would hear again the waves of Scottish applause that had greeted his extraordinary double peroration. And no doubt his 'train of thought' would remind him that he was Scottish too. In this respect, it is interesting to note that when Rosebery himself died in 1929 at his country house near Epsom it was not to the sound of a Burns air but to the strains of the *Eton Boating Song*.

Unlike Lord Rosebery, Sheriff Campbell Smith did not have train to catch when he addressed the Burns Club in the Kinnaird Hall on that same night – 21 July, and he gave his enthusiastic listeners the full benefit of his forensic fondness for the spoken word. The following is an edited version of his tightly-worded, tightly-printed but tightly-thought-out address:

> I follow Coleridge in thinking that the individual memory is the imperishable record – the book of the recording angel out of which each man and woman will be judged for the deeds done in the body. The perfect record, the actual balance sheet of Burns's life, as a life, has been closed and is unknowable, whatever profane, sulphurous bigots may think and say about it; and I daresay Burns will be far from sorry should he find himself excluded from their special department of Paradise. But during the time since his death, the human, imperfect record has been searched into by many curious inquirers some friendly, some hostile and the details of it are better known I believe, than that of any man's life that has ever lived. The printed books in which they are recorded are enough to a fill a considerable library, and the speeches that in private and on platforms have been devoted to them, if recorded and printed, would fill ten times as many books. These details, so far as for edification, and it may be a good deal further, are known to all who are likely to occupy places in an audience like this. I therefore take the general knowledge of them for granted, that being the only course at present competent for me, and recommend to all men, especially young men, who do not have that general knowledge, to get it as soon as they can...
>
> Let the aspiring, hopeful, determined young man who desires to acquire knowledge, take note that Robert Burns, by facilities for education far inferior to those that are forced upon all by the modern machinery of compulsory education, became the skilful literary artist, and one of the most widely, most accurately informed men of his day upon all vital subjects; and let those who are impulsive in temperament, and liable to be beset by temptation, take double and treble note of the way in which uncontrolled impulse, fiery unbridled passion, lays waste the highest powers, whirls the attention into the clouds or into the mire, paralyses for the time all intellectual efforts, wrecks the bodily health into premature ruin, and leaves the conscience no function, except to punish by remorse the vice and folly which it has been powerless to prevent.
>
> To the best of my judgement, not a single dishonourable or dishonest deed has been proved against him. I think he was a

true man through and through, and that the strong irrepressible instinct of veracity in him that made him the poet he was – one of the truest of the true – kept him far from everything that savoured of deceit in all the relations of life, even those that were passionate as well as the dull and prosaic. Unlike many poets, perhaps most, he honestly paid his debts. I don't believe that he was a heartless seducer – indeed, I doubt if he was ever a seducer at all. No doubt he did not use Jean Armour well, but it is my belief that not one man in ten thousand would have forgiven what she – easy tempered, soft, squeezable mortal – at the instigation of her gruff, severe, elder father, did to him. He was his own worst enemy, and the conscious enemy of no other human being. No man knew his faults so well as himself, and no man was ever more free from all manner of wilful falsehood...

Burns was the greatest gift of Providence to our country in his own generation. In point of gigantic force of intellect I think he was the greatest Scotsman of all time. And how did his contemporaries receive and appreciate this unprecedented, this priceless gift? That is one of the most searching questions that can have been put to Scotland and its thoughtful sons and daughters for the last hundred years, and it starts up tonight with importunate pertinacity, looming its biggest through the misty memories, the multitudinous opinions, fluctuating between the carping superfine gentility of Jeffrey and the inspired reverence of nature worshipping, sympathetic Wordsworth, struggling and advancing to victory over prejudice, stupidity, and religious bigotry in the wide battlefield of the Anglo-Saxon world, under the sunlight, starlight, lamplight, midnights of a busy, restless, hundred years. I think I can say with a good conscience that the peasant brotherhood of Scotland, upon the whole, behaved loyally, tenderly, and justly to their gifted, impulsive peasant brother; that they rejoiced with their whole nature in his poetry as they had never before rejoiced in poetry – not even the inspired Psalms of David; that they sang his songs tunefully, or the reverse – with thorough appreciation of their strong sense and fiery sentiment; and that they gathered while they could – the cleverest of them – to hear him talk wherever and whenever they had an opportunity, as they never before or since crowded to hear any mere secular conversationalist, nor any one except a very few popular preachers.

The representative intelligence of the peasantry of Scotland, repressing all manner of jealousy, and doing their utmost to gag the howling of cant and bigotry, have stood faithfully by Burns, from the time they discovered his abilities – and they discovered them early – till now. The moderate or rationalistic clergy of Scotland stood by him in his lifetime, and they have done so since. Carlyle laments that he became their 'fighting man,' but what else could he have done had he not steered clear of religion altogether, a quite impossible thing for any true poet who is bound to deal with the great social forces, and especially with religion, which is the greatest of them all? The religion that cannot bear to be scrutinised by the highest talent of the age, that is, or ought to be, ruled by it, that cannot bear the purification of the acutest reason and the keenest satire, is too superfine for the realities of erring fallible human nature – is fit only to throw a putrid, phosphorescent glory over the mummeries, the hypocrisies, the phylacteries of those that do their worship by machinery, and that have no rooted convictions because they have never been perfected by suffering or proved by the tempests of doubt. To the best of my understanding and conviction, the educated, rational classes of Scotland, high and low, rich and poor, from the first appreciated and honoured Burns as no poet has ever been appreciated by the masses – I ought rather to say by the solid mass – of his countrymen. He was intelligible alike to peers, professors, and peasants; indeed, the peasantry had had, for understanding him, a better training than the peerage, because they had from childhood been learning his language and seeing the sights that were familiar to him.

Some of the tribe of professors who were also unfortunately pedants did attempt to criticise and patronise him. Their lucubrations, for the most part, have tended to show that a man may be installed in a University Chair and yet may be an ass. But Dugald Stewart, Dr Blacklock, Dr Gregory, even Dr Blair, whose sermons have afflicted so many young persons on Sunday evenings, and above all the rest, Professor Wilson showed that College learning does not destroy the power of appreciating natural genius when the critic is a man of strong intellect and clear insight, and not a mere parsing, philosophising, syllogising machine. However, I admit that the tendency of College criticism has been somewhat to forget that the thunderbolt of original thought which is to travel through abysses of time does not require to be geometrically accurate in its form, and perfectly polished all over the academic sandpaper. Its function is to fly far, to illuminate primeval darkness, to burn up the effete of bygone eras, to melt or crush out from rubbish the ore of truth that can pass as gold into the intellectual currency of coming generations.

My conviction, based upon more facts than I can enumerate, is that Burns never suffered from contact with any man of real intellect. He had something to teach the best, the cleverest of his contemporaries, and they had all something to teach him. His most dangerous and useless friends were his drinking friends pure and simple, for what valuable idea can emerge from the convolutions of a brain that is reeking with whisky? The writers of Ayr could drink, but they could also think; so could most of the clergy of that age and I am inclined to believe that their plentifully strong toddy was more dangerous than their stinted, watery theology especially to a man like Burns, who did not require a teacher in any field of temptation.

The ruling politicians of Burns's time, especially Pitt, 'the Premier youth,' have been greatly blamed for their neglect of Burns. Pitt was a bit of a poet himself – at least, he had tried his hand at translating Homer, and succeeded better than most University young men. When appealed to on behalf of Burns, he said 'literature will take care of itself'. I am not sure that many of his successors, unless, perhaps, Mr Disraeli, would have done more for Burns. Political magnates appear to be afraid of poets, and still more of satirists. Dean Swift and Sydney Smith ought to have been Bishops for certain, if unrivalled intellect could be discovered and appreciated by Prime Ministers. But the high political mind seems to be incapable of putting faith in any mental powers beyond high class, decorous, industrious commonplace, and to be bound by its limited practical nature to distrust genius as a force that is abnormal, beyond calculation and control, and therefore dangerous. I wish that Pitt could have found some more congenial and appropriate occupation for Burns than 'gauging auld wives' barrels', and in the meantime I believe that he would have done it if he could, for Pitt, like his father, was a noble, unselfish kind of man. But, of course, like all Prime Ministers, he was fettered by the traditions of the holders of his office, none of which are likely to take into account either the uses of the claims of genius. Pitt's latest, brightest, and liveliest biographer is to preside over a cognate monster meeting in Glasgow tonight and we will all feel inclined to believe all that he says in favour both of Burns and of Pitt, and anxious to learn what he, with his greater versatility and wider knowledge, would have done for Burns had he been in Pitt's place. How to utilise the gift of the highest genius must always be a difficult problem to the possessor of it, and not less to the people for whose guidance and advancement it has been given; and woe be to the dunces and the infidels who scorn and despise it, whether they be in high places or in low; woe be to the kings of the earth and their advisers who help to send poets, before the full maturity of manhood, the dreary ways traversed by Chatterton and Burns; woe, more terrible still, to the country that breeds 'mute inglorious Miltons' and Cromwells that cannot reach even through seas of blood the sceptre which they alone are fittest to wield. Notwithstanding of little help from high places, and of some obstruction from foolish men, as also, though not without a compensating inspiration, from unwise women, Burns has been one of the greatest benefactors of the human race, and more especially of the Scottish race; and we have reasons innumerable and inexpressible to be thankful to Providence that his message of freedom, of emancipation from the bonds of Royal and aristocratic tyranny, of Pharisaic pretence, and of priestly, though Presbyterian superstition, was thought out and delivered in our hilly, heathery, barren, toil-devoted country, which no mere superficial tickling can cause to laugh with harvests; and we have further reason to be proud that the Scottish race, probably alone of all the mixed races on the earth, or that have ever been on it, was fit to listen to his message, to understand it, and, in fair measure, to welcome and applaud its utterance; for, be assured, no orator can stand far above the level of his audience, no prophet be much in advance of his age, no poet can charm and inspire with his own heaven born revelation of the beautiful and the true, any multitude or race that has not been prepared by its history, its experience, and its destiny, to understand and joyfully accept that heaven born revelation.

Egypt, Judea, Greece, Rome, Germany, England, have each contributed to the miraculous, or all but miraculous advances of civilisation. Scotland, too, though a small country, has not

> failed in her share of the predestined work of human progress, and honour and glory be to the names of John Knox and David Hume, for they both fought for truth and freedom, though with very dissimilar weapons. Like honour to the names of Robert Bruce and of Robert Burns, for the one dealt a mortal blow to foreign, and the other to domestic tyranny; also, honour and gratitude to their successors in the host of the true and the brave that have continued the fight, and have helped us forward towards that liberty of thought, and word, and deed, which is the long delayed but inalienable birthright of the human race.

Following such an oration the Dundee Burns Club were wise in following the Sheriff with a special entertainment, especially prepared for the occasion, described as a musical lecture in song entitled *Robert Burns*. This was devised and performed by Madame Annie Grey but the report of the evening makes no further comment. Enough said. On the motion of Mr Alexander Macdonald, however, a hearty vote of thanks was passed to all who had assisted in the evening's proceedings. and the meeting terminated with the singing of *Auld Lang Syne*.

A bombardment such as that provided by those two Burns big guns, Rosebery and Smith, could not have been sustained throughout Scotland, nor Britain for that matter, but on that commemorative January evening (a Sunday on this occasion) they came out and let off their lesser cannon as best they could. All that summer a Burns Exhibition was held in the galleries of the Royal Glasgow Institute, the same event for which Stevenson was supposed to write the catalogue introduction and more than 3,000 Burns-related objects were shown to an astounded public. The success of the event was due mainly to Mr. W. Craibe Angus with the help of the inevitable Earl of Rosebery. Lord and Lady Kelvin had a Burns reception at Dunoon Castle for those involved in the ceremony of unveiling the statue of Highland Mary. This had been organised by a frail and ailing Colin Rae-Brown, who was witnessing his last Burns event and was to die not long afterwards.

However, even Rae-Brown would have been taken aback by the way in which women have increasingly played their part in Burns proceedings. They had come down from the gallery and balcony and taken their rightful place on the platform beside their men-folk in

Burns. In this commemorative year of 1896, and for the very first time, a woman spoke publicly on the poet. Well, it was a leap year. This brave woman was not a Scot, she was a Yorkshire lass, and she addressed a *conversazione* on Burns held at the Victoria Art Galleries, Dundee, a few days after their memorable Burns Banquet. It would only be fitting to leave such a charming and articulate woman with the last word on the year that has been. Mrs R.A. Watson said:

> I beg you to believe that I am not here of my own conceit. Like the old woman in the story, when asked to give her opinion of the minister, I would not have had the presumption. You know all about Burns, and there is nothing more absurd than telling Scots people what they know already. But you have paid me a great compliment, and what you want from me, I believe, is just a few words of personal testimony. Some may say – will say, no doubt – but what testimony have you to give about Burns, except to condemn his errors and deplore his influence? That was said to Gilfillan years ago, and might be said with more force to a woman. And then, again, the English man of letters, hearing of Burns festivals and Burns enthusiasm and all the rest, puts up his eye glass and says, with a look of great astonishment, 'Why do these good people make such a fuss about Burns? Scott was greater as an artist and more estimable as a man. He was one of the three mighties of the world. Why Burns and not Sir Walter?' Well, the answer to that question is what makes the great man of the people... Among all the poets he is the most real, the most frank, the most free. He is the type of Scotland alike in its good and its ill, and has given his people a treasure of apt quotation suited to their character, expressing the national temper, the beauty of the land, the keen energy of the life that is lived here. Only the Scots folk could have had Burns; only Burns, the critical, homely, tender and scornful, serious and wayward Burns, could be the voice of the country...

Although that same voice had written of Dame Nature,

> Her prentice han she tried on man,
> And then she made the lassies-O.

Even so, as the Victorians marched on to the close of the century, the male predominance resumed and their voices boomed from every top table as the Edwardian Age loomed. None more so than Dr William Wallace, who needed all his distinguished authority as the best 19th-century biographer of Burns with his 1896 re-working of Cromek's four-volume *Life and Works* of 1808, in order to face the famous Ninety Burns Club in Edinburgh on Burns Night, 1897. He was something of a catch for them that year, but they didn't expect the celebrated editor's rather frosty attitude to Burns Clubs in general, if not to the Ninety in particular. However, Dr Wallace had the highest regard for Lord Rosebery. The shorthand-writers did him justice in a very full report:

> Mr. Wallace, in proposing the toast of the Immortal Memory, said that six months ago their distinguished neighbour and fellow citizen, Lord Rosebery, put a very memorable Iliad into a nutshell, when, in the course of an address which was not only a masterpiece of Burns criticism, but a masterpiece of British eloquence, he spoke of 'the miracle called Burns.' It was that miracle which made the year 1896 an eventful one in the history of literature, for it evoked, not from Scotland merely, but from the whole Anglo-Saxon world, the second most remarkable demonstration of hero worship that this century, or indeed any century, had witnessed. It was that miracle which, in spite of a centenary year full of overflowing of love and admiration, made Scotsmen all over the world give up that night to the worship of their true patron saint, St Robert, with unabated enthusiasm, with unsated passion.
>
> Burns before his death said to his wife that he would be better appreciated a hundred years after that event that he had been during his life, and expressed the pious but quite ineffectual hope that the awkward squad would not be allowed to fire over his grave. That century had passed away. It had done its best, and its worst. An awkward – a very awkward – squad of biographers, editors, critics, to which, he regretted to say, he belonged, had been firing over Burns's grave ever since he was laid in it, the only satisfactory thing about the performance being that having, in their awkwardness, loaded with ball cartridge, they had been firing into each other, to the edification of the many and the amusement of all. Still, that century of Burns appreciation could not have been altogether useless. At all events, the very fact that it had passed away suggested three questions – What

has the century done for Burns, for the man as well as the poet, so very thoroughly that no further work of the same kind requires to be done in the years that are to come? What remains to be accomplished in the century that has commenced? Above all, what is the fundamental reason why, looking into that century as far as we can, we should continue the work of 'realising' the miracle called Burns? In the first place, then, what were the most remarkable of the Burns achievements of the century? The most noticeable of these was the existence of that unique propaganda for keeping Burns's memory green in the heart of the world, and for giving circulation to his ideas, known as the Burns Clubs.

The Burns Clubs comprised the big battalions of the sense and worth of Scotland and of Scottish communities all over the world. But members of Burns Clubs were often subjected to attacks from another quarter, and one entitled to respect. Critics and other men of letters almost every year censured such celebrations as that of that night, because 'the orators of the 25th' did not understand Burns. To a certain extent he agreed with the critics. No man thoroughly understood Burns – except Burns. Yet even in the matter of imperfect or approximate understanding he questioned whether men of letters were entitled to be assigned a position of superiority to that occupied by those men of business, those men of action, whether on a large or on a small scale, whether belonging to the classes or the masses, who did the bulk of the hard work of the world; who, because they loved Burns, formed themselves into Clubs, and who, forsooth, were guilty of the incredible presumption of luxuriantly indulging their well-placed love one night in the year of revelling in Burns's unrivalled lyrics and his equally unrivalled good sense, in doing their humble best to cross in imagination form the seen to the unseen, and to give the cordial shake of brotherhood to that vanished hand! He had the highest respect for men of letters – when they stuck to their last and their letters. But he held with Burns himself:

Our friends the reviewers,
Those chippers and hewers,
Are judges of mortar and stone, sir;
But of meet or unmet,
In a fabrick complete,
I'll boldly pronounce they are none, sir.

But the century that had passed since Burns's death was to be credited with other achievements than that of establishing Burns Clubs. It had firmly established Burns in his true position both in the world of literature and in the heart of Scotland. Carlyle by his famous essay did a great deal for the reputation of Burns. But he pronounced the opinion that the national poet was, as he put it, 'a little Valclusa fountain' compared with such 'mighty rivers of song' as Shakespeare and Milton. Post-Carlylian criticism had gone a step further. It had not only recognised Burns as the Eclipse of British lyrists, the rest, including Herrick himself, being practically nowhere, but, as represented by Taine in France and Arnold in England, it had place the author of *The Jolly Beggars* on the same shelf with Shakespeare, Aristophanes, and Goethe. As for Scotland, was it at all necessary for him to say here that she had long ago accepted Burns as her foremost lyrist, satirist, and everyday moralist, as incomparably the greatest exponent of her full-bloodedness, of her moods of ecstasy, despair, all embracing brotherhood, and that love which cast out the fear of death and the fear of man? So far as Scotland was concerned, indeed, the danger was not that they might admire and love Burns too much, but that they, or at least their successors, might get confused about the historical position of his achievement, or even the facts of his life.

And now, what of the special work that lay to be done in this second century of Burns' appreciation? For the last few years he had been thinking not a little about Burns. He started his thoughts and his inquiries with two impressions, and at the end of his journey these impressions were stronger than they were at the beginning. The one was that it was absolutely impossible to understand Burns or his hold upon Scotland and humanity, unless his character and genius were considered together as parts of one truly stupendous whole. The other was that the more carefully his character was examined the better it appeared.

Much was to be said for the suggestion thrown out by Mr Lang and other Scottish critics, that Burns Clubs should set about the preparation of adequate editions of those authors who preceded and prepared the way for Burns. If, further, they could devote some of their resources of time and money to the examination of Burns traditions, he was certain they would perform a valuable service to Scotland, because experience taught that the examination of Burns traditions meant the exposure of Burns falsehoods. But now he came to the main question – Why should Burns be recommended for the admiration of another country? He died a hundred years ago. Innumerable poets had succeeded him, and had attained a more or less enduring fame. Were none of these deserving to be put in his special place, as the supreme poet for men of action? To this the answer was obvious.

He was not prepared to discuss the question whether, viewed simply as a poet, Burns was the inferior or the superior of his brilliant half-brothers in revolt against conventionality – Byron and Shelley – much less of Wordsworth or Tennyson, who, although their lives were cast in pleasanter places than his, understood him thoroughly and loved him tenderly, yet not more tenderly than the simple great ones gone from the United States within living memory – Longfellow and Whittier and Whitman. All that he had to contend for was that Burns was different from his successors, that he touched more closely the realities of present day life than they had done, and that in virtue of his doing so his name evoked more general enthusiasm.

In his eternal youth, in his eternal hope, in his eternal sympathy which made the weak strong and the poor rich, in that courage which converted misery and despair into stepping stones to fame and power, Burns appealed to Scotland for all time as emphatically her strong man rejoicing to run a race, and to their own generation as the most lovable, the most daring, the most modern, nay, the most Shakespearean of all the poets that influenced present day conduct as well as present day literature. Therefore it was that, taking a liberty for the first and last time with the text of one of his poems, he asked them once again to

Fill their cups with generous juice,
As generous as your mind,
And drink with him the generous toast,
The Bard of Humankind!

An interesting afterthought to Lord Rosebery is provided by Dr Jim Connor, that indefatigable Canadian Burnsian, and Past President of the Burns Federation. When he and his wife, Elma, were in Peebles, Scotland, for the 1999 Burns Conference they visited a local antique dealer with a view to any Burns 'stuff' he might have available.

Among the 'stuff' he was shown was a letter from a certain Alex Pollock, Joint Honorary Secretary of the Rosebery Burns Club in Glasgow addressed to a William Haddow, Secretary of the Hamilton Junior Burns Club, regarding a publication of Burns for the blind. Apparently, a book of Burns in Braille had already been published in seven volumes, but the year was 1914 and events had occurred in northern Europe that would lead a whole generation of young men, blinded by gas on the Somme, to find Burns by touch rather than sight because for nearly six years the supposedly civilised world closed its ears to poetry and had no eyes for anything beyond mere survival. The essential verities were regarded as dispensable in a jaundiced age and for a time Burns's ideal of worldly brotherhood remained for many no more than poetical pie in the sky. By 1919, it was a difficult time to be a poet. Even a dead one.

Is there a man, whose judgement clear
Can others teach the course to steer,
Yet runs, himself, Life's mad career,
Wild as the wave?
Here pause – and, through the starting tear,
Survey this grave.
(A Bard's Epitaph)

5

20th Century Burns

> Poor Burns! I have always deplored his hard fate. He has always been a favorite of mine. The child of genius and of misfortune, he is read everywhere and by all classes throughout the extent of our country and his natural pathos has reached all hearts.
>
> (James Buchanan, President of the United States 1857-61)

The events of 1896 had been so momentous in a Burnsian sense, that it was inevitable that a reaction would be felt in the immediate years that followed to close the 19th-century. The Toast, of course, went on but they were pistol shots compared to the loud cannon of the year before. Nevertheless, even if they aimed lower, they hit their mark. Take, for example, Dr Kerr, whose address was given before the Edinburgh Burns Club on 25th January 1897:

> I have had little experience, less skill, and, if possible, still less liking for speech-making, and I very earnestly ask your kind indulgence for my attempt to add one small stone to the ever-increasing cairn of Burns. Though the subject is inexhaustible, I cannot hope to say anything new – anything that has not been said as well or better before.
>
> It is, however, a subject of ever fresh interest, and awakes a responsive echo in every Scottish breast, and I indulge the hope that the enthusiasm, admiration, reverence, and love you all feel for Coila's bard will more than make up for my defective treatment of so lofty a theme as his immortal memory. The salient features in the life and works of unquestionably the greatest of Scottish poets are known to you all. His humour, his pathos, his marvellous tenderness, his patriotism, his sympathy with all that is noblest in human nature, have been lovingly descanted on for a century by men

of every rank and profession, and the cry is 'Still they come.' The secret of a popularity which has no parallel in any age or country is that there is no aspect of life in this workaday world, whether of joy or sorrow, which he has not flooded with the light of his genius; no nobility of action which he has not invested with a dignity which makes it an example to be followed; no meanness or hypocrisy which he has not denounced with scathing indignation; no weakness against which he has not set up a warning beacon; no shades of feeling which make up the complicated network of our emotional nature which he has not touched with a tenderness and truth entirely his own. We can name scores of men of genius whom we admire and reverence, but there are none whom we love so much as Burns, because he is incomparably the most human and sympathetic. In spite of his God-sent genius we still feel that he is one of ourselves. His words reach our hearts because they came warm and straight from his own... Nothing truer or more beautiful has been said of him than that he had 'a true poet soul, for it needs but to be struck and the sound it yields will be music.'... No one can believe that the whole breadth and depth of Burns was fully developed during the few years of his mature life. What might not the man who in these few short years sounded all the depths and shoals of human feeling, and left an undying record behind him – what might he not have done had it been his fate to live out the allotted span?

It is, however, in his songs that Burns shows unique power. While all poetry, whether epic or lyrical, implies highly intellectual power, the element of sentiment, the mainspring of which is the heart rather than the head, plays the most important part in song-writing. Songs are emotional rather than intellectual. Songs are the language of passion – passion in its widest sense, whether it be like the tender and amorous cooing of the turtle dove, the manly fidelity of friendship, the jovial invitation to good cheer, or the trumpet blare that nerves the arm for battle. In this field Burns was peculiarly fitted to shine.

As to his prose, considerations of time and your patience prevent me from saying more than that I thoroughly agree with eminent critics who think it is as remarkable as his poetry for terseness, vigour, and grip, and that we know Burns imperfectly if we judge him only by his poetry. In estimating

> the man as separate from his writings, all his contemporaries declare that in overmastering personality he was far greater than his works. His greatness as a poet was simply a part of that colossal personality.
>
> We must also remember that through his transparent openness of character in making known his own faults and failings, through the unwise zeal of his friends and the hatred of his enemies, everything he said, or wrote, or did, is known to the world. Before that world his great soul stood, and stands, unveiled. Is there a man in this room who would not shrink from such a microscopic examination of all his words and actions? Is there one of us who could pass through such an ordeal unscathed? In the name, then, of all that is – I do not say charitable, but fair, manly, and which obeys the golden rule of doing as we would be done by – in the name of all this, let there be an end of this contemptible garbage-loving, unchristian search after blemishes – a crew of pigmies girding at a giant. Let us decide once for all whether Burns was a gain or a loss to the world. Let us say, if we dare, that it would have been better if he had never seen the light. Let us admit, as we must do, that we have never looked, and probably never shall look, upon his like again, and, having done so, let us relegate to the limbo of oblivion errors inseparable from weak human nature; errors that sprang from that high strung sensibility which often accompanies and always gives living force to poetic fervour; errors that were bitterly repented of with many tears, and atoned for by terrible retribution. He has tooled his assize; let him have his acquittal...

Well said, sir.

And on the same night, on the other side of the country, schoolmaster T R Stuart, MA, addressed the Ayr Burns Club.

> De mortuis nil nisi bonum – 'Let the dead bury its dead.'
> He is far away from all praise or blame now, and in loving trust let us leave him to the God who endowed him with all his marvellous powers, who alone could understand his complex nature, and who cared for him more than he cared for himself. On an occasion like this it seems to me more fitting for us to think not so much of Burns the man, as of Burns the poet – a living and active force in our midst today,

exerting by the power of his genius a wider and a mightier influence than the vast majority of the men who are alive and working around us. The poet still lives. He breathes still in his works, and through these we come within the circle of his charm, the halo of his inspiration. The quintessence of poetry is the lyric; the quintessence of lyric poetry is distilled in the poems of Robert Burns. True, the grandest moments of human thought, preserved in poetic form, are the stately epics, the lofty dramas of some giant – a Homer, a Virgil, a Milton, a Shakespeare; but in each of these we have more than a poet. We have an historian, a psychologist, a philosopher. In these productions we have history, psychology, philosophy, and poetry. But in the exact, elastic sonnet, in the slender, sturdy, stirring song, we have poetry; and we have poetry pure and simple. The loftiest flights of the imagination, the deepest feelings of the heart, the vividest images of the fleeting thought, are arrested at their very best and bound captive in the velvet chains of the short lyric. Are not such themes, in their simplicity, the true quintessence of poesy, and is not such poesy 'the precious life-blood of a master spirit, embalmed and treasured up on purpose to a life beyond life?' Is not this especially the case with the poems of Burns? It has been sympathetically said of the man that he 'died of being Robert Burns.' Might it not be said with equal truth of the poet that he lives by being Robert Burns?

'The Immortal Memory' of Burns is, then, the immortal memory of his lyric poetry, and that immortality is only limited – pardon the 'bull' – by whatever limitation there may be to the immortality of Nature. For Burns is a true son of Nature – no artificial, made-up fop, and his songs are actual, integral parts of Nature; that is, of course, the best of his songs. The poets of the age immediately preceding Burns had been sagely discoursing about Nature, unnaturally, though perhaps prettily, writing about it in their prim studies, and with the backs of their chairs to the window. They had also studied men and women – 'over the tea cups.' Burns had no prim study. He went out into the fields and lanes, and was on nodding, even speaking terms with field mice and daisies. He went up the glen, and over the hill, and along by the brook, and here he met real men and real women with whom he was on even more familiar terms of nodding and speaking. When he sings of these people and these scenes, we listen to human voices, to human laughter, to human sobbing. And so with his magic wand of sympathy Burns touches every passing phase of Nature.

One of the deepest, the most enduring qualities of Burns is his humour, for he is never more genuine than when he is humorous. It is amazing how his powerful, trenchant statement of plain fact turns to laughter. Just recall the first stanza of *Holy Willie's Prayer*. And in a kindlier vein consider the riotous fun of *Tam o Shanter*, or that powerful masterpiece of the ludicrous – there is none greater in literature – *The Jolly Beggars*. In his best work he sees life with them exactly as it is, and putting it down so, sets every table in a roar – ay, and makes even the solitary reader shout with delighted laughter. From merciless satire this humour ranges through every grade to the gentle smile of archness, never distorted, always true.

But, great though Burns's pre-eminence is in the various forms of lyric poetry, it is in his love songs that he specially excels. Sappho, Horace, Beranger, Ben Jonson, Moore, have all left behind them love sonnets which are among the gems of literature; but in this branch of lyric art, even these masters must yield the palm to Robert Burns. Here he is unsurpassed. Here we have the music of the heart 'breathed by love in beauty's ear – thoughts that breathe and words that burn,' and in 'that wedded verse and music you feel that love is heaven and heaven is love.' The grand secret of Burns's power in those songs is that they were composed in honour of no mere phantom of a poet's fancy, but were the outpourings of a man's devotion to the then reigning divinity of his heart. His songs came from the heart, and they appeal straight to the heart.

The heart! Ay, 'there's the rub,' gentlemen; therein lies the secret of Burns's popularity with his fellow countrymen; there the irresistible charm which pervades his poetry. 'Touch the heart,' did I say? Yes, in very deed, he has touched it, more deeply than, in his most sanguine moments, he ever dreamt he could have done; touched the heart of a nation till its tenderest chords have vibrated at 'the touch of a vanished hand and the sound of a voice that is still.' To your feet, then, gentlemen, and with pride and joy let us pledge 'The Immortal Memory of Robert Burns.'

And the Rev Hugh MacMillan was doing likewise at Greenock.

> We are reminded by this remarkable anniversary that the character of the season in which great personages are born is very often found to correspond with their own character and destiny. Our national poet himself noticed the strange harmony between the character of the month in which he was ushered into the world and his own nature and life. We cannot imagine him a child of summer or autumn, with their settled sunshine and mellow fruition. The opening month of the year – looking, as its name implies, before and after, with the desolation of the past winter and the promise of the coming spring – seems to us to be analogous with his mixed nature and storm-tossed life; full of sorrowful memories and bright hopes, of desolations of passion and beautiful realisations of a nobler ideal. The wailing winds and the lowering clouds, and the clear afternoons that shed a mystic gleam of sunshine on bare pastures, and the lengthening eves with wistful sadness, that marked his natal month, seemed to repeat themselves in his own human experience.
>
> And the gifts of life, the beginnings of bird –life and flower – life which January shakes out of its grasp into the storm, and keeps warm by breathing upon them between its hands, were emblematic of the gifts of song cast into the tempest of his fortunes, and nurtured into beauty by the warm breath of his genius. The earth was a wintry landscape to him, and his life a January day. He came early into the world, and went away early out of it, ere he had time to warm both hands at the fire of life. His intellectual life, too, may be said to have been born in a January season in the history of our literature, when it returned from the decay and barrenness of a highly conventional style to the simplicity of Nature. On a great scale the world was beginning at the time to awaken to all the qualities of a vigorous and beautiful youthhood.
>
> There are prosaic souls that wonder why, year after year, we meet to honour the birthday of our national poet in the same unchanging fashion. They feel as if we ought, like themselves, to get tired of it and give it up. But I am sure that those who take part in this annual celebration do not experience any weariness or monotony in it. Each new occasion comes with fresh interest and zest. We do not grow tired of our own birthday; and the birthday of our immortal bard may well be

a significant time to thousands who owe the first dawning of their intellectual life to the inspiration of his poetry...

It is well to have such commemorations as this, if only to keep in remembrance our nationality. At one time, not so long ago, Scottish names connected with the Scottish capital were at the head of our English literature, and Edinburgh was in truth the Modern Athens. England, by the attraction of its superior wealth and political importance, is gradually assimilating our country to its own likeness. In such circumstances, we are called upon to maintain and assert our individuality as a nation and country with greater zeal and resoluteness than ever. And the best way of doing so is, not by echoing the parrot-cry of 'Justice to Scotland' in regard to its political interests, but by such commemorations as this, which fan the fire of our patriotism through our homage to our great national poet. Scotsmen are cosmopolitan, and Scottish blood everywhere has a peculiarly cohesive property; and in every country under heaven our kinsmen tonight meet together, and while they speak with rapture of what Robert Burns has done for their native.

What Scottish song was before his advent it is difficult for us to imagine. At an earlier period the ballad poetry of Scotland embodied all the romantic life of the land with a genuine pathos and passion, and imaginative power, and humour, and directness of expression which thrill our hearts even at this distance of time. These ballads were comparatively pure, and lived on the lips and in the memories of several generations, as they were sung over the land at fairs and feasts, and at the fireside by the wandering beggar, who paid in this manner his lawing for his supper and couch of straw. But after these ballads succeeded a period which can never come back again, when the exquisite music of many of our best known songs was associated with foul and bacchanalian words, giving them a false charm like that of the iridescence that shines on the surface of a polluted pool.

Such songs could not be sung without spreading an infectious evil atmosphere around them; and that they were popular at all showed how low was the state of morals. From this unholy alliance Burns divorced the lovely music, and married it anew to words that were worthy of it – words and music forming, as our own Hamish MacCunn has so beautifully shown, a harmony most pure and perfect. Those

> familiar songs that form part of the emotional inheritance of every Scottish man, woman, and child, and that raise a lump of yearning tenderness in our throats when we hear them sung in foreign lands, have all had this origin. Had Burns done no other service for his country than this elevation of our national song, he would be deserving of everlasting remembrance.
>
> 'He died of himself,' as some one has graphically said, in his thirty-seventh year. He had no autumn of reflection. It was all wind-born spring of growth and a summer of passion. And on his grave fell many of the blossoms of his genius, from which no fruit to quench the thirst of the soul could ever be grown... And the earnest wish of us all is, that this and all similar commemorations of Burns may do what Burns himself did for our Scottish song – elevate our minds and prove to us a source of the purest social pleasure. I ask you to join with me, in most respectful silence, in the toast of the evening – 'The Immortal Memory of Robert Burns.'

Finally, in the specimen year of 1897 with typical Addresses as the core of its Burn Night commemorations, we have Mr Walter Black at the Kelso Burns Club. His speech was reported and a brief extract is given as follows:

> Mr Black, in submitting 'The Immortal Memory,' said:
>
> Our monarch's hindmost year but ane
> Was five and twenty days begun,
> 'Twas then a blast o'Janwar' win'
> Blew hansel in on Robin.
>
> And surely Mother Nature never gave a more boisterous welcome to any man destined to play so great a part in the drama of life. His words to the mountain, daisy are applicable to his own birth:
>
> Cauld blew the bitter biting north
> Upon thy early humble birth;
> Yet cheerfully thou glinted forth
> Amid the storm.
>
> For out of trouble and distress, out of misery and despair, out of the storm and tempest of his chequered life, Burns rises high and clear, until today he stands on the highest pinnacle on the temple of fame. Tonight, not only in our own land, not only across the Border, but all over the world, wherever 'Scotchmen gather,' admirers and lovers of our national bard

are accepting his own invitation – an invitation which is still given, and will be given, to all those who choose to accept it, as long as the works of Burns occupy a place in the hearts and lives of men:

> A' ye whom social pleasure charms,
> Whose heart the tide o' kindness warms,
> Wha hold your being on the terms,
> 'Each aid the others,'
> Come to my bowl, come to my arms,
> My friends, my brothers!

Much has been said about the circumstances of the life of Burns; but we must not forget that those very circumstances have given to us this precious wealth of poetry and song. His loves, his joys, his hopes, his disappointments breathe in and through almost every line he has written. Out of the fullness of his heart the poet speaketh; and his was a large and a full heart. But there was no room in it for the tyrant and the oppressor. He loathes and curses the 'wretch of humankind'; he detests the haughty lordling who spurns the poor petition of the o'erlaboured wight; but he sings in praise of the 'simple rustic hind,' the 'buirdly chiels and clever hizzies,' and the 'social, friendly, honest man,' and tells us ' 'tis he fulfils great Nature's plan, and none but he.' Burns estimated man according to his worth – 'The honest man, though e'er so poor, is king o' men for a' that' – and points out the goal of social perfection, for further we cannot go:

> For a' that, and a' that,
> It's comin' yet for a' that
> That man to man the warld o'er
> Shall brithers be for a' that.

The twentieth century was only half a year old when the population of Barre, Vermont turned out en masse on the occasion of the unveiling of Burns's likeness in dark, Barre stone by J.Massey-Rhind. The Hon. Wendell Phillips Stafford of St Johnsbury, in the main speech, made a clever plea for Scottish-Americanism in Burns. He was fully reported in the local paper.

> Hon Wendell Phillips Stafford of St Johnsbury, the orator of the day, is a native of Barre and of Scottish descent, and his selection was owing to those facts, in addition to his known brilliancy as a speaker. We give the following extracts from his speech:–

Most of Burns's poetry was only another form of his conversation. It dealt with the same topics and was addressed to the same persons. His brightest and pithiest words are often to be found in those rhyming epistles he sent his friends. One year he made his tax inventory in verse. It offers still a half humorous, half sorrowful picture of his poverty. Some of the poems – and some of the best, too – bristle all over with the names of his neighbours. So it is, for instance, in *The Twa Herds*. It was never printed while Burns lived. It was handed about and laughed over among the unregenerate for the slaps of wit and stings of sarcasm, all unhappily too well deserved. It was exactly as if a great genius should drop down here in our midst, take a hand in all our quarrels, ridicule our weaknesses, avenge himself upon us for our slights, and draw with merciless fidelity the characters we meet day by day upon the street.

Macaulay said truly that no man ever wrote an immortal work in any language except the one he heard about his cradle. These are the words in which thought kindles into flame. It is in moments of tremendous excitement that the finest poetic expressions have birth, and in those moments the soul always speaks in the tongue of its childhood – all other language is forgotten. You may give a Scotchman all the culture of the school, until his ordinary conversation shall not betray his race. But the first excitement will betray him. Let him get angry and, if he swears, he'll swear in Scotch. If he falls in love, he'll woo in Scotch. When he tells a thrilling story he'll tell it in Scotch. And if he gets 'fou and unco happy,' he'll sing in Scotch.

Now Burns could have received no education that would have given him a mightier command of this tongue – to him at once a harp and a sword. Perfect knowledge of his subject, perfect sympathy with his audience, perfect mastery of his instrument – and for not one of these gifts or acquirements was he indebted to any school or university. But let us not make the common and silly mistake of calling him uneducated. He was well educated, thoroughly educated, for the great place he was to fill. No other training would have answered. The mills have been running at Edinburgh, Oxford, and Cambridge for centuries. Why haven't they produced a few Burnses? They have given us many a man of learning, they have polished and adorned many a man of genius, but they have never given us a single poet of the people. There is only one school that can produce him, and that is the school of hardship, privation, and daily toil, that Burns attended.

He had one gift, generally considered to be rare among poets, but of priceless value anywhere. I mean great, rugged common sense. With all his fooling, bantering and dreaming, he never overstepped this bound. You can point out many things that are coarse, that ought never to have been written; but you cannot lay your finger on a single line and say it is silly. There is that substratum of good sense under everything he wrote. This cannot be said of all poets, nor, indeed, of all great poets. Wordswoth wrote much that is good, and a little that can never die. Many who judge wisely in such matters rank him third in English poets – Shakespeare, Milton, Wordsworth; but Wordsworth cannot bear this test. When he was proposed for Poet Laureate, a member of Parliament recited some of the weakest of his writings, and then asked, amid the jeers and sneers of the House, whether a man who could be guilty of such stuff as that was fit to be the Laureate of England! He could never have done that with Burns. We may laugh with Burns; we never laugh at him. You may strip him of all his poetic gifts, and still have left the man of ability and brains.

He had likewise the gift of leadership, of magnetism, of eloquence. Women loved him at sight; children hung about his knees; and men followed him like children. When it was known that he was at the tavern farmers forsook the fields, work in the village was laid aside, and if he would talk, the crowd would hang upon his lips until morning. And it was not the peasantry alone who admired him. Men and women of the best birth and breeding in Edinburgh testified that his conversation was even more wonderful than his poetry. This awkward ploughman was transformed in the presence of beauty. He could greet a lady with the grace of a knight. 'Sic an e'e in his head!' was a common exclamation among those who saw him. His countenance beamed with intelligence, and his smile was as winning as a child's. who wonders that women loved him? Over his rugged and manly strength was thrown the charm of wit, the grace of speech, and that indefinable suggestion of greatness. Here was that rare blending of sweetness and strength which captivates the heart and leads men where it will.

But over and above all this he bore the rare, mysterious, magnificent endowment of poetic genius. This was his crown. Here aspiring nature burst into flame. The rarest and most splendid gift God ever bestows upon the world is a great poet.

We see now that it was Nature's purpose to make a poet, and that she took the surest means. She took the best blood of Scotland, peasant blood pure and undefiled, that had flowed for hundreds of years close to the kindly earth – gave him a father of nature and hardened manhood, a young mother with a glad, warm heart – a father of rigid virtue, ardent piety, but independent spirit and almost ungovernable temper – a mother of poetic soul, responsible to every appeal of beauty, and so smitten with the love of song that she went about her work crooning the old Scotch airs day after day while bearing her baby in the womb. 'When a man is born,' said Emerson, 'the gage of gifts is shut behind him.' Why, Nature had made sure that Burns should be a poet before ever he was born.

If somewhere in the other world, that spirit-land, which may be nearer than we think, this great should is looking down upon our doings here today, believe me, nothing in them has touched him more than that his form was wrapt about with the stars and stripes – the glorious ensign of that young republic he saluted from across the sea! You, men of his race, who cherish his fame, and out of the love and sacrifice of loyal heart have reared this monument to his memory – you shall be better Americans for being true Scotchmen. You have cast in your lot with us, in a land dedicated to the very principle for which Burns sang his earnest song. We have a great task before us still, and you must help us. We must see that the sublime idea of our fathers is realised better, year by year, in a wide and wider spread of these blessings which they intended to secure for themselves and their posterity. The stream of your natural life must be the richer for your coming. Bring us of your thrift, your energy, your loyalty. We need them all. But bring us your finer gift, bring us your poet, too. He is too great for Scotland – he belongs to the world at large.

Queen Victoria died in January 1901 and the Edwardian era finally began. That summer, the Burns Federation held its Annual Meeting that summer in Dunfermline. Mr Andrew Carnegie of that town and a self-confessed Burnsian sent a note of apology. He was unable to attend because he was entertaining the Principals of the Scottish Universities at Skibo Castle. The meeting, nonetheless, conferred an Honorary Presidency on the millionaire. Also absent was Dr William Wallace, whose idea of a University Chair of Scottish History and Literature was foundering due to lack of funds. Professor Lawson of St Andrew's University made a plea for more support from the Clubs who had so far contributed one-tenth of the amount required. The meeting responded by making Dr Wallace an Honorary Vice-President.

And so the idylic Edwardian sundown continued in its unruffled, complacent way. The annual voices were raised at Burns Suppers but in this one hundred and fiftieth anniversary of the poet's birth, no one thought to get very excited, except perhaps Mr Rae-Brown who showed all his old enthusiasm for anniversaries but, compared to the explosions of 1859 and 1896, hardly a ripple was heard. Typical perhaps was the quiet, reasoned voice of a Scottish clergyman who spoke at the annual supper of the Glasgow Ayrshire Society. It was January 1913 and theirs was a kind of world that was, in the following year, to disappear for ever. In that lull before the storm, there was still time to pause, reflect and reason, and the Reverend David Dickie did just that for his fellow-Ayrshire men in Glasgow and for that other man o' Ayr.

> In endeavouring to interpret the oracle of Burns, necessity is laid upon us to obtain an honest medium – a veritable life-likeness. Before his personality can possess us, our imagination must capture the stamp of man he was, as well as his attendant atmosphere. In other words, if we are to come within the full sphere of his influence we must secure a view-point with nothing to obstruct. Too many of the prints and paintings, the marble busts and sculpture monuments, are but misleading commentaries. In the main they are too Parisian – too suggestive of a dandy and a foreigner – and altogether outwith the traditions of time and place.
>
> Happily, in the artistic creations of these later days, we are getting back to nature first hand – back to plain and simple truth – looking fact in the face. So that while Burns is still set before us as a figure to fill the eye, he is no longer presented after the fashion and modes of indoor life – the broad jaw, the high cheek bones, the strong head, the sturdy upstanding

frame speak to us of a man true to type – a man like the world – the world of farmer folks. With such a human likeness we can all stand in, and start communion, and the ground on which we meet is not less holy because it is common ground. Standing at his shrine as we are this evening, most essential it is at the outset that we lay down his life-work on legitimate lines. On no account must we regard his development as an exhibition, solitary and apart. No mere 'sport' of human kind was he, nor intellectual accident. His genius was genuinely related to the dwellers round about – was but the high water mark of the spiritual spring-tide of his native country.

One other natural factor in his composition we must not overlook. We must not forget 'the rock out of which he was hewn'. Poverty, his bedfellow all through, was not his only patrimony. In more ways than one his father was a man of might. In his economy, the elemental forces of genius were pent up and imprisoned. The power that burst forth as poetry in the son, slumbered as piety in the sire. So truly was he the high priest in his home, that the bard held him in awe even in his wildest moments. As you note the father's grave, puritanic pride, you can easily discern whence Burns drew his manly independence and native dignity. And in the old man's fine respect for Deity, you can trace the subtle religious influence that ever stood like a good angel between the poet and his works.

Happily in our appreciation of Burns the historic sense obtains. We have passed from the period when the real man could not be discerned in the heat and dust of the day. The whole kindly economy of life has laboured to resurrect him as he was in heart and principle. So that what outstands today is Burns at his best – Burns the Immortal. After a century and more the sheer sincerity of the man has saved him. In spite of everything else his innate native 'rightness' has come through and won its way to the front. One cannot help contrasting time's tender treatment of Burns with its rough handling of men of a different stamp – men never done affecting the pious pose – whose life-labour it is to keep their own goodness in evidence, and if possible under the lime light. In most wondrous and unreckoned ways life's interaction works off their veneer – discovers the joints in their harness, quite quietly brings the real man out of his guard – searches him through and through, as with a lighted candle, and shows him up – not a man, but only the phantasm and wrappings of a man. It may be in this same city you have seen under wintry conditions 'the bird of Paradise' in the moult.

If, like many another prophet, Burns received but scant honour in his own day and from his own folk, history has handsomely righted the wrong. From being a mere popular rhymer, he has been lifted into the front rank of Scottish Reformers – our acknowledged national liberator. Underneath all his writing runs one continuous emancipation act – not for a class, but for humanity, bringing freedom not into one department of duty, but into the whole domain of life. Hard-mouthed purists hold it rank heresy to reckon Burns a religious reformer, yet assuredly that was his peculiar ordinance. Out and out and through and through, his life-work made for betterment in conduct as in creed. In this respect he served his kirk and country, as neither kirk nor country realised. Had the preachers of the day but known it, he was ministering with high distinction at the same altar with themselves. His lyrics have simply transfigured the whole spiritual outlook and economy of humankind.

In the most ordinary mortal this Scottish seer discerned a very heaven of human interest and charm – unroofing the plough-man and the milk-maid, he surprised situations surpassingly idyllic – revealing a wealth of sentiment that carried further than mere emotional response – sentiment not merely winsome and clean, but empathetically redemptive, simply incalculable in its moral uplift, ennobling the whole tone of life's relationships. Into the natural commerce of the swain and his sweetheart he glinted a new light from above, lifting it out of the level of sense, and transmuting the challenge of sex into 'the sacred lowe o' weel placed love.' Pecksniff & Co. have made a mighty ado about his side stepping, but at its worst, it was not a feather weight over against the lift his lyrics gave to sex relationships, and the best interests of morality.

Not less in the world of thought than in the world of feeling was his unique power advertised. More perhaps than any scientific theologian, Burns banished distorted notions of Deity, recovered and established the standards of truth. There are those who assert that only a burning desire to clear scores, made him lash out at the dogmatists of his day, whereas we all know that it was his antagonists' contradictions that called him forth. There before him was an order of teachers, genial and human-hearted, even jovial, but who, the moment they adventured into theology pulled down the blinds, and threw life into shadow. No wonder it maddened him to see men – lay and cleric alike – the very soul of good company, when they came to appreciate the Divine management, go straight back on their own personal enjoyments, right in the teeth of daily experience, and altogether against the grain of human nature.

Those blasphemous caricaturists Burns did not condescend to combat, he simply laughed them out of court. Like the breath of spring on the stubble, his scathing satire and resistless humour withered the undergrowth of mock piety in Scotland. First and last an earnest truth-seeker, he could not away with men in a sacred office who only peeped and muttered, and no quarter did he give them, and no quarter did they deserve. To his eternal honour be it testified that his was the supreme genius that undermined the fabric of superstition and brought the house of lies down, and Scottish theologians ever since have been but helping to remove the rubbish.

Only those familiar with the literature of the 18th-century will rightly appreciate his services to poesy – how he redeemed our lowland lyrics from coarseness and obscurity, sweetening and purifying the whole atmosphere of song. His patriotism still makes men's blood run fire – vibrant yet the ring he gave to the 'rights of man.' Never another mortal preached the gospel to the poor with such homely vision. His sheer humanness makes him kin to every life in distress, concerning itself even with 'the sorrows of Satan'. Time would fail me to review the long procession of his ministries, and I humbly venture to think that at a meeting like this, better work can be done for our hero. The pledge is laid on every member of a Burns Club to put the poet right with the world, and to turn his memory round and round till the true light – the light of life – falls upon it.

Far be it from us to throw a halo of glory round what is wrong, or dress up evil in the garb of holiness merely because a genius did it. Such is not our intention, nor is such our painful necessity. The tears of time have long since blotted out the stains on his memory. Affection's offices have healed the wounds, and covered over the scars in his character. The instinct of justice in human nature has firmly put its hand on

> the mouth of the defamer. For all the follies that laid him low, atonement has been made a thousandfold. But even in his lifetime, Burns wrought out his own redemption. In spite of all the dark passages and tragic breaks, his character had an integrity of its own. Spiritual deliverance came along its own private path – along the line of his hard, unhappy life. Religion with him was not an attainment of rounded corners and completed achievements. All the while the divine purpose seemed thwarted and turned aside, the fierce fires of penitence were burning within, cleansing his soul, and keeping his conscience hard at work. Behind no plausible subterfuge did he ever conceal himself from Deity. Out into the open he came, confessing his errors with the frankness and candour of a little child. And what more could mortal do, bound as he was by past infirmity!
>
> I confess, to me he has always seemed greatest when the world turned its back on him – greatest when his life lay sunken in the shadow of a terrible eclipse. Where another and shabbier soul would have lain down and grovelled, begging the public pity, Burns stood up to his disgrace, meeting the sneers of the crowd with the full might of his manhood – sending back scorn for scorn. Not lowering his mien for a moment – but carrying himself in his own grand way – peerless in the region round about – a king in his own right. Why the convention has obtained to honour this sentiment in solemn silence, I fail to understand. We are assembled to celebrate a nativity. Why, then, should we strike a wrong note by turning the festive occasion into the scene of a funeral service? Why should solemn silence black border rejoicing? We are not come to bury Burns, but to praise him. I give you – with all the honours – 'The Immortal Memory'.

There is such calm, good sense here that it is a pleasure to put it whole on the page. One can not only understand Burns the better but one gets a glimpse of the balanced man the Reverend Dickie must have been. This is the kind of unshowy Memory that shows up the essential Burns best, but then in 1914 the insanity and absurdity of war broke out like a sore and spread like a cancer all over Europe. All memories gave way to the nightmares of Mons, Ypres and Cambrai and every kind of young man was sunk in mud and blood for four hideous years in the obscenity of out-dated trench warfare saved only by the arrival of tanks and the Americans.

With the end of the war the countries involved only took time to recover from their wounds before beginning their preparations for its continuation in the Second World War just twenty years later. 'Between the Wars' the period is called and it comprised those two decades known broadly as the 'Roaring Twenties' and the 'Hungry Thirties'. Man was still a long way from Burns's ideal of brotherly love, and in many cases it was more like *Buddy, can you spare a dime?* This was an American popular song of the Depression years and it was in America that the focus turned for new thoughts and new writing on Burns.

James Buchanan wasn't the only American President who knew his Burns. According to Milton Hay, President Lincoln could recite the whole of *Tam o Shanter* and President Roosevelt was known to have enjoyed Ray Noble's sweet-swing version of *Auld Lang Syne* broadcast every Hogmanay from the Rockefeller Centre, New York. The very first president, George Washington, would have known Burns as the first American edition of his poems was published in Philadelphia in 1788, and ever since then his popularity, surprisingly, has grown in the United States to a degree even greater, or at least, more widely-spread than in the United Kingdom.

We have acknowledged the tributes paid to him by poets like John Greenleaf Whittier and Ralph Waldo Emerson, but it was the scholars of America who advanced him most in the twentieth century. The study of the letters of Burns in 1931 and the legend of Burns in 1932 by J. DeLancey Ferguson were important additions to Burns scholarship and the Life by Franlyn B. Snyder in 1932 was rightly regarded as monumental. Oliver Wendall Holmes put it succinctly when he said:

> Burns ought to have passed ten years of his life in America, for those words of his: 'A man's a ma for a' that' show that true American feeling belonged to him as much as if he had been born in sight of the hill before me as I write – Bunker Hill.

This American accent is still heard today in Burns scholarship in the work of such as the already-mentioned Professor George Ross Roy at the University of South Carolina, although his native voice is Canadian. In this context, it is worth quoting at length the final few paragraphs of the late Donald Low's excellent edition of *Robert*

Burns – The Critical Heritage (1974). Here, Dr Low concluded:

> Scotch blood explains only a little of the American regard for Burns. In this country he receives a profounder and sincerer homage than any that springs from the sentimental claims of race and nationality – a homage that is rendered, not by reason, but in spite of much that is intrinsic in the poet's character and work; a homage that takes us beyond the limited range of Burns's patriotism, and reveals the true horizon of the poet's greatness. Notwithstanding his excessive Scotchness Burns has struck home to the American heart as no other outside writer has done before or since, and won from a practical, but essentially non-poetic, people an appreciative homage which is the most eloquent tribute yet accorded to his genius...
>
> The literary, like the political revolution of the 18th-century, consisted chiefly in the assertion and establishment of the dignity of individual man; it lay also in a return to the healing powers of nature, and in both of these respects the Napoleon of this revolution was Robert Burns. Nature was his high priestess in song; and when equality and fraternity were being branded with blood and fire on the face of Europe, Burns gathered as into a burning focus the whole human sentiment of the revolution in 'A man's a man for a' that'. This was a voice straight from the democracy, speaking for the democracy with an unexampled directness and dignity – the voice of one who stood on his own rock of independence, and esteeming every man at his mere intrinsic worth, proclaimed the new creed and gospel of humanity.
>
> In this Burns is more in sympathy with American than with Scottish life. The principle of individual worth and the spirit of independence which are to us in this country commonplaces of our daily lives are not so familiar in Scotland of today, and in the days of Burns they were startling in their novelty. It is true that Burns seemed to have failed miserably, that he was silently crushed out and down by the allied respectabilities of social caste, whose extinction he so proudly heralded. But despite his apparent failure there is in the life and poetry of this heralded of the dawn an immortal record of the true majesty of manhood. Therein lies the great ethic of his work, therein lies his just claim to sit among the great and beneficent spirits of the human race.

There is also a transatlantic connection in one of the first voices raised for Burns soon after his death, and in a woman's voice at that. Interestingly enough, she also had a relation with the only part of the Americas Burns might actually have visited had his book not sold – the West Indies. Maria Banks Woodley was the daughter of the Governor and Captain-General of the Leeward Islands and in 1788 she accompanied him to the West Indies. She met there the doltish Walter Riddell and returned with him to England in 1792. They had earlier visited Robert Riddell at Friar's Carse and there she met Burns. They were mutually attracted at once but various unfortunate events caused a quarrel which was not made up until the last few months of his life. Before this, however, with Burns's encouragement she had written *Voyages to the Madeira and Leeward and Caribee Islands* and when he died, Maria wrote a memoir of the poet which W.E.Henley thought 'so admirable in tone, and withal so discerning and impartial in understanding, that it remains the best thing written of him by a contemporary critic'. However, since the concentration in this book is on the oral or verbal evocation of Burns in oration, we must pass it over.

Maria Riddell's 'pen-portrait' brings to mind at this point the matter of the portraits of Burns and how he was seen by painters in his own day. Unfortunately, none was a great painter in the classical sense, although Sir Henry Raeburn, one of the few genuine Scottish masters, was reputed to have made a likeness at one time even if it was only a copy of Nasmyth's portrait rather than an original. Raeburn was in Rome when Burns first came to Edinburgh and although they might have met during the later visits, they did not. This is to be regretted as Sir Henry, from his Edinburgh studio in York Place, painted many of the leading figures of the golden age of the Scottish Enlightenment and might have, had the opportunity arisen, given us the real Burns in oils instead of a copy of a copy, even if it is by his own hand. Letters, dated 14 November 1803 and 22 February 1804, from him to the publishers, Cadell and Davies, in London, state:

> I have finished a copy of Burns the Poet from the original portrait painted by Mr Nasmyth. I have shown it to Mr Cunningham who thinks it very like him...

and

> Nothing can be more gratifying to me than the approbation you expressed of the copy I made for you of Robert Burns.

George Thomson, according to his biographer, J.Cuthbert Hadden, in 1898, considered the painting he (Thomson) had of Burns by Raeburn 'was the best extant...' [and]

> who, on my solicitation, did me the great favour of revising and retouching the face in my own presence, and gave much to that lustre in the eyes which I well remember in the living man, and upon which I could not help gazing during the only day I ever had the pleasure of dining in his delightful company...

He then went on to say:

> The charms of Burns's conversation may well make us regret that he was not, like Johnson, attended by a Boswell...

This has been a regret felt by many, including the present writer who, in a volume dealing with the spoken word on Burns, would have dearly liked to have included the spoken word of Burns himself. However, enough exists in anecdote to give us the flavour of this exceptional man, and for that we must be content.

What became known as the Auchendrane replica of this same portrait was bought by Lord Rosebery but the basic portrait was the work of Alexander Nasmyth and it was executed while Burns was in Edinburgh during 1787. The result is what amounts to the passport portrait of Robert Burns. It is the one everybody knows – the wispy hair plastered over a high forehead, long sideburns, dark, lustrous eyes and almost womanly lips. This is the ubiquitous Burns, Burns as icon, and it is the brand-image that represents Burns to the world today. Various engravings were made from this original by such artists as Neagle and W.F. Fry but did Burns really look like this?

Apparently not. The family considered that the portrait done by James Tannock, a Kilmarnock-born, London-trained painter who was apprenticed to Nasmyth in 1803, was 'the best likeness in existence'. According to Gilbert Burns – 'To make the poet min-mou'd will not do.' Illustrators seem determined to give him prissy lips and a weak chin. Perhaps they considered this the poetic look.

The very much family resented this. His sister, Isabella (Mrs Begg) was typically explicit – 'He was far bigger and tougher than his portraits. They make him look like a gentleman which he never was.' Sir Walter Scott says much the same thing – 'His person was strong and robust…his countenance is more massive than it looks in any of the portraits…' For Scott, it was the face of a 'douce, guid man, who held his own plough.' John Beugo may have got something of this in his engraving and the John Meirs silhouette suggests a fuller face. Peter Taylor and Alexander Reid in their works suggest the artisan rather than the artist, as does the Tassie medallion of 1801 but, generally speaking, most portraits, including the admirable copy of the Nasmyth made by Archibald Skirving in red chalk, and another in oils by John Faed, give us a 'pretty', highly idealised Burns who is portrayed as less than he was in life.

Modern opinion was well illustrated by an essay on Burns in Latitudes (1924) by the Orcadian, Edwin Muir. Muir, as one of Scotland's leading poets in the 20th-century, claimed that the only contemporary verdict on Burns free from 'a touch of cant… something morally or socially superior' was that of Allan Cunningham's father, who said:

> Few men had so much of the poet about them, and few poets so much of the man: the man was probably less pure than he ought to have been, but the poet was purer than he ought to have been, and the poet was pure and bright to the end.

That is Burns in a nutshell.

Despite having lost a whole generation of members to the Great War, the Burns Clubs resumed their activities soon after the Armistice in 1918, and with them the annual January supper. These might be best be typified by the programme offered by the Bridgeton Burns Club of Glasgow in its 58th anniversary dinner at the Grosvenor Banqueting Hall on Wednesday 25 January 1926 at 6-30pm for 7. The Chairman for the evening was the Club president, Dr David McKail, and the Croupiers attending him were the Vice-President, Mr Templeton, with the club office-bearers, Messrs Shaw, Stobo, McDonald, Whyte and Cowper. The traditional Scottish 'Bill o' Fare' was offered as follows:

Caller Eysters

Cockie Leekie an' Baps

Fush: Fried Filleted Sole an' Ballochmyle Sauce
Haggis wi a' the Honours
(This would mean it was piped in and served with a dram)
Roastit Chicken an' Ayrshire Bacon
Mauchline Puddin' an' Droukit Sauce
Cauld Cream
Dessairt
Coffee

After an appropriate interval there followed what was termed *The Nicht's Ongauns*. This really meant the Toasts of the evening interspersed with Burns readings and songs as well as, in this case, a collection for the Schools Burns Competition Prize Fund. The Chairman proposed the first toast, which is always to the reigning sovereign, in this case, King George V. This was followed by the National Anthem given by the company who then rendered the Scottish anthem (*Scots Wha Hae*) after which the cigars came out with the relevant *speerits*.

To honour him, we've met aince mair,
Come fill your glass and rise from your chair.

Professor Bowman then gave the toast to the Immortal Memory on this occasion and, as was the custom at this club, the toast was followed by:

ONE MINUTE SILENCE

as announced in the programme in bold type. This was strictly observed and no doubt was in effective contrast to all that had gone before – and what was yet to come. The chief toast is always, or should be, the watershed of the evening. Things rise towards it and then fall away from it. This is why the minute's silence is so effective a bridge. The solemnities had been properly observed and now the fun can start. The toasts are lighter and are wholly at the discretion of the club. In this instance, the subsequent toasts were 'To the Lord Provost, Magistrates and Town Council of Glasgow', 'To *Oor Guests*' and finally, 'To Our Chairman and Croupiers' before the company joined *Auld Lang Syne* and repaired to the respective trams, trains and taxis.

It is worth quoting this programme in detail for not only is it typical of its day it is very much the format still offered at the formal dinners known as Burns Suppers all over the world. Particulars may vary and superficial rites may be added appropriate to the club and its locality or tradition, but in the main, the meal serves to prepare the company for the toasts, the chief of which is, of course, the Immortal Memory. This purpose should never be lost sight of, whatever the circumstances or the standard of the Supper or the status or rank of the chosen speaker or even the price of the ticket. Robert Burns is the alpha and omega of whatever is organised in his famous name.

This was still true no matter what language was used in the ceremonies. Translations of Burns continued and, by this time, had been translated into all the main tongues. Norwegian and Rumanian were added in 1923 and 1925 respectively, but, as has been previously mentioned, 1926 saw a version of the works appear in Esperanto. Henryk Mink dealt with this at some length in the 1996 Bicentenary edition of the *Burns Chronicle* and the following remarks are taken from that article. He first of all acknowledges the work done by William Jacks in 1896 which has already been referred to, but he differed from that compiler in that he (Mink) insisted that the translator be fluent in both in Scots and the language into which it is being translated. This was asking a lot of even a polymath like Mr Jacks. Mr Mink, for his part, was fluent in Esperanto and used Scots who knew their Burns and who were also familiar with that artificial language.

Esperanto was a language communication invented by Ludwik Lazar Zamenhof, a Polish Jew who practised as an oculist in Warsaw and became known as 'Doktoro Esperanto' after his new language was adopted in other countries and Esperanto Associations set up. It is based on an international root-word vocabulary adapted to a simplified 16-rule grammar. It was intended as a kind of *lingua franca* between nations and to break down the barriers of difference in line with the Burns precept of international brotherhood, but today English has become the international language of commerce and culture even where it has been reduced to the jargon of information technology or cell-phone text. Doktoro Esperanto deserved better. But for those who enjoy the challenge, *Afton Water* can be sung as:

> Fluadu Altono lau verda kampar, Fluadu trankville al vasta
> la mar...

Or *Bonie Wee Thing, Cannie wee thing* as:

> Bela eta estajo, afabla eta estajo...

All the translations of Burns into Esperanto were of his songs. As Henryk Minc says, the main purpose of the translators was to:

> make available to Esperantists some of the most beautiful songs ever written. The translators have endeavoured to produce lyrics for these songs that fit the original tunes and render Burns's lyrics as faithfully as they could. These translations were meant to be sung and enjoyed at Esperantist gatherings and not to be studied in minute detail.

Yet the article mentioned went into considerable detail. However, his point is taken.

Mention has already been made of the fact that the first Immortal Memory was given in verse and many speakers since have followed that example as will be seen in these pages. However, no one yet has attempted to describe a whole Burns Supper in verse but this is exactly what the heroic anonymous rhymer of 1927 did in describing the events of the evening at the Chryston Burns Supper before he capitulated to the call of Nature. No apology is made for including it here in slightly re-ordered form because this unknown pen gives us real a picture of a West of Scotland Burns night as acute as any report in the *Herald* or *Bulletin* of the day might have done.

Ae nicht, a lang while back since,
Foregetherin' at Davie Jackson's,
We a' sat roun' the ingle crackin'
The time the supper was a- makin',
An' aye the crack took random turns
Till Davie spak o' Rabbie Burns.

The mair he spak', the mair I lis'ened,
And Davie's e'en wi' ardour glis'ened,
Sae weel his language he direcked
That a' that heard him were infecked,
An' I, afore I left for hame,
For Chryston Burns Club gi'ed my name.
In consequence o' whilk deceesion,

Ae Janwar' nicht, wi' much precision,
I dressed mysel, an', carefu' happit,
Aff tae the Burns Club Supper stappit;
I cared na' though the roads were slippy,
Or frost had made the air gey nippy.

I reached the Ha', the door unsteekit,
And ben intae the lobby keekit;
There, seein' mony weel-kent faces,
My shyness kicked oot-owre the traces;
Sae ben I gae'ed, an' ane an' a'
A welcome gi'ed me tae the Ha'.

The sicht I saw- I'll ne'er forget it;
Four tables braw, wi' flo'ers deckit,
An' roun' them sittin', jokin', laughin',
The wale o' men frae Chryston Clachan;
Douce Davie owre the scene presides,
An' carefu' he the meetin' guides.
His audience he wi' pith addresses
An' on us as a study presses
The life an' works o' oor Scotch Robbie
An' a' through life tae mak' a hobby
O' speakin' in the auld Scots tongue
In which oor poet proodly sung.

Ere he sits doon, his gless he raises,
'The King,' quo' he, 'he needs nae praises,'
An' we like loyal Scottish people
Sang till we rocked the auld kirk steeple
'God save the King'; lang may oor race
Gi'e this gran' toast its honoured place.

The echoes o' that anthem glorious
Had haurdly de'ed when loud, uproarious,
We hid the widden rafters ringin'
Wi' whit's noo ca'ed communal singin',
An' rendered in the auld Scots style,
'There was a lad was born in Kyle.'

But I maun pause to ca' attention
Tae twa-three chiel weel worth the mention,
Chiels we were glad tae ha'e amang us,
Led by the geniel Geordie Angus;
Gran' waiters a', alert when summoned,
Were Wallace, Beattie, Bell and Drummond.

Ye've heard o' Glesca's waiters,
Compared wi' oors, they puir bit craturs
Were hirplin wrecks, wan, feckless dreevils,
But Geordie's men were loupin' deevils;
Ere empty gless had left your mou'
Yer jug wi' reamin' swats was fou'.

Nae mair my time on waiters wastin',
Through the lang programme I maun hasten;
Sae young Philip wi' the yill stops flirtin'
Whan Davie bids him tak tae liltin';
Bauld Philip gi'es us a pawky smile
And starts 'The Lass o' Ballochmyle.'
The chorus o' that sang subsidin',
The lichtnin' waiters sprang frae hidin'
In ante-rooms, an', souple-j'inted,
Each gallops tae his place app'inted,
An' splash! afore ye'd coont up four
Your gless wi' usquebagh rins owre.

Then hark! Upon my ears comes dirlin'
The music o' the bagpipes dirlin'
An' heid erec' an' pipin' brawly
In steps oor piper, young McAulay,
An' close ahint him, short but bulky,
Comes marchin ben' oor ain Jock Wulkie.

Jock tae the haggis tray is yokit,
His Tam o' Shanter's deftly cockit,
An' prood as Lucifer he's smilin'
Tae cairry in the haggis b'ilin';
His fingers wi' the the hot tray burnin',
But fient a hair is Jockey turnin'.

Still – wi' regard for burnin' fingers –
Nae meenit on the road John lingers,
But aye his dignity maintainin'
An' pride his manly heart sustainin';
The Chairman's table sune he faces,
An' doun the haggis tray he places.

An' I maun e'en say, 'Weel dune, Jockey,
Ye've played ye're pairt, pert an' cocky,'
An' whan I feel douncast or sulky,
The memory o' wee Jock Wulkie
As he cam' smilin' doun the Ha'
'I'll drive my sulky mood awa'.'

Noo, Jim McFaurlin tak's position,
An' his nae learned disquisition,
But word for word, as Burns indited,
'The Haggis Ode' bauld Jim recited;
F'eth, Jamie lad, an' Burns had seen ye
A hearty cheer he wad ha'e gi'en ye.
When Jamie's recitation finished,
An' cheers an' noise had a' diminished,
The lichtnin' waiters, pechin', sweatin',
Set doun a meal weel worth the eatin';
Wi' reverent voice an' solemn face
Douce Davie said the Selkirk Grace.

I lookit roun' the gleesome getherin'.
An' some were gorgin', ithers bletherin',
But whether daein' ane or ither,
Each felt his neebo'r was his brither,
The bonds o' fellowship were strengthened,
New frien'ships made an' auld anes lengthened.

The supper's owre – an' fu' each bag is
Wi' tatties, whisky, beer an' haggis.
Oor Chairman gi'es us a' a warnin'
Aboor the sair heids i' the mornin,
'But noo,' says he, 'the time is fleein'
I tae the programme maun be seein'.'

He intimates the next event is
A sang by oor guid cronie, Prentice,
Wha lilts tae us sae sweet an' canny
The poet's love for winsome Nannie;
Sae earnestly he sings an' well
Ye'd think he lo'ed the lass himsel'.

The Chairman frae his seat noo bounces,
An' tae the gatherin' announces
That the Address on this occasion,
Combinin' baith Toast and Oration,
Was due tae come frae Johnny Broun,
The best-kenned man in a' oor toon.

'Mid loud applause, but nae whit worrit,
John tae the platform stappit forrit;
He clears his throat, adjusts his glesses
An' th'expectant thrang addresses.
In simple words, yet-weel-turned phrases,
The genius o' oor bard he praises.
Tae gi'e again John's dissertation
I've neither time nor inclination,
But I'll say this, nae critic fearin',
That his discourse was weel worth hearin',
An' for it I'll remain his debtor
Nor ever wish tae hear a better.

Ere his address the speaker closes
'The Immortal Memory' he proposes;
Nae word is spoken-nae gless clinkin',
But each the toast in silence drinkin'
Wi' reverent thochts an' tribute mental,
We drink tae genius transcendental.

The solemn silence noo is broken,
The Chairman aince again has spoken:
The program lang he puts his haun' on
An' asks Muirhead tae be upstaun'in'
An' sing that sang nae Scotsman spurns,
Kenned as 'The Star o' Rabbie Burns.'

Then Davie, withoot hesitation,
Ca's for Jock Wulkie's recitation;
Jock shoves aside a toom decanter,
An' risin' gi'es us 'Tam o' Shanter',
He reels it aff withoot a flaw,
Hoo he can min' it beats us a'.

An' sae on wings the nicht quick passes
Wi' story, sang, an' clinkin' glesses;
Lang Murchie tells some pawky stories
An' young Philip's sangs ha'e rousin' chorus;
His cultured voice an' tunefu' ear
Mak singin' a delicht tae hear.

Wull Broon an' Jamie Hunter singing'
Frae a' that hear them cheers are bringin',
But Davie sune subdues the clatter,
An Archie Orr sings 'Afton Water';
Expression sae his sweet notes saften,
Ye a'most heard the murmurin' Afton.
An' noo oor men o' elocution,
On Burns warks mak' execution;
Wull Bell lays aff a lang epistle,
Verse efter verse as clean's a whistle;
McFaurlin's 'Man was made to Mourn'
Shewed Jimmy was an actor born.

Rab Wilson next recites 'The Vision';
He's studied it wi' sic precision
That through it he gangs glibly skelpin'
Withoot a single word o' helpin';
Hoo he can dae it gars me won'er
I couldna dae it in years a hunner.

Tim Gray upon him tak's the duty
Tae tell o' Hornbook an' Auld Clootie;
Weel he relates the eerie story
Hoo Auld Mahoun, wi' scythe a' gory,
Vows that the doctor's pride he'll end,
An' swears tae nick him in the end.

O' speeches, tae, we had fu' measure,
Whilk tae repeat I ha'na leisure,
But Gibson, Broun and Willie Duncan
Withoot the slightest sign o' funkin',
Gie'd speeches that set hearts a-steerin',
An' prood were we tae gie them hearin'.
An' here, my frien's, I had tae leave
Though I maun say, sair did I grieve,
For ere I frae the Ha' departed
Young Jamie Broun 'The Twa Dogs' started,
And sae, again' my inclination,
I had tae miss his recitation-'

Any one who has attended such a Burns Supper will know exactly how the anonymous bard felt, and would sincerely hope that he made it.

As the Twenties moved into the Thirties, the world wide depression bit deeper, but by 1934 the Brigton Burnsians were again at the Grosvenor for their 65th Supper and this time the principal speaker was Sir John C Watson, KC, Sheriff Principal of Caithness, Orkney and Shetland, who said that a mass production in economics was a lesser danger than mass production in thought, and it was the mass production mind that labelled Burns the sinner. 'Burns, however, never pretended to be a saint,' he said. 'And in *Auld Lang Syne* he had written a litany for the English speaking people of the world.' 1934 also saw the *Glasgow Herald* publish a review of Burns Suppers in the city around that time. This is a random selection from some of the speeches made.

> If ever there was a poet who sympathised with man's laughter and tears, his hopes, labours, and failures, that poet was Burns.

This tribute to Burns's qualities was put forward by the Rev J Russell Miller of Kilsyth, who proposed The Immortal Memory at the dinner of the Glasgow Haggis Club in January 1934. He went on:

> Burns not only expressed the soul of Scotland as few others had done, he expressed it in songs that none other had equalled. He lived and died little above the line of poverty, but he left a rich inheritance behind him...

> Never had man paid such a ribute to womankind as did Robert Burns in his love songs. He was the love poet of the world of man. We sang what he wrote, we felt what he felt, but he only could express it. Those songs were so many and so beautiful that it was almost an impertinence to select from them.

It was another minister called Miller, this time the Rev James, who was a last-minute replacement at the Sandyford Burns Club dinner and ball in the Ca'doro, Glasgow. The Earl of Elgin was to have proposed the principal toast, but because of illness, unable to attend, and the duty was undertaken by Mr Miller, who was chaplain of the club. In proposing The Immortal Memory he made the following comment:

> Twelve thousand men of all ranks and persuasions attended the funeral of Robert Burns. Was that the life or passing of a debauchee, the record of a wasted mortal span?

'Poetry was only a small part of the man,' said Colonel A.D. MacInnes Shaw, who proposed The Immortal Memory at the jubilee dinner of Rosebery Burns Club, held in the Grand Hotel, Charing Cross, Glasgow. He also said:

> The evidence proved that the man was far more remarkable than his work. They had the testimony of an accomplished lady of his day that none ever outshone Burns in the charm and fascination of conversation, the spontaneous eloquence of social argument, or in brilliant repartee. 'No man's conversation ever took me so completely off my feet,' said the Duchess of Gordon, then the queen of Scottish Society.

'I have the right to be protected against certain Peeping Toms, Spying Sallies, gutter scrapers, and dunghill rakers,' stated Mr A.M.Williams when proposing the toast of The Immortal Memory at the anniversary dinner of the Glasgow Ayrshire Society in Glasgow. He was speaking of Robert Burns, of course. Mr Williams went on:

> This might, in view of recent books, be part of the declaration of Burns were he to return to earth today...In approaching the life of an eminent man, poet, politician, or author, there were two aspects from which his life might be considered, the public and the private... In recent times there had been a

> tendency to seize upon a reputation and examine it for the purpose of unearthing scandal. There was a body of literary resurrectionists who sought a diseased side in any reputation in order to show it to the public... It was common still to talk of that Ploughman Poet. It was quite true that Burns was not a University man but neither was Shakespeare...Burns sang as the birds sang – because they must. His songs flowed from his pen like liquid gold, and time, the great thief, plucked no laurels from his brow.

'He was the multitude articulate' declared Mr Donald M'Kay Kerr, PPGSW of Burns when giving The Immortal Memory at the annual dinner of the Glasgow Masonic Burns Club in the Trades House Restaurant. Burns, he said, used everyday words in his writings but with a magic sweep of his pen he produced a phrase which swept the imagination and enthralled the mind. Thus he made us wonder at the beauty of our own language. Burns portrayed the feelings of the masses in the language of the masses. He was, in fact, the multitude articulate, and, because of the simplicity of his themes, the directness of his message, and the beauty of his writings, Robert Burns became not only the National Bard of Scotland, but the bard of humanity.'

The Immortal Memory of Robert Burns was proposed by Dr Catherine Graham Dow at an all woman Burns Supper held in the Grand Hotel by the Glasgow branch of the Women's Educational Union. True to the tradition of the Union, the haggis was borne in by a woman chef and piped in by a woman piper in full Highland dress. In her oration Dr Dow said that Burns was Scotland's magnificent challenge to England in the realm of poetry, and the greatest folk poet of the whole world. He was a pioneer in the message of liberty, declaiming the ideal that laws and conventions could and must be overthrown before a new world could be built; his was the challenge of the unconventional man, the liberator. Dr Dow concluded by saying that the poet's biographers were too apt to ignore his collected letters, in which he emerged as a man of strong masculine judgement, whose social beliefs helped to build the Scotland of his day.

The *Herald* report also touched on gatherings outside the city, especially that hosted by the Mother of all Burns Clubs, Club No 1 at Greenock where, at the Tontine Hotel, the 133rd dinner of the club was held. The Immortal Memory here was proposed by

Professor J.L. Morison, Durham University, a nephew of the late Mr J.B. Morison of Greenock. The good professor said, in the course of his oration:

> Recently I have been trying to fathom the shallow but troubled depths of modern Scottish nationalism in letters, and through comparison with the sane and fundamental 'Scotchness' of Robert Burns to define what are the true qualities of rational Scottish nationality. It is rather startling to be asked by Mr Grieve to believe that 'apart from the Scottish renaissance group the rest of the people in Scotland today are not Scottish to any real sense of the term'...For Mr Grieve the Union is, of course, the culminating disaster; but when he writes of 'the cultural poverty of post Union Scotland,' I thought of that great period from Burns's birthday onwards, the age, in imaginative literature, of Fergusson, Burns and Scott; in philosophy, of Hume, Reid and Dugald Stewart; during which Boswell wrote the greatest of biographies, and Adam Smith the most authoritative of treatises in political economy; when Principal Robertson was publishing histories which we still consult, and Raeburn was doing his best to rival Sir Joshua Reynolds. If this, I thought, be cultural poverty, we could do with more of it today.

The *Herald* noted that special features marked the celebration of the Burns anniversary in Dumfries. In addition to the usual ceremony of laying wreaths from representative bodies on the tomb in St Michael's Churchyard, there was a special ceremony in the reopening, after renovation, of the house in which Burns died. The house had recently come under the direct management of the directors of the Dumfries and Galloway Royal Infirmary, who are the trustees of the property under the will of the poet's son, Colonel William Nicol Burns, and they have carried out its renovation and improvement while still preserving its character as at the time of the poet's death… At yesterday's ceremony, which was broadcast by the BBC, the chairman of the Infirmary, ex-Provost Brodie, presided, and there was a large gathering of representatives of the Town Council, the various Burns clubs in the town and district, and other bodies to see Miss Jean Armour Burns Brown, great-grand daughter of the poet, formally open the door of the house.

Still with the women, a rather novel approach to Burns in this period was shown by Miss Winifred McQuilkan in far-away New Zealand. As a student at Otago University in Dunedin she was well acquainted with Burns through that city's links with the poet's nephew, Thomas, and with the long tradition of Scottishness in that part of New Zealand. In 1935, Miss McQuillan was awarded the University's triennial MacMillan-Brown Prize for 'Excellence in English Composition' for her verse monologue entitled *An then she made the lasses-O* which appeared in the *Otago Times* for Wednesday 22 May 1935. The writer had James Boswell report on happenings in Hell, and of course every writer who was anybody was there – including Burns. It is he who provokes Dr Johnson to a tirade against women and the action deals with how the other famous names respond to this. Naturally, Burns wins out in the end, with the help of the wives of those speaking most against women, but possibly this is one of the most effective – and longest – Toast to the Lassies ever set down. Regrettably, space precludes the insertion of all this very original work here but the following passages will give its distinctive flavour. Boswell is speaking:

I just had noted down Johnson's fierce condemnation
Of Burns, so was ready and free to supply the quotation
I altered a little the swing of the verses
A word here and there – which not for the worse is:

'When Nature, our parent, beloved and benign
First attempted the creatures of earth to design
Inexperienced to fashion our sex she essayed
And then, gaining skill, she created the maid:
So nature, the 'prentice, unused to her tools,
Produced us, my friends – callow bumpkins and fools
While the elegant female, supreme in her pride
Shows what Nature, with practice could do when she tried.
I think, Mr Burns, that is how you express it?'
'The meaning is there – if you pause to undress it,'
Said he with a laugh which I could not explain
In any case Johnson was speaking again:

'I knew, Mr Burns, you were lacking in sense!
Dame Nature with tools: an incongruous pretence!
A poet should not be prevailed on to prate

But Gray was the same – he bade rivers orate
In trumpery ballads what follies can lurk!
Then you say that our sex is a 'prentice's work
While the female, for sooth, is the polished creation!
I attribute such nonsense to inebriation
The place held by women need not be disputed
She is lower than man; and that can't be refuted
Only think to what heights of caprice she can reach!
Why, some of the sex even hanker to preach!
I hear by the radio now of a person
Who actually does – Aimee Semple McPherson
And this is the sex that you laud to the skies
You'll have to retract, Mr Burns, to be wise.'

Said Chesterfield then, 'but we must recollect
The context to which the expression belongs
Remember that Burns is a writer of songs
In those merry trifles, why, what does it matter
To quibble a little in order to flatter
Especially for women for whom as we know
No flattery is ever too high or too low
Of course, we are always superior in fact
To flaunt our supremacy, though, is it tact?
Mr Burns has said this from his true perspicacity
What cause then have we then to impune his veracity?'
'That's cant sir!' cried Johnson 'whatever we write
Must be honestly meant and not merely polite
I know as a man I am very genteel
But yet I have never disguised what I feel
And it's easy to find what this Scotch fellow means
When he glorifies women, his Marys and Jeans
He must understand such a view is absurd
If you've any defence, sir, then let it be heard.'
He turned to the poet expecting to floor him
But Burns remained lounging in silence before him
A good humoured smile as his only reply...

Finally, and only more slightly more seriously, in this survey of pre-war Burns-related happenings, the *Herald* reported that the Prime Minister, the Right Honourable James Ramsay Macdonald, was proposing an Immortal Memory in Swindon. Macdonald, the orphan boy from Lossiemouth who became Britain's first Labour Premier, was then uneasily leading the then National coalition of Labour and Conservative parties which was to bring him down in 1935. Nevertheless, he took time to pay eloquent tribute to Burns at the dinner, where he claimed that:

> Burns's place among the immortals was indisputable...

By 19th September 1937, however, he was no longer Prime Minister but Lord President of the Privy Council. Even so, his words still had an eloquence that had nothing to do with office but came from the heart of the man.

> If our children, if our young men and women today, read more of their Burns, felt more of the manliness of the man, felt in themselves more of that tremendous power of human capacity and human idealism, – the prospects of the next generation would be better than they are...Why is it that Burns lives? It is because Burns was a simple, natural man. He was like a harp, across whose strings the emotions of life had passed and made music...

But the music heard was the wail of the air raid sirens as they announced, on Sunday 3 September 1939, the start of World War 2. It wasn't 'Haughty Gaul' which threatened invasion this time, but haughty Herr Hitler and his Nazi Germany. Like everyone else, the Burns Club members took to their air raid shelters taking with them their gas masks and only their most prized possession – family photos, insurance policies, the family Bible and the Works of Burns. It would be five years before 'normal service could be resumed'. Meantime, in the windows of bombed-out shops and houses framed photos of King George VI and Queen Elizabeth could be seen through the dust and rubble swinging defiantly on what was left of the walls...

The wretch that would a tyrant own,
And the wretch, his true-sworn brother,
Who would set the mob above the throne
May they be damn'd together!
Wha will not sing 'God save the King'
Shall hang as high's the steeple;
But while we sing 'God Save the King'
We'll ne'er forget the people!
(Does Haughty Gaul Invasion Threat?)

6

The Austerity Burns

1945

> His works bear impressed upon them, beyond the possibility of mistake,the stamp of genius.'
> (William Ewart Gladstone)

Unlike the first hostilities in 1914, the 1939 outbreak did not cause a complete cessation of Burns activities in Britain. The *Chronicle* came out in 1940, almost as usual, during what was called the 'Phoney War' and token conferences were held in Glasgow from 1941 and throughout the war, thanks to the initiative of its Lord Provost, Sir Patrick Dolan. The only continuing annoyance was how the clubs dealt with Entertainment Tax levies on all fees paid to speakers and singers engaged for the annual Burns Suppers. Considering they were meeting to honour a former Customs and Excise Officer it seemed ironic that they were now being harried by his 20th-century equivalents.

However, it was in 1941, to mark the Golden Jubilee of the *Burns Chronicle*, that James Ewing, it editor, summed up its aims and intentions and his report is worth repeating here for the clear light it throws on the periodical and its work for Burns and Burnsians since 1885. Mr Ewing wrote:

> During its life the *Chronicle* has altered to some extent in appearance and content, but its original purpose has retained its vitality through times of immense change and upheaval. It is broadly speaking, the voice of the Burns Federation and of people interested in Burns everywhere. It puts on record all aspects of the Federation's aim to disabuse the memory of the poet, to excite admiration for his works and honour for his name. More especially, it acts as a repository of facts relating to Burns and his writings. It likes to leave the facts to speak for

themselves as far as possible, to narrate rather than explain, to put forward authenticated evidence and not wage ghostly wars among theories. Some of its material is specially directed to future writers upon, and critics of, Burns. In other items old ground is sometimes resurveyed, to clear away confusion and error. Numerous inaccuracies in biographies of the poet have been corrected by articles in the *Chronicle*. Innumerable conjectures and mis-statements have been investigated.

In justification of this purpose, it is a fact that nearly every book on the subject of Burns published in the course of the last generation has been indebted for much of its information to articles in the *Burns Chronicle*. The function of being a comprehensive cleaning house for Burnsiana for all sorts has, indeed, proved a substantial part of the *Chronicle*'s achievement, and one of which it is uniquely equipped.

On the other hand the *Chronicle* has also devoted much of its attention to serving in all the ways open to it the more social and personal side of the Burns cult which finds its outlets in annual suppers and dinners and in meetings and lectures. These are recorded, outstanding orations and lectures are published, and notable personalities and events centring round the cult have attention given them.

The *Burns Chronicle* has gathered its material from far and wide during its lifetime, and it may be claimed that it would be hard to find any other possible repository for so much discovery, inquiry and opinion than this tenacious publication, kept alive by nothing more or less – than affection and reverence for the memory of one humble Scotsman whose short span drew to its obscure close more than a century before the *Burns Chronicle* was even contemplated.

James Ewing retired in 1948 after steering through 23 issues. Wartime paper restrictions had prevented any enlargement of the circulation but they didn't stop a record printing of more than 3,000 copies of the 1947 edition. The Third Series began in 1952 and ran to 24 volumes under James Veitch but by 1974 it was losing money and something had to be done to save it. Veitch's sudden death in January 1975 did not help and Arthur Daw was brought in from the *Scots Magazine* in Dundee. He was not a Burns man but he was a newspaper man as indeed was the founder, Colin Rae- Brown, and he kept the ship afloat until James Mackay took over in 1977 and steered it into its modern harbour.

The Registered Office for the Federation is still at the Dick Institute in Elmbank Avenue and the 350 clubs around the world that form the Federation today are still the kind of enthusiasts that Rae-Brown, Mackay and Sneddon would recognise. There is still an annual Burns Supper. There are still meetings to attend, rules to fuss over, traditions to uphold, quarrels to be made up. There is still a President to be elected each year. At the time of writing that office is held by Jim Gibson from Symington who follows in that long line from Provost Sturrock. The average membership age today may be older than it once was, and getting older by the year, but what does age matter when one is dealing with something immortal?

The present administrative offices of the Robert Burns World Federation now look out in baronial splendour from a bower house administration complex in Kilmarnock's Dean Castle Country Park. It is now a limited company with a Chief Executive (Shirley Bell) and an e-mail address that says it all – robertburnsfederation @kilmarnock26.freeserve.co.uk. The old Federation had been finally dragged into the 21st-century recognising that Robert Burns doesn't belong to Scotland but to the world. It is a long way to have come in 200 years – from the Victorian Thames Embankment to cyber space and www.worldburnsclub.com. But some things never change. As long as the Burns focus is maintained its essential message will remain – that hope expressed by the man himself, and by almost every proposer of an Immortal Memory ever since, the Brotherhood of Man. Sadly more than a little ironic in May l945 when atom bombs were dropped on Hiroshima and Nagasaki and the war was over in Europe at least. At the end of the year the Federation announced that 228 clubs were fully paid up and federated and an amnesty would be granted for clubs not paid up. This brought 18 clubs back into the fold, allowing 246 clubs to be represented at the last austerity Conference held at the Mitchell Library, Glasgow in 1946, the 150th anniversary of the death of Burns.

The importance of Glasgow's Mitchell Library to the Burns scene cannot be overstated. Over the years, thanks to careful purchasing and extensive donations, it has built up the largest collection of Burns material in the world, amounting to more than 4,000 items.

There are no less than 900 editions of the Works, including the famous Kilmarnock Edition of 1786, the Edinburgh and London printings of 1787 and that of Philadelphia in the following year. There are ten original manuscripts by Burns including his only letter in Scots and a full set of the Burns Chronicles dating from 1892. If one adds to this examples of translations into more than thirty languages, plus recordings and videos, it can be seen that there is not much about Robert Burns that the Mitchell Library does not know. On Level 4, within the Arts Department, Curator Donald Nelson organises regular exhibitions and lectures relating to the Bard, and from day to day deals with every kind of query about him from every sort of quarter. The present writer, for one, is glad to acknowledge a great debt to this source.

The highlight of the 1946 conference at the library was the speech made by Sir Patrick Dolan. Dr Jim Mackay reported it extensively in his highly-readable 1987 history of the Burns Federation, and part of it is reproduced here with his kind permission. Sir Patrick's motion was:

> This Conference welcomes the formation of the United Nations Organisation. It has been constituted to give effect to the basic principles of the teaching of Robert Burns, namely, the Brotherhood of Man. We recommend that federated Clubs and their members give wholehearted support to this movement. The success of UNO would realise world peace and security, to the furthering of which Robert Burns dedicated his life's work.

Dolan attended the conference as a very sick man, and was not allowed to stand and move this resolution himself. John S Clarke, the Federation's president for that year, spoke for Sir Patrick and rose to speak to the motion in terms that were as meaningful in 1946 as they are today.

> Today it was not so much the greed that came after the last war that was making the people so angry at these conferences. It was fear. Russia was scared of something. America was scared of something. Russia was possibly scared of the atomic bomb which happened to be in the hands of America. It was s great pity that the last secret of Nature had to be used in such a sinister fashion. It was a pity these bombs were ever

> dropped, because mankind now knew that certain people had the power of destroying not only humanity and civilisation but the very planet we lived on. It behoved every Burnsian not to say anything that was going to cause enmity between the nations...

Something of a stir was caused when Alexander Emslie, seconded by William B. Harkness, unexpectedly moved as an amendment:

> That, while in full sympathy with the idea of the brotherhood of man, the Conference pass to the next business, as the resolution is not within the scope of the Constitution of the Burns Federation.

The report continues:

> This was too much for Sir Patrick who, against all medical advice, struggled to his feet to reply. He was astounded that in a meeting of the Burns Federation there should be any opposition to this statement of principle which he had always regarded as fundamental to the Federation. He came to the conclusion some years ago that is world peace was to be established it would have to be by means of an organisation that held men of all parties, all creeds, all nations and all colours, and the only organisation he knew, outside of religious or semi-political bodies, that did that was the Burns Federation. In his opinion this was not a Scottish organisation, but an international organisation founded in Scotland for the purpose of making its message accepted internationally ... if they in that organisation, with affiliations in twelve different countries, were not going to give a lead in the endeavour to build to temple of peace and make security possible, and emancipate the world from the dread and horror of atomic warfare, then he thought they were losing one of the best opportunities they ever had. Not surprisingly, Sir Patrick's resolution was carried by an overwhelming majority.

Although the war was over, war-time restrictions still applied in what was left of the Forties. Lord Woolton ruled at the Ministry of Food. Ration books were still in force and hospitality at dinners and receptions was seriously affected. This did not prevent everyone having a great time at Dunoon where the Federation hosted a dinner-dance at the Pavilion Ballroom – with spam in place of the haggis no doubt. Fortunately, the Burns Clubs of Australia got together to create a 'Britain Fund' which sent food parcels to their hungry brother clubs, and these helped achieve a reasonable 'bill o' fare' when required. The roll of clubs at the time numbered 679, of which two-thirds were active, so there were a few mouths to feed. It was in this time of restraint and restriction that Edwin Muir took time to take a fresh look at the image of Burns in the post-war world. In *The Burns Myth* (1947), he wrote:

> For a Scotsman to see Burns simply as a poet is well-nigh an impossibility. Burns is so deeply imbedded in Scottish life that he cannot be detached from it, from what is best in it and what is worst in it, and regarded as we regard Dunbar or James Hogg or Walter Scott. He is more a personage to us than a poet, more a figurehead than a personage, and more a myth than a figurehead... here is a poet for everybody, a poet who has such an insight into ordinary thoughts and feelings that he can catch them and give them poetic shape, as those who merely think or feel them cannot. This was Burns's supreme art. It seems to be simple. People are inclined to believe that it is easier to express ordinary thoughts and feelings in verse than complex and unusual ones. The problem is an artificial one, for in the end a poet does what he has a supreme gift for doing. Burns's gift lay here; it made him a myth; it predestined him to become the Rabbie of Burns Nights. When we consider Burns we must therefore include the Burns Nights with him, and the Burns cult in all its forms: if we sneer at them we sneer at Burns. They are his reward, or punishment (whichever the fastidious reader may prefer to call it) for having had the temerity to express the ordinary feelings of his people, and having become a part of their life. What the Burns Nights ignore is the perfection of Burns' art, which makes him one of the great poets. But there is so much more involved that this, his real greatness, can be assumed and taken for granted.

This was a cool, dispassionate voice but it wasn't heard by the great majority of Scots who only wanted to put the war behind them and pretend that it had never happened. While the feeling in the country did not equate to the hysteria of 1920, the end of the Forties was a time for trying to pick up the pieces again. The burning topic of debate at the 1948 Conference at Stirling was the projection of a Robert Burns Memorial Theatre or as some delegates saw it, a National Theatre for Scotland. Other delegates, however, had a deep-seated Presbyterian horror of all things theatrical, and saw the hand of Satan behind all the machinations of the stage. This attitude had much to do with the Federation's reaction to an offer made to them by Sir Billy Butlin, the holiday-camp millionaire. Again, resort is made to Dr Mackay's account:

> In September 1947 Billy Butlin, the holiday camp proprietor and entrepreneur, approached John S Clarke, Past-President of the Federation, and said that he was prepared to donate a site, together with the sum of £10,000 towards the building costs, for a Burns Memorial Theatre. The proposed site, within the complex of the Butlin camp at Heads of Ayr, was subsequently inspected by members of the Executive and a plan approved in principle. Consequently Butlin handed over a cheque for £10,000. Presenting his first annual report, at the Stirling Conference in 1948, however, William Black merely added laconically: 'In the interval, the Executive, after full and earnest consideration, have advised Mr Butlin that they cannot commit the Federation to the project envisaged in his offer.'
>
> The President later added, by the way of explanation, that the site offered by Billy Butlin, though very attractive, was too remote from the town of Ayr for the theatre to be a success outside the holiday season. The Federation soon discovered that a theatre such as they had envisaged would actually have cost about £10,000 to build, while the necessary permit to erect it was not likely to be forthcoming for several years anyway. They had hoped that Mr Butlin would allow them to keep the £10,000 until conditions were more favourable, but Butlin believed that the theatre could be built immediately and nagged them into proceeding with the work. They told him that they were not prepared to go ahead at that time and suggested various alternative ways of using the money.
>
> One suggestion was a museum of Scottish folklore to be built on the site. No such museum existed at that time and it was felt that something of the sort, showing country life in the time of Burns, would be an admirable project. The second alternative was to use the money to build ten cottages for old

> people. Sir Patrick Dollan, the President of the Federation, thought that this would have been the most beautiful way of spending the money. Thirdly, it could have been used by the Federation for educational purposes, or fourthly, devoted to literary schemes in which the Federation and other Scottish organisations were interested. None of these ideas appealed to Mr Butlin. That being so, 'they felt that the only course, in keeping with the dignity of the Federation, which they could take, was to return the £10,000, thanking Mr Butlin for his offer and wishing him well in any scheme he might undertake. If a theatre, to be called a Burns Memorial Theatre, was to be provided they hoped that the plays and the programmes to be presented in it would be in keeping with what they regarded as the dignity and the philosophy of the man whose memory they honoured'.
>
> Reading between the lines, we can perhaps afford a wry smile at the contrast between the Federation, trying to maintain pre-war values and standards which must have seemed old fashioned and outmoded to some, and the whizz kid of the holiday camp world, bristling with gimmicks and bustling to try them out. While it is a matter for regret that no way could be found of bridging the cultural gap, in hindsight there is absolutely no doubt that the Federation took the only honourable course open to them.

As a theatre man myself, I can only regret that the chance to build a Robert Burns Memorial Theatre was so simply lost. This is not to deny the highly-charitable alternatives that were put forward. They were worthy, certainly, but they were dull. Small wonder that Sir Billy turned them down. But then there were few visionaries in the Federation at that time. They were all worthy men, but it needed just one with panache, with daring – another Rae-Brown perhaps. Jock Thomson unfettered. Sam Gaw? Certainly, one with faith and trust in Burns himself to realise that a theatre in Burns's name built as early as this would now be just as established as that other Memorial Theatre at Stratford which is a cultural centre in its own right and a continuing Mecca for tourists world-wide.

One remembers that Burns himself attracted tourists in his own day. While he was 'enjoying the fruits of his retirement at Ellisland', according to the London newspapers, the Glasgow coach would often stop at the road end to set down West Country passengers who:

> trusting in the accessibility of the bard, made their way to his

> door... Such visitations – from which no man of genius is free – consumed his time and wasted his substance, for hungry friends could not be entertained on air.

A Robert Burns Theatre might have been the same kind of magnet and not all the Theme Parks, Information Centres, museums, libraries and wee shoppes in all their sum make up for the impact a successful theatre might have had on the local community and on the nation generally.

With this building as a *locus*, we would have had by this time new Burns plays and musicals, concerts, recitals, seminars, talks and illustrated lectures, parties and the whole pan-jamboree of Burns events and all in one recognised centre in Ayr. We might even have had that long-awaited Burns opera. It would be now the focus for all things Burnsian and the world would have flocked to it. The lost opportunities hardly bear thinking about, but a gathering of grey hairs, no doubt highly suspicious of anything 'theatrical' – it was so UN-Scottish – decided in their collective wisdom to spurn a generous offer and it was one that would not be repeated. But then few at Stirling were *entrepeneurs*. They can hardly be blamed for refusing to think outside the parameters of their experience which for the most part were small business practices and the respectable professions. They followed the normal reaction of all committees: 'When in doubt – do nowt'.

Yet it did not prevent this same company of gentlemen acting as artistic censor in the name of Burns. When Robert McLellan's play 'Rab Mossgiel' was belatedly televised on 22nd September, it gave a view of the poet which upset many Burnsians, despite an excellent cast, which included Bryden Murdoch as Burns, Gwyneth Guthrie as Mary Campbell, Eileen McCallum as Jean Armour and Rona Anderson as Clarinda. An anonymous review in the 1960 *Chronicle*, stated:

> The playwright's conception of Burns was of a depressed, distraught, skulking, two-faced sex ridden lout...it is characteristic of some Scots to disparage greatness. If one of their own kind is larger than life, it is their mission to cut him down to size. No matter how the rest of the world regards him, they must dwell upon his failings and his weaknesses.

A young actor-singer, Robin Hall, not yet paired with partner, Jimmy MacGregor, also drew criticism of a long playing record launched by Collector Records as a bicentenary tribute. The *Chronicle* took him to task for his rendition of *A Man's a Man* – 'he himself was at fault, his Doric being suspect'. When Iain Hamilton's *Burns Sinfonia for Two Orchestras* was performed at the 1959 Edinburgh Festival it provoked the ire of that year's conference. To be fair, the first performance also had rather a mixed reception from the music critics. Christopher Grier, in the *Scotsman*, pointed out that:

> There are not many in Edinburgh, even in mid Festival, who are sufficiently versed in this musical language to deliver a judgement of much weight. But of the imagination, seriousness of purpose and skill that went into its making there is no doubt whatever.

David Harper in the *Daily Mail*, however, voiced the more popular reaction:

> Burns must have revolved rapidly in his grave. Tolerant though he was, he could not have been expected to bear with the unpoetic sounds created by modern dodecaphonic composers.

In more recent years, however, the Federation, to its credit, has been more aware of the practical value of cultural events in relation to Burns and has become more involved in the Burns festivals and symposia which have been held in all the Burns centres – Ayr, Kilmarnock, Edinburgh and Dumfries. However, it was in none of these centres, but Bristol in England that the Annual Burns Conference, postponed from 1939, took place in 1950.

As soon as the decade turned, all Burnsian minds were directed to the prospect of the Bicentenary of the birth of Burns in 1959 and these thoughts focussed entirely on the demand for a Burns stamp in time for that great celebration, especially as at that time, Russia's Postmaster General had already issued a Burns stamp. This was a matter of great pride to them but it caused some consternation among Burnsians in Britain.

I have three Russian books in my Burns collection, that is three books of Burns in Russian, each of them given me by Russians in

Moscow. I mention this because around this time, an inspiring speaker and teacher was the leading Burns scholar of the age and the best-known translator of Burns into the Russian language, for which he was suitably honoured by the Burns Federation. This was the famous Samuil Marshak. One of my books on Burns was by this same man and was given to me by his son Immanuel Marshak. However, not even Professor Marshak's prestigious presence could procure the promise of a British stamp for Burns, despite the heroic efforts of British MP Emrys Hughes in Moscow. Mr Hughes was then the MP for South Ayrshire and even made the point of learning Russian so that he could speak the language when he went to Moscow in 1959. We anticipate the next chapter here, but it is all germane to Burns and Russia.

Emrys Hughes had begun battling for a 1959 Burns stamp since 1953 and in 1958 he was part of a Scottish deputation which met with the then Prime Minister, and part-Scot from the Isle of Arran, Harold Macmillan. The urbane Macmillan said he would 'consider the matter carefully' which meant he would pass it on to the then Postmaster General, Ernest Marples, who was not a noted Scot, and who of course rejected the idea completely. However, Hughes obtained a kind of revenge on Macmillan when they were both in Moscow in 1959. The Prime Minister was there on Government business and Hughes was there to speak on Burns in the Tchaikovsky Hall in reply to Samuil Marshak. It was here that the Russian Postmaster General handed Hughes a letter with the Russian Burn stamp affixed. As the MP said, 'It was a moment of humiliation for me'. The next night, both Hughes and Marshak were invited to a reception in the British Embassy hosted by Macmillan. Marshak presented the Premier with his translation of Burns, and was given in exchange a first edition of a Dickens. Hughes took the chance to slip the Russian letter with the Burns stamp to Macmillan who asked, 'What's this?'

'Send it to Marples,' said Hughes.

Government wheels began to turn from that time.

Meantime Scottish enthusiasts made their own preparations for the great mailing day. Things were hurriedly arranged to get a special Alloway postmark out on the actual birthday and, even though it was a Sunday, thousands of people availed themselves of the once-in-a-lifetime opportunity. So much so that extra offices were opened in Dumfries, Edinburgh and Glasgow to deal with the rush. Despite this obvious popular demand, London remained unimpressed. The whole of Scotland then seemed to take up the cause but the Civil Service mind was tightly closed and took cover behind the rubber-stamped parapets of its own regulations. There would be no stamp that year. It was the Burns Federation that had been licked. London still ruled. 'That great city' as Burns had termed it remained quite indifferent to Burns, to Scotland and to Scots. Never mind, the Scots knew that the stamp of greatness on the high Burns brow was still there and that no amount of London indifference or civil service apathy could efface it.

It made no difference to officialdom that Russia had issued not one, but two Burns stamps and had linked Burns with its own Pushkin as twin-poets of all the Russias, Aleksandr Sergeyvich Pushkin. The Robert Burns-Alexander Pushkin Friendship Club still exists in Moscow and its list of honorary members includes such names as Bertrand Russell, John Steinbeck and Emrys Hughes of course. In 1964, this club, with the help of Professor Peter Henry, then head of Slavonic Studies at Glasgow University, would produce a bilingual booklet, *The Immortal Memory of Robert Burns*. Interestingly, Pushkin himself, although Russian, was a black man or at least a half-caste. This prompts the thought that Burns, in the course of his short life never met a coloured man of any kind, even in Edinburgh. A man's a man and all that, and it certainly would not have bothered him, but it might have intrigued him.

There is no record of his ever coming face to face with an Asiatic or any kind of brown skin in Edinburgh, despite the fashion in high society then for Moorish pages and attendants from the Indies and Burns did write later of going to the Indies himself as a 'negro-driver'. During the Border tour with Ainslie Captain Rutherford at Jedburgh captivated him with his tale of being captured by the Chippawah Indians during the War of Independence. This was all very exotic stuff for a young Ayrshire farmer and worlds away from his experience. But we digress.

In 1957, the Glasgow Ayrshire Society invited Dr Ronald Mavor, that well-known man about Scottish letters, drama critic, director, playwright, painter, pianist and Fellow of the Royal Society of

Surgeons, to propose the Immortal Memory at their annual Burns Dinner. 'Bingo' Mavor is also the son of the late Osborne Mavor, otherwise, James Bridie, the playwright who was also a doctor, and who, in 1943, founded the Glasgow Citizens' Theatre. Bingo has grown up with a literary and theatrical as well as medical background, so it was no surprise when he opened his Burns speech with Gertrude Stein. It appears that she, on her death-bed, kept asking: 'What is the answer, what is the answer?' A friend, sitting by the bed, hurried to reassure Miss Stein, by saying, 'There is no answer, Gertrude, there is no answer.' To which Gertrude Stein replied 'If there is no answer, what then, what is the question?' Bingo then went on:

> A distinguished anthropologist was studying the problem of telepathy in South America. It seems that it is still the custom of some tribes to communicate telepathically. The wife will go out and speak to a tree, saying that she wants her husband to come back early from the town and he will come back early. This anthropologist was most interested in the phenomenon and asked one of the women of the village – 'Why do you go and speak to a tree when you wish to send a message to your husband?' Her reply was immediate. 'Because we are poor,' she said. 'If we were rich we would have the telephone.'
>
> As I rise to my feet this evening it is borne in upon me, as it was upon Miss Stein, that there is no answer. But if there is no answer, as she rightly said. what, then, is the question? You will perhaps forgive me if I do not start at the beginning with 'what is the chief end of man?' Nowadays we ask different questions like 'Should I let my daughter go to a Rock n Roll concert? Or 'Would I have a better opportunity in Canada?' If we are going to do more than take a cup of kindness yet for auld lang syne this evening, it is among such questions that we must find our questions and it is in such a world that we must seek for our answers. To be sure, there is something rich and strange in sending one's messages echoing through the ether from the wind- borne branches of an ancient oak but let us, as they say, let us face it, the telephone is more reliable. Our world of today contains not only the lark on the wing and the snail on the thorn but the Archers on the Light, and the Groves on the Tele. Have we room for the poet Burns?
>
> I have had the pleasure of attending a fair number of Burns

Nights one way and another and under the most variable of auspices. At all of them I have been impressed by the constancy with which the orator projects his personality onto the life history of the poet. I was at a Communist dinner in which Burns was held up as a looking glass to Lenin. A jovial fellow saw him as the most jovial of fellows, a wild man as the king of bawdry, an underdog as the daringest snapper at the heels of the mighty. Catherine Carswell saw him as a heroic DH Lawrence-like figure rising from the good earth to smite the Philistine. Maurice Lindsay as a Lallans poet – which, of course, he was...So it is with a full consciousness of my on foolhardiness that I venture to turn your thoughts to the life of Robert Burns. But I will not shirk my commission. I am aware that I am celebrating a rite. At this point in the ritual I must lay out before you – as an oriental dealer his carpet – the pattern of that short life.

In the play *The Lark* by Jean Anouilh – which is about Joan of Arc – there is a noble scene at the end when the stake has been prepared and the fire is about to be lit. The Dauphin comes right out of the play and across the centuries and says, 'No, it mustn't end like this. It wasn't a sad story at all. We have been playing the happy story of Joan of Arc.' And the faggots are torn down and the banners are brought in and we are back at the crowning of the King of France at the Cathedral of Rheims. So this will be the happy story of Robert Burns.

Certainly there were hard times. It was hard times that drove William Burnes of the Mearns down to Edinburgh and out west to Alloway village. Even in that hard winter of the middle of the eighteenth century in Scotland may he not have felt in Edinburgh the rising of the sap that was to bring the new spring in less than fifty years and make Edinburgh the cultural capital of the world? Times were hard at Mount Oliphant and little better, or only for a time at Lochlie with the father growing prematurely old and the boys doing all the work. But when William Burnes died and the farm was teetering on the verge of bankruptcy the brothers found a good friend in Gavin Hamilton to lease them Mossgiel and let them start again. It was a hard life but the Burnes family were used to hardness. It was neither squalid nor soul-destroying.The young Burns (as he came to call himself) was frustrated, displeased and dissatisfied with his lot. The social stratification of Ayrshire society offended him – 'proud man'. 'The great misfortune of my life,' he said, 'was not to have an aim – I had felt early some stirrings of Ambition, but they were the blind gropings of Homer's Cyclops round the walls of his cave.'

In this state of mind surprising? Is this out of date? Are not our present day aspiring men of letters still so? Colin Wilson is termed an 'Outsider', John Osborne is the 'Angry Young Man', wasn't Burns both? Suddenly, it seems to me, he comes into focus at this point – as we gaze back through those hundred and seventy years. Here is Rab Mossgiel, age twenty five, farmer. He has a local reputation as a rhymester and rustic bard. A good man at a party but always a bit of a rebel. As I said, an angry young man. Proud and outspoken on many subjects, notably the Auld Lichts of the Kirk with whom he has crossed a sword or two. For some years his friends have recommended him to send some of his poems to the reviews. This is in Mauchline, in Ayrshire, in 1784 and 1785. And then suddenly it all changes.

In relating history one must be careful to avoid false emphasis and giving false impression by changing the sequence of events.

Anyway, in the first half of 1786 Jean Armour, the daughter of a neighbouring and wealthier, farmer became pregnant to Robert Burns. He proposed her marriage, her father opposed the marriage and she rejected him. The fact that old Armour preferred a bastard grandson to himself as a son in law was a severe blow to Burns' hypersensitive pride. He decided to go to Jamaica. Where before he had idly thought of publishing his poems, it now became an urgent compulsion – a last gesture. He would show Scotland what sort of man she had driven out to the Indies as a 'negro-driver'.

Events followed thick upon the other – old Armour sued him for the upkeep of the child. His fated affair with Mary Campbell was at its perihelion. The Reverend Mr Auld summoned him to the penitent's stool. And then, out of the blue – or rather, on the 31st July 1786 the *Kilmarnock Edition* appeared – and everything changed for Robert Burns. He was suddenly the hero of the day. The Sheriff's Officers daren't touch him. Armour withdrew his writ – and his daughter – and Burns found that he was famous. At least locally.

Two months later Burns set off for Edinburgh for his first

taste of the high life and, like many another since, became a less angry young man and less of an Outsider. He did a few grand tours through Scotland of which he was now the crowned bard and arranged for the second edition of his poems. More importantly he met James Johnson, an engraver and music publisher and was begun on his life-work of saving songs. I am not an Auld Licht. I do not believe in predestination. Therefore I believe that Burns had a choice; three choices. But perhaps we only think we choose; and we are so made that at such a point in the weaving of our lives we can follow the thread only one way.

Burns was the Golden Boy of the Edinburgh *literati*. The Man of Feeling had clutched him to his breast, praising to the sky all the poems that today we blush for. Could he not have become a literary gent contributing to the weeklies, odes and verses on the lines of 'Edina, Scotia's darling seat' and 'Something like moisture conglobes in my eye?' Could he not have further wrought his considerable skill in producing literary poetry in the styles of Montgomerie, Dunbar and Fergusson and have become a Scottish Masefield, a Scottish Tennyson, a Scottish T S Eliot? In fact it is virtually only in *Tam o Shanter* that this brilliant 'academic' skill is deployed again.

As I mentioned, the Edinburgh meting with Johnson set Burns off writing and collecting songs for Johnson's *Musical Museum*. With an industry, with an absorption and with a genius probably never equalled, he gathered, edited, adapted, and frequently wrote what is to all intents and purposes our whole heritage of song in the Scots language. He would accept no money. He would not acknowledge the extent to which a published song was collected, adapted or written by himself. It was an astonishing work for a man who had still financial difficulties in his new farm at Ellisland and who had recently had the most remarkable publishing success in Scottish history – soon however, to be somewhat outdone by the Waverley Novels.

David Daiches has suggested that Burns' total absorption in the work of the *Musical Museum* and the later *Select Scottish Airs* proved the one way in which he could escape from his split personality – 'from the basic conflict between Rab Mossgiel and Robin Burnes, between the son of William Burnes and the Caledonian Hunt's delight, between the lover of Jean Armour and the correspondent of Clarinda, between the peasant and the man of letters.' That is well said. Perhaps he could no other...

This is an unromantic age. It is not an age to speak of 'heaven-sent ploughmen'. Every second new novel is by Angus Wilson or some heaven-sent boot-and-shoe operative, or heaven-sent British Museum librarian or even heaven-sent secretary to James Joyce. Nor with Sam Beckett or with the third thousand of Hungarian refugees on our doorstep are we to bemoan the barren soil of Mount Oliphant too much. The shade of John Knox now thunders silently at the thousands who crowd the Assembly Hall for the music and dancing of Cedric Thorpe Davie and Edinburgh, occupied with its Festival, heeds him not. The Auld Lichts have moved to the southern suburbs of Aberdeen or to Sunday morning television. George the Third is dead. America is free. The French Revolution is over. Freedom is so much in the air that we have stopped asking for it in this country and have had to start giving it away in places like Africa. Even Canada is fighting for it – although they do it in French. Or a kind of French.

So shall we just roll up this life again for another three hundred and sixty five days? I think not.

I have suggested that the pattern of this life was of honest toil coupled with ill-defined ambition and aspiration. That there came a moment when something in that life seemed to catch fire and blaze up and shine, in a moment, across the world. In that moment of incandescence, Burns saw and clutched at and held to the one thread in design – the one path that his true spirit could follow. That the songs of Robert Burns – the songs of Scotland – are the result of that choice.

Here in the middle of Glasgow with the river gently flowing down to the Ayrshire coast and out into the Atlantic with the subway rushing like an old mole up to the Cowcaddens and down and across to Govan with Argyle street not a hundred yards away and with, above the lights and the buildings, the same old sky...the sky he once saw, and in it yet, however old it has become his star still shines.

Which is why. here in Glasgow in 1957, I give you with honour and with gratitude – and with no cant – the Memory of Robert Burns.

Dr Mavor went on to greater prominence, becoming the Director of the Scottish Arts Council and a Dean of Dramatic Studies in Saskatchewan, Canada, but he never bettered the eloquence he showed on behalf of Burns to the men of Ayrshire gathered that night in Glasgow.

Meantime, the Burns stamp business continued to bother the Burnsians. It occurs to me that one good idea might have been to send the Russian Post-master general a Burns stamped letter from that other Moscow in Ayrshire. Had they done so, however, they would have to have waited until February 1, 1966, when that ex-aristocrat become Socialist, Anthony Wedgwood-Benn announced in the House of Commons that a stamp commemorating Robert Burns would be issued officially. What is a surprise is that he did not call for the singing of the *Internationale* when he did so.

The only time I have heard this anthem sung at a Burns supper was years later, in 2000, when I was the non-speaking guest of the Milngavie Labour Club and the Immortal Memory was proposed by Danny McCafferty. He spoke that night having just had a serious heart operation, but there was no doubt his heart was still in the right place.

> After 204 years of speechifying about the Bard, there is little to be said, which has not been said or written a thousand times over. Having stated that, you're going to hear it again, and I hope again and again, for many years to come.
>
> Robert Burns, was not what we may call nowadays, politically correct, so if you are of that inclination...forget it. It would be a disservice to attempt to sanitize or rehabilitate Rabbie after 204 years...and I will not insult his memory by doing so.
>
> There is however a matter of accuracy. Burns did not drink himself to an early grave. Nor did he die of tuberculosis exacerbated by wild nights and loose living. His genius and clarity of thought remained until his last breath. He died of endocarditis, a form of heart disease brought on and worsened by years of excessive labouring in the field. The reputation of Robert Burns, as a decadent drunkard who consorted with whores and suffered from venereal disease is a reputation created largely by his first biographer, Dr James Currie, a Liverpool physician... moralist and strict teetotaller who to his shame, deliberately chose to present the poet not

only as a genius, but also in such a light as to promote Currie's own morality and 'tea-total' values. He used the fame of Burns to propagate the message that loose living and hard drinking can ultimately bring only doom.
(stop here for sip of whisky).

In short, Dr Currie was an eejit!!

Robert Burns enjoyed a laugh but he also had a melancholic, almost depressive side. On the opposite extreme he had a carefree spirit and an abundance of optimism. He was deeply religious, but no respecter of hypocrisy or cant. 'I am a sincere believer in the Bible, but I am drawn by the conviction of a man, not by the halter of an ass.' Burns bowed to the Church in penitence for his sins and went out to commit as many again... he was a fervent and passionate patriot of Scotland but found no difficulty in swearing allegiance to the Crown as a member of the Excise or on joining with the Dumfries Volunteers, a local militia. He had no great regard for Lords and Ladies, Earls and Dukes, yet he moved freely in their company like a latter day Billy Connolly. Speaking of the aristocracy, Prince Charles was once invited to a Burns Supper and turned up wearing a hat made of fox fur. His hosts, naturally curious, could resist no longer. 'May I ask you why you are wearing that hat Your Highness?' inquired one of the guests. 'Well', says Charles 'I was just about to leave the Palace when my pater, the Duke of Edinburgh, you know, asked where I was going.'
'To a Burns Supper in Glenshoogly,' I said, to which my pater distinctly said 'Wear a fox hat.'

Burns was not a Royalist but he was a Unionist, a Nationalist, a Republican and an Internationalist. Not all things to all people but a part of all people. He was not an unsung hero of his times, but widely acknowledged and acclaimed as a living genius as testified by the estimated 12,000 mourners of all ranks, classes and title at his funeral.

Discretion was no friend of Burns. When at a function the health of William Pitt was proposed, Robert was asked to leave on proposing the 'health of a greater and better man, George Washington'. He was subsequently accused of being a Democrat!! Despite that incident, Pitt himself later paid tribute, saying of Burns's poetry – 'I can think of no verse since Shakespeare that has so much the appearance of coming sweetly from nature.' [He] was a member of no political club or society, and when voices from such quarters were raised in revolutionary rhetoric his was not among them. Opinions, he most certainly had 'May your success in this war be equal to the justice of its cause.'

A lover of liberty, a lover of people, but tied to no one political ideology above any other... Burns deserves his Immortal Memory for his love of life, love of humanity and the gifts he has bestowed upon us all. All peoples. Not just in Scotland. But all over the world. That's what makes him international.Internationalism to many people is about football matches increasingly so at club level. So much so, that the cries now abound at games between Rangers and Celtic in a multilingual fashion. No longer Orange and Green, but a rainbow coalition of noise no longer sectarian, but internationalist. Sweary words in every language. In a funny sort of way it has its merits. There are those who bemoan the influx of foreign players into the Scottish game as a bad thing for home grown talent, because our young players can't compete at the same skills level. On the other hand it provides a perspective on the world, rather than the narrow constraints of nationalist vision which says home grown is always best. In its own way it helps to broaden outlooks. We inhabit a world and not just a country...

There can be no more appropriate subject, other than internationalism, that can be added to the annual celebration of the life and works of Scotland's other Burns. Very few figures in literary history have capture the imagination of world's population as did Scotland's most famous poet, Robert Burns. He did so through his blunt honesty, his subtle charm, his warmth and passion, his optimism and vision, as well as his despair and vulnerability. He was a genius, yet with a simplicity about him. He is claimed as a nationalist, a unionist, a socialist, a republican and a royalist. He was a man blessed with supreme talent and yet so insecure. He was no hypocrite despite these contradictory characteristics. He was human, a man of the people, all of the people, with no one, narrow section able to lay claim to him as theirs and theirs alone. Therein, I believe lies the international appeal of Robert Burns. A man who practised social inclusion before politicians got their hands on it. A man who believed in equality and social justice as being more than simply words. A man who viewed poverty as a condition not a requirement.

Burns is not only remembered by the international community, he did much to bring it closer together though a philosophical and ideological vision, 'that man to man the world o'er will brithers be for a' that'. I am sure he was a creature of his times as well as ours and meant no disrespect to our sisters when he wrote it. It equally applies in its sentiments of unity and comradeship towards women in our modern world.

Some people choose to practise international humanitarism through voluntary or charitable means sometimes physically assisting at the direct point of need, more often through financial contributions. Some are determined to bring about social and political change within suppressed or underdeveloped countries. Some campaign for peace to bring about change. Some go to war. If the underpinning ideology of international relations is that of social justice, healing, caring, sharing, loving and understanding then the world is the better. If it is a philosophy built on greed, division domination and exploitation then it must be opposed. Burns has contributed to the former philosophy through his poetry and music. He has not been alone. Other artists have made a great contribution too. But tonight belongs to Burns...

The great surge of international solidarity in our time such as the American Civil Rights Movement, Cuba, Vietnam War, Solidarity with Chile Campaign and the Anti Apartheid struggles coupled with the international dimension to the Campaign for Nuclear Disarmament helped shaped philosophies and outlook in life for any here tonight, myself included. Each generation is influenced by international events and actions. Burns was similarly affected by the American War of Independence and the French Revolution.

Internationalism draws the young and captures imaginations more than domestic politics. It is something which, as a labour movement, bemoaning the lack of interest of youth in modern politics that we have failed to recognise and channel. It perhaps says something about our own failings, ceasing to involve ourselves in the international dimension as we grow older, more comfortable and more complacent but we will not harness the spirit, energies and talents of young people without a global vision of socialism. And you have to remember that Robert Burns was always young.

Communication is at the heart of drawing people together

in a common global cause. In the 21st-century communication technology, especially in respect of visual media, has made the world a smaller place than it may have seemed before. There is no hiding place for injustice, no excuse of returning away from what we know to be wrong. Chechnya, Somalia, Rwanda, Bosnia, Croatia, Palestine, are no longer remote but on our doorstep and in our living rooms.

One hundred years ago, workers in far flung corners of the globe would read in trade union newspapers about strikes halfway around the planet. Sometimes they would dig deep into their pockets and send much needed financial support. The struggle may have been crushed before it arrived. Now there is instant access to the world's population. We are in the information age where knowledge is not only power but can create movements. The European wide campaign on fuel, the tactics used and the way in which physical forces could be mobilised points to a new dimension in how to harness the internet to bring about social change. Such change can be for the better or worse and we ignore the political potential at our risk...

Robert Burns had no time for humbug or hypocrisy, only for people, and not just the people of Scotland as can be seen in his support for the French Revolution, the birthplace of modern internationalism. He had time for the people of the world. In return, the people of the world have taken him to their hearts.

I ask you to stand with me for a toast to the Immortal Memory of Robert Burns and to couple it with it a toast to all the people of the world in his name.

The Internationale was then sung lustily by all assembled.

Arise you pris'ners of starvation,
Arise, you wretched of the earth;
For justice thunders condemnation
A better world's in birth.
No more tradition's chains shall bind us,
Arise, ye slaves, no ore in thrall,
The earth shall rise on new foundations,
We have been naught, we shall be all.

'Tis the final conflict, let each stand in his place,

> The Internationale shall be the human race,
> 'Tis the final conflict, let each stand in his place,
> The Internationale shall be the human race.

It is not the kind of song you hear often in douce Milngavie – even at a Burns Supper.

As the Fifties drew to a close, minds were already turning to the Bicentenary of the birth but Burnsians still had to get there by the usual route with regular stops for refreshments every 25th of January. And nowhere more so than in the United States where the anniversary flourished to a much greater extent than in Scotland, but then, even if Scots won't admit it, The United States are much bigger than Scotland. Never mind, there are plenty of Scots throughout America and Burns Clubs abound. One very enterprising example is in St Louis, Missouri where the members not only observe the Burns civilities on their due day or thereabouts but print copies in hardback of the proceedings and the following is taken from their printed account of several such suppers between 1955 and 1964 edited by their very capable secretary, Irvin Mattick. On January 25, 1956, the speaker was Michael Gerard and his theme for the Immortal Memory that night was 'The Education of Robert Burns'.

> My only connection with the Scottish nation was one year which I spent as a member of the Argyll and Sutherland Highlanders... During that year, and later with the 15th Scottish Division, I learnt to admire the supremacy of the Scotsman in two things: fighting a battle and singing a song, and it seems to me now that that is no bad qualification for discussing Robert Burns. In fact, what is most necessary is just a mind that is quick to respond to laughter and song sparked by a certain frankness and devilry. The only disqualification is squeamishness. One of the dullest and most unsympathetic accounts of Burns was written by a fellow Scot, Robert Louis Stevenson, and the reason for his failure may be found in the confession, – 'I made a kind of chronological table of his various loves and lusts, and have been comparatively speechless ever since.' Finding that I have survived the impact rather better, and am still comparatively articulate, I shall proceed to my subject. The formula I have found for Burns is that of the poet fighting to be free of the world, of the prisonhouse, and my theory is that poetry comes when the

world has been put in its place, and what puts the world in its place is education.

Similarly, it is true that a good deal of verse and some poetry came from Burns right from the beginning. There is no time when philosophy ends and poetry begins. There is no time when education ends and life begins. Still, it is true that much of the earlier verse is derivative, much of it – and that the most interesting – satirical; and satire is poetry meant to put the world in its place, not poetry for the sake of the thing itself. In a letter to Peter Hill he wrote, 'We are placed here amid so much nakedness and hunger, and poverty and want that we are under a damning necessity of studying selfishness, caution, and prudence.' He opposed all the genial warmth which society, love and poetry inspired in him. Never vicious, but always susceptible, he wrote for himself when he said, 'To the sons and daughters of labour and poverty, the ardent hope, the stolen interview, the tender farewell, are the greatest and most delicious parts of their enjoyment.' And love led to composition: 'My passions when once they were lighted up, raged like so many devils, till they got vent in rhyme.'

In the account written to Dr Moore he dwells less on the details of his family's poverty and his own ruin, than on the details of his initiation into Love and Poesy, and equally with these the details of his reading. From *The Vision of Mirza* and a hymn of Addison's, through school books, farming manuals, and religious works, to poetry and novels, they are recorded. In later letters we find him reading Dryden's Virgil, and Pope's Homer, and a whole list of 17th and 18th-century dramatists. At the surveying school at Kirkoswald, he says, 'I had met with a collection of letters by the Wits of Queen Anne's reign, and I pored over them most devoutly. I engaged several of my schoolfellows to keep up a literary correspondence with me,' and 'literary correspondence' remained a great solace and delight to him the rest of his life. Social life was the sovereign remedy for Burns' ills, and in that, too, he knew that it was his 'reputation for bookish knowledge, a certain wild, logical talent, and a strength of thought something like the rudiments of good sense, (that) made (him) generally a welcome guest.' He was also in the habit of writing, for the imaginary company every man keeps when alone, in a series of Commonplace books, to which he would confide, for example, the 'uneasiness and chagrin' with which he compared the reception of a poor genius (like himself) with that of a rich dullard 'decorated with the trappings and futile distinctions of Fortune.' By these means Burns educated himself to meet poverty without rage or frustration. When he expressed himself on the subject in verse, always more concentrated and final than prose, as in *An Epistle to Davie*, a Brother Poet, he began,

> I tent less, and want less
> their roomy fireside;
> But hanker and canker
> To see their cursed pride.
> It's hardly in a body's power
> To keep at times from being sour
> To see how things are shared,

But concluded,

> Misfortunes 'gie the wit of age to youth;
> They let us ken oursel;
> They mak'us see the naked truth,
> The real guid and ill.'

Thus the fight against poverty was won.

'In this country,' he wrote to John Beugo, 'the only things that are to be found in any degree of perfection are stupidity and canting. Prose they know only in graces, prayers, etc, and the value of these they estimate – by the ell!' just how uncharitable the church was, just how far its petty tyranny could go, none knew better than Burns. His own father never forgave him for attending a Country Dancing Class. He came under fire for his drinking and wild talk. And when finally Jean Armour bore his illegitimate child, he had to listen to the minister rebuke him before the congregation with the words, 'like the dog to his vomit, or like the sow that is washed to her wallowing in the mire.'

Again his reading came to the rescue. He had fed his mind on Stackhouse's *History of the Bible*, and Taylor's *Scripture Doctrine of Original Sin*. A year or so later, while still on his father's farm, he was active in founding a Bachelor's Debating Club. It would be worth much more than all our discussions and speculation to hear Burns with his 'wild logical talent' armed with the arguments of John Taylor, holding forth

> before the bachelors of Tarbolton. He had long been, he tells us, so active in polemical divinity, and used to 'puzzle Calvinism with so much heat and indiscretion' that (he) raised a hue and cry of heresy against (himself)... At the end of this period he wrote to William Nicol, 'I have bough a pocket Milton, which I carry perpetually about with me in order to study the sentiments – the dauntless magnanimity, the intrepid, unyielding independence, the desperate daring and noble defiance of hardship – in that great personage, Satan.' But Burns was never 'of the Devil's party without knowing it.' Later, when he had turned from satire to song, he made it abundantly clear that his education, in arming him for this fight also, had not delivered him over to any violent extreme.
>
> In 1789 he confided to Mrs Dunlop that he still remembered his childhood reading of *The Vision of Mirza*, Addison's allegory of the dangerous bridge of life over the tide of eternity, and that he still felt on certain days 'an elevation of soul like the enthusiasm of Devotion and Poetry.' The letter is of course one of his literary compositions, in which he played for membership of polite, rational 18th-century Society, but that need not mean that he is insincere. Certainly we believe him when he ends, 'I am a very sincere believer in the Bible; but I am drawn by the conviction of a man, not the halter of an ass.' And there, Gentleman, I shall end...

And why not? In the following year (1957) St Louis was treated to the theme of 'Scotland in the Time of Burns' by Thomas S. Duncan:

> It seems appropriate to preface this sketch with a sentence taken from F Fraser Darling's little book, *The Story of Scotland*. The members of the club will have reached the point in their celebrations where the mood is genial and they are not inclined to take offence at what may be only a partial judgment. Darling says, a propos of Burns as one of the leaders in the Scottish renaissance, 'Burns, 1759-96, was a poor Ayrshire cottar's son, a child of the soil and a lover of nature. He has suffered in reputation from his too perfervid admirers, usually exiled Scots who have formed societies in his name wherein they may indulge their nostalgia, their convivial proclivities and their capacity of adulation of their own race.' When one considers how difficult it was for the Scots to have any important part in government affairs after

> the union, the following facts afford some satisfaction. In 1758, Horace Walpole said of them, 'The Scots are the most accomplished nation in Europe.'
>
> Two of the men who did most to shape the age's mind shaped theirs in Scots classrooms and round Scots dinner tables. They were David Hume (1711-76) and Adam Smith (1723-90). Professor Sorley said of them, 'There is no third person writing in the English language during the same period who has had so much influence on the opinions of mankind.' Leslie Stephen considered Hume to be 'the acutest thinker in Great Britain of the eighteenth century, and the most qualified interpreter of its intellectual tendencies.' Hume's famous *Treatise of Human Nature and Causes of the Wealth of Nations*. It is noteworthy that John Buchan on Edinburgh, which, of course, was the centre of the new Scottish life, says 'Edinburgh was a true capital, a clearinghouse for the world's culture and a jealous repertory of Scots tradition. Below the comely surface there were new forces working of which even the illuminate Whigs knew little; but the surface was all cheerfulness, good fellowship and a modest pride – an agreeable cosmopolitanism – but the scene was idiomatically Scottish.'
>
> In this brief sketch we have indulged a good earl in 'the adulation of our own race' as the critic mentioned at the beginning accused us of doing, but it is to be noted that our adulation has consisted chiefly in the statement of facts and not in the claim of qualities possessed by the Scot. But should anyone apologise for adulation where the subject is the great Scot who, while proud of race, included all in his broad sympathy, and could think of nothing better than the coming of a time when he might call all men brothers?

Quite so.

And finally, in this triumvirate of views from St Louis, we have a discourse dealing with 'Robert Burns – From Alloway to Lochlea' given on January 25 1957:

> One hundred ninety eight years ago the 'banks and braes' of Doon bloomed as fresh and fair as today. Long before, Roman legions fought their way through its valley, and memories of strange deeds, some brave, some bad, clung round the walls of the castles by its banks. Doon was then

unknown to fame. The fortress on Loch Doon is now a neglected ruin, overgrown with weeds, the haunt of hawk and heron. The very site of many an ancient keep has been forgotten, yet an 'auld clay biggin' has become a shrine to which pilgrims come in thousands year by year. An 'auld Kirk,' scarcely even picturesque, is protected with jealous care. An 'auld brig,' no longer fit for traffic, is more famous than the greatest triumph of engineering skill, and 'bonnie Doon' is known wherever men speak the English tongue.

To the banks of this stream in Ayrshire, William Burnes, who had labored for some years in the neighbourhood of Edinburgh as a gardener, found his way in 1752 to become gardener to Mr Crawford of Doonside. He was a frugal man, and industrious. He was deeply religious and disliked bigotry in any form. He best loved plants, animals, small children and his own dignity. William Burnes rented a piece of ground in Alloway, and while continuing his service with Mr Crawford, he planted a market garden and built with his own hands a humble clay cottage. It was a simple 'but and ben,' with byre and barn adjoining, all roofed with thatch. So it can be seen today, and no stately Holyrood, no Scott's 'romance of stone and lime,' not any other place, or cot, or castle in all Scotland, is held in deeper reverence than this clay cottage by the Doon. Here in 1757, William Burnes and Agnes Brown began their wedded life. It was a happy union between that heavy-browed, deep thinking, solemn man from the shores of the North Sea and this merry-hearted, sweet-voiced, sunny, Carrick maid. Thirteen months later, Robert Burns was born.

As [he] grew older, his father noticed with satisfaction the quickness of his son's mind, and with misgiving, the even greater quickness with which one mood succeeded another. The dark, obstinate little fellow, often gloomy, was astonishingly vocal, and in states of emotion, his eyes, as indeed his whole body, spoke for him as well. One day at Mount Oliphant Burnes stated to his wife 'Whoever may live to see it, something extraordinary will come from that boy.' The beginnings of his wisdom are to be sought in the wise counsels of his father. His love of Scottish song awoke as he listened to the sweet tones of his mother's voice.

Too soon his boyish frame had to bear a man's work. His shoulders were bent with holding the heavy four-horse plough, which turned a furrow fifteen to twenty inches broad.

The physical effects of this toil remained with Burns throughout his life, until an overworked body and a strained heart hastened his death. The moral effect – the loss of a steady aim, the stifling of ambition, and the desire to seek pleasure while it might be found – was no less disastrous. In this stern school he learned the unheroic philosophy which he thus set forth:

Then, sore harrass'd and tir'd at last, with fortune's vain
  delusion,
I dropt my schemes, like idle dreams, and came to this
  conclusion:
The past was bad, and the future hid – its good or ill
  untried;
But the present hour was in my power, and so I would
  enjoy it.
Thus, all obscure, unknown, and poor,
Thro' life I'm doomed to wander,
Till down my weary bones I lay in everlasting slumber;
No view nor care, but shun whate'er might breed me pain
  or sorrow;
I live today as well's I may, regardless of tomorrow.

In 1781 when Robert was twenty two years of age, a few of his rhymes appeared in print. These included *Winter, a Dirge*, the *Death of Poor Mailie*, *Mailie's Elegy*, and *John Barleycorn*. Of several of Burns' effusions that have been translated into the German, we are informed that no one delighted the illustrious Goethe more than *John Barleycorn*.

We need not linger over the last sad days at Lochlea – the quarrel with the landlord, the law-suit, and the father's broken health. The grey light of a February morning stole through the little window of the 'Spence' at Lochlea, and fell coldly on the bed in which William Burnes lay dying. By his side his favourite daughter knelt, listening amid her tears to gentle words of farewell counsel. Suddenly, the dying man raised his voice: 'There's ane o' ye,' he said, 'for whom my heart is wae. I hope he may na fa'.' The tall, stooping figure beside the window started and trembled. 'O father,' he said, 'is it me you mean?' For an instant their eyes met in a full deep gaze. Then slowly the father's eye-lids fell, and his head sank on his breast in affirmation. He spoke no more. Shaking with

> sobs, Robert Burns turned the window. 'Father! Father on earth and Father in heaven! I will be wise.'

It should be noted that the name of the speaker of this address at St Louis in 1957 was Robert Burns.

As we have shown in this chapter, the Robert Burns we all honour is not a Scottish monopoly. Minds like his belong to the world and his work therefore is the commonon property of all humanity. So perhaps it is appropriate to close with lines written by Samuil Marshak in 1959 and quoted by John Armit in his Immortal Memory given to the Paisley Burns Club in 1992.

> To us – your friends as well –
> Your barefot muse is dear.
> She has walked through all the lands
> Of the Soviet Union.
> We remember you
> Amidst the banquet's merry noise
> And we're beside you in the struggle
> For the peace and happiness of the world.

> I like to have quotations ready for every occasion. They give one's ideas so pat, and save one the trouble of finding expression adequate to one's feelings... [but] I have no great faith in unlaboured elegance. I firmly believe that workmanship is the united effort of Pains, Attention and Repeated Trial.
>
> (Letters to Mrs Dunlop of Dunlop 1786-96)

7

The Bicentenary Celebrations 1959

> I could never fancy that Burns had ever followed the rustic occupation of the plough, because everything he said had a gracefulness and charm that was in an extraordinary degree engaging.
>
> (Miss Jean Jeffray, 1789)

1844, 1859, 1896, 1909 and now 1959. The anniversary dates toll like an anthem down the years. sounding the passing of one man's life into a legend and now into a legacy for Scotland and all things Scottish. The sesquicentennial year of 1909 had virtually passed without notice coming so soon as it did after 1896 and, in any case, by that time the large-scale anniversary dinners associated with his name in the main centres had given way to the smaller, more intimate gathering appropriate to each local Burns club. By the time the Great War had made its ghastly interruption in 1914, it may be said that the formal Dinner had become the cosy Supper.

However, with each passing milestone the man that was Burns grew inevitably distant. At the same time the myth expanded proportionately till it was almost impossible to separate the fact from the fiction. He was either a god or a ghoul to many and in 1959, to the Anglified Edinburgh establishment at least, he certainly did not err on the divine side. Permission was refused to have a plaque put up on the wall of St Giles and the legal profession, almost to a man, refused to attend a special service at St Giles dedicated to the memory of Burns, saying that they only attended such services when members of the Royal Family were likely to be present.

No such qualms attended the annual gathering at St Louis, and once again we return to their records to see how they acknowledged the bicentennial anniversary. This time, there was no invited speaker. At their annual dinner on January 24 1959, secretary Irvin Mattick presented a roll-call of previous St Louis Memories.

> This is not my address. What I have to say to you has been said before, in this very room. I have culled from the books of Burns Night speeches published by the club, what I considered the best. They are excerpts from the addresses by those who have long gone before throughout the 55 years of the Club's existence. And I have taken such excerpts, which bear most on the subject of Burns, the man, the poet, the lover. Really, in Burns there can be no true separation of those three classifications. He was a genius in all three. In him they overlapped, fused, flowed one into the other. As living the part of a man of his day he was always the poet. As the poet he was always the lover.
>
> What you will hear is a symposium taken from the great of our Club, again speaking to us tonight from beyond, on the 200th anniversary of the birth of our Bard.
>
> From the many available, I chose parts of the talks made by the following members, once with us:
>
> From the 1911 Dinner – John Livingstone Lowes, then head of the English Department, Washington University.
>
> From 1912 – William Marion Reedy, editor of Reedy's Mirror and literary lion of St Louis.
>
> 1913 – The Reverend Dr W C Bitting, once Pastor of the Second Baptist Church here.
>
> 1928 – W Roy Mackenzie, former head of the English Department of Washington University.
>
> 1938 – Thomas Shearer Duncan, classic scholar, and a Professor of Washington University.
>
> 1939 – Read from a reprint from an article by Dr Otto Heller, Professor of German, and of Modern European Literature, at Washington University.
>
> And this is part of what they said:
>
> If we could tonight take ourselves back some 200 years, and review the Passing Parade of the 18th-century, we would recognise many men and women of genius and renown. Among others there would be Newton, Pope, Bach, Mozart, Beethoven, Goldsmith, Frederick the Great, Gainsborough,

Franklin, Washington, Goethe, Schiller and Haydn. And in the procession, during the latter half of the century, there would be walking, sometimes upright and defiant, at other times bowed by toil and depressing hypochondria, but more often singing and laughing, or wittily scourging, a Scottish Ayrshire peasant, sturdy and keen, wearing the hodden grey of the ploughman as proudly as any Louis of France wore his ermine and gold. He is dark and handsome, a magnetic man, his eyes flashing right and left and up and down, on all the scene around him. His hand at whiles is either firmly on the plow, or gripping a quill wet with burning ink, or raising a bumper, or chucking a girl under the chin... Robert Burns took his part manfully, toilsomely, and not vainly. Only those who sought to destroy him wrought in vain. They were either destroyed themselves, or, if any are left, they shall be destroyed if they try to upset what Burns started for the liberation of man and womanhood in that intolerant 18th-century. For, after the parade had passed, after the mob had stamped on his sheafs, and the clowns had jostled him along until he turned the corner, there still was music and laughter and pity which he had wrought for all mankind.

And the wonder continues to grow, that here was a man, a spirit, who gave more life away than he ever himself lived; who dipped his pen in his own blood and so fused his genius with the universal heartbeat of mankind that today what he left is immortal, aye, will remain even after the name of Robert Burns is forgotten, as the names of the psalmists are now unknown to us.

It is not with most, as perhaps it was not with you, when reading Burns for the first time, that the whole new planet swims into our sight. And as our reading progressed it is borne in how great a poet Burns is by the number of his lines that have been absorbed into the language of all people. There they are, passage after passage, enough to make a biggish bibelot. Often these passages are whole poems. I suppose that *Auld Lang Syne* can almost be called the whole world's *Internationale*... Burns came here dowered in head and heart, and gifted with a grasp upon and a hunger for life and all that it contained.

His life and work show that good sense and sentiment, reason and passion, waged a mighty struggle in his heart all his days. The push and the pull of those opposite forces gave him the full swing of the pendulum – all the ecstasies of life, from rejoicing to despair. Burns's spirit seized upon each detail of experience, warmed it, fanned it, and fashioned it into forms of beauty which still speak their truths to all the children of men.

He had the ink in his veins, and as things moved his thought or emotions he wrote them off. Life was the matter and breath of his singing. It had to be released from him as a valve releases pressure. He claimed:

Yet when a tale comes in my head,
Or lassies gie my heart a scried,
As whyles they're like to be my dead,
(O sad disease!)
I kittle up my rustic reed:
It gies me ease.

But Burns had studied life. He had met with smugglers, sailors and roisterers, and had found them human beings often of better and more honest stuff than most of the gentry he knew. He had met and gathered with those fine fellows who are so bad for good fellows. Drink and doxies fascinated him, for his was the temperament that finds generous pleasure resistless, all, ironically stimulating to a poet's genius. He was yet to find, and to write that:

Pleasures are like poppies spread,
You seize the flower; its bloom is shed;
Or like the snow falls in the river –
A moment white, then melts forever.

At Mossgiel, the ploughman failing in his crops, wrote 133 poems in three years, 60 of them undying songs. Burns knew by now that he was a poet. In his letters and verses he was referred to himself as 'Bardie'. And he made a high resolve:

That I for poor auld Scotland's sake
Some useful plan or book could make,
Or sing a sang at least.

Written out in his round, brave handwriting, never before was such verse so circulated since certain sonnets of Shakespeare's among his friends. They were composed at the plow and after the 'countrawark' written out by candlelight in a low garret. And later, all the better was this flash of song, for through the meditations at the plough and at the driving of the kind there flitted the face, and we must not forget the figure, of Jean Armour: 'Bonny Jean.' Much of the great work of the world in all times has been done for, and to the audience of one woman – not necessarily for the same woman. Jean Armour stung Burns into song and glory! For all the sordid details of that story, as we might call part of it now, Burns married Jean, and, as he wrote, 'made a decent woman of her.' We know that Jean grew in womanly dignity and loving kindness, well content, not to understand, but to love the genius who was her husband. Some observers believe that the reason Jean and Robert finally were so happy was that Jean was the only woman who really loved Burns. Her trials and patience certainly substantiate that belief.

In three years at Ellisland, 132 poems and songs were written. Here, *Tam o Shanter* was created. Ellisland failing, Burns moved to town, to Dumfries. In Dumfries, where life was gay after a fashion, Burns was exiled. He was never a townsman. He had a sharp tongue – a tongue that spoke the truth too often. He said things he shouldn't have said, and in the worst places: the tavern and the marketplace. He uttered treasons before the Royal natives. To a toast to Pitt he responded: 'To George Washington, a better man!' Burns was a Jacobite by romantic tradition, but republican by his reason. A democrat with a small 'd', he was still Jacobite because he loved the lost cause, the unfortunate Stuarts, and misfortune never appealed to Burns in vain. Satirist though he was, he had a vast common sense. His judgments upon himself and others were always fair. In his *Epistle to a Young Friend*, he wrote:

Adieu, dear, amiable youth!
Your heart can ne'er be wanting:
May prudence, fortitude, and truth,
Erect your brow undaunting!
In ploughman phrase, 'God send you speed,'
Still daily to grow wiser;
And may you better reck the rede
Than ever did th' adviser!

The last five years in Dumfries brought forth 100 more poems and songs, some his most brilliant and immortal. The lower the flame of the man burned, the higher the divine muse soared! The end came one afternoon, on July 21 1796. He had sung Scotland back to something like nationhood. And on the day they buried him, many high and low were heard to murmur: 'Who will be our Poet now?' Well, no one else has

> been their poet since. He still is. They who had cast stones were now ready to bring bread. There is little else to say.

The annual Burns Conference was held in Ayr that year but it was a low-key event. One would have thought the 200 years milestone would have inspired them but it limited itself almost entirely to a review of the various bicentenary events and a bemoaning about the falling sales of the *Burns Chronicle*. It was time for a whole change of attitude, but, alas, the mills of the Burns business turn slowly and no far-seeing changing decisions were made – yet. But they would come. Meantime, the Immortal Memories flourished among the celebrations. Dumfries drew an interesting double. Sir Alan P.Herbert, the writer, proposed the Immortal Memory for the Burns Club at their Bicentenary Dinner and the falconer and sometime film star, James Robertson Justice, followed a few days later doing likewise for the Scottish Southern Counties Association.

Niall Macpherson, the Under-Secretary of State for Scotland introduced Alan Herbert, as 'a man of independent mind' who was going to speak of another of the same cast. Sir Alan certainly spoke his fertile mind.

> It would be a wonder indeed if, after 200 hundred years of due, sincere and unremitting commemoration, there could be found a man who had anything new to say concerning the shining soul, the splendid singer, Robert Burns...It would be more surprising still if that man were a 'poor, wee timorous, English beastie' of Irish extraction. Yet I see no reason why an Englishman should not be invited to try. It is true we do not know the poet so intimately and well as the sons of his own soil; yet he is a part, a familiar part, of the life of every Englishman, more so even than any poet of our own. Only the great Kipling perhaps – another singer – is so often on the lips of the Common Man.
>
> It is not only on New Year's Eve, on Ludgate Hill before St Paul's – nor by Scotsmen only – that *Auld Lang Syne* is sung. Through all the year, wherever two or three Englishmen are gathered together who wish to express their love of life, their affection for their fellow men, their simple gratitude for simple happiness, how do they do it best – not with solemn speeches that begin the feast, but with a friendly Scottish song that sends them home to bed. And this

is not in England only. All round the world, on every ship that flies the British flag; all round the world, wherever the sons of Britain are dwelling or serving, are sweltering or shivering, they sing that song whenever they are in company... It is safe to say, that there is no moment of the day at which, somewhere under the circling moon, some company of men, in merry or melancholy mood, is not singing *Auld Lang Syne*. How happy any one of us would be if he thought such a thing would be said of his work 162 years after his death...

Burns loved all natural life and beauty but was condemned to wreck himself by cruel labour in the country he loved. But among the many men that filled that brief but fruitful span of eight and thirty years there was one, I believe, who governed and survived them all:

For thus the royal mandate ran
When first the human race began,
The social, friendly, honest man,
Whate'er he be,
Tis he fulfils great Nature's plan
And none but he.

We call that man, rather proudly and patronisingly, the Common Man.

But Robert Burns discovered and glorified him 200 years ago.

Two hundred years ago, Robert Burns was born. A little more than two thousand years ago, the Roman poet, Horace, was born. He, too, was a lyric poet, with strong powers of satire. He, too, is sung a little in England, at least in the schools. He, too, had the gift of putting a few common words together so that they shone like a posy, or a cluster of jewels of wit and wisdom. He, too, has left many a saying that is still a part of the coinage of life for those who studied him in youth – and, indeed, for many who did not. Near the end of his days he wrote –

Exegi monumentum aere perennius
(I have built a monument more lasting than
brass.)

That, I believe, was the grandest boast, the boldest prediction, that a mortal has ever made. Yet it was true. The Rome he knew is dust and ruin – the Latin tongue, they dare to say, is dead; yet his polished pearls of verse are as fresh and fascinating as ever. If you ever need a new motto for your

> annual celebrations you might do worse than take these tremendous words of the poet Horace...for it is safe to say that 200 years from now, if the human race is still alive on this rash and undeserving planet, at every moment of every day, someone will be singing, under the circling moon –
>
> Should auld acquaintance be forgot
> And never brought to mind
> Should auld acquaintance be forgot
> And auld lang syne?
>
> No song, I swear, will go round the world unless the poet is as worthy as his words; and by worthy I don't mean an example of all the usual virtues but an honest witness and interpreter of the human heart and mind...
>
> Behind the singer there must be a soul...

Sir Alan went on for several pages more of sound sense and acute observation of the poet's craft which reminded the hearers that he was no mean writer of verse himself. At the end of his speech, he was rewarded with an ovation and a scroll that declared him to be, like John Buchan, an honorary life member of the Dumfries Burns Club.

No such honour came Mr Robertson Justice's way. This bluff, blunt, bearded man of many parts, who described himself as 'by nationality a Scot and by profession, a scientist' had never been to a Burns Supper in his life and he astounded his Dumfries audience by saying immediately, and not so foolishly:

> Of course it was pure twaddle to maintain that everything Burns wrote should be inscribed on tablets of pure jade. No artist in the history of the world had produced 100% pure gold.... I speak, I hope, as an intelligent layman, and though so to say will probably result in my heel dangling in the air and a halter round my neck suspended from a neighbouring lamp post, I venture to say that Burns wrote a great deal of rubbish...*John Anderson, My Jo* is a sentimental monstrosity and *The Cotter's Saturday Night* must have been written with a remorseful hang-over or with tongue in cheek – or both...
>
> *(Murmurs)*
>
> The real miracle is that he wrote so much that is immortal and that his prose is so good it could be used today...He was a great lyrical poet and had a magical personality and a gentleness that would not allow him to harm a living creature – BUT – it is the uncritical worship of his work which I

> personally find enough to make a sensitive student take a scunner against the entire haggis. Burns was a victim of his time, a time which made it possible, or even desirable, for him to become, at least outwardly, a toady, a shocking sentimentalist, and, at times, a cad.
> *(More murmurs)*
> I cannot believe in the 'great lover' nonsense that was talked about Burns...
> The psycho boys have a word which describes the promiscuous male, the inference being that, at heart, he despises women. But even so, Burns behaved in a detestable way towards his girl friends, if only because he kissed and told – (*Loud shouts*) – a habit against which I was always warned. It must have been poor consolation for the girls to be immortalised in verse though the surprising thing is that none of them seemed to protest and accepted his advances as willingly as they forgave him later-'
> *(Uproar)*

Just as many of his audience did, we must leave Mr Robertson Justice at this point, although it must be said that for a certain type of man this was a reasonable view of our Bard, and, remembering him from Pinewood Studios, he was that kind of man. His essential thesis, it must be said, had a lot going for it, but not enough, it would seem, to impress Dumfries.

There was no report of such controversy at the London Burns Club No 1, which had a record turn-out, nor even when 700 Americans – or Scottish Americans – rallied to a dinner in Cuyahago County, Ohio. That was a big turn-out but an even bigger moment was experienced by the Glasgow and District Burns Association at the opening of the Jean Armour Burns Houses at Mauchline. This had been for so long a project of theirs and in the warmth of a sunny afternoon they had the great satisfaction of seeing it finally realised when the Houses were officially opened by Mrs Myer Galpern, the Lady Provost of Glasgow. Edinburgh's Burns Clubs did their part by producing an Exhibition of Children's Art on Burns Themes which was displayed at Riddle's Court before going on tour around the country.

Arbroath at last got its Burns statue in time for the bicentenary – after 70 years of talking about it. The Arbroath Burns Club had first proposed it all that time ago and now they had their wish realised in the only statue raised to Burns in modern times. It is a striking work. The sculptor had given the town a seven-foot bronze, uncompromising in its defiant outward stance. Scott Sutherland's fresh-faced, neat-headed Burns stands with hands clasped in front of him, facing out, legs apart, his plaid across his shoulders. The 15-inch clay model for the work was given to me by Mr Sutherland's daughter and it now stands, just as defiantly, on a bookcase only a step or two from my desk. You can never move far from Burns in my study.

January 25 fell on a Sunday in 1959, and almost the first flag raised for the bicentenary was a red one. Three thousand people packed St Andrew's Hall in Glasgow for an event organised by the Scottish Committee of the Communist Party of Great Britain. Hundreds were turned away at the door. The actor, Alex McCrindle, delivered the prologue, and Alex Clark, later to be secretary of Scottish Actors' Equity, chaired the proceedings and read out the messages to the demonstration that had come in from all over the world. Dr C.M.Grieve (Hugh MacDiarmid) spoke eloquently, claiming that nowhere else in the world would so many ordinary people gather together to honour a poet. (See his Immortal Memory below) John Ross Campbell, editor of the *Daily Worker*, (one remembers Colin Rae-Brown's weekly *The Worker*) took up MacDiarmid's point that Burns is the only authentic voice of the Scottish people and then asked who is speaking for them today if not the *Daily Worker* and the Communist Party.

Bob Horne, a noted Burnsian was also present. He had been brought to the Bard by hearing the same John Ross Campbell deliver a stirring Immortal Memory in London twenty years before. Horne quoted Edwin Muir, like MacDiarmid, a Scottish poet of the time, who wrote of Burns:

> He is so deeply embedded in Scottish life that he cannot be detached from it, from what is best in it and what is worst in it.

Burns songs and poems were performed thoughout the evening but the highlight was undoubtedly the closing sequence. This was a production by Scottish Television's Jimmy Sutherland of *The Jolly*

Beggars performed by members of the Young Communist League under the direction of James Callan with the *recitavo* spoken by David McDowell. This well-rehearsed presentation roused the huge audience to such an extent that they rose to their feet as the cast gathered under the specially-painted banner for the finale of the cantata which came in a thunder of applause and went on for minutes on end. So great was the enthusiasm for this climax to the evening that Willie Stewart, who had designed the Burns banner hung behind the performers, was asked to create a painting of that wonderful finale. This now hangs in the Burns Room of Mitchell Library,

There has long been an accepted link between Burns, the natural rebel and Burns, the radical red. In fact, Ross Campbell, the proposer of the Immortal Memory during the evening, was also the author of *Burns the Democrat*, a booklet published by Scottish Arts and Letters in 1945 which sold for ninepence. In this Campbell argues for Burns's life-long hatred of the ruling gentry however much he had to mix with them. His view was that Burns:

> looked rather to the gradual economic progress of the tenant farmers, small manufacturers and the middle class in general to create the elements of a better order, with, of course, the more intelligent members of the working class admitted to their ranks. The political reforms which he supported were to contribute to this end by the removal of unjust privilege. As he wrote to the Earl of Mar:
>
> > Does any man tell me that my feeble efforts can be of no service and that it does not belong to my humble station to meddle with the concerns of a nation? I tell him that it is on such individuals as I, that for the hand of support and the eye of intelligence a nation has to rest. The uniformed mob may swell a nation's bulk; and the titled, tinsel, courtly throng may be its feathered ornament, but the number of those who are elevated enough in life to reason and to reflect; and yet low enough to keep clear of the venal contagion of a court, these are a nation's strength.
>
> Burns takes his place, and a foremost one, in the procession of great Scottish Rebels who have striven to make the lot of

> the common people a happier one. And now the common people themselves, with ever-growing unity and determination, go forward to achieve their freedom and to make our beloved country a land of which Burns would be proud.

1959 was important in another Burns respect as it was also the year of the first publication of Maurice Lindsay's seminal *The Burns Encyclopaedia*. As J.B.Hardie, the then President of the Burns Federation, said at the time – 'A study of this Encyclopaedia is a generous education in itself'. Dr Lindsay, a poet and writer of some standing, and one who had shared many a platform with Hugh MacDiarmid and others, had written on Burns before in *Robert Burns; his Work; the Legend* (1954). It was while working on this he had the idea of a simple reference work giving the basic information on Burns to the general reader. It is much more than that of course, and over the years, with further printings, it has enlarged from the basic 'hand rail' the compiler envisaged and has become a whole Burns staircase in itself. It is mandatory reading for anyone embarking on a Burns project, this writer included, and Dr Lindsay has to be thanked for his contribution, not only to Burns scholarship, but to the added pleasure it gives to the reading of the Burns works.

This element of entertainment was to found in Dr Lindsay's many other sides which offset his day-to-day work as a director of public companies, administrator of arts foundations and public servant. He continues as a published poet as well as a lecturer on every aspect of Scottish letters, particularly on Burns. One of the most recent of these was to the University of Glasgow on *Burns and Scottish Poetry*, part of which, with his kind permission, is reproduced here.

> It is difficult, if not virtually impossible, to imagine English literature without Shakespeare, broad and generous as is England's literary heritage. It is absolutely impossible to imagine Scotland's literary heritage without Burns. In making this claim I am not comparing Shakespeare and Burns. Leaving aside the fact that Shakespeare's greatest poetry is meant to be spoken on the stage, mainly by kings and the great – or not so great – rulers of the past, while Burns wrote, so to say, for the mind's ear – by far the subtlest way to enjoy poetry, in my view – there is the fundamental difference which, broadly speaking, distinguishes the two literary traditions.

Recently, a daughter who teaches English in a Southern English school in the Home Counties, as they used to be called, found herself involved in a scheme where the pupils in the English department were exposed to a selection of contemporary work by English, Welsh and Scottish poets. The comparison most of the youngsters chose to make was between the English and the Scottish attitudes. One youngster, my daughter remarked, seemed to put it particularly well when he described how he saw the difference. 'The Scots,' he opined, 'seem to be inside looking out. There's much more people poetry than in the English work.' I'm sure he'll go far, that lad, for it seems to me that he hit the nail on the head – which is, of course, where you are suppose to hit them.

'People Poetry.' That, indeed, I think, is the outstanding characteristic of Scottish poetry down the ages...While it is true that Dunbar, but more particularly Sir David Lyndsay of the Mount, to some extent did their share of celebrating the ways of kings and queens, the religious turmoils of the seventeenth century partially drove poetry underground. When it re-emerged, so to say, in the eighteenth century, though stimulated by the threat to the sense of nationhood caused by the Union of 1707, Scottish poetry was already firmly people-orientated.

There are, I suppose, two kinds of artist: those who forge new forms or ways of expression; and those who take the forms already to hand and use them with greater richness than any of their predecessors had done. An analogy with music comes to mind. Two of the sons of the great Bach – Carl Philipp Emanuel and Johann Christian – were innovators; the former both formally and with the personalisation of expressiveness, the latter stylistically, giving an elegance to the *gallant* manner which has, happily, been re-appreciated in our own day. Mozart, on the other hand, though greatly broadening and extending their use, took the forms that were to hand and by substituting genius for great talent, endowed them with a perfection not hitherto achieved. And so it was in Scottish literature.

Allan Ramsay –himself of fairly humble origin – and the other lesser literary figures around him, were essentially 'people poets'. Ramsay, indeed, through his anthologies and his library – the first circulating library in Scotland – wanted to make literature more widely available and was only thwarted by the clerical establishment from setting up a theatre in Edinburgh the better to reach the people through drama. He wrote about 'low-life' people – a brothel madame and a keeper of a tavern, for example and he was unsparing with the verbal lash against the Kirk-Treasurer's man, whose sanctimoniousness oppressed the people.

Robert Fergusson, his successor, was even more of a people's man, and – as befitted the growing urban influence being brought about by the Industrial Revolution – more or less our first town poet. He, too, had no hesitation in applying the satirical lash to pompousness and social pretension.

The 'people' business – like the 'Standard Habbie' stanza they often favoured and which was imported from France – was used by one of the comic characters in Sir David Lyndsay's one surviving play *Ane Satire of the Three Estates* – a comic masterpiece, as we all know, which surely couldn't have been Lyndsay's sole dramatic endeavour. So it was the practical poetic heritage which Burns came to heir.

Like Mozart, Burns took the materials of his immediate predecessors and enriched them beyond anything hitherto imagined. Incidentally, there are two other significant links between Mozart and Burns. Mozart's opera *The Marriage of Figaro*, tilting ridicule at the unacceptable 'droit de Seigneur' privileges of the aristocracy, appeared in 1786, the same year as Burn's Kilmarnock poems, satirising the unacceptable practices of the Scottish establishment. Both were Freemasons, much favoured by socially conscious late 18th century intellectuals. And both paid for their temerity: Mozart through the withdrawal of Viennese upper-class support during the late 1780's; Burns by the growing coolness with which the Edinburgh upper classes came to regard him after the novelty of his year or so as 'the wonder of all the gay world', as Mrs Cockburn called him, began to wear off.

The notion that poetry had to be written in a high-falutin' manner and be about exalted topics, while a romantic fallacy already widely believed long before Romanticism ever raised its introspective head, was never one that fully pertained in Scottish poetry. Scotland never seriously succumbed to an Augustan phase. James Thomson, the leading Scottish Augustan, decamped to England and the circle of Pope beside the Thames. With so much cultural publicity focused on the Augustan English poetry of the time, it is hardly to be wondered at that, from time to time Burns should have raised his eyes from his true preoccupation with the people, to emulate, almost always unsuccessfully, Shenstone's 'bosom-melting throe'.

Virtually anything can provide the subject-matter of poetry, and one of the reasons for Burns's astounding success with the Kilmarnock Poems was that they proved just that. The ways of country folk, and of the animals with whom the farmer necessarily worked in the closest contact, rather than, for example, the pampered lady at her toilet in front of her dressing-table mirror, were shown to reflect the basic values that matter in life. It is not without significance that out of all the stilted upper class affectation – the Clarinda and Sylvander nonsense of Burns's affair with Mrs Maclehose – there was finally distilled the one last note that summed it all up and rang true – the song, *Ae Fond Kiss*, a people's poem if ever there was one.

From the particular, Burns could draw the universal generality. Probably arising out of his love for an unattainable country lass, Alison Begbie, came the song *Mary Morison*, with its heartache line celebrating the uniqueness of the beloved, 'Ye arena Mary Morison' – incidentally, thought by Hugh MacDiarmid to be just about the greatest line in Scottish poetry. And from the exposure of the secret lust of that poor old sanctimonious local, Willie Fisher (who died miserably freezing to death in a ditch) came what is possibly the wittiest and most devastating denunciation of religious hypocrisy to be found in European, if not in world literature, *Holy Willie's Prayer*.

Burns's people's instinct rarely faltered – momentarily, perhaps in Edinburgh, when he was subjected to the patronising flattery of the social glitterati: and certainly in his over-enthusiasm for the French Revolution which ended, as most violent Revolutions do, in the establishment of a repressive and cruel dictatorship: but Burns was not the only poet to be carried away by the French Revolution's initial breath of democratic liberty: Wordsworth made the same misreading of the situation, though he at least lived long enough to be able to question his earlier unqualified enthusiasm before descending into stultified conservatism.

In his best work – and, ultimately it is only a poet's best work that really matters – Burns's democratic sincerity rang clear and true... It was, I believe, a combination of his use of ordinary subject matter and everyday imagery, coupled with this unflinching sincerity that brought him, almost immediately, in 1786, the wide range of his readership. He was writing at a time when the old agrarian way of life, the time-honoured country values, were being assailed by the very different social and economic conditions evolving from the Industrial Revolution. In a sense, therefore, Burns perhaps seemed to enshrine the very qualities which were then regarded – and, indeed, have been ever since – as the fundamental qualities which constitute the Scottish character.

It is difficult to find any other explanation for the phenomenon of the cult of Burns Supperism which established itself within a couple of decades of his death and, institutionalised by the establishment of the Burns Federation, has flourished ever since wherever in the world a handful of Scots find themselves gathered together around January 25th... Now, as in his lifetime – despite, in the intervening years, such sentimental absurdities as *The Star o Rabbie Burns* and the often stultifying attitude induced by the Burns Cult – it is the quintessential honesty of his poetry and its accurate capturing of the basic tenets of our Scottishness that has preserved his popularity among readers from generation to generation.

When we come to consider his influence – or rather the influence of his work – on later generations of Scottish poets, it is quite another story. There was, for instance, the mistaken belief that it was his having been a ploughman, a former Excise-man, that explained the secret of his genius. So, with vastly mistaken energy, a certain Mr Edwards, in 52 volumes, proceeded to collect a wide assortment of worker poets, categorising them trade by trade. Virtually all of them were Burns clones, not only without the genius but without even raceable literary talent. At a rather higher level of imitation, or at least model-copying, there were writers gifted in varying degrees – some, like James Hogg, a writer of imaginative distinction (as we are at last discovering) in other forms and literary fields; others, like Robert Tannahill, with some individuality and ability (albeit, in his case, 'a too-quick despairer', leading to his suicide). There was also, of course, a vast and now utterly forgotten horde of local versifying followers who thought the touch lay in the couthy use of the Doric.

Scots, like Gaelic, must come under increasing pressure in the years ahead. Gaelic, for the time being, like Welsh, has the support (at very considerable cost) of special promotion by the most powerful media arm of our day, television: the same arm of the media that is exercising increasing pressure even against English as spoken in England, with its ever-increasing quantity of imported transatlantic material. The 'talkies' in the 'Twenties' no doubt made some small impact against Scots and its dialects. But the BBC charter, when concerned only with sound radio, contained provision for the nurturing of local languages and dialects, a condition that it was obviously quite impractical to impose upon television. 'Market values' have now been, of necessity, let loose against 'the guid Scots tongue'. It has, indeed, been under sentence of death for many decades; yet is still of literary use. But for how much longer, who can say? Yet it seems unthinkable that a time should ever come when the people of Scotland would no longer understand the language of Burns, let alone that of Henryson, Dunbar and MacDiarmid.

The fact is that Burns virtually perfected the use of the poetic tools which lay to hand when he 'commenced poet', to use his own quaint phrase. Even quite gifted poets in later years who tried to don his mantle like Stevenson (though, fortunately not exclusively) or John Buchan – walked, so to say, as if in antique guise; indeed, in literary fancy dress. It simply isn't possible to be sincere wearing the borrowed clothes of your literary ancestor Hogg, as I've already mentioned, though much influenced by Burns, and who, indeed, though that the Ayrshire poet's mantle had descended on him, had himself a touch of genius, though it is only in our own times that his stature, both as poet and novelist, is being properly reassessed.

The link between the major influence on Scottish literature during the 19th century and Burns is a tantalisingly minor social one. The boy who became Sir Walter Scott was present at a social gathering where Burns was the centre of attraction and was able to supply him with the identification of a poet, which had slipped Burns's memory. What Burns did for the Scots tongue, Scott, through the Waverley Novels, did for Scotland's history. As a lasting influence on their preservation of our sense of nationhood, the two must be seen in tandem. We are apt to forget that the ordinary Scot did not have easy access to the history of Scotland before Scott popularised some of its main confrontation points through fiction. Thus the stemming of the tide which threatened to engulf Scotland and North Britain was achieved jointly by Burns and Scott, spreading knowledge both of the Scots language and the old Scots ways of rural life as well as the actions and decisions which shaped her destiny in the dubious years.

In any case, the first half of the 19th-century was not a rich gleaning field for poetry in Scotland, the novel taking precedence in readership popularity. In the weedy rural sidewalks, of course, there were plenty of versifiers imitating Burns in form and content. Indeed, it was not until the middle of the century that the rural shadow of Burns was finally shaken off, poetically speaking. Urban and industrial influences began to be felt in the work of John Davidson and James B.V.Thomson, the one born in the industrial Clydeside town of Greenock, the other in the neighbouring town, Port Glasgow. The work of neither of them showed any Burns influence whatsoever, unless one counts anti-Calvinism, indeed anti-religion, as to some extent a Burns influence... Nevertheless, Scots itself trickled on, not ineffectively, into the early years of the 20th-century in the work of such writers as Charles Murray, Violet Jacob, Marion Angus and Helen Cruikshank; no longer Burns-influenced perhaps. The ladies struck an original rather plangent note and demonstrated that the Scots tongue whose demise had been prophesied since the 18th century, was certainly itself a gey long time a-dying!

It has been said that the creative energy flung into religious disputation in 17th-century Scotland and into cultural pursuits in the 18th, found its true expression in the 19th through engineering. There may be something in this, of course. Yet the great Scots concentration in providing engineered products for the world market – mainly, of course, a Glasgow and Clydeside preoccupation – did not in any way stem public enthusiasm for Burns's poetry. It has often been remarked of the English in recent years that they have never really taken to industrial urban society; that they believe the countryside to be their natural habitat. Thus, when they make money out of industry (or however), they buy themselves back into a kind of sanitised countryside; a countryside that has nothing, of course, to do with the hard work, low pay and battle with harsh elements of the real agricultural workers. I think the same social phenomenon probably also exists in Scotland. At any rate, Burns as a creative literary influence – though not, of course, as a source of delight to successive generations of readers – waned as the voices, mostly in English, celebrated, or denounced, Industrial Society gathered in strength. And so we come to our own century – 'the Age of Anxiety', as Auden called it; the decade of bloody wars, as many have experienced it; or 'The People's Century', as the BBC Television service currently calls it. All are true definitions in their way.

In Scotland, what part has the Burns influence played in shaping our literature and our sense of nationhood which, during the last three quarters of the century, has, slowly but surely, been showing signs of renewed strength? On 'the-sense-of-nationhood' business, undoubtedly an enormous invisible influence, so to say, though difficult to quantify since impossible precisely to define. But on creative Scottish writing, I should have thought, very little; beyond, perhaps, reminding Burns readers and the vast army of passive Burns-Supperites, that in a master's hands, the Scots tongue awoke and still awakes ancient, still valid values deeper than the marketplace 'value for money' attitudes increasingly urged upon us today.

The main influence on, and to a large extent the heart and centre of, the Scottish Renaissance movement, which flourished in Scotland from about 1925 to 1975 or so, has undoubtedly been Christopher Murray Grieve, the poet Hugh MacDiarmid. *Sangshaw* and *Pennywheep*, those two books of superb lyrics, are broadly speaking, rural inspired in content and imagery. *A Drunk Man Looks at the Thistle*, however, ranges widely over contemporary life and thought as it existed in the 1920's. 'Not Burns – back to Dunbar' was MacDiarmid's cry for many years. For his own exquisite early lyrics the by then debilitated state of the Scots tongue as used so wonderfully by Burns was an insufficient tool; so, as everybody knows, MacDiarmid set about constructing Lallans, Plastic Scots – call it what you will – reviving words with latent imaginative potential out of Jameson's *Scots Dictionary*. Against all odds, it worked.

No one with an ounce of feeling for true poetry can fail to thrill to the lyric wonders of *Sangshaw* and *Pennywheep*, or be excited and impressed by the wit, the satire and the sheer energy of the *Drunk Man*. But MacDiarmid's success and what he achieved in these early years though surely imperishable – was built upon an intellectual structure poorly able to withstand the tides of chance and change that swirl up the deposit that is history. It had several flawed planks in its construction. It is sadly, a well-proven fact that a language can only survive if it is used in commerce and the everyday business of life. The most obvious example of the failure of Government legislation artificially to revive a language not so used is the lack of success in Eire over the long-standing official programme to revive Erse as the daily Irish tongue.

By the time MacDiarmid burst upon the Scottish scene, Scots had largely fragmented into a series of local dialects. Most non-Gaelic speakers by then spoke a kind of Scoto-English, the thickness of the dialect depending to some extent on education and social class. Now please – and I don't want anyone to get me wrong about all this – I treasure and revel in our Scots literary heritage as much as anyone; every word of it. And I applaud all the gallant workers in the language section of the Association for Scottish Literary Studies – of which, indeed, I am a past-President – not to mention the School of Scottish Studies, who labour so enthusiastically on its behalf. But no matter how vigorous their endeavours, the artificial – if I may put it that way – restoration of Scots as a used tongue is, in my view, even less likely to succeed than the late-in-the-day efforts to lift Gaelic off the rather low-lying plateau where, happily, for the moment at least, it seems more or less to have stabilised.

In his early days, MacDiarmid inveighed against the only Scots tides that showed any signs of stirring popular living Scots at all. I refer, on the one hand to the honest efforts of the Burns Federation to stimulate interest in Burns's Scots among schoolchildren; and on the other to the vibrant use of it, albeit in a thin, debased strain, by Scots comedians like Harry Lauder and Will Fyffe – 'Music Hall Scots', if you like. At least *that* kind of Scots was undoubtedly people's tongue. The faulty planks I referred to as being built into the MacDiarmid Scots Revivalist structure were: firstly, that he was a Communist who, in old age, even supported the brutal suppression by the Soviet Army of the Hungarian and Czech popular democratic risings – and that's a far cry from Burns's 'Liberty's in every blow / Let us do or die'.

As it happens, I got to know him very well in the post-war years, because he lived in a house in the West End of Glasgow almost back-to-back with my father's house. I saw him frequently. Basically, I think he didn't much like people. Certainly he could not brook any suggestion that he might be wrong over some things, or that not everything he wrote was necessarily a manifestation of genius. Secondly, he ceased to practise what he preached, abandoning Scots in favour of a fairly rhythmless, quotation-larded English sprawl. There have been many explanations for this curious reversion. The most probable, however, seems that told to me by Norman MacCaig. MacDiarmid, who was accidentally tossed from a London double-decker bus in the late twenties, lost his sense of rhythm as a result of the injury sustained in that incident.

But this is not a lecture on MacDiarmid. It is, however, important in my view, to establish that however great the Scots lyrics written between 1924 and about 1932 – and they are very great indeed – they will never likely ever make him a popular poet. There has never been any question of its being 'move over Burns'. Whatever may be the future course of Scots, MacDiarmid's influence is to be found not so much on his use of the Scots tongue, as in the internationalising of Scots thought. So low had the esteem in which Scotland held itself become that until the post-Second War years, Scottish literature was not taught in Scotland's schools; not, at any rate, systematically and as a requirement. All that has changed for the better. Young people in future should come out of some Scottish schools at least able to understand what Burns was writing about.

If I had a criticism to make of the work of the Burns Federation over the years – apart from its perhaps incidental encouragement of Burnsolotry, a mindless condition which has nothing to do with the merits of this poetry – it would be that for years they treated Burns as if he were an isolated phenomenon, springing, so to say, fully armed to the forefront of Scottish letters. Obviously, that view is nonsense. Great poet that he is, it is simply not the case that he is so much better than all the other earlier Scots writers that none of them are worth reading. I hope this is an attitude which no longer prevails anywhere. 'Back to Dunbar' was thus not such a bad cry, if it could have been held to apply also to all other so-called Scottish Chaucerians or Makars.

It is probably true that Scotland's three greatest poets have been Dunbar, Burns and MacDiarmid. By far the greatest of the three, however, is Burns. It would appear from Dunbar's verse that, like MacDiarmid, he wasn't awfully fond of other people. Certainly, like MacDiarmid, Dunbar never was, nor ever can be, in any real sense a 'people's poet'. But he was a master technician, a creator of great bursts of verbal music: one of many of Burns's predecessors who should certainly still be studied and enjoyed by the general reader.

Finally, there is the influence of Burns, the man, to be considered. I once did a rough check in a library to try to find out who had inspired the greatest number of books in English. Leaving aside Jesus Christ as being a special case, numerically, Burns is rivalled only by Shakespeare and Napoleon. That was some years ago. Many of these Burns books, of course, are worthless. Those that fulminate against strong drink as the cause of his death – it was a contributory cause, no doubt, but not the main cause. Those which simply regurgitate the common facts of his life story – and we still get those regularly appearing – and those (a minority) which genuinely advance our knowledge of the facts of his life or result in an increased understanding of his work or the texts which contain it.

All this regurgitation, however, at least suggests that, whether conveyed in strictly factual form, in semi-fictional, like the biography by Catherine Carswell, or wholly fictional, as in the novels of James Barke, our interest in the man and his milieu seems to be more or less insatiable. And no wonder. What a story it is! Born in an agricultural labourer's cottage – though Burns's father never thought of himself in quite such lowly terms – part of the thatched roof of which was blown off in a storm; smitten by the charms of love and poetry at an early age; as a boy, engaged in a heart-dancing labour in the fields; easily – perhaps too easily – successful with women; a hater of social injustice and an upholder of the rights and dignity of the ordinary man; an exposer of fake pretence and hypocrisy; fond of the good things of life, or such as he could afford; one with a talent for friendship, regardless of status or rank; one capable of making enormous mistakes and bitterly repenting them afterwards; here, if ever there was one, is a man whom nearly everyone who reads his story warms to and can identify with.

Then again, some people like to assume that he would have

supported this or that cause which happens to involve their own interest. Take religion, for example. When Burns was writing to his 'mother-confessor', Mrs Dunlop, knowing that she was of religious turn of mind, he larded his letters with pietistic references; for example, 'I hope and believe, that there is a state of existence beyond the grave where the worthy of this life will renew their former intimacies'. Yet a few weeks earlier, to Alexander Cunningham, he was declaring: 'Of all Nonsense, religious Nonsense is the most nonsensical.' Probably his true beliefs were agnostic – again, pretty well echoing the general modern view, so well expressed by Burns to Robert Muir on 7th March, 1788:

> 'If we lie down in the grave, the whole man a piece of broke machinery, to moulder with the clods of the valley – be it so; at least there is an end of pain, care, woes and wants. If that part of us called Mind does survive the apparent destruction of the man, away with old wife prejudices and tales! Every age and nation has had a different set of stories; and as the many are always weak, of consequence they have often, perhaps always been deceived. A man conscious of having acted an honest part among his fellow creatures; even granting that he may have been the sport, at times, of passions and instincts; he goes to a great unknown Being who could have no other end but to make him happy; who gave him those passions and instincts, and well knows their force.'

The story of 'a man, conscious of acting an honest part among his fellow-creatures...' particularly when he happens also to have been the greatest literary genius Scotland has produced – the story of such a man never ceases to absorb our interest and involve our deepest feelings...

Hugh MacDiarmid claimed, like Walt Whitman, 'I am large. I contain multitudes.' Maurice Lindsay is too diffident a man to make such a claim but he has worn an amazing number of hats in his time. As well as his literary and bureaucratic concerns, he has also acted as an articulate interviewer on television and was a noted presenter being especially remembered, like Frank Muir, for his range of colourful bow ties. He once interviewed MacDiarmid when that poet was being sculpted in the BBC studio by Benno Schotz. The result now stands in the foyer of the BBC studios in Glasgow. Later in his broadcasting career, moved to become Controller of Border Television in Carlisle, and in that capacity, he presented a Burns programme with Moira Anderson, Bill McCue, Mary Marquis and the present writer.

It suddenly occurs to me, that in my professional life as an actor, I have not only been presented by Maurice Lindsay on television but I, too, have shared a platform with Hugh MacDiarmid (at Kirkcaldy Art Gallery with Alan Bold) and I have had my bust sculpted by Benno Schotz. It stares stonily over my head as I write. Much of what I write goes over my head, and even more of what I read, except when I read of Burns. As Dr Lindsay has said, his story is compelling in every aspect as far as I am concerned, especially when I have the help of commentators such as Lindsay, David Daiches, Tom Crawford and Donald Low – all, except the last, still extant in Scotland. It says much for Burns's calibre that he has engaged, and continues to engage, such eminent Caledonian minds. Yet, with all due respect to these names, perhaps the finest Scottish literary mind of the 20th-century was the pugnacious, mischievous, elf-like figure already much mentioned – Hugh MacDiarmid. A little man with a big head, piercing eyes, a squeaky voice and beautiful hands, MacDiarmid was a poet and polemicist, a true colossus in letters, internationally respected and, arguably, Scotland's best poet since Burns himself.

Dr Christopher Murray Grieve, otherwise known as 'Hugh MacDiarmid', was born in Langholm, Dumfries, the eldest of the two sons of a postman who died when they were very young. Chris, as he was called in the family, was first trained as a schoolteacher at Broughton, where he came under the influence of a good teacher, George Ogilvie, but, in 1911, his most promising pupil was expelled for stealing books. Grieve then became a journalist with the Edinburgh *Evening News* where he was sacked for selling the books he had been given to review. Fortunately he was saved from a life of crime by war service with the RAMC in Salonika from 1915. The army experience turned him to poetry. On his release in 1918, he had various journalistic jobs before settling with the *Montrose Review*. In Montrose, he met and married a girl in the office, Peggy Skinner, despite having been unofficially engaged to a Langholm schoolteacher, Minnie Punton, before joining the army. He soon became a father, a respectable town councillor and Justice of the Peace and began to edit the Scottish Chapbooks. It was around this time that he adopted the nom-de-plume by which he was to become known.

He also took up his life-long cause of Scottish Nationalism and in 1928, helped to found the Scottish National Party, taking as his cue, Burns's own comment:

> What are the boasted advantages which my country has gained from this Union with England that can counter-balance the annihilation of her independence and her very name.

MacDiarmid always had a remarkably clear idea of what the International Burns movement could become. That is a world-wide organisation that would uphold:

> Burns's essential motives applied to crucial contemporary issues as he applied them while he was living to the crucial issues of his own time and generation. What a true Scottish Internationale that would be – what a culmination and crown of Scotland's role in history!

There was also an uneasy parallel with Burns in MacDiarmid's own love life. He had never married his childhood sweetheart, Minnie Punton, and in 1929, he lost his wife, and mother of his two children, to a local coal merchant. In his despair, he took off for London to work for Sir Compton Mackenzie, but the first thing he did was to fall off the top of an open double-decker bus and land on his head on the pavement. He might just as easily have been killed but instead suffered severe concussion, which resulted in headaches for months. Various other mishaps occurred in England and drove him back to Scotland as far north as the Shetland Isles where he suffered a serious nervous breakdown in 1935.

However, Valda Trevlyn, a fiesty Cornishwoman, whom he had met in London, gave him all the support he needed. She also gave him a son, Michael, and after a hard spell in the Shetlands, the family spent the Second World War in Glasgow, at 35 Havelock St. By this time, MacDiarmid had been conscripted into an engineering firm and Valda got a job behind the counter in Smith's, the bookshop in St Vincent St. Finally, in 1951, through the influence of William MacLellan, the kilted Glasgow publisher, they moved to a farm cottage outside Biggar. It was very basic but it became their first real home. Called Brownsbank, it also became a mecca for the constant stream of literary and artistic visitors who found their way there for the remaining 27 years of his life.

Hugh MacDiarmid wrote much and most of it was good but his undoubted masterpiece is *A Drunk Man Looks at the Thistle* from 1926. This meditative monologue in Scots vies with Burn's *Tam o Shanter* as the greatest long poem produced in the Scottish language. At 2,685 lines to Tam's 229, it is certainly longer.
The following is a brief excerpt.

To prove my saul is Scots I maun begin
Wi' what still deemed Scots and the folk expect,
And spire up syne by visible degrees
To heichts whereto' the fules ha'e never reeked.
But aince I get them there I'll whummel them
And souse the craturs in the nether deeps,
For it's nae choice, and ony man s'ud wish
To dree the goat's weird tae, as weel's the sheep's!
Sic transit gloria Scotia – a' the floors
O' the forest are a' wede awa'. (A blin' bird's nest
Is aiblin biggin if its brood is like the rest!)
You canna gang to a Burns Supper even
Wi'oot some wizened scrunt o' a knock-knee
Chinee turns roon to say – 'Him Haggis, velly goot!'
And ten-to one the piper's a Cockney.
Crouse London Scotties wi' their braw shirt-fronts
And a' their fancy freens rejoicin'
At similar gatherings in Timbuctoo,
Baghdad – and Hell, nae doubt – are voicin'.
Syne, here's the cheenge – 'The Star o' Rabbie Burns!'
Sma' cheenge. Twinkle, twinkle, the memory slips
As G.K.Chesterton heaves up to gie
The Immortal Memory in a huge eclipse.
Or somebody else as famous, if less fat.
You left the like in Embro in a scunner
To booze wi' thieveless cronies sic as me.

And a' the names in history mean nocht
To maist folk, but ideas o' their ain,
The very opposite o' onything
The deid 'ud own gin they come back again.
A greater Christ, a better Burns may come,
The maist they'll dae is to gie bigger pegs
To folly and conceit to hang their rubbish on...

MacDiarmid, as a card-carrying Communist, had a life-long admiration for Burns's work and philosophy but he did not have quite the same feeling for Burns Clubs although his links with the Burns Federation went a long way back. He attended the Birmingham Conference in 1921. At the delegates dinner, in replying to the toast 'To Scottish Literature', he tried to make a case for the retention of the Lallans in Scots writing but it was poorly received. Some felt that he was wrong-headed in his approach, but MacDiarmid, a poet in the direct line from Dunbar, was unrepentant. As he said – 'Wrang-heidit? Mm. But heidit! That's the thing.'

He fell out of sympathy with the Burns movement in general as many good Scots minds did, like Dr David Daichies, for instance. There was a common feeling that the Federation held themselves to be high priests of all things Burnsian and that they kept him to themselves, in a rarified strata just out of reach of everyone else. However, in 1958, just to be awkward, MacDiarmid and friends formed the 200 Burns Club at Milne's Bar in Hanover St, Edinburgh. Sydney Goodsir Smith and Norman MacCaig were admitted as his fellow Bards. MacDiarmid said, 'While we may not be the Three Musketeers, we were a great trio.' They certainly were. The club was a great success and held many Burns Suppers thereafter. From the proceeds of these they were able to re-published MacDiarmid's *A Drunk Man Looks at the Thistle* and *A Scottish Noel* by Fionn Mac Colla.

In 1959, to mark the birth bicentenary, the 200 Burns Club arranged to have a special envelope made substituting the head of Burns, created by Aba Bayevska, for the head of the Queen on the stamp and hundreds were addressed to people of influence and power around the world but the postmaster at Alloway refused to accept them. By this time, MacDiarmid had become the Grand Old Man of Scottish Letters and travelled extensively to speak for the Chinese and

Russian Friendship Societies in Peking and Moscow. For the bicentenary year he toured Rumania, Bulgaria and Hungary on behalf of Burns. None of these countries, incidentally, boasts a Burns club although their interest in the poet is great. MacDiarmid, by this time, and mellowed sufficiently towards Burns Suppers to propose the Immortal Memory for a special BBC broadcast Bicentenary Burns Supper from Edinburgh. A private tape of this event was sent to me by Norrie Paton, that well-known Burns espouser, and the following text is taken from it with his permission:

> Mr Chairman, my lord, ladies and gentlemen. I regard it as a great honour to have been asked to propose the chief toast on this auspicious occasion.
>
> The bicentenary of Robert Burns has shown no diminishment of homage to him, but on the contrary, an increase. Within the past few years a vast new public has accrued to him – in the Soviet Union, China, Hungary, Bulgaria and elsewhere. In all these countries leading poets have published new translations of his poems and songs and these have circulated in hundreds of thousands of volumes. But North America is of course the great strong hold of Scottish sentiment, and consequently of the Burns movement, not only because both Canada and the United States have an element in their populations of hundreds of thousands of Scots with a great array of St Andrews societies, Edinburgh associations, Clan societies and Burns clubs, most of which celebrate Burns every January but because the preferred Scottish feeling is continually refreshed by the huge and ever increasing number of visitors to Scotland, most of whom visit the places associated with Burns and carry back a renewed enthusiasm.
>
> Nor is that merely emotional. There is a sound background to it, of practical interest in Scottish affairs and of intensive scholarship. It is for this reason that most of the best books of Burns, and of Scottish literature generally, are being written in the United States. The radio too, has played its part in broadcasting Burns to many millions of listeners in every part of the world. The way in which Burns continues to be celebrated annually is a phenomenon unique in literary history. Sir Alan Herbert was right when he said, ' At the present time, there's a lump of metal going round the sun. I

heard the other day,' he said 'that some solemn ass described the dispatch of this lump of metal as the supreme achievement of man. How much grander is the fact that Robert Burns put a girdle round the earth with a single song – *Auld Lang Syne* – owing nothing to electricity or science, his only instrument the hearts and tongues of ordinary men.' (Hear! Hear!)

The secret of the whole thing is in that last phrase – 'the hearts and tongues of ordinary men'. I have said elsewhere [that] Burns remains the authentic and almost the only voice of Scotland in the world today. The reason for his unparalleled fame is not far to seek. It is based on his belief in the creative power of the broad masses of mankind. His glory lies in his tremendous faith in the common man and woman everywhere. No one who does not share, and live by this faith really appreciates Burns. Wordsworth said of [him] – 'he showed my youth / how verse can build a princely throne on humble truth'. Longfellow put the whole thing in a nutshell when he wrote 'the burden of his song is love of right, disdain of wrong, its masterchords are manhood, freedom, brotherhood!' *(Hear! Hear!)*

Many famous poets have expressed their love of Burns but all of them at the same time have denied him a place among the world's greatest poets. Even Walt Whitman was constrained to say 'while Burns is not at all great in the sense that Isaiah and Aeschylus and the Book of Job are unquestionably great, he is not to be mentioned with Shakespeare. He has a nestling niche of his arm, all fragrant and quaint and homely; a lodge built near, but outside the mighty temple of the gods of song and art.' Nevertheless Whitman continued to say – 'that after a full retrospect of his works and life that Burns remain almost the manliest, tenderest, and even if contradictory, almost the dearest flesh and blood figure it all the streams and cluster of bygone poets!' *(Hear! Hear!)*

How is this paradox to be resolved? If Burns is not one of the world's greatest, why has he this unprecedented world-wide acclamation? Whitman again came nearest the solution when he wrote – 'Think of the petty environage and limited area of the poets of past or present Europe. No matter how great their genius, it almost seems as if a poetry with cosmic and dynamic features, of magnitude and limitless suitable to the human soul were never possible before. It is certain that a poetry of absolute faith and equality for the democratic masses never was!' Burns comes as near to that perhaps as any poet has yet done. Carlyle was right when he said that if Burns had been a better intellectual workman he might have changed the whole cause of European literature. As it is, despite his worldwide fame, Burns has had no real successors. Most subsequent voices of any rank have appealed, not to the broad masses of mankind but to a very small, specialised reading public.

To reach the common people is a glory not often achieved by the great artistic poets but Burns has achieved it (and) in greater measure than any other poet so, if he is not to be counted among the world's greatest poets, he nevertheless appeals to an immensely greater public than all these other poets put together. A public that has little or no use for any other poetry, no matter how great the literate might think it. *(Hear! Hear!)* For it is above all true of Burns that he wrote, not to extrovert his personality, nor to comply with the demands of taste, but to voice the common thought of masses of men. His poems and songs express something clamouring for utterance.

> The glory and generous shame,
> The unconquerable mind and freedom's holy flame.

That is why, two hundred years after his birth, the star of Robbie Burns is beaming more busily than ever all over the globe.

(applause)

The language he wrote in had a great deal to do with it. Because Scots poetry is almost entirely a poetry of song whereas English poetry is extremely deficient in song. Song is nearer to the hearts of all people and Scottish song owes its immense effect to the open vowels of the Scots language. Whereas the narrow, clipped sounds of modern English are no medium for song at all. It would be very sad thing if the language in which Burns wrote is allowed to die out and if the independent Scots literary tradition to which Burns owed so much ceases to be carried on. Burns would never have done his great work if he had not been concerned, as he said, to see subsequent bards carrying on that tradition to endless generations. *(Hear! Hear!)*

Over 3,000 books have been devoted to Burns. I think the best of them is Hans Hecht's critical and biographical study

> first published [in English] in 1936. Hecht summed up the whole matter splendidly when he said that into little more than 37 years of life there is compressed in Burns such a wealth of love and sorrow, of passion, success and disappointment of errors and triumphs, as seldom fall to the lot of any individual. He has been granted the happiest lot that can fall to any poet. He is enshrined forever in the hearts of his fellow countrymen and has became such an essential part of their spiritual possessions that it is impossible to imagine Scotland without Robert Burns. He has remained a living force in the nation. The sun that rose over the grave by the churchyard wall in Dumfries was the sun of immortality.
>
> Nulla crux, nulla corona!
>
> We toast the immortal memory of Robert Burns and the whole world agrees. But homage is not enough. We must continue his great work and carry it on in the conditions of a world that has changed out of all recognition since Burns day. Only in so far as we inherit Burns spirit at its very best and carry forward his work to new levels of achievement are we worthy to call ourselves Burnsians. Immortality is a word really beyond our comprehension, whereas it is within our power to ensure the future of Robert Burns and develop his influence on the world.
>
> And now, ladies and gentlemen, I ask you to be upstanding and drink with me to the immortal memory of Robert Burns. To Robert Burns!

The gathering repeated the toast then gave prolonged applause to the speaker until the piper entered playing *The Floors o the Forest* – a tune that speaks to ancient Scottish loyalties. In his speech, Dr Grieve had mentioned that Burns 'had no real successor' but modestly omitted to mention himself in that category. Finally, as far as Christopher Murray Grieve is concerned, it is good to keep in mind that while Burns had his red, red rose, MacDiarmid's was white.

> The Rose of all the World is not for me,
> I want, for my part,
> Only the little white rose of Scotland
> That smells sharp and sweet – and breaks the heart.

It was MacDiarmid's latest editor, and my good friend, Dr Alan Riach of Glasgow University's Department of Scottish Literature, who, when I told him I was involved in the preparation of this book, said, 'You know what MacDiarmid said such a book would *reveal*, of course...?'

> Hear, Land o' Cakes, and brither Scots
> Frae Maidenkirk to Johnnie Groat's,
> If there's a hole in a' your coats,
> I rede you tent it;
> A chield's amang you takin notes,
> And faith he'll prent it.:
>
> (On the late Captain Grose's
> peregrinations thro Scotland)

8

The Dramatic Burns

1960

> I have been in the company of many men of genius, some of them poets; but never witnessed such flashes of intellectual brightness as from him,the impulse of a moment, flashes of celestial fire.
>
> (John Ramsay of Ochtertyre)

In his *Bicentenary Review* of 1959, John McVie, a distinguished Past President of the Burns Federation, made this with regard to the future of the Burns Federation and the Burns movement generally:

> It is a record of which it has reason to be proud, but no organisation can have much of a future if its members are satisfied merely with basking in the reflected glory of their predecessors' achievements...The present members should re-dedicate themselves to carrying on the work of the founders of the Federation who built better than they ever imagined. In particular, they should redouble their efforts to encourage the development of Scottish literature, art and music.

Significantly, there is no reference in that laudable injunction to theatre, or perhaps as 'dramatic art', it would come under the general label of Art. Mention has already been made at some length in these pages of Burnsians and their attitude to the stage, their high suspicion or is fear of it? Yet a feature of that same 1959 Bicentenary Year had been the presentation of a pageant in Green's Playhouse, Ayr, entitled *I, Robert Burns* by 'Sandy Thomas Ross', a pseudonym for a writing collective led by Alex Macmillan, the Convenor of the

Bicentenary Committe of the Burns Federation. The Federation had joined with Ayr Town Council to produce the work and the Town Chamberlain of Ayr, Thomas Limond and Alec Ross Taylor, a teacher at Ayr Academy were the other authorial parties involved. Funds were made available to assemble a first-rate cast – Andrew Keir as Burns, Annette Crosbie as Jean Armour and Gwynneth Guthrie as Mary Campbell. Eileen Price and Charles Greville were the singers. Despite the calibre of the participants, and the presence of more than 200 local players in the supporting cast, the summer run of the piece was not successful.

The Burns Clubs were conspicuous by their absence, as so often happens when culture intrudes in their annual calendar of events. Once again, the bias against the theatrical was evident. This does not happen when the event is musical, particularly when good singers are involved, but the Burnsian shy away from repeated attempts to portray their hero in a musical. Yet what a natural musical hero he is. But so far he seems resistant to greasepaint. One has to wonder why this is so. It's not that people haven't tried – myself included – to put Burns on stage in the full colour of his story in song – his own songs – and also with original material specially commissioned – but despite initial encouragement, the public reaction has been moderate at best, and from the Burnsians, consistently apathetic. Why? Is their kind of Burns too big for a theatre. Or are our theatrical talents too small?

The matter of Burns and the Drama is dealt with comprehensively in my own book, *The Daring Bard*, but in this context you might wonder at the relevance of things theatrical in a book dedicated to the Immortal Memory of Burns. The point I want to make is that anyone in the theatre is in the memory business. There is no more potent art machine for creating a memory than a stage performance when it strikes a chord or hits a note that resonates between the performer and the 'house' as he calls it. This is why one can feel 'at home' in a theatre. In my experience of playing Burns on stage I have seen audiences come to him in the course of the evening and go away at the end of it with an new understanding of this remarkable man. As I said at the time, this was my solo once-nightly Immortal Memory. That was the reason I persisted in the theatrical interpretation over the years and wished for others to follow my example – for Burns's sake. There is an audience who will never read him but will gladly listen to him in performance.

In many ways, his poems and songs are performances, a word he himself used to describe them. They are 'made', in the sense that they are carefully constructed just as a play is. There is a professional at work here. He explores roles within his poems much as the playwright does. He offers a pure and spontaneous point of view, that is born of the moment and immediately pressed on the work, deftly and with assurance. The beauty he sees, we seize at once. This is the artist at work. He knows what he is doing, almost subconsciously. He 'plays' unabashedly and the result is often an unforced and unexpected insight that frees the image immediately. He can do and be whatever he likes. Which is why Burns was so capable of writing in an old man's voice, a young girl's voice, even a sheep's voice when required. In the ensemble poems, where more than one voice is heard, he was already proffering an auxiliary theatrical experience. In effect, the dramatic Burns was writing little plays all the time.

His main *milieu* as a poet however, was the personal. He excelled in the miniscule, the miniature, the daintily deft, and was at his best when he could be intimate, especially in the one-to-one relationship of lover and sweetheart. Their poetic exchanges are often conversational, and to all intents and purposes, pure dialogue. In a small way, each poem or song is a playlet. See *'Indeed will I,' quo Finlay* for example. and the verse duologues like *The Twa Dogs* and *The Brigs o Ayr* not to mention *Tam o Shanter*. One feels that any of these might be staged with no lessening of poetic effect. It all points to the loss of the playwright when he was not allowed to live long enough to carrying out his stated ambition to write, as he said himself, 'a drama for Scotland'.

There was something like drama going on in St Louis, Missouri in 1960. A Professor Alexander M. Duncan was invited to give the Immortal Memory and his subject was *The Burns We Praise*. On January 23, he rose with the proviso:

> I doubt it's hardly worth the while to be sae nice wi' Robin.

He then proceeded, in a long and learned address, to take the poet at his word.

Twenty six years ago, this evening, one of the great Burns scholars spoke to this Club, – Professor DeLancy Ferguson, the editor of the poet's Letters. The purpose of his address was to defend the reputation of the poet against the charges brought against it in what he termed 'smoking car legends,' and to show that Burns 'was no worse than the standards of his class and his century.' He claimed that the character of the poet was all of one piece, and that the man 'whose immortal memory the Burns Clubs annually celebrate' was the same man who could, on occasion, annoy even his best friends, such as Mrs Dunlop and Maria Riddell.

Some three years later, an honoured member of this Club found himself in the awkward position of rising to refute another pronouncement by Professor Ferguson. Our member was Dr Taylor, and the scholar's opinion that he arose to contradict was an article which appeared in The American Scholar in the autumn of 1936. it was entitled *The Immortal Memory* and was a devastating attack on Burns Clubs, the Burns Federation, and the pleasant ritual of the Birthday Dinner... 'The Burnsians,' wrote Professor Ferguson, 'are not students, either lay or professional; they are a cult. Cult members subscribe to certain orthodox interpretations of their founder and his writings and show marked hostility to views which challenge any part of that orthodoxy.' It seemed to Dr Taylor, then, as it must still seem to readers of this article, that Professor Ferguson was being both tactless and inconsistent. Before the members of the Club here, and as their guest, he had in 1934 defended the poet's memory against the moralising of his biographers and the slanders of the ill informed, giving his audience the credit of being on the side of justice and good will. Only a year or two later, he was railing at the Clubs, – this one among the others, presumably, – for clinging to a favourable interpretation of the poet's life and work. And, while not many Club members are in a position to know the ins and outs of Burns scholarship, he denied them even the right to be called 'students' and branded them, amusingly and rather bitterly, as mere 'worshippers.'

Apparently Dr Taylor's remarks in defence of our 'cult', as Professor Ferguson was pleased to call it, made little impression on him or did not reach the scholar's ears. When his study of Burns, entitled *Pride and Passion*, appeared in 1939, it repeated a number of the more acrid comments of the article in *The American Scholar*, and more criticism in the same vein was added, in almost total condemnation of our rather innocent desire to keep the memory of Burns and his work alive. He called it a 'movement' and traced it back to the first meetings in honour of Burns held shortly after his death:

> ... the movement acquired the characteristics of a minor religious cult, complete with ritual meals...In itself this establishment as hero of a national cult might be harmless. After all, if any writer was to fill the role, Burns was the inevitable candidate, for he alone of the great Scottish writers was truly a man of the people. No the existence of the cult, but the direction it took, is the tragedy of Burns. The sentimentality which lies, like the soft core of an over-ripe pear, at the heart of writers like 'Ian Maclaren,' Sir James Barrie, and A.A. Milne, is widespread in Scotland. In the Burns cult this softness yearns to the answering softness of *The Cotter's Saturday Night*, *To a Mouse*, and *To Mountain Daisy*, extols its hero as the Bard of Humanity and Democracy, and rejoices in the bathos of Clarinda and Highland Mary. Meanwhile the ribald magnificence of *Holy Willie* and *The Jolly Beggars* is neglected, the homely realism of satires epistles, and dramatic monologues goes unread. Worst of all, the splendid treasury of more than three hundred songs, Burns' most truly patriotic work, lies almost untouched on the shelves...

The charge, I think, need not bother us too much. If the general public has preferred *Sweet Afton* and a rather inferior version of *The Banks o' Doon* to some other, and perhaps better, songs by the same hand, the Burns Clubs are hardly to be held responsible. It may simply be, as has happened with a number of the Burns products, that the dialect has been a handicap even in Scotland, and that some of the tunes have had a more general appeal than others. It has seldom happened that the popularity of a song has had much to do with the quality of the verses written for it. Perhaps Professor Ferguson feels that his great service to Burns scholarship has not been richly rewarded and takes out his sense of neglect, – which, after all, is often the scholar's lot, – on the wrong party.

There is, however, another charge which he levels against the Burns followers that must be taken more seriously. In the article for *The American Scholar*, he put it quite bluntly: '...his worshippers,' he said, 'are ashamed of him.' In *Pride and Passion*, he went into fuller detail:

> The flattery of being a national hero would delight Burns. If his followers were only mealy-mouthed where he was outspoken, they would merely amuse him. He would not mind if they slobbered over his sins, (a practice, by the way, noticeably lacking in this Club!) for the unco guid were old acquaintances of his. But at the very thought of his worshippers exalting his weakest work and ignoring his best, his very soul would scunner. The real Burns was not the dropper of tears over ploughed-under weeds but the man who brought in the neighbours for a kirn-night and kissed the lasses after every dance, the man who sat by farmers' ingles and on ale house benches listening to the racy earthy talk of his people and storing his mind with folk sayings and old songs. He was not ashamed of being a Scottish peasant, the heir of all the picturesque and frequently bawdy tradition of Scots folk literature. Neither was the man who wrote, 'But yet the light that led astray was light from heaven,' ashamed of his human nature. But his worshippers are ashamed of the best part of his nature and his work. And nobody else reads him at all.

As Professor Ferguson states it, the emphasis is a renewal of the verdict given by Henley in his famous essay of 1897:

> The master-quality of Burns... is humour. His sentiment is sometimes strained, obvious, and deliberate... and often rings a little false, as in much of the *Saturday Night*. But his humour – broad, rich, prevailing... is ever irresistible... I, for my part, would not give my *Holy Fair*, still less my *Halloween* or my *Jolly Beggars*...for a wilderness of *Saturday Nights*.

If we add to this preference of Henley's for humour rather than sentiment, realism before the elegance of fancy, the gist of Hans Hecht's magnificent chapter on *Burns as a Songwriter*, we catch the drift of Ferguson's choice. He prefers

> the Burns of *Tam o Shanter* and *The Jolly Beggars* to the seemingly other Burns of the *Saturday Night* and the sentimental poems to animals; and he believes with Hecht that the poet's nine years of devotion to the writing and revising of 350 songs is the true gift for which his admirers ought to be most grateful. As Hecht summarises this gift, (the translation is Jane Lymburn's)
>
>> He had the luck to find a still living tradition, with whose purest forms he was in close contact because of his peasant origin; he had the noble mind to recognise the national importance of this tradition, the inspired patience to study its technical peculiarities down to its smallest details, and the great genius to preserve and at the same time to rejuvenate what had come down to him, to save the old tunes from extinction and at the same time to sing a new song...
>
> This, of course, is excellently said and, as the considered judgment of scholars, must be kept in mind by any lover of Burns. If it is possible to distinguish a 'real Burns' and to decide on good evidence what part of his nature and work was best, as Professor Ferguson believes, it may be our duty to know this Burns and reject any image of him that is essentially false.

Actually, I find much to agree with in what DeLancey Ferguson and Henley had to say and, to my personal knowledge, Dr David Daichies in Edinburgh is of much the same opinion. Professor Buchan did Burns scholarship a service by bringing these views forward but his speech sparked off a reaction which caused some consternation in St Louis. Professor Buchan went on:

> The address by Professor Ferguson was followed, next year, by one of a very different sort which may deserve the bitter reproof of the lover of Burns. It referred to the poet as 'giving the license to his passions that ultimately proved his moral ruin,' – an example of the moralizing that disturbs many of us. About the Irvine episode it declared that 'there (he) fell into company that was not good for him, and he gave vent to his indiscrimate philandering,' – surely a harsh judgment on love affairs out of which came the stimulus for the songs. It maligned Burns' friends in Tarbolton as 'the graceless lawyers

and topers of the locality,' though it was to these graceless young men that Burns turned for encouragement when he began to write, and his great gift might never have been known had it not been for those groups of rowdy companions. The address reprobated the satires on the Kirk, *Holy Willie's Prayer*, *The Ordination*, *The Holy Fair*, and called 'most serious Scotsmen' to witness that it would have been better if they had never been written. Against every bit of evidence, it asserted that 'Burns adorned the commonplace and cast the glamour of genius about it, till even the coarse and grotesque becomes refined,' – a strange judgement, indeed, in the light of Burns's own repeated outcries against refinement in every shape and form.

It looks as if here, among our own records, is a paper of the kind that scholars dislike, – one that pretends to worship Burns and is yet ashamed of him. If there is a real Burns, his picture cannot surely be found among those who use his life as a theme of a sermon against license and philandering or who would gladly eliminate from his work whatever offends their tender sensibility. It is of the very essence of the understanding of Burns that the best of him, as man and poet, came of something unregenerate in his nature and tradition, and any effort to conceal this fact denies the clear evidence of the letters and the poems. He loved ardently and not always wisely, and yet, having a gift of quick speech, he wrote fine lyrics about a number of women.

He hated the Kirk and its ways and many of its elders and preachers. Ignoring this hatred does him an injustice. In the company of graceless people whom he met in shady places, and almost certainly over a glass, he listened to old tunes and bits of rhymes out of which he could make poetry. One rowdy visit to the most disreputable tavern in Mauchline, along with two quite unregenerate companions, Jimmie Smith and Johnie Richmond, furnished the inspiration for *The Jolly Beggars*.

We have no right or need to make excuses for him – the only excuses required are his own broadcast through his letters and his poems, – and what he accomplished in song, satire, and description would be inconceivable without this unregenerate streak in his nature and imagination.

There has been, however, a persistent attempt to offer apologies. His earliest editors from Currie on were willing to print some of his poems and reject others. *The Jolly Beggars* and a number of the satires on the Kirk were not at first allowed to appear alongside *Bonnie Doon* and *The Cotter's Saturday Night*. Even intelligent fellow Scots, like Carlyle and Robert Louis Stevenson, seemed to feel that they had to build up a case for him. A proper and stuffy writer like the middle-aged Wordsworth would not believe that his ploughman poet could write some of the verses ascribed to him – 'He must be a miserable judge of poetical composition who can for a moment fancy that such low, tame, and loathsome ribaldry can possibly be the product of Burns' – a remark calculated to prove that even a great poet may be a poor judge of composition unlike his own. The highly improper Lord Byron professed, as Professor Ferguson reminded us, to being shocked at a collection of letters loaned to him by Robert Cleghorn's stepson:

> Allen has lent me a quantity of Burns's unpublished and never-to-be-published letters. They are full of oaths and obscene songs. What an antithetical mind' tenderness, roughness – delicacy, coarseness – sentiment, sensuality – soaring and grovelling, dirt and deity – all mixed up in that one compound of inspired clay.

Yet Burns was completely honest about his own nature and the kind of literary product that expressed it, – not one kind of product but many, and the rough among the others. 'There is,' he wrote to Robert Cleghorn, 'and must be, some truth in *original sin*. My violent propensity to bawdry convinces me of it. If that species of composition be the sin against the *haly ghaist*, I am the most offending soul alive'... Although given a more decorous form by Burns himself and the respectable demands of the *Musical Museum* and the *Scottish Airs*, the songs keep far more traces than is often realised of the indecorous world of folk-song and ballad out of which they emerged.

For various reasons it has only recently been possible for the common student of the poet to learn much at all about this tradition. In a well known passage of the Centenary Edition, T F Henderson wrote about the difficulty he had in tracing the originals of the song:

> Much of the materials he (Burns) collected... has been destroyed – by his relations, or by Currie, or

> by later owners – in the interests partly of Scottish morals, partly of that cheap, decorous chromo-lithograph ... which bids fair to supplant the true Burns – ardent, impulsive, generous; but hypochondriacal, passionate, imperfect – in the minds of his countrymen ...

Less of the material may have been done away with than Henderson imagined, and it is possible today to bring the image of the poet into clearer focus than ever in the past, but his picture of the 'true Burns' appears substantially the one to be looked for.

Among lovers of Burns, a willingness to accept the prodigal in the man and the poet is as important as to the scholar. Great editor as he was, T F Henderson may have been inclined to emphasise too heavily the plain spoken tradition of the old Scots poets, and the clandestine literature of the chap-books and the oral record, but if his preference is backed up by a careful study of all the work, – not one or two pieces regularly chanted at our Burns dinners or those served up in anthologies for college sophomores, – the common reader benefits by opening up the pages and discovering what they have to say.

A word or two may be worth while on two topics of the poetry that frequently come up for mention, – his attitude toward the Kirk and its beliefs, and his feeling for animals. The picture of family worship in *The Cotter's Saturday Night* has charmed believers for many generations, because the sentiments arose, during the troubled years of the poet's apostasies, out of a fond memory of childhood under a god-fearing father. It ought to be noticed, however, that the service takes place in the home, not in the Kirk, and that it is reduced to the simplest of elements, – the singing of the old psalm tunes, the reading from the Bible, and the father's prayer. Apparently beyond these, the essentials of simple faith, Burns's memory and observation found nothing to please him in the rituals of the Kirk. He saw its ministers straining at the gnats of theology and swallowing the camel of their own personal sins and lack of charity. In the conventicler that he describes so vividly in *The Holy Fair* he finds all of the features of circus, much of the operation of the De'il and not a shred of religion. Against the one picture of sincere devotion found in the cotter's family, and one that includes, it must be remembered, a family meal and a country love-affair, may be set a half dozen of bitter portraits, the ferocity of which is hardly lessened by raucous laughter and acid wit. It is scarcely to be expected, even today, that men of the cloth should be generous enough to a man who showed so little patience or sympathy with the institution they serve. Maybe one reason for a 'false' image is the intrusion of too much pulpit eloquence at the Birthday Dinners.

Neither is it all certain that Burns had for the animals of the field and the yard more affection than the average countryman displays. He had a finer gift of noting and recording the little ironies of an animal's existence, – that his pet ewe was almost throttled by her tether, that the dog seemed to behave like the master, and that the auld mare of the farm became, in course of the years, a part of the life of the man who rode her. But for the most part he saw himself as he looked at animals, his own disaster in the wreck of the mouse's nest, his own ideas in the head of Luath, the ploughman's collie, and a warning for himself in Poor Mailie's hopes for her first born:

My poor toop-lamb, my son an' heir,
O, bid him breed him up wi' care!
An' if he live to be a beast,
To pit some havins in his breast!
An' warn him – what I winna name –
To stay content wi' yowes at hame;
An' to no rin an' wear his cloots,
Like other menseless, graceless brutes.

In the familiar *To a Mouse*, where the poet feels sorry for himself because his fate and the mouse's are alike, he appears far less happy as a writer than in the much gayer, *To a Louse*, in which the 'ugly, creepin' blastit wonner,' finding thin pickings in the gauze and lace of Jenny's bonnet, achieves a vivid disreputable life of its own. Like the creators of animal fables from Aesop to Disney, Burns found the animals rather amusing cartoon copies of men and women, creatures fit to fill in the diagram of human littleness. As a farmer, he liked to have his ewes, his auld mare and his collie with him on the fields, but he lavished on them no tear-filled sentimentality.

It is through the songs, however, that there may be traced, if they can be found, the elements that go to the understanding of a 'real Burns.' Though the satires and the poems about animals reveal some qualities of their maker, all of them were, in a way, occasional, the expression of moods of wry humour or of irritation that came and went. But Burns began and ended his life as a writer in the pleasure of making songs, and, during the Mauchline years, as well as in Ellisland and Dumfries, it was to songs that he returned after every excursion in verse prompted by a political quarrel or a moment's swift observation. Any reader of the letters to Johnson or Thomson, as well as to the other correspondents who had their sheet of news filled out with stanzas of new experiments in tune, can immediately recognise the deep, continuous passion for song and song writing that allayed the drudgery of the farm and the tedium of excise duties. It was around this interest that he built up his small library of books, and for its development that he took time out for talk and singing by anybody who had a contribution to make to the store of tunes in his head and fragments of lyrics that he jotted down.

If is now possible, as it never was in the 19th-century, to trace to their sources in the folk literature and the older writers of Scottish verse many of the fragments that Burns adopted and modified for his purpose. Manuscripts have been authenticated and compared, and we are able to read various versions of many of the songs. Burns was not easily satisfied with a first draft and kept revising a number of songs again and again. What concerns us is the kind of song that interested him, in the first place, and, in the second, what happened to the original material once it came into his hands. A common critical remark has been that he spent the years in Dumfries cleaning up, for the decorous pages of Johnson's *Museum*, a quantity of indelicate songs out of the past, adding verses to some, changing words and phrases in other so as to meet the demand of the respectable. To some extent this process went on, but it appears to have been only part of the story.

The poet was aware of the body's hunger and knowledgeable in the ways of satisfying it. So long as he stayed away from Chloris or Clarinda and the affected English in which he wrote to her, he never claimed that the hunger was other than it was, and this honesty is a finer thing than the indecent pretence that love is ugly or too serious to be made the subject of a jest. The difference is apparent in an emphasis where the strict moralist may never agree with the comic artist, and it is clearly set out in two versions of *Bonnie Doon*. The common version first appeared in the *Museum* in 1792, and all of us have felt agreeably sad while singing it:

Ye banks and braes o' bonie Doon,
How can ye bloom sae fresh and fair?
How can ye chant, ye little birds,
And I sae weary fu 'o' care!
Thou'll break my heart, thou warbling bird,
That wantons thro' the flowering thorn!
Thou minds me o' departed joys,
Departed never to return.

But an earlier version of the song went in a letter to Alex Cunningham, a year before it appeared in the *Museum*. While the changes are not very great, they mark the difference between a sweetly sentimental song, and one that had the clear marks of the poet and the comic artist upon it, – no 'flowering thorn' or 'warbling bird' wantoning through it, and no departed, departed joys. Much simpler, much finer:

Thou'll break my heart, thou bonnie bird,
That sings upon the bough!
Thou minds me o' the happy days
When my fause Love was true.
Thou'll break my heart, thou bonnie bird,
That sings beside thy mate,
For sae I sat, and sae I sang,
And wistna o' my fate.

It is in the second stanza, however, that the early version far excels the other, and in the meaning of the figure of the rose and the thorn.

Wi' lightsome heart I pu'ed a rose
Upon its thorny tree,
But my fause lover staw my rose,
And left the thorn wi' me.

Wi' lightsome heart I pu'ed a rose
Upon a morn in June,
And sae I flourished on the morn,
And sae was pu'd or noon.

What Burns first did, and then had to undo for the pernickety Johnson, was to sketch the episode and temper its sweet sentiment with the use of the rough, colloquial phrase about pulling a girl's rose: he cut the sweetness with a drop of the lemon of wickedness. And, because this dash of tartness came to him from the local Scottish speech, he felt more at home with it, more apt to turn out good poetry in it, than when he tried to imitate the sentimental English writers of the time.

The image of love making that went into *The Bonie Moorhen* so offended Mrs McLehose that she begged her Sylvander not to print it, – not for her sake or his own. The euphonious little phrase about going 'tapsalteerie' that we associate with *Green Grow the Rashes* was clearly associated in the poet's mind with the lasses, as well as with wardly men. When one of these lasses sang about her ploughman, she was even franker:

Snaw-white stockings on his legs,
And siller buckles glancing,
A guid blue bonnet on his head,
And O, but he was handsome!
Commend me to the barn-yard
And the corn mou, man!
I never got my coggie fou
Till I met wi' the ploughman.

To the country lover, the fou coggie spoke of the same pride in masculinity as a similar vessel did, in token of his drinking prowess...Quite often, as in this kind of slang everywhere, the sense, as here in the filling of the coggie, is one thing to the innocent mind – to the pure of all things are pure, poor dears! – and another to the mind tempered by laughter and experience. The farmer's wife who hired the man at Martinmas because he could 'labour lea' gave him his three arel-pennies for ploughing up the pasture, but when she cried, in one of the versions of the poem 'O Can ye labour lea?'

But my delight's a Ploughman lad
That well can labour lea

She was approving of him for quite another kind of service. And Burns, we are certain, did not disapprove of the service that was not paid for in cash. He sang so, often enough:

O, kissin is the key o' love
An clappin is the lock;
An' makin of it's the best thing
That e'er a young thing got.

The tinker, the weaver, the ploughman, the tailor, the highland laddie and the sodger, even Prince Charlie himself on his wanderings, – all receive their meed of lyric praise from Burns for being 'braw wooers' who did not have to stand at the door too long asking to be let in. An unforgivable offence in his own day, and for the strait-laced ever since, is that he sang about how

The minister kissed the fiddler's wife,
And couldna sleep for thinking o't

And showed pillars of the Kirk sharing in the same human activity, – though apparently without enjoying it.

O, wert thou, love, but near me,
But near, near, near me,
How kindly thou would cheer me,
And mingle sighs with mine, love.

They were not long happy worshipping one another from afar. Their road of love making was short and led to a mattress of clear rushes, or a plaidie, shared breast, as bield from the cauld blast of everyday living.

To make a happy fireside clime
To weans and wife;
That's the true pathos and sublime
Of human life.

By the frequency with which those lines are recited at gatherings such as this, one would imagine that they voiced the sole and characteristics utterance of the poet about home and its loyalties. There is no need, of course, to pass by this desirable sentiment which did credit to the friend for whom the *Epistle* was written and to such poems as Thomson's and Shenstone's to which it was indebted. The lines express simply and well, if in rather general terms, an ideals of home, the same ideal as is reflected in *The Cotter's Saturday Night*.
The poet, however, drew a clear mark between two kinds of writing to both of which he was prone, the sermon and the song:

But how the subject-theme may gang,
Let tune and chance determine:
Perhaps it may turn out a sang,
Perhaps turn out a sermon.

Of the sermon variety there is quite a store in Burns, and the popular taste seizes upon this as its favourite, – the shrewd comment on experience rather than the simple cry of experience, the song, on which a poet's chief quality rests. Memorable as are many of Burns's comments on his own and other people's living, he seems to have been more himself, and certainly a finer craftsman, when he sang out of the heart of simple events, leaving the reader to draw his own conclusion... Almost always, when he achieved the song rather than the sermon, it had a wry, arch lively flavour that the reader or the singer quickly begins to recognise. Quite a trace of the archness came out of the ballads and bits of rhyme on which, in many instances, the songs were made. The liveliness is felt in the tunes of olden times that the poet soughed through his head as he wrote, and they were mostly merry tunes for reels, strathspeys, and jigs – not hymn tunes by Stainer or Dykes or melodies concocted by the musicians. The quality of the life they contain is not by any means as sedate as in the *Blacklock Epistle*, but rough and humorous and often far from sublime. It contains Maggie of 'Whistle o'er the lave o't', meek and mild, sweet and harmless as a child, before marriage, and another Meg after the wedding:

Wha I wish were maggot's meat,
Dish'd up in her winding-sheet,
I could write (but Meg wad see't) –
Whistle o'er the lave o't.

In this world is Willie Wastle's lady, as disreputable an old harridan as even Chaucer could depict:

She has an e'e (she has but ane)
The cat has twa the very colour,
Five rusty teeth, forbye a stump,
A clapper-tongue wad deave a miller;
A whiskin beard about her mou,
Her nose and chin they threaten ither:
Sic a wife as Willie had,
I wad na gie a button for her.

Auld badrons by the ingle sits,
An' wi' her loof her face a-washin;
But Willie's wife is nae sae trig,
She dichts her grunzie wi' a hushion;
Her walie nieves like midden-creels,
Her face wad fyle the Logan Water:
Sic a wife as Willie had,
I wad na gie a button for her.

In thus unkempt world, the wife of the Cooper o'Cuddy deceives her guideman with any number of strangers, and he is so doited and blin' that he doesn't know what is going on.

The lass that makes up the bed for the visitor does him the courtesy, – it is Burns's word, – of sharing the bed with him.

In incident after incident, sketch after sketch, of the sort if built up a picture of a home-life rather alien to the happy fireside clime, much closer, in fact, to Hogarth than to Gainsborough or to Millet. It is as if the poet put into practice his own little ditty,

I'll be merry and free,
I'll be sad for naebody.

The professors and divines turned their fine noses aside from the stench of the causeways and the taverns, but Burns walked into the tavern and made friends with the orra bodies who frequented the place. As he wandered in and out of hovels in which most of the farm folk lived, he found more of a strong sap of life in the reek filled rooms than in the fine drawing rooms of the gentry. There is a chance that he was mistaken, but to refuse to look at what he saw and recorded is to do him a grave injustice.

Very few of the 19th-century biographers or critics knew enough, or had a sound enough stomach, to describe Burns honestly, and far too many of them, even the great Matthew Arnold, lacked even a rudimentary sense of the value of laughter. They made the easy mistake of lumping the work of a magnificently realistic and Scottish poet with the romantic lyrics of Englishmen who came soon after, or, being far from robust in their likings, they praised him for his least admirable qualities. About the songs we are now able to accept Hans Hecht's good judgment:

> There are no poems containing subtle analyses of the poet's mind... His work contains no nature poems as such, and ... no examples of (an) ascent into the metaphysical... there is no trace of the romantic-visionary element... Burns's lyric poetry is, rather, markedly unromantic. It avoids the mystic twilight, it builds no new world in the blue wonderland of Fancy, but clings to the clear realism of its chief sources – the Scottish popular and traditional songs.

In those sources he found a healthy, hearty manhood and a background of a piece with the bitter-sweet irony of your life and mine when we have the good sense to temper its ardour's with fun. Through it courses a passionate love of the common

> human pleasures, – food and drink, love making in the cottage and love making in the open fields, quarrelling and making up. If there is no great abundance of reverence, the sturdier is the independence of mind, and, if refinement may on occasion be noticeably lacking, – well, who wants to be too refined when Willie brews a peck o' maut or when a braw wooer has come striding down the lang glen?

It would seem that the members of the St Louis Club would have preferred a more refined Professor Buchan judging by the comments made in the minutes dealing with his long oration.

> Minutes of Annual Dinner Meeting – January 23 1960
> And then we came to that highlight of every dinner: the main address.
>
> Professor Buchan was our speaker, and his paper was titled *The Burns We Praise*. It was a scholarly, incisive approximation of the Bard, and went deep into the earthiness of the poet. There were some who wondered whether this was their Burns. There were others who knew it was. Some seemed to hover in between. Professor Buchan had his own ideas, and expressed them. Several of the members were called upon to respond to the speaker after he had finished. These men were legion about the scholarly explorations the speaker had made in preparing his paper, but could not hold altogether to all of the ideas.
>
> After Mr Stewart and others had responded, Mr Skinner was asked for his comments. Mr Skinner contributed the view that the speaker had, perhaps, used the apparatus and scaffolding of scholarship to do nothing more than reconstruct somewhat preciously a three dimensional image of Burns that already existed in the minds of common readers of common sense. Mr Skinner suggested that we did not really need to have pointed out to us – with footnotes – the fact that Burns was a man who liked women, liquor and libertine language. All that, he held, must be apparent to everyone. And all that, he insisted, has little to do with our reasons for our holding Burns so high in our minds and hearts. Burns was, Mr Skinner observed – and he gave thanks for it – a man of sense and solar plexus like the lave of us. But he was, further a genius of high intellect, rare insight and warm humanity – and it is for these special endowments rather than

> for his common clay that we honour him. Burns has shown us, Mr Skinner said, what clay can aspire to become.
>
> Your secretary was asked by the speaker to make comment, but excused himself for having opportunity to make such comments in these minutes. He agrees with the scholarly approach of the paper. He also knows the things about Burns that were mentioned.

Appropriately, the writer of the minutes had the last word:

> There is an old choral glee, which used to be sung around the campfires by soldiers far way from home. One of the couplets in that choral is:
>
> Though each one thought a different name,
> They all sang Annie Laurie.
>
> And that is just what all of us do who follow Burns.
>
> Though each one thinks a different man,
> We all sing Robert Burns.

It was all very powerful stuff, but perhaps North America's Burns is a much more romantic figure than Scotland's. The myth is the man as far as many of them are concerned. North Britain, by the same token, as Scotland was struggling to resist becoming throughout the 18th century, was far different from Burns's Jacobite Caledonia, which itself owed more to myth than fact, but at least it served his Muse, and spurred him to songs like *My Heart's in the Highlands*.

> Wherever I wander, wherever I rove
> The hills of the Highlands forever I love.

The problem today is that Scotland is a place in the heart to many as much as it is a place on the map. It is an attitude which owes nothing to latitude, an imaginative recourse rather than a real country to live in. The whisky and haggis industries are evidence enough of this and Scotland as a country measured in mere miles isn't large enough to contain all those Grannies in their Heilan' Hames or Heather Hills. The real Scotland is a different matter. The vital fact is that its cultural heritage is not confined to Scotland itself but extends to the many Scotlands that exist beyond its borders. The Scottish diaspora is only a little less than that of the Jews and has touched as many countries around the world. One has only to travel outside Scotland to realise this.

On Burns Night, St Andrew's Night and New Year's Eve, these expatriate Scots will suddenly appear, easily recognisable in self-conscious kilts. In Scotland itself, the kilt is now only worn at weddings. Yet despite this, it cannot be denied that the Scottish cultural inheritance has an international influence notwithstanding, and as such, it is much too important to be left to the Scots themselves. It is something that should be freely offered to the world as further evidence of its identity as a distinct, separate, social, political and cultural entity. Hitherto, the Scottish artist in Scotland has been overwhelmed and inhibited by his own vulnerability and insecurity with regard to his natural identity as a Scot in his own country. The shadow from south of the border looms large north of the Tweed and, as a result, the Scot finds it difficult to 'find his light' as they say in the theatre.

Meantime, in Ayr, on Burns Night in that same year, David D. Murison proposed the Immortal Memory. Mr Murison was then editor of the *Scottish National Dictionary*, so his words would have some weight. As a man of words, he knew their value, and used them sparingly, but unerringly:

> Scotia! My dear, my native soil…'
> That I, for puir auld Scotland's sake,
> Some usefu' plan, or book could make,
> Or sing a sang at least.

> There can be no mistaking the note of the true patriot there. The true internationalist who sang of a time when 'man to man the world o'er shall brothers been for a' that'. You see, when pledging his immortal memory we are really passing judgement, not on Robert Burns, but on ourselves. We are reminding ourselves of our duty to keep the knowledge and love of his poetry, and of the country of which he wrote, alive in our own generation and to pass it on to those that come after us as part of their heritage.
>
> No nation's culture can be passive and live. It must be forever active. It must be creative. We shall all have to make it our principal aim as Scotsmen, and Scotswomen, and as lovers of Burns, the preservation of our own way of life. And for that we have no better example than Burns – who, in himself, gathered together the many threads of our Scottish and re-interpreted them for generations to come.

> He prayed indeed for world brotherhood but he never prayed for the obliteration of Scotland. Nay rather, he gave all his genius to the restoring of her name and repute as an emancipated and civilised nation, and to make her people freer and happier. And God forbid that the day shall ever come when we cease to understand and value such things...

The name Murison will remind Burnsians of the excellent Murison Burns Collection at present in the charge of the Dunfermline Central Library where nearly two thousand items relating to Burns are stored for the benefit of readers and enthusiasts. These include everything from a Kilmarnock edition to the latest CD recording and the whole thing began with John Murison, who was born in Glasgow in 1852. He became an extremely successful commercial traveller throughout Britain for a seed merchant and in his later years became friendly with the great Burns collector, W.Craibe Angus. It was he inspired Murison to start his own Burns library.

From a collection, it became an obsession and forty years later it had become too large for him to control properly as a private project and so, very reluctantly, he had to dispose of it, which is why, in 1921, Sir Alexander Gibb, of Rosyth Naval Dockyard, bought it for the City and Burgh of Dunfermline, where it has remained and prospered ever since. What is noticeable, however, is that the smallest section by far, is that dealing with 'Fiction, Drama and Parodies'. There are some concert programmes but John Murison's own collection of playbills would indicate that even in his time there was some acknowledgement of Burns and the Theatre.

Meantime, in St Louis, the flow of annual speakers was unstoppable and we now feature four more from Missouri. In 1961 their speaker was Francis C. Lloyd Junior and his topic on January 28 was 'The Letters of Robert Burns'.

> The letters of Robert Burns cover a span of fifteen years. From 1781 to the year of his death in 1796, seven hundred and ten (710) of his letters have been published. There is reason to believe that a number of important letters were destroyed by overzealous and prudish admirers of the poet. The outstanding scholar in the field of Burns' letters is Professor DeLancey Ferguson, who published in 1931 a two volume edition of Burns' letters known as the Clarendon Press

Edition. In 1953, Professor Ferguson edited a one-volume edition for the Oxford University Press which published them in its Worlds Classics Edition.

The scholarly care of Professor Ferguson is notable and in sharp contrast to earlier editions published in the late nineteenth and early twentieth centuries, for instance, the collection edited by J Logie Robertson and published by Walter Scott in 1887. So prudish were these early editors that Robert Burns was portrayed as a stuffy, pompous, self-conscious man. Most of the humour and all of the carefree gaiety of our poet had been deleted.

It can be said that letters of any significance were only written to some thirty-three persons, with his wife, Jean Armour, and one of his most faithful patronesses, Mrs Frances Anna Wallace Dunlop receiving a very high percentage.

Although the poet often referred to his peasant origin in his letters to Mrs Dunlop, he obviously wished to appear as a cultured, literary man. To quote from a sensitive lecture on Burns given last year by the poet Robert Hillyer: 'The fact is that when Burns wrote in English – and this applies to his prose as well as his verse – he did not write naturally, because for him English, as written language, was a literary medium heavily influenced by the books he had read in that tongue. In English his humour strained toward the epigram in the manner of Pope, his romantic of Gray or Thomson, his odes, also influenced by Gray, took on rhetorical flourishes that did not quite ring true to his own genius. In other words, he had too many predecessors in English!'

In sharp contrast to the letters to Mrs Dunlop and others of her social level, are the very intimate and natural letters written to some of the members of a convivial club the 'Crochallan Fencibles' which was formed during his stay in Edinburgh. In these letters colloquial expressions, and earthy and red-blooded phrases are often found.

The longest letter that Burns wrote was to Dr John Moore. This letter was written after Burns had become famous in Scotland for his poetry and after his first set of twins had been born to Jean Armour, but before the second set of twins had arrived. As he says, 'To divert my spirits a little in this miserable fog of Ennui, I have taken a whim to give you a history of myself.'

This autobiographical letter does reveal a number of

important things to us. It fills in details of his early life which show on the one hand the rugged and simple existence of the farm hand and on the other hand the absorption by this sensitive, intelligent youth of every bit of great literature that came his way. The idea that so skilled a poet as Burns could spring from the new turned furrow into a famous poet is obviously absurd. The details he gives us of his reading and the influences on his life show how great was his training, self taught though it was. Another thing this letter reveals is that Burns felt it necessary to put on a polished front when he wrote to the gentry. This letter is not in the vernacular, does not have the freshness and humour that the letters to his close friends reveal. Despite the details of his life which he has given us we would know very little about Robert Burns the man.

The end of Burns' correspondence is indeed poignant. His last two letters, one written to his beloved Jean and the other written to her father, speak for themselves. Basic love and concern speak out in these two letters written without false sentiment, theatrics, or self pity. The language of these letters is pure and unadorned.

> My dearest love, I delayed writing until I could tell you what effect sea-bathing was likely to produce. It would be injustice to deny that it has eased my pain, and I think has strengthened me; but my appetite is still extremely bad. No flesh nor fish can I swallow: porridge and milk are the only things I can taste. I am very happy to hear by Miss Jessy Lewars that you are all well. My very best and kindest compliments to her, and to all the children. I will see you on Sunday. Your affectionate husband, R Burns.

And then the final letter to Jean's father written on the eighteenth of July, 1796, just three days before his death,

> My dear Sir, Do, for heaven's sake, send Mrs Armour here immediately. My wife is hourly expecting to be put to bed. Good God! What a situation for her to be in, poor girl, without a friend! I returned from sea-bathing quarters today, and my medical friends would almost persuade me that I am better; but I think and feel that my strength is so gone that the disorder will prove fatal to me. Your son-in-law, R Burns.

On January 27th 1962 it was Thomas B Sherman with 'Impressions of a Newcomer to Burns'.

A human being born in poverty and sentenced to hard labour for a considerable part of his life is likely to view the world with a kind of numb fatalism. Burns was such a man but he escaped the brutish consequences of poverty partly because he had an educated father and became educated himself, but mostly, I think, because he was endowed with a poet's vision. A poet, almost by definition, is an alchemist. He turns base metal into gold. He converts the random and inexplicable commonplace events of life into something that is not only beautiful but also significant.

It is easy to fall into a wrong view of Burns by assuming that his verses dealing with familiar events and places are no more than rhymed aphorisms. It is easy to be misled by the fact that his verse is intelligible and his subjects are homely. There is much of Burns's poetry, no doubt, that is not exactly transcendental. There are tag lines that have become ravelled from overuse. But such is the fate of most poets. The phrases that are bandied about in the market place of popular ideas are the ones that represent some plain concept that seems to be unassailably true.

What has been rewarding to me in my brief contact with your patron poet is that he really has a poet's range and that his reputation need not rest entirely on his lyrical use of the Scotch dialect; nor on simple declaratives set in rhyming couplets.

Many admirers of Burns are really just admirers of Scotland for persona reasons. A few weeks ago I was talking to a gentleman whose name betrayed his origin and whose manner suggested that he had been influenced by one of Old Scotia's most famous exports. I asked him what he thought of Burns. 'A great Man' he said 'and the greatest poet that ever lived.' I mention this not as a prelude to an assessment of Burns in relationship to other poets. It is not necessary to establish the superiority of one artist to another to know his value. Burns's fame is beyond the need of proof. The existence of this club is an indicator of how his works have been cherished.

The relationship of a man to his work, however, is a relevant subject to all who are devoted to one or to another. Sometimes in making a comparison between the man and the artist we see at first a startling contrast. Richard Wagner, for instance, had defects as a human being that his most dedicated admirers could not overlook. He was arrogant, he was not loyal to his friends, he put himself and his interests above every other consideration. Yet his music expressed tenderness, love, and heroism. Actually, I believe there was no great discrepancy between the man and the artist, but to make that clear we would have to show the causal relationship between all the minutiae of his art and his personal life.

In the case of Burns I think the one suggests the other. Without knowing anything about the facts of his life one could assume that he had personal charm, that he could make friends on several planes of society, that he had a natural attachment to the soil, to nature and to humble men, and that he himself had known hardship.

The rigors of coaxing a living from the soil of Scotland were more severe than in most agricultural countries and we see that a reason for Scottish frugality which is sometimes interpreted as stinginess.

But this misconception is no greater than many others that afflict the minds of men. In Europe all Americans are regarded as dollar chasers and in America the French are frivolous and immoral and the English have no sense of humour.

As for Burns, it is remarkable that he wasn't hard as a rock and bitter as gall. He might have been if he hadn't become convinced in the early stages of his life that he had a 'muse' who would presently wait upon him.

He realised, of course, that a man couldn't make a living from poetry; nor did he want to. From the beginning of his young manhood he intended to find an occupation that would provide his bread and salt and still leave him time enough to pursue his muse. He liked to use that word.

I find it touching that Burns wanted to keep his muse free of the market place. Implied in this attitude is the belief that to write or paint or sing for money is to demean one's mission in life and to corrupt the product of one's mind and spirit. I cannot believe this is a valid proposition. Many artists get paid for what they do without being adversely affected.

It seems to me that an artist will inevitably draw on what's inside him – his ideas, his sensibility, his conceptions of significant form and the like – whether he is working for money or for nothing. He can't do anything else.

We know, however, that Burns was determined that nothing should tarnish his 'muse'. So he must assume that whatever he did was his best at the time he wrote.

> Whenever I want to be more than ordinary in song; to be in some degree equal to your diviner airs, do you imagine I fast and pray for the celestial emanation? Tout au contraire. I have a glorious recipe; the very one that for his own use was invented the Divinity of Healing and Poesy when first he piped to the flock of Admentus. I put myself in a regimen of admiring a fine woman; and in proportion to the adorability of her charms, in proportion you are delighted with my verses. The lightning of her eye is the godhead of Parnassus and the witchery of her smile the divinity of Helicon.

The highfalutin prose may have been intended humorously; it is not to be taken literally in any case. But there can be no doubt that he was highly susceptible to women and that he often pursues his fancy with more ardour than judgement.

When he and Jean Armour were hauled into the Kirk and publicly rebuked for their misbehaviour, he evidently thought that such humiliation was no more than he deserved. He made no public protest against it, but I can imagine that as he stood there, a convicted sinner, he was not wholly free from resentment. Perhaps he had reason to believe that some of his accusers were also no better than they should be.

Certainly he deserves to be honoured, remembered and read. He found sermons in stones and books in running brooks, and he made them tender and warm and well accessible to his fellow-countrymen and finally to the whole world of English speaking people. The foregoing sentence has a rounded oratorical flourish if I do say so myself. But I am not finished – not yet. It is more suitable, I think to call on another poet to bring this talk to a full close. So I will quote a verse by William Wordsworth:

> I mourned with thousands, but as one
> More deeply grieved, for he was gone
> Whose light I hailed when first it shone
> And showed my youth
> How verse may build a princely throne
> On humble truth.

> Thank you gentlemen – and long live Bobby Burns.

Why do Americans never refer to Bobby Frost – or Bobby Browning? Never mind, Mr Lloyd, as he said, was new to Burns. The next St Louis speaker, of 26 January 1963, chose to relate Burns to the French Revolution but at least Mr Lemoine Skinner Junior did not refer to the poet as 'Monsieur Robert Ruisseaux'.

> My job is to try to relate the mind, the character and the genius of our poet to the greatest intellectual and political upheaval in Western history. The last quarter of the Eighteenth Century posed all the big questions – all the questions we are still required to live with. What do we owe to tradition? What do we owe to reason? What in civilization can we hope to make better? Is there really a possibility of progress? What ought an intelligent conservative seek to conserve? What can a hopeful liberal expect reasonably to change? Where does religion fit in? Where is the place of patriotism? What does a man owe to himself? What does he owe to his family, his society, his country, his God?
>
> These are the terrible questions that broke up the old feudalism and Century to which the United States of America, the United Nations, the French Community, the British Commonwealth and – indeed, the Soviet Union – today are seeking to provide answers. We recognise, after 200 years, that our answers continue to be tentative and partial. The good society has still to appear – perfect and without spot. We have not so far got any alabaster cities. We have so far not built the new Jerusalem.
>
> We are, in short, still living in the half-light of the great Enlightenment, no matter how often we may wish we could draw again the comfortable covers of darkness up over our heads. We are the heirs of the Encyclopaedists, the scientists, the adventurers, the Montesquieus, the Voltaires, the Lafayettes, Washingtons, Franklins and Tom Paines. We have opened the Pandora's box of freedom. We have eaten the apple a second time. We – and the whole human race – have chosen to break loose and to be free. Even our Communist opponents accept the ultimate goal of individual freedom as they prescribe intermediate slavery as a necessary stage to be suffered through.
>
> We are all, then, descendants of that great Eighteenth

Century time of revolution and remaking – the time in which Burns lived, and a time in which I propose to show he was part of an influence that brings us today comfort, assurance and an enduring encouragement to believe that the human race can and will grow in goodness and in slow progress toward more complete individual freedom, responsibility and happiness. Charles Dickens gave me my first schoolboy impression of it – and still my most vivid impression – at the start of *A Tale of Two Cities*:

> It was the best of times, it was the worst of times, it was the age of wisdom, it was the age of foolishness, it was the epoch of belief, it was the epoch of incredulity, it was the season of Light, it was the season of Darkness, it was the spring of hope, it was the winter of despair, we had everything before us, we had nothing before us, we were all going direct to Heaven, were all going direct the other way – in short the period was so far like the present period, that some of its noisiest authorities insisted on its being received, for good and for evil, in the superlative degree of comparison only.

The first point that the historical record makes clear is that – Tories, monarchists, and established clergy aside – the bent of the intelligent, educated and optimistic Eighteenth Century mind was in favour not only of the libertarian philosophy of the Enlightenment; it was also outspoken in favour of political and revolutionary action to translate that philosophy into a real social order.

It would be, indeed, a fair generalisation to say that the leading men in the public life of Great Britain, taken as a group, initially applauded the revolution in France and wished for their neighbours across the channel the same benefits of personal liberty, security and freedom they were proud of having achieved in their own constitution with its Declaration of Rights after the Glorious Revolution following the deposition of James III a century earlier. As the wise, level-headed and practical politician Pitt observed, 'Tom Paine is quite in the right, but what am I to do? As things are, if I were to encourage Tom Paine's opinions, we should have a bloody revolution.'

It is clear that our poet, when the mood was on him, could go as far as any of the young revolutionary romantics of the day in looking to France for an example of absolute freedom – freedom approaching anarchy – freedom from all the old restraints of church and state and feudal privilege. There are moments when Burns makes even the fire eating Tom Paine seem like a model of restraint and conservative reason.

The fact of the matter is that Burns did not really have to change his view. He was no more committed with final intellectual conviction to any doctrinaire statement of the Rights of Man than he was to the divine right cause of the House of Stuart. He felt the glow of intense Scottish, national patriotism, and the exiled Stuarts became a symbol of this feeling. In this sense he was Jacobite. He felt the injustices of the established order of privilege; he suffered from the apparent unfairness of a society that gave its rewards to men for their inheritance rather than their worth. In this sense, hew as a Jacobin. 'Consistency,' he could easily have said before Emerson, 'is the hobgoblin of little minds, adored by little statesmen and philosophers and divines.'

Though Burns' verses and his letters disclose deep interest in the great events of the day and an astonishing knowledge of the personalities, politics and military campaigns of Britain, America and France, it is everywhere apparent that he was never the captive of any single viewpoint, party or doctrine.

He could be, and was, a liberal – even a revolutionary – in wide areas of his thought and feeling. He was at the same time deeply conservative in the very terms Burke himself uses to define his position in his speech, *On Conciliation with America*, 'Above all things, I was resolved not to be guilty of tampering – the odious vice of restless and unstable minds. I put my foot in the track of our forefathers, where I can neither wander nor stumble.'

Burns, for his part, put his foot in the track of his forefathers, and the strongest trait in his nature was what Virgil would have called a pious reverence for the traditions and the institutions of his native land and his familiarly society. He can mock the absurdities of narrow religion. But reverence wins in the end:

The great Creator to revere
Must sure become the creature;
But still the preaching can't forbear,

And ev'n the rigid feature:
Yet ne'er with wits profane to range
By complaisance extended;
An Atheist's laugh's a poor exchange
For Deity offended!

Burns, briefly, is the kind of paradox that is part of the make up of the homme moyen sensual of all ages. He is a devoted husband and father. But his eye wanders; his behaviour strays. He is disdainful of indolence. He works hard at his job. But he is again and again incapacitated by drink and debauch. He is restive against the narrow limiting rural society he was born into. But he praised its simple virtues with unmatched beauty in *The Cotter's Saturday Night*. He can be scathingly sarcastic on the subject of aristocratic pretension and yet frankly, openly admire a particular aristocrat he thinks admirable... Burns' radicalism, then, at its root can, I think, be compared to the radicalism of the Christian gospel. He saw the hope of the Enlightenment as a hope 'not come to destroy, but to fulfil.'

'Where Liberty is, there is my country,' said Benjamin Franklin. 'Where Liberty is not, there is mine,' said Tom Paine. Compare the words of Robert Burns in a letter to Lord Eglinton, 'I cannot,' he says, 'I cannot rise to the exalted ideas of a citizen of the world at large; but have all those national prejudices which I believe glow particularly strong in the breast of a Scotsman. There is scarcely anything to which I am so feelingly alive as the honour and welfare of old Scotia.'

How many read Tom Paine today? How many read Edmund Burke? How many remember, or care about, the issues of reform in England in the late Eighteenth and early Nineteenth centuries? How many know the differences among our own Bill of Rights, the Declaration of Rights of Man of the Glorious Revolution of 1688 and the declaration, based on both, of the French National Assembly?

It is, I think, no accident that Burns' voice – rising above the harsh particulars of the argument that still goes on around the world today – speaks the deep and universal meaning of our common inspiration for freedom and for brotherhood. It speaks so because it is a voice at once conservative and radical – a voice for change and a voice for preserving the best of our past – a voice requesting us to strive to make a better society – a voice that admonishes not to depart from the foot paths of

> our forefathers. But, above all, it is the voice of a unique, poetic genius – a bard in the deepest and most mysterious sense of that great name – who found images and words to touch men's hearts as well their minds, and in simple, moving, singing language to remind us all, generation after generation of our common humanity, our weaknesses, our loves, our loneliness, our danger and our hope.

Finally in this section, on Burns Night 1964, William Stephenson reminded his fellow-Americans that young Burns 'Wore the only tied hair in the Parish.'

> I recently invited a seminar of graduate students to jot down what they knew of Robert Burns. The replies, on the whole, were all 'doucey halesome.' A few, of course, said 'nothing at all.' One thought Robert Burns wrote the script for *Tight Little Island*. Or was he, another enquired, a roue of the Byron type? Another said that Burns was a British poet, 'who had a great love affair with someone – and didn't he write Tintern Abbey?' Several could recall a few poems – *Auld Lang Syne* especially, and a few familiar quotations – 'The best laid schemes o' mice an' men gang aft agley' – 'Oh wad some power the giftie gie us.' – 'To see oursels as others see us!
>
> Otherwise, Burns the man was variously described as 'A man with a lust for living, who put the barmaid into his poetry – a man who appreciated life and enjoyed living it – a man who believed in letting life attain the potential that freedom of choice – philosophical, moral, religious – implied. Convivial, but with a strong social conscience – 'a man's a man for a' that, etc – poverty-stricken, ill-healthed...who had a way of looking at the beauties of natural life. Happy, and thankful of what he had, especially his family – who loved life and happiness, not material things. – Lusty poet, born of poor parents. – gentle, hearth-loving Burns. – Robert Burns is about the only name of a poet I know.'
>
> Snyder remarks, as well, that Burns was interested in human nature, not scenery – he loved men and women, and found his happiness in associating with them – he was a citizen of the world. The graduates emphasised the lively enjoyment, lustiness and happiness, and in one or two instances the element of freedom of choice which Hecht describes as 'liberty of conscience,' and Snyder as 'passionate detestation' of all sorts of dependence.

But for me Robert Burns the man is more astonishing than either Hecht or Snyder could discern, and far more interesting than the popular view conveys. Speaking now as a psychologist, interested in the epochs of man's character, I propose to you that Robert Burns stands squarely as the first of modern men, 200 years before his time (and indeed far more, for few have reached his stature even now).

Some rhyme a neeber's name to lash;
Some rhyme (vain thought!) for needfu' cash;
Some rhyme to court the countra clash,
An' raise a din:
For me, an aim I never fash;
I rhyme for fun.

The genius of Burns shows primarily when he writes for 'fun': *Tam o Shanter* is the epic of absolute fun – he takes devil worship in one hand, holds the tail of Calvinism in the other, and sings a song well described as 'worthy to stand beside the best tales in the literature of the world.'

But by fun I do not mean the ribald verses with which his name is associated in much of the public mind. Instead, I mean pure joy which a man has essentially by himself. My graduate students caught something of this feeling, as the following remarks suggest: –

> He hit upon things we've all thought about before, but can't see as clearly, or express as beautifully as Burns does – his writing carry sorrow, pitifulness; yet he could find and accept gracious qualities in the most menial of subjects – he had a genius for placing reality in his poems.

It takes a great deal of something called self-consciousness to make a man autonomous. And by self-conscious I do not mean shyness, but an ability to look at oneself squarely, to recognise and respect one's own feelings. The child learns something of this as it freely plays, in pure play; Robert Burns, by great good fortune, learned what it meant and is its epitome. He became, then, an autonomous man. But this also made it possible for him, I believe, to be the great humanitarian he was, champion of freedom and independence more generally. He knew what existence meant, he had sampled the records, books, candies, cookies of a free store – and he wanted everyone else to have the same unbounded pleasure of existence. Gentleman, I give you

Robert Burns, the first of Existential, as of Brotherly, Man!

Here endeth this chapter and also the generous contribution of the St Louis Club of Missouri to this volume.

Then up amang thae lakes and seas,
They'll mak what rules and law they please:
Some daring Hancock, or a Franklin,
May set their Highland blood a-ranklin';
Some Washington again may head them,
Or some Montgomery, fearless, lead them.
(Address of Beelzebub)

9
The Burns Festival at Ayr
1975

> The books that have influenced me are –
> Coleridge and Keats in my youth
> and Burns as I grew older and wiser.
> (John Ruskin)

One wall of our dining room/library here in Auckland is devoted to various items of Burnsiana collected during my Burns-playing days, as an actor, which were almost as long as he had lived – thirty-seven years. One item is a framed certificate from the British Tourist Authority commending Shanter Productions (which was my company) for promoting a Burns Festival in Ayr during 1976. It amounts to about all I have to show for almost a decade of work on the project but it does bring back a lot of very mortal memories – good and bad – and we will come to them in due course. Since I first began with the solo Burns in 1965 with *There Was A Man* and later in 1967 with *The Robert Burns Story* it was often remarked how like the poet I was in the costume. This was borne out when I played at Dumfries Theatre Royal in 1969 and the local paper ran a cartoon showing the Amelia Hill statue standing on its plinth in the centre of a roundabout in the north end of the High Street. with a 'Sold Out' sign round its neck.

One of the local journalists responsible for the good business at the Theatre Royal was Frank Ryan. In 1971, Frank was asked to propose the Immortal Memory for the Dumfries branch of the Scottish National Party. His verse-address centred on this very statue and what it might have been thinking as it sat there since 1882. Frank imagined it had come alive. This is a short excerpt from his impish piece.

> When Hogmanay at last is past
> And Janwar' winds are at fu' blast

When winter sales are a' the rage
And posties fight to up their wage
Oor minds to ain great topic turns-
The life and works o' Rabbie Burns.
In spite o' wildcat strikes an' freezes
In spite o' blasts and bombs and bleezes
In spite o' hijacks, lunar shots
In spite o' they damned decimal dots...
In pubs and halls throughoot the land
Guid Scots are gather'd – some half-canned
Tae praise Burns' name in verse and sang
And honour him wi' speeches lang.

Yin speaker claims Rab was a Tory
An' proves his point wi' true blue story
Another says he'll eat his hat
If Burns was oucht but pure Scot Nat.
Some other swear the bard was red
As ony blood that Wallace shed
Nae matter speakin' guid or ill
They'll hae him fitting ony bill.
He's Jacobine and Jacobite
Charlatan and shining knight
Parochial poet, Parnassian Bard,
Reactionary an' avant-garde,
The Exciseman who loved the cratur,
Family man an' fornicator...

Like Tam o'Shanter in the tale
I'd had my fill o' potent ale
And as I staggered frae the howff
My brain reeled like a gormless gowff.
(Nowadays I'm worldly wiser
Thinks: thanks tae yon damned breathyliser!)
As doon the narrow close I rolled
I saw a sicht that turned me cold;
Like organ stops my e'en stood oot
My heartbeat raced, my feet took root.

'There was a Man? – or was it so?
Surrounded by a ghaistly glow,
Nae normal bod o' human mould

But yin frae yon immortal fold,
Wi' guid frock coat and fancy breeks
Wi' curly locks and hair-borne cheeks,
Wi' ruffled shirt an' buckled shoon
He micht hae been a hippy loon.
But yet his features rang a bell,
I felt I'd seen him whiles mysel'
But tae spier ootricht, I kent I darenae
I wondered: is it that man Cairney?

Frank goes on to have his verse-dialogue with the ghost of Burns and has the latter make the amusing point that if he ever came back to earth again the last place he would be seen would be at a Burns Supper.

Of course there are Burns Suppers and Burns Suppers. Gordon Ross tells of giving the Immortal Memory to an expedition 18,000 feet up at the Mount Everest Base Camp. He said they all got high that night. Gordon also tells about the Burmese gentleman, John Htet-Kin, who gave the Immortal Memory at the Cameron House Hotel in Burmese – with simultaneous translation from Mrs Htet-Kin, but it turned out that John had married a Scottish girl in Edinburgh nearly forty years before, and was able to continue in perfect Scots once he had the audience convinced they were hearing Burns in Burmese. Memories are made of incidents like this, but the oddest, and perhaps the saddest Immortal Memory was that given from a tape recorder in Spain. Jimmy Logan, the late Scottish actor/comedian and lovely man, and the one, incidentally, who started me off as Burns in performance, told the story in his autobiography, *It's A Funny Life* (1998). It concerned Bill Simpson, the Ayrshire actor who won fame as Dr Finlay, but who always harboured a secret wish, so he told me, to play Robert Burns on film. Sadly, Bill was to die in 1986 aged only 56. Jimmy says of him: 'I always called him Poor Bill...'

> He was drinking more than he should have been, and, ignoring his doctor's advice, he went back to Spain, where he had previously owned a house and still had a lot of friends. Unfortunately the drink took its toll and Bill ended up in hospital. He had planned to do the Immortal Memory at a Burns Supper with his friends in Spain, but he was suddenly called back to London. Bill recorded the Immortal Memory on cassette before leaving. He died shortly afterwards, and never

> saw those friends in Spain again. Bill's recording was spoiled by a hum on the tape, and the quality was terrible. But listening to that recording made me realise what a beautiful, toned voice Bill Simpson had. He was brought up in the same part of Ayrshire as Burns, and spoke about the bard with great authority. He was a kind of Scottish Richard Burton. On the day of his funeral all his friends in Spain put their dining tables out in the sun, filled them with food and wine, and had the kind of party Bill would have enjoyed. After his funeral in Ayr we went back to Bill's favourite hotel and drank a toast to his memory with his family. At the bar there was a chair known as Bill's Chair. And in that hotel Bill was always remembered by those who knew him. At the next Burns Supper Bill's friends played his Immortal Memory, even though the quality was poor. And they have done the same every year since in his memory…

It's that kind of extraordinary action by ordinary people that underlines Dr Lindsay's point about Burns's being a 'People Poet'.

This is evident to me in the hundreds of unsolicited poems I have received over the time I have been involved with Burns as a part to play. Some of the effusions are remarkably good and some are downright awful. Most are in-between but they are all sincere and it says much for Burns's innate sincerity that he can prompt people who are not writers or critics or academics into putting their thoughts about him on to paper. These kind of 'performances', as Burns would call them, never ever pretended to be great verse, but they said what they wanted to say and said it simply and directly.

Then of course, there is the other side of the coin. These writers would pay back Burns in another way. Their verses were often bitter but there is no denying their passionate sincerity. Why is it though that this sort of thing is always sent anonymously? The following piece came to me in four handwritten pages of white, ruled paper, with each verse neatly numbered from 1 to 17. The title was underlined <u>The Immoral Memory</u> and beneath it, the heading:

A poem written on Burn's Night, 1966 and
addressed to Robert Burns.

1 They congregate to worship you
They come to supper on this night,

Disciples (self-appointed) who,
In your name, preach of right.

2 They sing your songs, proclaim your verse,
Their eyes grown dim and misty
They quote as if they said it first
And sing duets with whisky.

3 They dine on haggis, broth and neeps
And call themselves right lucky,
For they hae meat and they can eat,
(they wish that it were turkey).

4 'Ye Banks and Braes' brings tears to eyes
'Of a' the Airts' a smile
These men who hide from wintry skies
And rarely walk a mile.

5 They weep because your 'Angel' died
That sweet, that favourite daughter,
Forgetting others died today
For want of food and water.

6 They've lost the man who lived and died
The man you were whilst living
The man who raged, despaired and cried
And begged to be forgiven

7 Good and bad, and weak and strong
A human man like I am
No silhouette against the sky
A Hector or a Priam.

8 A man who knew that life was short
Who lived the life of ten
As if each day would be your last
You shame us. Are we then

9 To die of creeping common sense
Who dip our toes in living
Whilst you were totally immersed
In taking and in giving

10 You felt more grief upon the death
Of one red-tipped flower
Than they felt when a baby died
Who'd lived for one brief hour.

11 They found him in a plastic bag
Motherless, lifeless flesh
A broken egg, spilled and cold
Dropped from a careless nest.

12 That baby died within their walls
They feel but little sorrow
They call it 'shame' they shake their heads
And laugh again tomorrow
13 You felt great pain. Your soul was marred
Scars marked your war with life
But life defeated even you
You wearied of its strife
14 But oh! You fought with splendid strength
You did not hide like most.
A living memory you left
But they worship now a ghost
15 And so tonight they fool themselves
That you would call them 'brother'
And puppet-like your words they quote
Then congratulate each other.
16 I know what you would want from them
Not praise or speeches pretty
But love for lonely, loveless men
And grief, and joy, and pity
17 This makes me speak to you in shame
I spurn a crown of laurel
Apologies are what I bring
For a mem'ry made immoral.

Voltaire is reputed to have said – 'I disapprove of what you say, but I will defend to the death your right to say it.' He also said – 'The secret of being boring is to say everything.' So we shall say no more at this point, and bear in mind what Robert himself said in his *Epistle to Davie*:

Then let us cheerfu' acquiesce
Nor make our scanty pleasure less,
By pining at our state.

1975 was designated as the Year of Architecture in Europe and Charles Rennie Mackintosh was beginning to be talked about seriously in Scotland. I was playing Cyrano de Bergerac in the theatre at Newcastle at the time, and one night a well-known Scottish businessman, R.W.Adams OBE, called backstage after the performance to ask if I were interested in developing a script on the famous Scottish architect but at that time my head was just full of an idea I had for a summer festival of Burns to be held at Ayr. I had discussed this idea with my manager and accompanist, Colin Harvey Wright as we travelled around the world with my solo shows on Burns and McGonagall and when I got home I tried to interest various likely bodies like the Arts Council, the Scottish Tourist Board, Strathclyde Regional Council and the Kyle and Carrick District Council in a summer Burns event but the unanimous reaction was that it was a wild idea, and anyway, in the good old Scottish phrase, 'there was no call for it'. Well, I was calling for it – and loudly, but to no avail. Deaf ears all round. The scheme might have been described as 'Hot Ayr' so derisive were the comments I provoked. Even my friends in the press were apathetic to its likely interest. Yet to me the idea of bringing Burns out of the snows of January and into the sun of July was irresistible.

The nine days between the date of his death, 21 July and the date of of his first printing, 31 July were an ideal bracket on which to hang a garland of different Burns activities centred around Ayr and the various Burns places. No speeches, no haggis, no immortal memories this time, but the spoken word or sung note in performance as in plays, musicals, solos, recitals, talks, symposia – anything that could entertain and edify an audience about Burns away from the unyielding, and often unsightly cement of the traditional winter Supper. And in the open air too. After all, it was the same air that Burns himself once breathed, in the fields, by the river and under the blackthorn tree. The whole concept had a fresh, bucolic feel and I could almost smell the red, red roses. Alas, I could convince no one. So the three of us decided to do it on our own – myself, Colin and his accordion. We had gone round the world with Burns, surely we could go round a few small venues in Ayrshire? So Colin made all the arrangements and organised some dates for *The Robert Burns Story*.

We opened at the Town Hall, Maybole with its fabulous acoustics. Cumnock Town Hall wasn't in the same class as a venue but it was given at no charge on condition we take a whole front row of Chinese from Chicago. They never moved a muscle throughout the whole performance but I gathered later that they enjoyed Colin's accordian. At Kilmarnock we were there on 31st July, the very day of the Kilmarnock Edition. We gave the show in the Grand Hall of the Palace Theatre with the audience seated around at tables. I enjoyed playing in the round but the ladies of Killie stole the show with their exquisite singing of *Ye Banks and Braes*.

We finished up with performances at Dalbeattie and Dumfries, back at my favourite Theatre Royal. Next day, I joined Provost Robertson at the Brow Well for an open-air service and I took the opportunity to reflect on the ten days that had just passed. As I have said before, these solo performances as Burns were my nightly Immortal Memory. Each evening was a toast in celebration of his life and work and I make no apologies for my career-long association with him. If I gave my audiences a memory they certainly gave me back as many in return. This exchange is exactly what live theatre is about. It's a sharing, not an imposing by any side. However, these aesthetic considerations aside, Shanter Productions, which was my trading name, lost money in the prototype nine days, so maybe the men in the suits were right after all.

Notwithstanding the cash facts, it had been a worthwhile artistic investment and audience reaction and numbers – especially among tourists – had been enough to provide me with enough field information to approach the authorities once again. So, more in a spirit of altruism than commercial acumen, I knocked on all the doors again. To my surprise two of them opened – the Scottish Tourist Board and Kyle and Carrick District Council. This time I traded under Theatre Consultants (Scotland), which was my Sunday name for Shanter Productions, so that my position could be seen as consultative as well as executive. The idea was accepted and dates were scheduled for the first official Burns Festival in the summer of 1976. The gamble of the year before had paid off and everyone looked forward to a bright summer. I could now get down to some serious Burns planning and take up Mr Adam's offer to 'do something about Mackintosh' over the winter. Quite honestly I welcomed the break from Burns.

Not so the great majority of Burnsians. The haggis season of '76 was on them and Immortal Memories were being brushed up. Or being created from scratch. In the latter category was Glasgow solicitor, Ian McCarry. In 1990, he wrote a little booklet about his initial Burns experience, and had it published by Ardlui Press. The following is taken from it. By the way, the line drawings illustrations in the booklet by his cousin, Thomas Docherty, are quite superb, but this is Ian's story of his first Immortal Memory.

He admits to always having been 'a great admirer of Robert Burns. To me, he is a great poet and a great Scot.' However, he didn't ask to do the Immortal Memory at the inaugural Burns Supper of the Arlington Baths. It seems that his name was put forward by someone at Glasgow University. In 1975, he had recently started his own business, so was quite busy. Anyway, on the night before the Supper, he was in bed in his 'wee flat in Maryhill' when he had the idea of doing the Immortal Memory in verse. He immediately got up and crept into the living room, 'not even taking time to turn on the electric fire', and started writing. He finished it about 5 o'clock the next day. Unfortunately, with all the hurry and all the amendments, he found it difficult to read , so his wife, Moira, then pregnant with their first child, wrote it all out neatly and Ian read it later that night. She hadn't intended going to the Supper but after writing it all out she was curious to see how it would go. 'We had a wonderful evening', said Ian later. He also said that everybody else who was speaking was great, especially Lavinia Derwent, whose reply for the Lassies was excellent. He was diffident about his own contribution but he trusted his inspiration – 'Burns won't mind my little bit of poetic licence...' Anyway, this is what Moira wrote out – or most of it at any rate...

...Poor Rabbie died aged thirty-seven
And went up to the door of heaven.
Auld Peter met him at the gate,
And fetched his scales tae test his fate,
'Now Rab,' he said, 'These scales will tell,
If you are doomed tae go to Hell,
Or if these gates will open wide
And ye will take yer place inside.
On one pan we maun place the ill,
The sins committed by your will
Frae when ye learnt o' richt an' wrang,
Until yer final fatal pang.
There's no much in yer early years,
Just wee trifles it appears...
Yer ither sins were as a man,

Of twa types only was their plan.
Ye'd fa' for ony lassie's wink,
An' times ye'd tak na tent o'drink.
But in yer plea in mitigation,
In this our haly litigation,
It must be said that ev'ry lass
That thro' yer span o' life did pass,
Forgave ye aught that ye did do,
They fand what love meant frae you:

And as for drink and socialisin'
In Scotland that is scarce surprisin'
For any race upon the earth
That took sic things o' little warth,
As water, barley, malt an' yeast,
Distilled the mixture which released,
A magic liquid, gold and pure,
Becoming whisky when mature,
Should be forgiven, if a lad
Betimes mair than he needs has had.'

Then spake the De'il's Advocate,
Wi' face as grey an' sharp as slate,
That while he on this earth was loose,
Defended murd'rers frae the noose
And shared wi' robbers in their spoils,
Protecting them frae judges' toils
For bags o' gaud, an' even worse,
Was pleased tae tak' a widow's purse,
An' empty oot each last bawbee,
In payment of his fancy fee;
And a' the while, wi' eiks an' feus
And dark conveyancin's every ruse,
He made her sign a wily missive,
Wi' stipulations sae permissive,
That when tae it she'd put her hand
She had lost a' her deid man's land.
Then bailies came wi' Sheriff's writ,
The wife an' weans refused tae quit,
She was dragged screamin' wi' her loons
And marched away by red dragoons.

'We wish to lay before this court
The De'il's Indictment and Report,
That libels seven past convictions
For sirin' weans without restrictions
Of yer ain haly marriage law;
And furthermore, a hunder twa
Offences of intoxication,
Including, that on one occasion
In seventeen hunder ninety three,
At Mistress Riddell's house for tea,
The company was most refined,
And after eating, all designed
Tae take part in a Masque that night
About the Sabine Women's plight.
At first the game was modest paced,
The gentlemen the ladies chased,
Until this Burns, who'd drunk too well
O' wine and port, forgot himsel;
A lassie's smile for stimulation,
Attempted complete simulation.
So Maister Riddell stopp'd the game,
And banned Burns frae his ancient hame.'

St Peter said, 'There's little doubt
That Robert Burns, wi' girls about,
Or drinkin' well in company,
Was apt tae stray tae some degree,
But now we'll hear guid o'the man,
An place it in the other pan.
He loved his wife, his girls and boys
Nae mair love turtle dove enjoys.
Upon the ploo he brak his health,
Tae earn for them a little wealth.
Tho' weakened by rheumatic fever,
He'd bend his back across the lever,
And o'er the field he'd guide the pair,
That swat before the hard ploo share.
At last he had to leave the ferm,
For truth, the land had done him herm,
An tak a job that few wad boast,
A Customs and Excise Man's post.
He warked at this wi' sic devotion,

That he had earned deserved promotion.
Before of this he had been told,
A wasting death had laid him cold.

But what a memory he left,
What wondrous lines, what sangs sae deft.
Around him there was pomp and poor,
But frae its might he didna cour...
Whate'er the rich be a' at,
A man's a man for a' that.
An' how he prized the haly faith
O' Minister and Cottar baith,
An' ranted at the self smug few,
That sat sae prood at their ain pew,
The Holy Willies, that wad drool
At ae puir lass on the kirk's stool
O' discipline, when they knew well,
They should be there instead themsel.

They think they're saved; too soon, I fear,
Nae man is saved till he's in here.
An' how Burns loved his native land,
When a' around him on each hand,
Were bowin', beggin', bendin', basin',
Before the English, for a place in
A Cabinet or Parliament,
A Royal box or regiment,
A colony or sinecure,
To lay the rod upon the poor,
And enter an Establishment,
That nae Scotsman e'er before had kent.
Rab didna write his sangs for treasure,
But used his auld Scots tongue wi pleasure,
Collecting sangs frae kintra folk,
An' addin' words and rhyme bespoke
So that a' the warld now sings his sangs,
Thrills wi' his loves, weeps wi his pangs,
Addresses haggis and wee beasties,
That start wi panic in their breasties.

Grim Russian Commissars declaim
About auld Tam O'Shanter's fame,

Americans now raise their glass
Tae toast his summer's red rose lass.
And simple folk the world o'er
Appreciate each year the more.
How he spak out tae mak' men free
And that a' men should brithers be.'

But lang before the saint had stopp't
The scales o'fate had firmly dropp't.
The pan o' guid had sic a load,
The weights had even overflow'd.
An' scattered loosely o'er the flair,
Was gaud wad saved a thoosand mair,
The gateman slowly turned his head,
But De'il an' advocate had fled....

And if Burns reached his heaven in Ian McCarry's charming verse-memory, then it could be said that I had reached mine with the first official Burns Festival in 1976. The *Burns Chronicle* reported on its progress and development from time to time with articles by its Editor, James A Mackay, James Glass of the Burns Federation and Judith Sleigh, at that time a senior executive in the Scottish Tourist Board. A selection of their comments is given here.

> The Robert Burns Festival is presented by Theatre Consultants (Scotland) Kyle and Carrick District Council, Kilmarnock and Louden District Council and the Scottish Tourist Board. Dumfries and Galloway declined to participate officially although some performances took place in their area. In its first established year (1976) that is, after John Cairney's original 'test run' in 1975, the festival won an award from the British Tourist Authority in its 'Come to Britain' competition and now, with John Cairney as its inaugural Festival Director, it bids fair to become an important date in the calendar of events which Scotland offers in the summer season.
>
> Most performances were centred around Rozelle House in Ayr and a charming little open-air Courtyard Theatre was created in the stable space before the McLaurin Gallery there. Mr Cairney's company presented local artists in an original Burns musical, *Bard* written and directed by him, which played to full houses despite the midgies – an occupational hazard for any outdoor event. It was noticed that many of the

audience were from abroad, particularly Canada and America. John Cairney, whose show *The Robert Burns Story* has been seen in many parts of the world, had obviously done well in his role of unofficial ambassador. Talks and readings with musical accompaniment were given in the room of Rozelle House and refreshments were available.

The following year saw the inauguration of the Land o' Burns Centre which was officially opened by the singer, Moira Anderson, an Ayr girl herself, and speakers included Provost Paton of Ayr, Mr Hutchison Sneddon and Mr Robin Maclellan, Chairman of the Scottish Tourist Board – who said that the Interpretation Centre – 'would add a new dimension to Scottish holidays and attract about a 100,000 visitors... it marked a new era in understanding Burns and telling the story of Scotland's poet... it would also serve as a further link in the chain of Burns Heritage sites around the west country and a landmark in what will become the Burns Trail... it is also extremely handy for visitors just off the plane at Prestwick. It might encourage them to stay awhile... in addition, Scottish teachers and their pupils will benefit from having their knowledge of Burns clarified by the wonderful audio-visual presentation which brings the story of Burns to life.'

An episode from that life was featured in Joan Biggar's play, *A Bird's Wing Beating* which premiered at Ayr and played at the Harbour Arts Theatre, Irvine. It also featured a young actor named Gregor Fisher in his first professional role. To the north, Dean Castle in Kilmarnock drew capacity audiences for performances under the aegis of Jock Thomson and in Dumfries Jean Redpath, recently returned from the States, demonstrated her wide knowledge of Burns songs. Extra events included traditional dancing, pipe bands and brass bands, sheep dog trials and side-shows – in short, something for everyone in one happy summer spell.

A focal point in each Festival so far had been the symposium, with the aim being to promote discussion on Burns and his work; this was an event which was always of special interest to Burns enthusiasts who could also contribute to the discussion, and in 1977 the platform consisted of Maurice Lindsay, speaking on 'Burns and Nationhood', Jean Redpath on 'Burns the Collector', John Weir on 'Burns the Mason' and Jock Thomson on 'The Merry Muses of Caledonia'. James Glass reported on this for the *Burns Chronicle*:

Maurice Lindsay's main theme was the disappearance of the old Scotland into what was termed 'North Britain'. He also acknowledged Burns's debt to Alan Ramsay and Robert Fergusson for the revival of the Scottish language in the 18th-century. Both men were heroes to Burns and they encouraged him to reverse the trend away from Old Scots which was carried on in the novels of Sir Walter Scott. This work in turn was continued by Hugh MacDiarmid and from around 1950 – 'there has been a reawakening of the Scottish spirit, leading to a strong feeling of being ourselves'. Scotland on her own can become part of the European movement but none of this might have been attained had it not been for the work of Burns.

Miss Redpath, to the delight of the audience, sung most of her contribution to the symposium but between songs she claimed that Burns was one of the first folk-lorists and it was his work preserved almost all that exist today of Scottish traditional song and work was now on hand to preserve most of these on disc. One pleasing aspect of Miss Redpath's contribution was the audience participation she encouraged.

John Weir concentrated on that aspect of Freemasonry which concerned Burns's introduction to the craft at Tarbolton where there had already existed a weavers' guild, a farmers' society, a universal friendly society and, at a later date, a branch of the Reform Movement.

By 1771 it had become a stronghold of Masonic activity and for such a small community it sustained two lodges for a time each with more than a hundred members, one of which, Lodge St James, Burns joined in 1781. What one has to remember about Burns is that once he became a mason he stayed a mason.

Jock Thomson, in considering Burns's collection of Bawdry, or 'Songs in the Oral Tradition', put the point that it might be thought of as a third Commonplace Book. It started as a collection of street songs and ballads to old Scottish airs which Burns sought to keep in order to preserve these lovely old melodies. The lyrics, however distasteful, had a therapeutic value in attacking the social evils of the time. However, by no means all of the songs in his handwriting were of his creation and this is what caused some confusion and embarrassment among his early biographers. But Mr Thomson was of the opinion that 'we should wish that Burns had collected enough street songs to fill a thousand Merry Muses...'

1977 was also the year of the Greenock Burns Club's 175th Birthday, and the Mother Club Bard, the Rev James L. Dow wrote a special Ode for the Occasion, on which, by the way, another clergyman, the Right Reverend Dr.Leonard Small, an honorary President of the Club, proposed the Immortal Memory. Rev. Dow wrote:

A century had just begun
The year, ye'll note, was eighteen one;
A wheen Greenockians, just for fun,
Yet mair than mirth,
Gathered tae honour Ayrshire's son
And Robert's birth.

For years a hunder and seventy five,
Whiles sair put on tae bide alive,
Your mother's managed tae survive
War's crucifix.
Kennin' that peace will ne'er arrive
By politics.

The men that aye for power yearn
And Cominform and Comintern,
Like a' dictators never learn
That what they've wrought
Will fade awa' frae man's concern
And be forgot.

But in the hearts of you and me,
Gathered in silence or in jollity,
Abides his spirit that is free
Of Storied urns.
Endures the Immortal Memory
Of Robert Burns.

And so another year passed, and yet another Burns Festival was upon us. Judith Sleigh reviewed the revised showing of *Bard* which was my previous The Holy Fair with a new director, Tom Raffell and musical direction by Tom Campbell. The leading parts were played by Jay Smith and Alison Hamilton and the production was given a page in the 1979 *Chronicle.*

The premiere was a resounding success...and there was a

general feeling of disappointment that it could not be prolonged for another week...It was the high point of a Festival which was studded with splendid performances, including *As Others Saw Him*, with John Cairney, Russell Hunter and others, a Courtyard Concert with Bill McCue, Patricia Carrick and others, a Town Hall concert with Marilyn de Blieck, Raymond Bramwell and others... As I write this, the third Burns Festival is only six weeks away and events over the past few months have laid the foundation for an annual event which will we hope, appeal to members of Burns clubs all over the world. Several organisations including the Scottish Tourist Board, local authorities and the Burns Federation have been working together to produce a programme of entertainment. Venues this year have increase to include Irvine, Moffat, Largs and Kilbirnie and visitors will also have the opportunity to visit Finlaystone House, once home of the Earl of Glenciarn, Burns friend and patron. The Burns Club in Irvine have also joined us and Sam Gaw will be giving a lecture on Burns Ayrshire...The members of the Committee which has been formed are aware of their responsibility in presenting events not only for those with a knowledge of Burns but also for those whose interest has stopped short at *Auld Lang Syne*. To some extent this is a matter of education and the visitor attracted to a film show on the Burns Country in Moffat or the Holy Fair in Ayr may well go on to all the Burns Heritage sites, or to join his local Burns Club – and perhaps become President of the Burns Federation... plans are now being discussed of the possible formation of a Burns Festival Society, now that the event is established as an annual promotion. This Society would be open to all – individuals, clubs, businesses – and would be responsible for promoting the Festival, organising some events, liasing with all concerned, offering concessions to members, organising a Festival Club. Members of Burns Clubs will be kept informed of our plans through the Burns Federation. Meanwhile the Burns Festival Committee would like to extend to all of you a very warm welcome to Burns Country and to Scotland in 1979.

For this Festival '79 I had written *A Drunk Man Looks at Robert Burns* which combined Burns and Hugh MacDiarmid, and since I was Burns (although now pushing it in terms of age) I hired Russell Hunter to join me as the Drunk Man (MacDiarmid). Looking back on this performance after more than thirty years it still remains one of the great comic creations that Russell Hunter managed in a long and busy career. The presentation was no more than a dramatic reading – on paper – but Hunter made it a supreme piece of theatre, funny, so funny and heart-breaking by the end – 'Oh, I hae a silence left...' he whispered, and the curtain came down in that silence before breaking into a thunder of applause. It opened at Ayr and played at Irvine and East Kilbride to the same wonderful reaction, and then was heard no more. But what a wonderful memory.

I am genuinely sorry to say, the Burns Festival sickened and died over the next three or four years. A series of stuttering, semi-celebrity concerts and half-hearted local events put paid to any imaginative leaps in a Burns Performance direction and the whole concept of aligning the poet with his places through live performance was quickly lost sight of. The high cultural aims of new work and commissions for Scottish artists and performers now became a dull re-hash of old concert-party and seaside holiday fare. One of the last shows to be featured in the final Festival of 1982 was the Garnock Valley Youth Theatre Puppet Show which used marionnettes to portray the life of the Bard. Nothing could have been more appropriate for the death-knell of live performance in the name of Burns. I mean no disrespect to the Garnock Vally Youth Theatre, but bloody puppets! The Burns Festival, as everybody admitted in the beginning, was a good idea. It was something which, in its sturdy infancy had promised so much for Burns and his work, and now it was dead. It may yet come again – this summer-time Burns. I hope so. But it will not be in my time. Meantime, the winter Burns carried on much as usual.

Orwell's year of 1984 opened and R.W.Adams OBE, the same gentleman who had foreseen the fashion for Mackintosh, found himself addressing the Aberdour Boat Club at their Burns Supper. Bob, who is an accountant by trade, and is now a successful playwright, had been commissioned in the Paras during the war, and knew how to deal with the orders he had been given – 'Burns if you must but a laugh if you can and not longer than fifteen minutes – twenty at most'. As a golfer, he also recognised that this request was par for the course at many Burns Suppers, so he got on with it – in his own way.

Commodore, Ladies and Gentlemen,
I would like to start by thanking you for inviting Mary and me to join you this evening. I have enjoyed myself very much – till now.

I have heard it said that the Aberdour Boat Club Burns Night is a bit of an orgy – and I thought of Ogden Nash's words –

Home is heaven and orgies are vile,
But we need an orgy once in a while.

Amongst the last recorded words of Rabbie Burns was the plea, 'Don't let the awkward squad fire over me.' He meant, literally, that he didn't wish the more inept of the local fusiliers firing a ragged fusillade over his mortal remains or – I wonder sometimes if he meant the battalions of after dinner speakers who would sound off over his immortal memory.

And forward though he couldna see, he guessed
and feared.

The very variety of the human conditions and emotions highlighted by Burns means that an equal or even greater variety of speakers can express the same or lesser sentiments as if Burns had taken the very words out of their mouths.

My own credentials for this momentous toast are few. But there is a coincidence. William Burns, or Burness, was born at Dunnotor, just south of Stonehaven, and I was married at Donnotor Church in Stonehaven – and there started a hard, grim, miserable life – for William Burns, of course, not me.

And my family name is once mentioned in a Burns poem, perhaps appropriately – I leave you to judge…

As father Adam once was fooled,
A case that's still too common,
Here stands a man a woman ruled,
The devil ruled the woman.

However, perhaps the best and only qualification is that I am an admirer of Burns without reservation. From me there will be no apologies, doubts or qualifications. To me, Burns was a great Scot – perhaps the greatest of all Scots – and certainly the world's most celebrated poet.

There is not and never will be an annual Shakespeare junket

in England. Or an annual Longfellow barbecue in America. Or an annual Omar Khayam glass of wine, loaf of bread and thou night in Persia. The Burns Supper is a phenomenon without compare – as the man himself is without compare.

George Orwell also 'forward looked and guessed and feared', but he was so specific that we will be able to say, I hope, at the end of this year, that he was wrong. Burns was too wise a man to fall into that trap.

The very range of his interests and his intellect makes the study of his life and words an academic work of pleasurable, but still considerable, work.

That work I have not undertaken, but when I was asked to propose this toast, I was told, 'It will be all right. Many of the guests will be English and won't know what you are saying, so will be bound to learn something.' I thought that has the same logic as the poster on the back of the Edinburgh bus. 'Illiterate? Please write for free booklet.'

Burns was born at a time and in circumstances when he might well have been illiterate. In the preface to the Edinburgh Edition, he said, 'I write to congratulate my country.' And well he might, as in no other country in the world at that time would a man in his station in life have received such an education. Nor in many countries would there have been sufficient people literate enough and with taste and discernment enough to buy and read the Kilmarnock Edition and thus make the Edinburgh Edition possible.

It may be this that gave Burns his fierce, but not aggressive, nationalism. He made one brief, very brief, visit to England in his life. On his return, he expressed his love of his own country in gentle terms and referred to it as 'My dear, my native soil.' Whereas a clumsier person like myself would express the same sentiment by referring to my favourite sign on a quiet border road which says, 'This is England. You are welcome to it.'

Not that Scots are arrogant. It's just that we are parochial.

As the two Fife soldiers showed when they were lost in the desert during the war, miles from anywhere and dying of thirst. The spirit of one of them as they staggered forward was getting lower and lower, so to take his mind off his troubles, his pal said, 'You know this is the day of the Burntisland Games.' The first soldier looked up at the pale, blue sky and the white hot blazing sun and croaked, 'Well, they're getting a great day for it.'

One of the talents I most admire in Burns is his succinct expression of eternal truths, at all sorts of different levels. I suppose everyone has his own choices. My own favourites include simple ones like: 'Up in the mornin's nae for me' and 'I'm o'er young to marry yet.'

And more complex ones like:

O wad some Power the giftie gie us,
To see oursels as ithers see us!
It wad frae monie a blunder free us,
An foolish notion.

Or

Ah, gentle dames, it gars me greet,
To think how monie counsels sweet,
How monie lengthened, sage advices,
The husband frae the wife despises.

But my favourite is, without any doubt, is 'To step aside is human.'

What a wealth of compassion, understanding and experience there is in that simple phrase. Has any man been able to put so much into so few words?

And it is a cause for sorrow that we cannot hear those words as spoken by himself. His voice has not been recorded for posterity. We can listen to Dylan Thomas himself reading the Reverend Eli Jenkin's morning service from under Llareggub Hill, we will never hear Robert Burns reading *Holy Willie's Prayer*. And this is especially sad because we read from many contemporary accounts that his supreme gifts were in conversation and eloquence, which some say even outshone his talent for poetry.

However he was born too soon for that.

But not, I think, too soon in other ways, because I am sure his influence and his representation of us is the main reason why Scots are highly regarded the world o'er – to our very great advantage over the years – perhaps more highly regarded sometimes than we deserve.

A lot of Burns poems rail against poverty, and the injustice of it. Not for himself, but more often for others as in those lines;

Not but I hae a richer share,
Than monie ithers,

By why should ae man better fare,
And a' man brithers.

Things have got better, but not for everyone, as the posh social worker learnt not so long ago when she had to make a call up a close in Glasgow.

She knocked on the first of the doors on the first landing, or stairhead, as they are known in my native city. The door was opened very slightly and a timid- looking lad peeped his head out.

'Is your father in?' she asked him.

'Naw. Ma faither went oot when ma mither came in.'

'Is your mother in then?'

'Naw. Ma mither went oot when ma big brother came in.'

'Well, may I speak to him, then?'

'Naw. Ma brither went oot when my big sister cam in.'

'Is your sister in then, please?'

'Naw. Ma sister went oot when a cam in.

'This is your house?

'Naw. This is the toilet.'

So there is much still to be done. Sometimes I fear that Burns' heartfelt plea for man's inhumanity to man to end, served as much purpose as the curt message received by the deep sea diver from his ship when he was far under the North Sea: 'Come up – we're sinking.'

Of course I tried to see if I could find some links between Burns and the sea, but I could find no sign that he ever set foot in a boat. But in his very rare mention of sea or sailors, he was, as usual, very perceptive:

The unwary sailor thus aghast,
The wheeling torrent viewing.
Mid circling torrent sinks at last,
In overwhelming ruin.

With sailors present, that's too distressing, so I won't mention it. Another, perhaps more relevant mention of sailing, starts a bit nearer to home.

The Queen o' the Lothians cam cruisin to Fife,
To see gin a wooer would tak her for life...

It's a longish poem, but later on in it, the shy wooer, Jockie, says:

But troth, Madam, I canna woo,
For aft I hae tried it, and ay I fa' thro'.

The mind boggles...!

But there is more damning stuff than that of you sailor lads. You all know of *Tam o Shanter* and how that low-minded, landlocked peasant picked out for his lascivious attention, the witch with the mini skirt, and he expressed himself thus:

'Thir breeks o' mine, my only pair,
That ance were plush o' guid blue hair,
I wad hae gi'en them off ma hurdies,
For ae blink o' the bonnie burdies!'
Then, roused to passion, bawled out,
'Weel done, Cutty-sark!'

No seafaring men would not have behaved like that. Or would they?

What happened to Cutty Sark? Why indeed was a great boat called after her?

We know that after that incident at the Brig o' Doon, when the end of the tale left her with the end of a tail in her hand, the sexy little warlock – quote from *Tam o Shanter* – was 'Lang after kenned on Carrick shore' and that she 'perished monie a bonnie boat'. Just like, in fact, the Sirens of Ancient Greece. As Burns might have said, if he had been a poor poet.

So, Yachtsmen, I would have you ken,
Have weaknesses like other men,
And Captains gaily wreck their ships,
For ae keek o' bewitching hips.
And ram their boats upon the shore,
When beckoned on by this wee whore.

Let us hope the unfortunate sailors did not suffer the same fate as Tam's grey mare, Meg. So there is often less than meets the eye behind the braw brass buttoned blue blazer – back again to:

O wad some Power the giftie gie us
To see oursels as ithers see us!

As always Burns had the appropriate words. And they are Scottish words, which gives us added pleasure – parochial again. But we have to be parochial. It is people who value their own traditions, who show most respect for the traditions of others. So we have to be on our guard against people like the dishonest tourist who went into a restaurant in Edinburgh, ordered haggis, paid for it, then sneaked out without eating it.

> So we must cherish the best of what is Scottish. And we must certainly cherish Burns. If this man we meet to honour tonight were to be judged by quantity we could contend that his poetry is read by more people than the works of any other poet. That his poems are read in more different languages than the work of any other poet. That *Auld Lang Syne* is sung more often even than Bing Crosby's *White Christmas*.
>
> But the quantity is only there because the quality is there.
>
> His poems are as varied as his life and his passions. They have wit and pathos. Some tell stories and some convey messages. Some condemn and others extol. Some are innocent and some are rude. They are easily read, yet they are profound. They have the common touch, yet they have universal appeal. But most of all, he says what *we* would like to say in the way we would like to be able to say it. And for that reason, this Toast will be proposed, all over the world, 'Till a' the seas run dry.'
>
> Ladies and Gentlemen, please be upstanding for the Toast to the Immortal Memory of ROBERT BURNS.

In this toast by Bob Adams, is exemplified the very best of the witty, gentle, but slyly wicked sense of fun shown by the speakers who understand their own and Burns's essential Scottishness. This is not quite so of every speaker but he is a man for a' that. Professor J.A.Weir was a kind of lad o parts who had made it academically in Middle America and was of such status that he could make time to come through a northern winter (with Mrs Weir) to deliver his Immortal Memory to the Edinburgh Burns Association in January 1985. Professor Weir spoke profoundly and at length. We enter his speech after the usual jocular preliminaries as the good professor warmed to his theme.

> After living with Burns for more than 50 years, without much exposure to other poets, I surely must belong to that strange cult that is anathema to Professor Daiches. For the most part it has been a solitary affair; and with the departure of Roderick MacDonald, a student from Aberdeen, there are now no authentic Scottish friends in our town. At the University of Kansas (with 24,000 students) there is a Hardy Society and a Johnson Society but for lovers of Burns the offerings are slim. In recent years I have been collecting books

and reading critical essays and since it is the Parish Poet, the National Poet and the World Poet, that brings us 'a' thegether' tonight (and not our private Burns) I would like to make a few remarks on the three stages in the life of the immortal bard... the Parish Poet, the National Poet and the World Poet.

The Parish Poet

Setting out to the capital on his adventurous quest, the bard wrote, 'I tost my plaid about my shoulders, and marched away to Edinburgh, determined, since no better could be, to push my fortunes as a literary man.' If this sounds vaguely familiar yet wondrous strange, I am not surprised. The year was not 1786 but 1810, the poet not Burns but James Hogg, the Ettrick Shepherd, then forty years of age. To quote from T F Henderson (1914): 'In all he (Hogg) was not more than six months at school, and, when he left, at the age of seven, he had only 'advanced so far as to get into the class that read the Bible'; and, in writing, he was able only to scrawl the letters 'nearly an inch in length'. In his early years, his poetic tendencies did not receive any instruction or fostering influence except that derived from his peasant mother's imperfect recital of ballads and fairy tales.

Considering his limitations, Hogg's success in Edinburgh was astounding. The parallel with Burns, too, is striking; but the point I wish to make is that Burns, who owed little to early Scottish predecessors (whose existence became generally known only after his arrival had aroused a certain curiosity) grew up in a land of native poesy and song (most of Burns' verse letters were addressed to local fellow rhymesters). However, in a local context Burns' education, though fragmentary, was superior; in Daiches' opinion, 'he knew Shakespeare, Milton, Pope and the Bible much better than the ordinary educated man of today knows them.'

...Before thoughts of 'guid, black prent' had ever entered his head, or necessity forced the issue – Burns tossed off his matchless works as trifles; to praise a lass, to enliven the tavern, to suit a mood, to amuse a friend. In the words of Henry Grey Graham, 'Local reputation was spreading, his verses circulated in the countryside, were roared over in every farmer's house and tavern, and chuckled over in laird's mansions and every moderate minister's manse'. And, you will recall, many of the poems that circulated locally would not appear in print until long after Burns' death.

The National Poet

> Yet long-lived pansies here their scents bestow,
> The violets languish and the roses blow.
> In purple glory let the crocus shine,
> Narcissus here his love-sick head recline ... etc
> (Obviously not Burns)

The writer of these lines may be forgiven for, though he was a poor poet, he was a good man. Thomas Blacklock, blind from the age of six months, was the son of a bricklayer yet was Scotland's recognised authority in literary taste during Burns' time. Even the almighty Dr Johnson, who found little to his liking in Scotland, 'beheld him with reverence'. Today, Dr Blacklock's sole claim to fame rests on his enthusiastic letter to Dr George Lawrie of Loudoun, who had sent him a copy of Burns' poems for his opinion. This was in 1786 at a time of crisis for the greater though almost unknown poet, who had resolved to depart for the West Indies. His chest was already on its way to dockside 'when a letter from Dr Blacklock to a friend of mine overthrew all my schemes by rousing my poetic ambitions... His idea that I would meet with every encouragement for a second edition fired me so much that away I posted to Edinburgh without a single acquaintance in town, or a single letter of introduction in my pocket.'

Incidentally, a lifelong friendship with Dr Blacklock did nothing to impair Burns' critical judgement for much later (1795) he wrote to James Johnson: 'The song to Ginland Geordie if my memory serves me right, is one of Dr Blacklock's. We all knew the Doctor's merit; but his songs, in general were very silly – I enclose you one to the tune which has much more merit, and I beg you will insert it.'

Thanks to a favourable review on the Lounger Burns' poems became widely known in Edinburgh not long after his arrival in November 1786 on a borrowed pony. The learned and the polite, who were prepared to accept the rustic genius 'with every allowance for Education and Circumstance of Life', were enchanted. From Burns' correspondence it is now clear that he was by no means overawed by men of high degree, which is not to deny that there were quite a few of deserved eminence in Edinburgh. Dugald Stewart, who had recently exchanged the Chair of Mathematics for the Chair of Moral Philosophy, was one. It was he who would introduce

Burns to the democratic Lord Daer, one of the few members of the aristocracy to make a wholly favourable impression on the poet. Burns maintained his poise and self-confidence throughout his stay in the city; it was the rich and polite who had reason to be nervous, for surely among them there must have been some who knew that circulating in Ayrshire were satires more biting by far than the *Twa Dogs* or any of the others in print. Moreover, the subjects were not hard to identify!

In the end it was not the excitement of the city that caused Burns to linger on and to return later but Creech, the wealthy publisher, whose reluctance to part with a guinea was excessive even by Scottish standards. Most of the 612 copies of the now priceless Kilmarnock edition – the one that propelled Burns from local to national fame – were eventually thumbed out of existence. (Harvard University, not surprisingly, has two copies – one in the original boards with pages uncut!) The 30,000 copies of the second edition, enriched by *The Ordination*, *Death and Dr Hornbook*, *The Brigs of Ayr* and *Address to the Unco Guid*, but rejecting *The Jolly Beggars*, extended Burns' fame still further.

Burns criticism is filled with references to the bard's indebtedness to Alexander Pope, but without elaboration. As a satirist Pope's attacks on his enemies were savage beyond anything Burns ever wrote with the possible exception of *Address of Beelzebub*. Much has been made of Pope's religious handicap at a time when Roman Catholics were barred from universities and public office, but this was not the major problem; nor was there ever threat of financial exigency –

Pope, plain truth to speak
Climbed Parnassus by dint o'Greek.

Burns was thirteen when he first became acquainted with Pope's works so he had an early exposure to a craftsmanship clearly superior to the prevailing genteel literary fashion. The conscious imitations in some English poems, From songs to Maria and *Epistle to Robt Graham of Fintry*, for example, are indifferent Pope but the barely discernible echoes that appear in scores of pages show a deeper and more subtle influence. The later image of the humble, heaven taught ploughman, and image that modern critics have taken great pains to erase, may not have been taken all that seriously at the time. As Professor Kinsley has pointed out –

> The evidence of Burns' reading in the English poets, and his appreciation of current political and social affairs, is everywhere in the Kilmarnock book. That the critics did not remark on it suggest, not that they missed it, but that they accepted it without wonder. Many of the Edinburgh literati were in one way or another countrymen, and knew that illiteracy was not a concomitant of poverty among Scottish farmers or cottars. What was really striking about Burns was not the fact, but the quality, of his poetic talent.

Put simply, in the best of his work, he was world-class.

The World Poet

Burns' international reputation, augmented by consequences of the migratory habits of Scots, may be second only to that of Shakespeare. I must confess that contemplation of Burns after an evening with Shakespeare always brings on a slight feeling of depression. No one in his right mind would compare Burns with Shakespeare, but to borrow a fragment from Pope, 'Fools rush in where angels fear to tread', or in more modern parlance, 'Damn the torpedoes'.

It does not require much effort to determine that the vast library holdings on Shakespeare contain a good deal of nonsense. He had no Boswell; there was no Shakespeare Federation; no letters survive; we do not know when he arrived in London or how he was employed; the first biography did not appear until almost one hundred years after his death. Among the many conjectures, G.B.Harrison believes that Shakespeare may have seen active military service between the ages of 23 and 25. The cause of death is unknown but one anecdote may be of peculiar interest to Burnsians: 'Shakespeare, Drayton, and Ben Jonson had a merry meeting, and it seems drank too hard, for Shakespeare died of a fever there contracted.'

Perhaps it is the absence of data and surfeit of conjecture that causes us to concentrate almost exclusively on the plays themselves. Today's audiences have no more need for advanced instruction in metaphysical meaning that audiences of Shakespeare's day; in the works of the universal dramatist we see ourselves and all humanity. Occasionally an apology or explanation may preface a modern production *The Taming of the Shrew* or *The Merchant of Venice* – but for the most part we are entertained by the humour, the startling insights and the power of language.

Now what, you may ask, has all this to do with Robert Burns? Making due allowance for differences in time and place, and station in life, I believe Shakespeare and Burns had a lot in common: neither attended a university, both had friends who did; in their most creative period neither cared about presenting his work for posterity – both understood and enjoyed the earthy language of common people. They were witty conversationalist and brilliant lyricists. It is not, however the similarities that I wish to emphasise but the essential differences in our perception of the works of Shakespeare and Burns. Compared to Shakespeare, our problem with Burns is of an opposite sort. Here we may at times be burdened by too big a load of prior knowledge. Could it be that the closer we come to Ayrshire or to the man himself, the less well equipped we are to detect the broader meanings?

In the Kilmarnock Edition, which Burns edited himself, we find most of the poems by which he is best known, all of them composed before he had left his twenties. The book succeeded in disarming the critics and appealing to Burns' own uncritical people – no mean feat. True, the threat of censorship may have led to suppression of some satires, but may it not also have served to sharpen Burns' natural sly wit and subtle use of innuendo? We lose something by ignoring the local context of the poems, but what might a reader discover without notes and commentaries, without Crawford's penetrating analyses or Maurice Lindsay's *Burns Encyclopaedia*?

Perhaps this is where a foreigner may have an advantage. *In The Twa Dogs* one may see, not the British gentry of Burns' day, but the present US Senate. 'The fear o' Hell's a Hangman's whip, / To haud the wretch in order', (slipped ever so innocently into the *Epistle to a Young Friend)* seems to characterise the foreign policies of both Russia and the United States. It is not hard to find Billy Graham or Jerry Falwell at the *Holy Fair* (and of course it requires no great insight to see which side Burns was on).

I understand that the humour in *Holy Willie's Prayer* is sometimes enhanced by a performance complete with nightshirt and candle. But, without knowing who the petty William Fisher was or how he died, might not the final stanza be applied to whole nations?

> But l-d, remember me and mine
> Wi' mercies temporal and divine!
> That I for grace and gear may shine,
> Excell'd by nane!
> And a' the glory shall be thine!
> Amen! Amen!

Professor Weir said at one point in his erudite presentation that – 'it's hard to know where to stop with Burns'. It is similarly hard to know where to stop with Professor Weir. But a couple of 'Amens' sound conclusive enough and so must regretfully leave Weir here, as one might say.

Just as regretfully, I said 'Amen' to my dream of a summer Burns Festival. I had hoped to have seen it take root in the grounds of Rozelle House which might have contained the Robert Burns Open-Air Theatre eventually – a kind of Hollywood Bowl by the lake – and Scotland might have had its own Stratford in Ayr. But it was not to be. Something of that summer atmosphere I had looked for was felt years later at the Brow Well on the Solway in 1996. The winter of my Burnsian discontent for that year in Scotland gave way to a glorious summer where, on Wednesday 17 July, on a beautiful, cloudless afternoon, hundreds gathered at the Brow Well on the Solway to join in a Commemorative Service conducted by the Rev Williamson of Ruthwell after which Murdo Morrison, President of the Burns Federation for that year, delivered the following oration:

> It's no in titles nor in rank,
> It's no in wealth like Lon'on bank
> To purchase peace and rest,
> It's no in makin muckle mair,
> It's no in books, it's no in lear
> To make us truly blest;
> If happiness has not her seat
> and centre in the breast,
> We may be wise or rich or great
> But never can be blest
> Nae treasures nor pleasures,

Could make us happy lang;
The hearts ay's the part ay
That makes us right or wrong.

Friends, how true the words of the Bard come to us through the centuries. Words which will continue to exist as long as people exist on this planet. Convenor, Provost, Councillors, friends from around the world, it is right proper and fitting that we should, as admirers of Burns, foregather here to pause and consider, in this setting, the real significance of this year of celebration and commemoration. A year when events in the world have yet again turned our attention to many of the aspects of human behaviour of which Robert Burns took a note and wrote. He saw and he heard and he understood some of the mystery of mankind.Some people, and some countries, acting as ever putting greed before need and cancelling out the appeal of Robert Burns imploring, exploring and wishing the thought that man to man the world owed shall brothers be for a that.

To this very spot came the Bard in 1796. To this place came a very ill man and brought with him his hopes, his thoughts and his Bible. Despite the depths to which to who decry him tend to sink – his Bible featured largely in his life and his times as did the people who had an eleventh commandment of thou shalt not be found out. He came here on the best medical advice available to seek a cure or alleviation from pain. The body which had been overstretched and overworked in youth when the work of a man was demanded from the framework of a mere lad was not in a terminal decline. Part of the belief of the time can now be politically parodied with the words of 'if it isn't hurting its not working.' In a letter to the Editor of the *Scots Musical Museum* on the 4th of July he admits that he is not well and goes on to say 'However hope is the cordial of human heart and I endeavour to cherish it as well as I can.' This is, of course, the spiritual heart and that which makes us right or wrong.

We live in a day and age of magnificent machines, tremendous technology and in our own lifetimes there have been many developments which, to our father, would have seemed highly unlikely and to our grandparents impossible. Despite the advance of technology people would appear not to have changed. The heart is still ay the part that makes us right or wrong. We can, of course, be wrong in our hearts and our minds and today it is as fashionable as ever to blame others. Not being able to see ourselves as others see us we point the finger of blame and accusation at someone else.

Conveniently we forget that if one finger is pointed forward there are three pointed back at ourselves. The address to the *Unco Guid* says it all. Again this is where and how we can dip into the works of Burns and retrieve the gems which he wrote which are as applicable today despite all our technology as the day they were written. The heart is aye the part ay, that makes us right or wrong... Hope is [still] the cordial of the human heart. Very often without hope we have nothing.

Within the Burns movement we must also have an option of doing something or doing nothing. That is something or nothing for the future of what we all believe in – the promotion and the protection of the works of Robert Burns – not in isolation but as part of our rich Scottish heritage. We have got to promote and protect what we believe in. If we do nothing we will be introverted into oblivion and that is surely something that is far removed from our mind and our hearts and our desire.

So here we are in the place where Burns walked and Burns thought. We are here in the place where burns faced the reality of his own mortality and forward he was guessing and fearing for the future. The future looked bleak – for him there was no option. Soon Burns was to be no more and departed this life to leave behind the treasure chest of words which he has passed on to us free of charge. The warp and the weft of his words form part of the rich tapestry of Scotland's history, and heritage and we, as temporary custodians have a duty to pass that to future generations...

As we leave this place, this day and this date of commemoration, let us, each and every one of us resolve to do something about the world of Burns and Burns in the world. Just this week we have seen what can be achieved. We can we should and we must ensure that is we are not already a member of a Burns Club or of the Federation that we should become one. We can, we should and we must start moving Robert Burns away from being an after dinner speech in January – important although that may be. We can, we should and we must make Robert Burns for all reasons a Bard for all seasons and in that way we can honour his memory and his gift to us all.

And what a gift is Scotland in good weather. Again, the idea of a summer festival nagged. A nine-day wonder of all the Burns world in the sun or under the stars would have been something to see. Nine days devoted to the memory of the young Burns in an open-necked shirt singing his songs in the open air and not choked by a black bow tie or cigar smoke. Summer is the time for celebration – even a Scottish summer – a time to wrest Burns from the old and give it back to the young; but it all ended with the usual Scottish eyes raised, grave shaking of heads, fingers put to pursed lips.

And from some, like me, with a bit of a sigh.

Then never murmur or repine,
Strive in thy humble sphere to shine...
Preserve the dignity of Man,
With soul erect,
And trust the Universal Plan
Will all protect'...
And, like a passing thought, she fled
In light away.

(The Vision)

10

The West Sound Burns Supper 1986

Burns is supreme in qualities of the heart
(Sir Arthur Conan Doyle)

West Sound Radio is now a subsidiary of Scottish Radio Holdings and a smallish cog in a large commercial radio wheel that radiates from Clydebank to over much of Scotland. In 1985, however, West Sound was a small town station in the corner of Ayr, which was then the small sea-side resort it had always been before it became a dormitory suburb of Glasgow. The manger of the radio station at that time was Joe Campbell, tenor and future President of the Burns Federation. Joe and I had met through a common admiration for Canon Sidney McEwan, the late, great Glasgow singer and Joe introduced me to the priest at his retirement home in Glasgow. I had wanted to do a documentary programme on him for television and had discussed it with the BBC and with Canon McEwan. 'Och, leave it until I'm away,' said that charming man with a deprecatory wave of his hand. So I did. He died soon after, but the programme was never made.

However, Joe Campbell had also talked about an idea he had for a Burns Supper to end all Burns Suppers and asked if I'd like to be involved. Of course I would. Joe wrote of that inaugural dinner for the 1987 issue of the *Burns Chronicle*:

> On Friday, 17th January, 1986, West Sound held a Burns Supper in the banqueting suite of the Hospitality Inn, Cambridge Street, Glasgow. This marked the bicentenary of the publication of the Kilmarnock edition of poems and the evening turned out a very important one in the Burns calendar. Assembled was the most glittering array of Burns talent ever to appear under the same roof. The principal toast

> of the evening, the Immortal Memory, was given by John Cairney, known throughout the world for his portrayal of Burns in *There Was a Man*. John flew back from the Pacific especially for this occasion and we were fortunate to have such an important speech in such talented hands. The Toast to Ayrshire and the Toast to Agriculture were delivered by George Younger and Ian Grant respectively. The Secretary of State for Scotland needs little introduction and Mr Grant is the current President of the National Farmers' Union of Scotland.
>
> The Burns singers are the finest of their generation, Moira Anderson and Kenneth McKellar. The irrepressible Andy Stewart recited *Tam o Shanter* as only he could. The Rev James Currie gave the graces. Ian Powrie, one of Scotland's greatest ever fiddlers, now happily returned to his native shores from Australia, played while the legendary Jimmy Shand stepped out of retirement to play a selection of Burns waltzes. West Sound's own John Carmichael with members of his famous band played throughout the evening. The current, and three times, world champion, Ian McFadyen was the piper. The Burns Supper menu was traditional with one notable addition: roast barons of Angus beef were served and carved at the table.

This dispassionate account is little more than a menu itself as it gives no real idea of the enormity of this, the largest Burns Supper ever held. A thousand people sat down at what seemed an airfield of tables under the chandeliers spreading out to the far horizon of the exit signs. The whole atmosphere might have seemed inimical to the essential close fellowship of the ideal Burns night but those thousand diners that particular night knew they were part of a special occasion and responded accordingly. Joe, in the chair, kept a tight but genial rein on things and the gargantuan affair rolled on through the long evening as if on oiled wheels. An LP was made of songs and speeches and sold later as *A Night of a Thousand Tributes* for charities of our choice. Even on the disc you can feel the atmosphere.

My only regret was that neither Joe nor I could persuade Moira and Kenneth to do a duet and all four of us found it difficult to get Andy Stewart to stop even after his brilliant mimicry in *Tam o Shanter*. It was that kind of night, with a lot of famous names living up to them. For me though, the highlight was not a song, or a recitation or a speech but it was the way in which a thousand people stood in absolute silence at the end of the Immortal Memory. It was only a moment, but it was powerful and unforgettable. And then the way that same audience at the end of a long night hummed the tune of *Auld Lang Syne* while I softly recited the words over. It was pure theatre, but, once again, the effect was created by the audience themselves not by the speaker.

Since that time, Joe Campbell has moved on to other and higher things but the West Sound Burns Supper has become a West of Scotland institution and is the hot ticket every January. They no longer strive for the thousand plus attendances but the figures are still very high and the calibre of the speakers reflects the quality of the evening. Tom Fleming, the actor and broadcaster, followed me in 1987 and sportscaster, Archie McPherson, followed him in 1988. The roll-call from then to the time of writing is like a 'Who's Who in Burns?' – Maurice Lindsay, George Bruce, Irvine Smith, James Mackay, then another actor, Iain Cuthbertson, who was followed by the American hostage, Tom Sutherland; then the newspaper man, Jack Webster, David Shankland, Murdo Morrison, a Past President of the Burns Federation; Howard Haslett, David Purdie, the late Donald Dewar and finally, Len Murray in 2001, who thus completed the two hundred years exactly since the first-ever proposer of the toast, the Reverend Hamilton Paul.

Not all Burns suppers of course are so grand, but they could be exotic, as William Adair reported to the *Burns Chronicle*:

> On Monday 27th January 1986, Provost Coyle of Strathkelvin District approached me and asked if I could assist with a proposed Burns Supper. I agreed, and he informed me that it was to be held on Wednesday 29th – rather short notice. Provost Coyle took the Chair, while I addressed the Haggis and also recited *To a Mouse* and *Holy Willie's Prayer*. The Immortal Memory was rendered by J Chalmers. The evening's ongauns followed the normal pattern, but the menu was certainly the most exotic that I have ever encountered and, I must add, quite delicious. The meal began with Cockie Leekie Pakoras and was followed by curried Haggis and boiled rice as well as the more traditional neeps and tatties. The supper was held at The Oasis Tandoori

> Restaurant, Bishopbriggs. The proprietors, Messrs Mahmmod and Khan, hail from Pakistan and looked quite resplendent in kilt, velvet jacket and lace jabot. They have an engineering business by day and run the restaurant in the evenings. It was a lovely evening but they plan something on more traditional lines for next year.'

Lochgelly and District Childrens Burns Supper has been a feature of the annual celebrations in Fife since 1883, but in 1986, the No 1 Gothenberg Supper Room in Bowhill was the scene of the Young Peoples' Burns Supper. The evening was supported by the Bowhill Peoples' Burns Club and Charles Kennedy reported that the Immortal Memory was given by 12-year-old Fiona Delaney.

> It is not easy to write well something that has been written a thousand times before. But I doubt if Robert Burns would mind a simple tribute to him because he liked the simple things in Life. We all know of the sorrow he felt at uprooting a common daisy and the gentle words he used:
>
> Wee, modest crimson tipped flow'r
> Thou's met me in an evil hour;
> For I maun crush amang the stoure
> Thy slender stem;
> To spare thee now is past my pow'r
> Thou bonnie gem.
>
> Scotland has had her fair share of famous men such as William Wallace, Sir Walter Scott, Alexander Fleming and Alexander Graham Bell to name but a few, but the most famous of all is Robert Burns. His fame is even greater now than when he was alive over 200 years ago. He understood nature, countryside and human, and because of this the Banks and Braes will always be green, sweet Afton will always flow gently and there will always be a Red Red Rose... Alexander Fleming gave us penicillin, Alexander Graham Bell gave us the telephone, but Burns left us all a legacy of understanding and this is my simple immortal memory.

On the point of Scotland's famous men, this super-patriot theme was followed by one Scots-Canadian recently who, in his Immortal Memory, gave nothing more than a list of Scottish inventors. It was probably at the same Supper that a singalong followed which featured the best-known songs of Harry Lauder culminating in Will Fyffe's *I Belong to Glasgow*.

The late Eddie Boyd certainly belonged to Glasgow but he was really an Ayrshire man. He was arguably the nearest thing to Dylan Thomas that Scotland has had, and like his fellow-Ayrshireman, Willie McIlvanney, had his own voice in dealing with the Scottish scene. Boyd became one of television's finest writers in its halcyon days in the Fifties and early Sixties, but in 1986 he addressed a Burns supper in the Glasgow Art Galleries and gave them the benefit of his acerbic viewpoint and sardonic tongue. Eddie could wield a word like a single-syllable stiletto. This can be seen in this all-too-short excerpt from the end of his verse-speech. He spoke, as it were, in Burns's own vernacular, in Burns's own voice, albeit in a tone rather more urban Glasgow than Ayrshire rural. At this point, we come in half-way through his poetic Memory. Eddie gave me a signed copy of the text which I folded away among all my other treasured Burnsiana, but I've lost the first page somewhere, which is why we begin where he was quoting from *The Twa Dogs*:

I've noticed, on our Laird's court-day
(An' mony a time my heart's been wae)
Puir tenant bodies, scant o' cash,
Hoo they maun thole a factor's snash;
He'll stamp and thraten, curse an' swear
He'll apprehend them, poind their gear;
While they maun stan' wi' aspect humble,
And hear it a' an' fear an' tremble!'

Then he (Boyd) extended the parallel to today's poor families.

Yer warl', this modern day, is filled
Wi' factors daein' naethin' else
Bit dream up snash for puir bodies tae thole;
The bureaucrats they're ca'ed nooadays,
The people without joy or faces,
The cuckoos claimin' every nest,
The institutionalised rinnin' the institution
Tae serve themsels an' no' the people:

'That Burns Family is a problem family, no doubt about it.'
An' next thing the social workers are fa'in a' aroon'
Llik' big pink snawflakes...

Ah'd better stop there. For, ye see,
Ah've answered ma ain question:
Whit wid Ah be writin' aboot gin Ah were alive the day?
Ah'd be writin' poetry for, an' aboot,
The Bader-Meinhofs.

Is there a poet livin' et this time
What kens the Land the wey Ah kent it?
The sight, the smell, the very taste o't:
The deep luve for its treacherous loveliness,
The deeper hatred o' its mindless cruelty.
Mount Oliphant
Lochlea – 'the poorest soil in Ayrshire
At twenty shillings an acre.'
Mossgiel.
The Carrick Hills, flat as the Ayrshire speck,
The Firth o' Clyde, glintin' lik' a broken gless,
The sma' rain that wis tae kill me
No' too mony years later.
Poor land,
Soor land,
It grew naethin' bit stanes –
An' poetry.

An' yit...an' yit – ah niver left it.
There wis some kinna recognition
Atween me 'n that land.
We took frae each ither 'n we gave,
Whiles a caress, whiles the back o' oor haunds,
Expectin', demandin' – naethin'.
It wis a hopeless love affair: an' Martial,
That Latin poet... fair summed it up:
'I cannot live with you nor without you.'
An' the Land wis a' ma wimmen,
They a' had the Land in their bodies 'n their breasts
An' the yins that didnae – weel,
That wis jist play-actin'.

A harsh mistress 'n jist the same the day;
Bit leave her – an' ye leave salvation.
Even the day
When the Lea Rig his become the oil rig,

She's jist as harsh
Bit leave her – an' ye leave salvation.
Adam Smith wis tellin' me jist yesterday
That only fower per cent o' the people noo wark on the
Land.
Leave her – an' ye leave salvation.

An' noo ah think Ah've deeved ye lang eneuch:
Bit yin last thing Ah'd like tae say tae ye.
During' the time ye've been listening' here tae me,
A hunner folk have, somewhere in the warl',
Died o'starvation.
If ye can live wi' that, then everything Ah wrote
Wis jist no' worth the effort;
Everything ah said
Wis wasted breath.
Ye say ah'm an immortal.
Not mortal.
Ma poems, ye say, imperishable.
Not perishable.
Ah've even been ca'ed immoral.
Not moral.
Every rebel is defined by negations;
Bit yin word naebody's ever yit applied tae me
Is 'impotent.'
Not potent? Ah kin hear the lauch ringin' roon' Ayrshire.
An'it... an'yit... it could happen.
Ah could be destroyed.

The poor we have always
The poor in heart,
The poor in charity,
The poor in deed,
The poor in compassion,
The poor in intention,
The poor in love.
Gin they inherit the earth, whit's tae become o'Burns?
Jist an Ayrshire ploughman wha wrote verses
In an incomprenhensible tongue,
Banished tae a dreary library 'n the key's been lost:
An' a' that stuff aboot the Brotherhood o' Man?
Banished wi' him.

It could happen.
Fegs aye, it certainly could happen.
Ah'm warnin ye, ye'd better stert mendin' yer weys.

How salutary to be brought up sharp like this. Eddie Boyd always knew what he was saying. He was a very careful word-maker, sharpening his point to thrust it home until it hurt. But it never bled. He chose to speak in Burns's voice as he might have spoken today. For me, it was a latter-day Burns exactly, and it was disturbing.

It is almost a relief to turn again to someone who speaks for himself. Robert Davidson Ogilvie, delivered a more conventional Immortal Memory in January 1987 to the Canberra Highland Society and Burns Club of Australia, but it was none the worse for that.

> Mr President, distinguished guests, members and friends.
>
> If a roll call of famous men were read over at the beginning of every century how many would answer a second time to their name? There would be no doubt or question as to Burns. The adsum of Burns would ring out clear and unchallenged. There would be a few before him on the list, and it is not now possible to conceive of such a list without him. In Scotland, Burns is more than a literary figure – he is a popular hero, whose birthday is celebrated by Scots all over the world. He sprang from the country people and their traditions and his undoubted genius owed nothing to fortune...
>
> The bare facts of Robert Burns life can be quite briefly told, since his life only extended over thirty seven years. He was born in the village of Alloway, close to the town of Ayr, on 25th January 1759. In a long autobiographical letter he wrote to Dr John Moore in 1787, he frankly admits the poverty of his home and his upbringing, and the unavailing fight of his father, a tenant farmer, to overcome that poverty, but in the same letter he dwells much more upon his own appetite for sociability. This appetite was a sure sign of the artistic temperament innate in Burns and it was to this, quite as much as to the very reputable schooling he had had from his father as well from various dominies, that we owe the poet that was to be.
>
> Burns' first love was song. He had a keen musical ear and a great feeling for rhythm. His first poems were song; the earliest were written when he was 15 years old. On his own

evidence he never composed a song without first having the tune in his head. When, in the year 1773, he 'first committed the sin of rhyme' it is significant that the lyrics he wrote in praise of the young girl he worked with in the harvest field should have been set to the time of her favourite reel. From his middle teens onwards it was obvious that Burns was conscious of the poet within him, that he was not going to be content to be an ordinary ploughman. Song was already in his heart.

An important part of his works are the epistles and satires, their style modelled on that of two earlier Scots poets, Allan Ramsay and Robert Fergusson. These show him as an acute Observer and critic of human conduct, with a warm heart, a strong sense of humour and a hatred for hypocrisy. His philosophy of the brotherhood of man was partly inspired by the ideals of Freemasonry.

Burns' character was not a complicated one, but it has been variously distorted both by admirers and detractors... He could read, write and remember. He surcharged with emotion, awareness and sensibility and despite his background and foreground of poverty, hunger and never-ceasing toil, he could laugh. The only mystery concerning Burns, whether in manhood or boyhood, is that of the quality of his genius... and this genius expressed itself in poetry. As a poet he could not be suppressed. As a poet he triumphed. Burns was pure passion and imagination pure fire. Burns power was his own mind. No other poet had the clarity of his vision.

It was the nature of Robert Burns's experience that conditioned his poetry... his experience, if searing, was fundamental and therefore universal. It is this wonderful quality that makes Burns the first world poet. Burns embraces all humanity. Humanity has in turn embraced him. One reason why Burns is universally loved and adored is because he expressed himself in the thought and speech of the great mass of his countrymen...

His songs and memory are today enshrined in the hearts of the people whilst the law-makers of his day are forgotten like the snows of yesteryear... Henry Wadsworth Longfellow wrote a handsome poem about Burns, written in the Burns style. I will read the last two stanzas.

For now he haunts his native land

As an immortal youth; his hand
Guides every plough
He sits besides each ingle-nook
His voice is in each rushing brook,
Each rustling bough.
His presence haunts this room tonight
A form of mingled mist and light
From that far coast
Welcome beneath this roof of mine
Welcome this vacant chair is thine
Dear guest and ghost.

Whether a man lives in Scotland, England, America, Australia or any part of the globe, he has the same sentiments for home or kindred, the same loves and fears, the same silent emotions whoever he may be.

In Burns' poems and songs these sentiments are expressed for which we cannot find words. These silent emotions are given expression, our lives are enriched and our loves are made more intimate. The *Holy Willies*, *The Hornbooks*, *The Cotters*, *The Man Made to Mourn*, *The Mouse*, none of these are exclusive to eighteenth century Ayrshire, they are universal and timeless.

So many of Burns' poems expressed his views to the fullest extent. There is no more flaming satire than *Holy Willie's Prayer*. There is no greater tale than *Tam o Shanter*. No poem has more love and feeling than the *Cotter's Saturday Night*. There is no more tender love song than *My Love is Like a Red Red Rose*. If *A Man's a Man for a' that* is the hope of humanity, then *Auld Lang Syne* is the world's national anthem. What greatness did this man Burns have? So great is he, in fact, that he belongs not to Scotland alone. He belongs to the whole world... As James Russell Lowell said.

> Burns is a citizen of a country of which we are all citizens, that country of the heart which has no boundaries laid down on man.

Burns takes his place with the marvellous William Shakespeare, with the great humanitarian, Abraham Lincoln, with Nelson, Wellington and Wilberforce, the great emancipator. All these men in various fields of endeavour have exerted an influence that extends far beyond the confines of their native countries.

He was endowed by nature with that vital spark which in

> him amounted to genius and his muse did touch the heart. That is one of the secrets of his greatness. He touched the hearts of men and what appeals to our hearts must appeal to our esteem. Scott, Keats, Milton, Byron are not revered the way that Burns is, and yet they were great men and great poets.
>
> As Burns Clubs prosper and Burnsiana froths across the globe, we hear him quoted in parliaments, learned judges recite his texts in courts, he is hotly claimed, for their own, by all political parties. The Russians still maintain he was a communist. The works of Burns are now taught in Russian schools. When the first translated works of Burns were published in Moscow 100,000 copies were sold in one morning. His face has appeared on their stamps...
>
> Today there are hundreds of Burns Clubs throughout the world and many of their members, as we have here tonight, are not Scotsmen. This, I think, typifies the power of Burns' poetry and song. And what of the future? Man cannot live on Burns alone. If we are to ensure that his immortal memory continues with any meaning other than sentiment and hero worship, then some positive action is required.
>
> Scotland, as a country, was dying when Burns emerged to re-popularise the Scots tongue and save some of its fast ebbing culture. Today, as far as native inspired culture is concerned, Scotland is probably at an even lower ebb, and there is no Robbie Burns to act the part of life saver.
>
> Scotia' my dear, my native soil!
> From whom my warmest wish to heaven is sent
> Long may thy hardy sons of rustic toil be blest
> With wealth, and peace and sweet content.
>
> Today, for the sake of the country he loved, we hope his prayers are heard and answered...

Mr Ogilvie concluded by reciting Colonel Ingersoll's poem written at Burns Cottage. As he sat down the company rose to him.

In 1989, the Burns Howff Club in Dumfries celebrated its centenary and as part of the celebrations, Dr James Mackay, the noted Burns authority and sometime resident of Dumfries, was invited, in the tradition of Hamilton Paul, to propose the Immortal Memory in original verse on Burns Night at the Globe Inn. Dr Mackay did so and the result is a unique survey of Burns from one who should know. This Burns knowledge is worn lightly but it is all there between the lines. 500 copies of the speech were run off for distribution. The following is an abridged and slightly edited version from copy No 16 which was presented to the present editor by the author.

Mr Chairman, Howff members an honoured guests,
Ah'm here the nicht after mony requests
Frae David Smith, your Secretary,
Wha said tae me – 'It's necessary
To get someone for oor Centenary do;
In truth, it micht as well be you'.
It didnae tak me lang tae pon'er,
Tae address the Howff's indeed an honour.
Ye've had some famous speakers here:
Men o mense an muckle lear.
As Ah look roun, ah'm verra prood
Tae think I staun whaur Burns ance stood...
This is the case, ah hae nae doot,
The bard himsel, in letters, put
The word around for a' tae see:
The Globe Inn was his howff. Thus he
Describes it in letters, if ye please.
Within these wa's he'd mony a squeeze
Wi stamp-house Johnie an Samuel Clark.
Upstairs he dallied wi Anna Park –
Fair Anna o the gowden locks –
Ach-
Ah wullnae dwell on maitters randy,
Whit Burns himsel cried 'Houghmagandie'!
But ah've digress't.

This auld inn's fu o interest.
Little mair nor a but an ben
When it was fun't in saxteen ten,
By Burns's time a leading tavern,
Its close-mooth gloomy like a cavern,
But through yon door was hospitality,
A place o warmth an conviviality.
Ae time, the Hyslops o Lochend –
Will an his wife Jean, the poet's friend –
Possess'd the globe, a nice sideline.

Will was a merchant wha dealt in wine,
Jean was a Maxwell o Terraughty.
'Tis said that she was rather naughty,
Conspiring wi Anna Park tae trap
Oor guileless hero, Burns – puir chap!
Whit truth there's in't ah canna tell –
Ah dinna believe a word mysel!
In Burgh Archives ah've search'd in vain,
Explored each clue, turn'd owre ilk stane.
Altho she cast a puckle stigma,
Anne Park is aiblins an enigma.

But if this girl remains a mystery
Ah've solved the Hyslops' family history.
In editing The Works, Ah must confess,
Jock an Meg had me in a mess.
Ah thocht Will an Jock were ane an the same,
An for that confusion Ah tak fu blame...
Ah've recently discovered that Jock
Entered intae holy wedlock
Wi a Margaret Geddes; an tae gie them a job,
Will Hyslop installed them baith at the Globe.
This happened in 1795
When Burns was verra much alive.
An thus this theory, please I beg,
Accept that Mrs Hyslop must be Meg.
'Twas she who dealt wi the poet's seal.
She was a guid freen, tried an leal.
Meg was a niece o Bishop Geddes,
An frae her uncle she had his
Copy o the Edinburgh Edition,
Wi Burns's manuscript addition.
In turn Meg Hyslop gied the buik
Tae a Dr Goadby, who it took
Tae America when he emigrated.
And in the Huntington Library it's nou venerated.

Ah'm suir ye'll also bring tae mind,
That Burns tae help Jock was inclined,
An asked James Johnson if he could
Engrave a billhead on a block o wood.
Ye may remember Rabbie tellin'

Johnson aff aboot his spellin.
He muddled postage, if ye please,
An spell't tobacco wi twa b's.
But his heart was in the right place;
The odd mistake was nae disgrace.
Far better than Thomson, yon stuck-up snob!
But –Ah digress again – back tae the Globe.

The King's Arms might profess gentility;
This Inn was a haven o tranquillity.
A refuge frae a' cares an woes,
A bed for the nicht when the need arose.
He needna heed o slaps an stiles,
Or wearied, hameward ride sax miles.
An efter he moved intil the toun,
The welcome here was aye a boon.
Ah like tae think, in his last years,
That here at least he shrugged aff his fears;
A' thae worries that sairly raxed him,
A' thae problems that sadly taxed him.
Fast by yon ingle bleezin finely,
Wi reamin swats that drank divinely –
Ye might have heard these lines afore!
Ach – ye ken what ah mean! Ahint yon door
Was the cosy snug, the elbow chair
In which he sat, Ah do declare.
The ambience was satisfyin.
Today, the atmosphere's electrifyin.
Sat in yon chair, Ah get a shiver,
The hair on my neck begins to quiver.
Whit ah'm tryin tae say in essence
Is that ye can truly feel his presence.

Ye members o the howff are blest,
Nae ither Club is thus possesst
O premises wi the stamp o Rab
On every brick, and tile, and slate an slab...
Let's face it – we a' tak for granted,
Dumfries has got mair that it wanted.
See yon Vennel flat, ance sae negleckit?
But nou restored and much respeckit.
See the cobbles o the Millbrae Hole

An think how hard it was tae thole
Yon last dread illness frae the Brow,
That brought puir Rabbie doon sae low.
The times he must hae trod thae stanes:
In happier days, the vennels an lanes
Rang wi his manly, independent stride.
His was the toun in which we bide.

Thae Ayrshire birkies hae the gall
Tae state that, of the poems, all
The anes of any substance real
Were written 'fore he left Mossgiel.
The Kilmarnock Poems are verra fine,
But Rabbie added mony a line
In the last decade o his life,
Spite a' his fears for weans and wife:
Thou Lingering Star an *The Wounded Hare*,
Scots Wha Hae an mony mair.
Discernin fowks agree that *Tam*'s
His best wark; but his epigrams
Are masterpieces o shairp satire;
Fu' o bite an tinged wi fire.
The wey he rhymed extempore
When he an Syme toured Galloway,
Whene'er he was in fightin mood,
E'n then the the witty lines ensued.

Oot at Ellisland, so they say,
Tam o Shanter, in a single day,
By Rab the Rhymer was composed;
Whit manic energy was here exposed!
It was regarded, as we learn,
The best day's wark since Bannockburn.
Ye could argue just as forcibly.
If Burns wrote naethin after he
Published in se'enteen eighty-sax,
His reputation wad hae suffered cracks.
He wad wi Fergusson an Ramsay
Enjoy a standing rather flimsy.

The poet's years in Dumfriesshire,
When Nith, not Afton did inspire,

Produced some o his finest wark.
On Scotia's ballads he left his mark.
The fragments o the auld Scots sangs
He saved an mended. He belangs
Within the makars' great tradition.
There's nane o that in the Kilmarnock Edition!
By fittin words tae an ancient melody
Burns demonstrates his versatility.
His genius maks it seem sae easy.
He cleaned up sangs that were gey sleezy.
The *Cumnock Psalms* an ither bawdry
Had words that strike us nou as tawdry.
Mony an auld sang was gey coorse
Wi words obscene – an sometimes worse.
The sentiments oor Bard refined –
He had ministers and maids in mind ...
The sangs o Burns run intae hundreds.
And maist are still considered standards...

Ten monuments to Burns ye'll find
In Canada. If you're inclined
Tae try the States, there's anither score.
As ye'll see frae shore tae shining shore.
Thae plaques an busts an cairns an statues
Generally extol his poetic virtues,
Wi scenes frae *John Anderson my Jo*,
To a Mountain Daisy – and oh –
The Cotter's Saturday Night an many
A tam o shanter still pursued by Nannie.
But ane that really took ma fancy
Is the braw statue that stauns in Quincy.
Now yon's a toun not really famous
For its Scots roots; its name is
Taen frae an ancient Pilgrim line
That spawned twa Presidents langsyne.
In much more recent times it seeks
Tae blend the Irish wi the Greeks.

Whit wey's oor Rabbie's figure here?
As Scotland's national Bard? No fear!
The statue was planned in twenty-three
For the hunner an fiftieth anniversary

O the opening round o the American War
O Independence. An therefore
They hae anither quality waled.
Burns here is as a champion hailed
O liberty an democracry,
An opponent o bureaucracy.
Upon the base are sax lines quo'd
Frae Burns's famous *Birthday Ode*
To General Washington: 'Nae Aeolian lyre
Awake – tis liberty's bold notes inspire.'
Tae sing the praises of a recent
Enemy was thocht hardly decent.
Dootless some fand it quite outrageous.
Mysel' – Ah think he was courageous.
Oor Rab was aye a maverick
That for convention cared na stick...

Some think that Burns was irreligious
An *The Kirk's Alarm* sacrilegious.
But Burns abominated cant
Hypocrisy an humbug. Scant
Attention has been given, it seems,
Tae Rabbie's views, express'd in reams
O letters tae his valued friend
Mrs Dunlop. In these he penned
At length his weel-thocht-oot opinions
On God an His divine dominions,
Showin how he'd worked oot for himsel'
The way tae Heaven –or need be, – tae Hell.

Sae too, in maitters gey political,
Burns was candid an highly critical.
Sometimes he could be rather tactless;
And was advised to think mair, act less...

Sometimes he had a second thought
An tried tae undo what he wrought.
Those hasty words o dedication
Inscribed in De Lolme's 'Constitution';
The ambiguous toast 'May our success
In the present war' (he did profess)
'Be equal to the justice of our cause'

Gey nearly brocht oor Bard tae blows.
He had tae watch his step, however;
Being an Exciseman he could never
Afford tae tak too bold a stan'
In advocating the 'Rights o Man'.
There were those quite ready tae betray him
As being disaffected. And wi him
Wi the reddest radicals acquainted
An wi democracy so foully tainted.

In makin his impassioned plea
Tae Robert Graham o Fintry, he
Became quite fearful, as well he might:
The loss o job an pension right
Were bad enough for a family man.
But even waur – the savage ban
On anythin the least seditious
Meant Burns was prey to tongues malicious.
There are aye plenty tae inform
On those who advocate Reform.
Burns was conscious, a' too well
On what tae Muir an Palmer fell.
Ilk day he walked by the Midsteeple
He'd mind the fate the Friends o the People
Had suffered for their plea 'One vote
Per man'. A frightened government smote
Them an sent them tae Botany Bay.
'Twas this inspired *Scots Wha Hae.*
It's strange tae think our national song
Should hae frae an injustice sprung.

But we remember Rab for his love songs tender
An his nature poems: tae the Daisy slender,
An *To a Mouse* – sae fu o pathos.
Burns ne'er descended into bathos.
We mind his digs at people's vanity,
But maist o a' we mind his humanity;
It's this knack o conveyin a'
The emotions, great an sma,
That strikes a chord in ev'ry heart;
That turns his verses into art
Burns is poet for a' time,

Appealing tae fowk o ev'ry clime,
Race, colour, creed, an tongue.
It's this'll perpetuate his mem'ry long...

I gie ye the Toast – the Memory
O Robert Burns, Poet o Humanity,

Gentleman – the Immortal Memory of Robert Burns.

And if Jim will allow a lesser rhymer to add:

The applause for the feat was loud and long
For Jim, with the Bard, could do no wrong
The men of the Howff did not reason why
They knew they had had the real Mackay!

It was at another inn, the Open Arms at Dirleton, just outside Edinburgh, that Iain Crawford proposed the Immortal Memory in 1993. The unusual aspect of the speech was the way it allowed for the insertion of Burns songs and recitations by others, but then Iain Crawford always did the unexpected. All the same it made very pleasant punctuation in the address. Crawford has been in his time been many things – actor, journalist, war hero, and a writer on wine and golf, but not necessarily in that order. What he is essentially, is a good talker, and here he talks about Robert Burns.

> The most amazing thing about Robert Burns is that he ever happened at all. Chaucer's father was a vintner and honorary butler to the King Edward III of England; Dante was a lawyer's son; Shakespeare came from yeoman stock and his father was a prosperous tradesman; Michelangelo's father was mayor of Caprese and owned a marble quarry; all the earlier Scottish literati were either aristocrats like Gavin Douglas and Lyndsay or university men like Dunbar and Fergusson. Even Allan Ramsay's origins were prosperous middle-class. But Burns was the son of a failed gardener and bankrupt small-holder. He was a man born out of time and out of place, perhaps the greatest example of that assiduous passion for learning which a few generations later was to make professors out of crofters' sons and scientists and bankers from the families of fishermen and weavers.
>
> He made his own time and his own place but never really

reconciled the two. Yet with that irrepressible quality which is perhaps the most admirable thing about humanity he managed to make passion and poetry, laughter, music and magic out of the ingredients of misery, poverty, triumph and failure. 'To treat these two imposters just the same' as Kipling was to say much later.

MY LOVE IS LIKE A RED, RED ROSE (Song)

It was the romantic songs which Burns wrote and rescued from oblivion in two collections made at the end of his life – and for which he earned nothing for more than 250 songs – which are part of his most enduring and endearing legacy. He played the fiddle himself and, although he declared he was not much of a singer, he had a fine ear for a tune. You only have to listen to the old tunes he rescued from extinction by providing them with new words, to see how accurately and with what grace, he matched the poetic rhythm to the music. The relatively small world offered by the Ayrshire community in which he lived added reality to his book learning.

'The joy of my heart' he wrote to his schoolmaster and friend, Murdoch, in 1783 'is to study men, their manners and for this darling subject I cheerfully sacrifice every other consideration. I am quite indolent about these great concerns that set the bustling busy Sons of Care agog.' Sometimes however, other 'darling subjects' got in the way. As when, at the age of sixteen, he went to his mother's home village of Kirkoswald to learn Mensuration and Mathematics. 'I struggled on with my Sines and Cosines until, stepping out in the garden one charming noon to take the sun's altitude, I met with my Angel

> Like Proserpine gathering flowers/Herself a fairer flower.

It was vain to think of doing any more good at school. The remaining week I did nothing but craze the faculties of my soul about her or steal out to meet with her; and the last two nights of my stay, had sleep been mortal sin, I was innocent.'

AY WAUKIN O (Song)

He confessed in the autobiographical letter he wrote to Dr John Moore in 1787, 'Far beyond all other impulses of my heart, was un penchant à l'adorable moitié du genre humain; my heart was complete tinder and was eternally lighted up by some goddess or other.'

But was Burns any more than a lyrical lecher – as it is

fashionable to portray him nowadays? He doesn't win many brownie points from the feminist cabal – especially that selection of it which holds that lust is a male imposition on womankind. A point of view likely to threaten the extinction of the human race, I would have thought. Not that the human race was in any danger of dying out as long as Robert Burns was around...but he was concerned with other aspects of humanity. He lived in a time of revolution – the American Revolution, the French Revolution, fellow excise officer Thomas Paine's 'The Rights of Man', Jefferson's 'Declaration of Independence'. He saw the social injustice and the hypocrisy which surrounded him with a dangerously beady eye.

A MAN'S A MAN FOR A' THAT (Song)

Not all of his scorn was directed against the larger structure of 18th century society. Some it struck nearer home, even taking on the extreme doctrines of Calvinism and the Divinely Chosen Few of the Elect, pre-ordained for Salvation, immortalised in his portrayal of a Kirk elder in the parish of Mauchline in *Holy Willie's Prayer*.

HOLY WILLIE'S PRAYER (Recitation).

However, the Holy Willies ganged up on Burns when his hand-fasted marriage to Jean Armour was denounced by her parents and 'the holy beagles and the houghmagandie pack' were threatening such dire punishments that he made plans to emigrate to Jamaica. He must have thought back fondly on an earlier, idyllic and less tempestuous love affair.

CORN RIGS (Song)

That was one of the two songs which appeared in the book which stopped him going to Jamaica. His own book, Poems, chiefly in the Scottish Dialect published in Kilmarnock in 1786. *The Printed Proposals*, by which he raised the subscriptions to publish, contained a justification by another, earlier Scottish bard, Allan Ramsay:

Set out the brunt side o' your shin
For Pride in Poets is nae sin
Glory's the prize for which they rin
And Fame's their jo;
And wha blows best the Horn shall win;
And wharefore no?

In his Preface he said: 'Unacquainted with the necessary requisites for commencing Poet by rule, he sings the sentiments and manners he felt and saw in himself and his rustic compeers around him, in his and their native language.' But further on in the pages of the Kilmarnock volume he was more forthright:

...Your Critic-folk may cock their nose
And say, 'How can you e'er propose
You, wha ken hardly verse frae prose
To mak a sang?'
But, by your leaves, my learned foes,
Ye're maybe wrang.
What's a' the jargon o' your Schools,
Your Latin names for horns and stools:
If honest Nature made you fools,
What serves your Grammars?
Ye'd better taen up spades and shools,
Or knappin hammers.
A set o' dull conceited Hashes,
Confuse their brains in College-classes!
They gang in stirks, and come out Asses,
Plain Truth to speak;
And syne they think to climb Parnássus
By dint o' Greek.
Gie me ae spark o' Nature's fire
That's a' the learning I desire;
Then, tho' I drudge thro' dub and mire
At pleugh or cart
My Muse, tho' hamely in attire,
May touch the heart.

And hearts *were* touched. And the Kilmarnock edition became a literary smash hit. Jamaica and emigration were forgotten. Edinburgh and a second edition beckoned. And Robert Burns listened even more avidly to the music of his time.

FIDDLE TUNE (Instrumental)

In Edinburgh, Burns was lionised... 'The town is at present agog with the Ploughman Poet' wrote Mrs Cockburn, author of *The Flowers of the Forest*. 'The man will be spoiled, if he can spoil' she added 'but he keeps his simple manners and is quite sober.' He concluded a deal for a second edition of his poems but he had to wait a long time to get the money from his publisher. Some things never change. During that time he made friends, useful acquaintances, who discovered what his friends back home already knew...

Sir Walter Scott, when a boy of 16, met Burns in Edinburgh. Years later he told J.G. Lockhart:

> His eye alone, I think, indicated the poetical character and temperament. It was large and of a cast which glowed (I say literally glowed) when he spoke with feeling and interest. I never saw such another eye in a human being, though I have seen the most distinguished men of my time.

Burns enjoyed Edinburgh – and being lionised, although that wore off a bit as the 16 months dragged by. He enjoyed the company of people who were his intellectual equals – rare back home – but beneath the polite and witty façade, the rebel lurked. He wrote to one of his less genteel Edinburgh cronies, Willie Nicol, classics master at the High School.

> I never, my friend, thought Mankind very capable of anything generous but the stateliness of the Patricians in Edinburgh, and the servility of my plebian brethren, who perhaps formerly eyed me askance, since I returned home, have nearly put me out of countenance altogether with my species.

He was fond of schoolmasters, for they had the learning which he admired, usually without the social pretension. For Willie Michie, schoolmaster at Cleish in Fife, he wrote a mock epitaph:

> Here lie Willie's Michie's banes:
> O Satan, when ye tak him,
> Gie him the schoolin o' your weans,
> For clever deils he'll mak them!

He was good at this kind of thing. He'd always been a kind of 'jobbing poet' who could turn his hand to versifying any occasion – from solemn commemoration to digging his friends in the ribs with words. He was better at the second:

> Lament him Mauchline husbands a',
> He aften did assist ye;
> For had ye stayed hale weeks awa',
> Your wives would ne'er hae missed ye.
> Ye Mauchline bairns as on ye pass,
> To school in bands thegither,
> O, tread ye lightly on his grass –
> He micht hae been your feyther!

Edinburgh offered lots of opportunities for pompous

declamation and too few for friendly jibes – and none at all for the rebellious fire which burns at the heart of his 'human rights' poems – like *A Man's a Man for a' That*, *Holy Willie* and *The Unco' Guid* which like *Scotch Drink* opens with a lilting Biblical paraphrase:

My Son, these maxims make a rule,
An' lump them aye thegither:
The Rigid Righteous is a fool,
The Rigid Wise anither:
The cleanest corn that ere was dight
May hae some pyles o' caff in;
So ne'er a fellow creature slight
For random fits o' daffin.

But the most radical of them all was *The Jolly Beggars*, written before the Kilmarnock edition but never published in Burns' lifetime, the nearest thing he ever wrote to a play – or a piece of music theatre (although he was planning a drama at his death) – a rumbustious appeal to humanity's 'unofficial self', an anarchic assembly of gangrel bodies outside the pale of social acceptance. No idealisation of the peasant as in Wordsworth or Yeats; the dark side of humanity caught in the act, sordid, lustful, drunken but also independent, comradely, scornful and courageous. Here's the raucle carlin, the female vagabond in her unlugubrious elegy for her Highland lover:

A HIGHLAND LAD MY LOVE WAS BORN
(Song)

On one of the two tours to the Highlands he made while he waited in Edinburgh for publisher, Willie Creech, to disgorge the miserly £100 paid for the copyright of the Edinburgh edition of his poems, Burns collected another rebellious and defiant ditty which he made into a lively song:

MACPHERSON'S FAREWELL (Song)

In 1788 he gave up the gilded – and gelded – life of being a poet in Edinburgh, regularised his marriage with Jean Armour and her now-fawning family, who had originally torn up his marriage lines, and took the lease of a farm at Ellisland, near Dumfries. Later, he became an excise officer to give his family the stability that neither poetry nor farming ever offered. There were more poems – a few great ones like the immortal *Tam o Shanter*, probably the finest narrative poem ever written in our tongue – and many songs in the labour of love to which he devoted the last few years of his tragically short life, until the endocarditis contracted in his youth and the bad advice of the medical profession, finally killed him in July 1796.

The novelist, George Eliot, (Mary Ann Evans) said:

> It is an easy task to write severe things about the transgressions of men of genius by making ourselves over-zealous agents of Heaven and demanding that our brother should bring usurious interest for his Five Talents, forgetting that it is less easy to manage five talents than two.

No lyric poet has been so much talked about and so often misunderstood and vilified as Robert Burns. His early biographers made him a pious example of their own narrow-minded philosophies of temperance and social probity but even they could not entirely evade the impact of his genius.

And the world at large has shrugged off their hypocritical judgements, to take him to their hearts as the poet who got closer to the lives and feelings of ordinary people than any other. The world o'er remembers him in many languages and meetings and partings, with the wonderful legacy of songs which he left us, in particular in friendship's international anthem *Auld Lang Syne*.

AULD LANG SYNE (Song)

And having said his piece, Iain, no doubt resumed his place, took up his dram and winked to the world over the rim of his glass.

In 1990, to everyone's surprise (except Glaswegians), Glasgow was named European Capital of Culture. To mark the honour, President Bryan McKirgan and his fellow-members of the Glasgow and District Association of Burns Clubs asked me to prepare and present *Burnsiana 90 – A Celebration of Burns in Glasgow*. Thanks to subsidies from the Glasgow District Council under their Lord Provost, Susan Baird, and a hefty donation from Marks and Spencer Ltd, whose store now occupied the site of the Black Bull Hotel (where Burns himself once stayed) a company was assembled and rehearsed for the three day run at the City Hall in the Candleriggs.

For the opening on 22 November, the Glasgow clubs produced a flashy brochure which contained details of everything that was ever to do with Burns and Glasgow and notes on the tripartite programming which consisted of *Burnsang* with Anne Lorne Gillies on the Thursday, dramatisations of *The Cotter's Saturday Night* and

Tam o Shanter on the Friday and a concert performance of the Burns Musical. *There Was A Lad* on the Saturday. Something, one would have thought for every Burnsian. People did come, and a good time was had by all, but once again, the Burns Clubs were notable for their absence. 'It was too near Christmas,' some said. Others, that they were getting ready for their own Burns Suppers in January. Even more incongruous, given the publicity it got among the clubs, some said they hadn't known it was on. Whatever the reason, they stayed away in droves.

Or was it that they were saving their resources for the next big Burns milestone – the 1996 Bicentenary?

For the future be prepared,
Guard whatever thou can'st guard;
But, thy utmost duty done,
Welcome, what thou canst not shun.
(Lines written at Friar's Carse)

11

The International Year of Burns

1996

> Burns – the truest and sweetest of all
> who have ever sung of home and love,
> and humanity.
>
> (John Greenleaf Whittier)

The year of 1986 had been my first attempt to retire from the world of Robert Burns. The book had been written, the recordings made – 'and all was done that I could do' with this part of my life. I thought that was that and prepared for other things. However, I had reckoned without a certain Philip Raskin of Glasgow who was about to open a tiny restaurant called the Inn on the Green in the East End of that city, and had the idea that a Burns Supper with me would be just the thing to get him started.

Well, he talked me into it. 'Just a wee Burns Night', he said, and has been talking me into it ever since. As a result of his efforts the annual Burns Supper at the Inn on the Green attained almost cult proportions in Glasgow and sold out from year to year. So much so, that extra nights were put on to meet with the demand. Once again, there was no room at the Inn. Why was this so? And why did the same people come back again and again? The answer was that Philip Raskin did small for less than a hundred patrons what Joe Campbell and West Sound did big for more than a thousand. What both nights had in common, however, was *style*. The ambience was special, the meal was superb and the Robert Burns Story was told simply and effectively throughout the evening. At the Inn on the Green there was no top table, no speeches, no toasts – just the words of Burns in verse and song fed through a single voice engaging an audience at close quarters throughout the night. Burns was allowed to speak for himself and when he did he never failed to make his magic.

The lesson is there to learn. Burns's own words are better than anyone else's if it's a Burns Night that is wanted. For thirty-seven years, his whole lifetime, as I said, this show has been my perennial homage to Burns. I have grown old in its service and will retire from it one day. Philip has now moved on to *The Tavern on the Green* in sylvan Strathaven *but* there is no reason why the Robert Burns story shouldn't go on being told in this distinctive way throughout the meal as long as people want to hear it. After all, the material is timeless and the memory of this man Burns is forever. At least it lasted until something they called the 'International Year of Robert Burns 1996'.

It all started off well enough. David Shankland, the Burns orator from Lochmaben, gave the toast at the West Sound Bicentenary Burns Supper, held, as usual, in the Hospitality Inn, Glasgow on Saturday, 13 January 1996.

> Time; like and ever rolling stream
> Bears all its sons away
> They fly forgotten as a dream
> Dies at the opening day.

> These lines from a favourite hymn serve to remind us how transitory, is our earthly being before, all too soon, we are whisked away to join the withered leaves of time. Once in every thousand years or so, however, there flickers into flame a light that does not dim or die, is not snuffed out, but burns brightly, ever more brightly, until it fills the whole world with the brilliance of its light. Such a light was and is the sheer genius of Robert Burns, Scotland's National Bard, whose natal day we are celebrating here in Glasgow tonight..Ladies and Gentlemen, when one considers the tremendous torrent of words that are written and spoken about the Bard at this time, is it not a tribute to his durability, his versatility, his staying power, that when the last word has been spoken, the last song sun and the last toast drunk, he emerges unscathed, his crown untarnished, his star shining more brightly than ever before? Tonight, in the presence of this distinguished company, I should like to pay my own modest tribute but rather than add materially to that mass of verbiage I have alluded to, rather would I draw upon it and try to extract from it the essential elements, the essence if you like, of the poet's genius. How does one define 'genius' however? In a sense, it is indefinable, like the gem it has so many facets. All

I can hope to do, therefore, is to pinpoint or pick out one or two constituents of what is a complex chemistry. Let me begin therefore by asking a fundamental question:-

What kind of a man was Robert Burns? Obviously, intellectually he was alert and intelligent. He was well-informed on what was going on in the world and was capable of hammering out abstract ideas on the intellectual anvil of debate. We are also aware that he was a master of words and these tools he used with devastating effect to immortalise a humble mouse and to deify a daisy. The thing that sets him apart in my view – and an Immortal Memory is a subjective opinion – was his tremendous emotional intensity, his sensitivity to the world about him. Here was a man of passion, a gentleman of compassion, a sensitive spirit able to feel the faintest flutterings of the human heart. These then I submit were the seeds of his genius and planted as they were by sheer chance in the barren soil of 18th century Ayrshire, they grew and flourished into the full flowering of his Muse. Our presence here in such large numbers tonight would suggest to me that the fragrance of that flower is still with us 200 years further on. Like all men, the poet felt the need to express himself and the only suitable vehicle for the imprisoned splendour of his mind could but be those poems and songs which poured forth in such profusion. His pen a brush, each poem or song a picture painted in vivid colours, he spans the whole spectrum of human experience; he runs the whole gamut of our emotions. He makes us proud and patriotic; he makes us ashamed of man's inhumanity to man; he shows us the beauties of nature; he opens our eyes to the pathos of the human situation. Listen to these lines:-

> Still thou art blest compar'd wi' me!
> The present only toucheth thee;
> But och! I backward cast my e'e
> On prospects drear;
> An forward tho' I canna see
> I guess an' fear.

But ladies and gentlemen, when the poet's words are added to the old tunes he picked up from round about, he achieves a new stature. Here is a marriage of Beauty and Perfection. Here, Burns is the master of our soul. Music you see expresses our innermost feelings, more eloquently than any other medium. Burns' music does that and more; little wonder then

> that a Burns' evening when properly orchestrated, is the perfect type of perfect pleasure. He writes the script, he chooses the music.
>
> Two other aspects of Burns' genius I must mention...
>
> The first of these is his relevance for today. Why does this great physician of the heart, still sit eternally at the bedside of our mind, although he has been dead for exactly 200 years?! Why are we here tonight? In my opinion, the Bard is relevant for today not only for his contribution to our culture but also because of his belief in the Brotherhood of Man. Now in matters material, the world is much advanced from that which the poet inhabited. Burns lived in a rural rustic agragrian society, whereas our world is one of automation, automobiles and the hydrogen bomb. Ironically, human nature hasn't altered since Burns' day. We are still the same old type of people with the same faults and failings, the same vices and virtues. Because of this, there are still wars and rumours of wars. The only difference is that man has now the capacity to destroy the whole world. In our time as in Burns' time, there is still great inequality – one half of the world has reached out for the moon while the other half reaches out in vain for a crust of bread. There is still hatred, hypocrisy, bigotry and bloody-mindedness. For all these reasons, there has never been a greater need for a belief in the brotherhood of man. It acts as a beacon to lighten our darkness.
>
> The second point I should like to comment on is Burns' universal appeal. It is not only we Scots who celebrate his birthday every January, but people of every class and creed, people of every hue and colour, people of every political persuasion. Why is this? First of all, I think the Bard speaks in a language we can all understand. Part of his genius lies in his ability to distil great thoughts into simple stanzas – we don't need to be a genius to get the message. Likewise, we can all identify with Burns the man. He is in fact a paradox. He is a Saint because he was a 'sinner' – he is a success because he was a 'failure' – he is internationally famed because he was a patriot. In summary, he is 'immortal' because he was so very mortal. Burns had his faults but who are we to judge? It is difficult to carry out a full cup without spilling some...

What a beautiful metaphor that is, and a good note on which to leave Mr Shankland's well-paced oration so apt and relevant to the splendid West Sound occasion. They always try to be the first Supper of the season but they also aspire to be the first in quality. Mr Shankland maintained that standard. Like many good speakers, he rose to the moment and we are left with the lovely taste in the mouth of that full Burns cup he conjured up, full and brimming over with all the talents but so early taken from his hand. What is nearly as tragic was the way in which all those who should have known better let the cup that was known as the International Festival of Burns 96 fall from so many hands so that what promised so much instead spilled away so disgracefully to so little effect.

Scotland has had her share of disasters, from Flodden to the Darian Scheme, but the Burns Year of 1996 would surely rank among the worst in recent years. Yet it wasn't for the want of thinking ahead. As early as January 1993, the Burns Industry Group comprising all the interested bodies like Enterprise Ayrshire and the Scottish Enterprise office in Glasgow as well as other ancillary interests had commissioned a report from consultants in Edinburgh on how to prepare for a great European event, and in due course, this was delivered in a 50-page ring binder but with all the appropriate sales jargon. One could see the suits behind every phrase: 'Product Enhancement', 'Event Matrix', 'Market Fatigue' and 'Menu of Activities' were only some of the phrases bandied, although the eventual 'Mission Statement' was plain enough:

> To use the bicentenary of the death of Robert Burns as a catalyst to generate additional economic activity in the South West of Scotland by organising events, helping market the area and promoting Burns.

Two 'impact-driven' general objectives had been recognised and these were to raise the profile of Scotland's south-west while 'countering any unfavourable perceptions' and to increase visitor numbers 'and thereby raise levels of ...derived benefits'. Dumfries and Alloway were recognised as 'core locations' and the 'incorporation of international activities' would be looked for on 'an opportunistic basis'. Then, almost as an afterthought, there was a mention of the main theme which was to provide a 'Cultural Festival' projecting Burns as a focal point of wider Scottish culture' and this was aimed for the month of July. Which was exactly what the original Burns Festival had proposed in 1975. This original Festival, incidentally, was never mentioned.

A gross cost of 940,000 pounds was projected which included a Hogmanay launch, the biggest-ever Burns Supper and an International Festival of Burns and a year-long tour by the Burns Youth Theatre Company. All this was very worthy and laudable but very little of it happened in actuality even though Her Royal Highness, the Princess Royal, was appointed President and patron of the year. Other patrons were Moira Anderson, Jean Redpath, Dr James A.Mackay and the present writer, although, as I recall, none of us was asked to do anything. Princess Anne took time to come to Kilmarnock to help get things under way but, in reality, it all came to little more than a Burns Look-Alike Competition and a ploughing contest. In typically Scottish fashion, everyone went their own way and only Burns was the loser.

However, provision had been made for the appointment of a Burns Festival Director and to 'provide a strategic plan for the appointed person'. I went to see this 'appointed person' at his newly-opened office in the Sandgate in Ayr to find that he had flown to London to try and engage Signor Luciano Pavarotti for the Burns Festival. Failing that, I was told, he was trying for Dame Kiri te Kanawa for a special outdoor concert by the banks o Doon. I had a scheme for the year to re-enact the Burns Border and Highland tours on horseback, with fellow actors who could ride joining me along the way. The 'appointed person' and I finally met to discuss the idea over a good lunch in a Glasgow hotel and he seemed most excited by the possibilities it offered on many counts. Later, we met in a theatre in Edinburgh to sort out the final small print and he went away to draw up the necessary contract. I never heard from him again.

Few did. And there were other artists and organizations left similarly high and dry. I just went ahead and did the tour anyway – by horsepower rather than on horseback but I felt an interesting project had been missed, not least its television potential as a documentary. I salvaged what I could of the idea, and while I went round the Borders and the Highlands in my car, the International Year of Robert Burns, or half-year, as it had now become, from 25 January to 21 July, seemed to lurch from crisis to crisis. Despite all the boasted high intentions, the beautiful brochures and press packs and leaflets and fliers nothing much appeared to happen on the ground and soon there were money problems. The press had a field day with each new scandal and even those respectably involved to have misgivings about the whole affair.

The promise faded further with each resignation, all the big talk fell into a smaller case, and when the 'appointed person' absconded into that obscurity for which he had worked so hard, the public outcry brought the house of cards tumbling down and the mirage that was the Burns International Festival of 1996 faded into the empty vessel it had always been. To be fair some of the projects came off, like the exhibition, *The Pride and the Passion* which opened at the Royal Museum in Edinburgh and went on to Kilmarnock. This was a splendid piece of work, the brainchild of Gavin Sprott in tandem with the National Library and National Gallery of Scotland and the Museum. If everything had been of this standard, Burns, and Scotland, would have been proud.

Instead, there was no great performance to remember, no new play, no new opera, no great speeches, no acts of daring, no ingenuity, no imagination, no FUN. In short it was no use, and everyone was glad to sweep the dirt under the carpet and shut the door on a large waste of time and money. Every District Council in the South-West had put in a stake, all the enterprise boards, the Arts Council *et al*, but the only one to show a return was the 'appointed person'.

It was almost a relief to get out of Scotland for a while. In that other Scotland, Eastern Canada, the metropolitan city of Toronto, Ontario, got itself a new subway station. For a week at least, the Old Mill Station will be known as Dufftown Scotland. The temporary change of name for the Bloor Street West station comes in honour of Robbie Burns Week, which was held in honour of the poet. For the renaming ceremony, pipers from the 48th Highlanders ascended the station stairs, coming to attention and flanking Metro Chairman, Alan Tonks, as he read the official decree giving it its Scottish designation. Everyone was invited to be there – even non-Scots.

Still in Ontario, in Alliston, George Douglas of Orangeville, gave the Immortal Memory. Despite a stormy night, more than 200 people turned up to hear George and enjoy this Supper. The following good point was made in his conclusion:

> One special note for those of us who are Scots. From the time

of the Union of the Crowns with England in 1603 and still more from the time of the legislative union in 1703, Scotland had lapsed into obscurity. The Scottish dialect was in danger of perishing. Burns seemed, at this juncture, to start to his feet and reassert Scotland's claim to national existence. Mankind will never allow to die the eternal language in which his songs and poems are enshrined. That is a part of Scotland's debt to Burns and which we are dealing with at this very moment, by our presence here. Friends, I propose a toast to the Immortal Memory of Robert Burns.

I must explain in this Canadian context that I knew John Maxwell McCuaig. I knew him as an ex-Scots guardsman, ex-Glasgow policeman and excellent contact man and broker for visiting theatricals across Canada. I also knew that he knew his Burns, having received his book, *The Return of Robert Burns* on one of my Burns tours, but what I didn't know was that he was such an accomplished public speaker as he showed when he addressed the 9th Annual Banquet of the Burns Club of Vancouver, extracts from which are now given. John was introduced by the Chairman, Fraser Lawrie.

Thank you Fraser for your kind, generous and altogether accurate introduction. I wish now I had written more.
Mr President, Mr Chairman, Honoured Guests, Fellow members of the Vancouver Burns Club. Gentleman all.

Recently I had the privilege of delivering this address to the inmates of one of British Columbia's finest Law Enforcement and Corrections Establishments, so if any of you gentlemen present here tonight are listening to it for the second time, please accept my apologies.

Now I'd like to take a moment to offer my sincere thanks to this year's Burns Supper Committee. Gentlemen, I am grateful for the honour you have accorded me by inviting me to address this distinguished assembly on such an auspicious occasion. It is my wish, and I can only hope, that fifteen minutes from now you will feel that your choice was not imprudent and that your confidence was well placed.

Tonight is of particular significance to all Burns lovers in that, not only are we celebrating the anniversary of the birth of Burns, which as most of you are aware, occurred on this night 237 years ago, but we must also remember that this year marks the 200th anniversary of his death. Robert Burns died on the 21st of July 1796, aged 37.

Thirty seven years from the cradle to the grave.
Thirty seven years to Immortality.

The story of Robert Burns is the story of one man's struggle to overcome extreme poverty and adversity, rampaging personal emotions and frustrated ambition. It is also the story of a poor Scottish farmer's meteoric rise from total obscurity to recognition, during his own lifetime, as a world class poet. Despite the rigours and hardship of farm labour for fourteen hours everyday, Burns was busy writing literally hundreds of songs and poems, the vast majority of which not only survived but have flourished to this very day...

It has often been said that one of Burn's many attributes was charisma...charisma is rare and few of us have it...it is difficult to describe or explain, but here is a little story which might illustrate how it worked for Burns.

One late summer afternoon, Burns was walking along a country road leading a goat on a string, and he had pig under one arm, a hen under the other. He also had a bucket under his chin. As he walked along he met a rather prim young lady coming towards him. As she approached Burns called out asking if it were far to the village. She replied that it was long way off but if he was in a hurry there was a short cut through the woods. He then said that he was indeed in a hurry and could she show him the short cut. She was alarmed that he should think she would go through the woods with a strange man.

'Why not?' asked Burns.

'You might take advantage of me?'

'What? Look, lassie, I've got a goat on the lead, a bucket round my neck, a hen under one arm and a pig under the other – how could I possibly do anything?'

The girls looked at him for minute then said quietly;

'Well – you could tie the goat to a tree, put the hen under the bucket, and I'll hold the pig.'

Now, that's charisma!

Burns was a man of many and complex dimensions. He was proud, passionate, charismatic and romantic. He was also driven and flawed. To say that he loved wine, women and song is simply to say that he loved life. Unfortunately, he was restricted by the father, the church and its elders and any effort on his part to display or express his feelings on the subject of personal freedom, or for that matter, freedom of any kind, met with resistance and disapproval. Considering the hardships and frustration he endured, one can well understand why, on occasion, Burns sought solace and comfort wherever it was to be found; whether it was in the arms of a woman or at the bottom of a glass...

There is no doubt that Burns enjoyed a drink, he also enjoyed the company and merriment that went with it, something he saw very little of during his lifetime...but much of what he saw and heard provided inspiration for the songs and poems he would write later. His genius expressed itself in his poetry. Poetry was his raison d'etre and where poetry was concerned he was triumphantly articulate. There isn't anything in Burns's poetry that cannot be universally applied or appreciated and it is sadly all too true that Burns's observations on the human condition are more relevant to today's world than they were to his. *Man was made to Mourn* is a classic example, wherein Burns observes that 'Man's inhumanity to man makes thousands mourn'. This was never more true than it is today.

Burns was many things other than a poor farmer. As I said earlier, he was a romantic, and as such, he bequeathed to the world some of the greatest love songs ever written... but in 1788, he gave to the world the song which is unquestionably the universal anthem of friendship and remembrance of bygone days. I refer of course, to *Auld Lang Syne*. There are those who believe that Burns would have achieved immortality had he written nothing else. It is a song which is sung by all races in every corner of the globe and will no doubt be sung by generations as yet unborn...

Burns embraced all humanity: humanity in turn has embraced him. Once each year, on the anniversary of his birth, Scots the world over foregather, just as we are doing here tonight, to mark and celebrate the memory of Robert Burns. However, we are not alone. Burns's unique universality is confirmed in similar celebrations by Americans, Germans, French, Italians, Russians and Chinese – to name but a few.

The years pass. His name has long been numbered among the great Immortals and gilded in the light of beloved memory that will never fade in the hearts of Scotland's worthy sons

> and daughters. The star that rose over the banks of Ayr on that cold January night 337 years ago is still rising and grows stronger yet with each passing year.
>
> Gentlemen, I ask you to rise, raise your glasses, and join me in a toast to Scotland's most illustrious son:
>
> To the Immortal Memory of Robert Burns.

A few days later, on the other side of the world, Mrs Nancy Norman of Masterton, New Zealand, an individual member of the Burns Federation, entertained a few friends in her own home to remember the bicentenary of Robert Burns. Being winter down under at that time, they gathered round the fire, and quite spontaneously, Mrs Norman spoke about Burns to the little gathering. Without knowing it, she delivered a completely natural Immortal Memory. As far as she can remember, this is the gist of what she said:

> Robert Burns experienced all the emotions that we're all aware of – sadness, joy, depression, grief, frustration, failure and genuine love. His poetry and songs testify to this. He knew the sadness of losing a beloved father, the joy of meeting his Jean, the depression of headaches and sickness, the grief over a dead daughter, the frustration of farming, the failure of Ellisland, and the real love he knew for all animals and everything in nature...
>
> Two hundred years ago on the 21st July, a few hours from now, Robert Burns died at 37 from the illness that had troubled him all his life. And he died worrying about his wee ones and about a bill he had to pay for a militia uniform I don't think he'd ever worn. But think of the goodness of the young girl, Jessie Lewars, who nursed him during his last days while Jean was lying-in with another child, a son who was to be born as Robert was being laid into the grave in St Michael's Kirkyard.
>
> Robert Burns loved life and the company of good friends... but being a wife and mother, I can only imagine how Jean must have felt through all their ups and downs and to lose him so young on that last sad day... leaving her with four boys to bring up...

Mrs Norman doesn't remember making any great toast or anything. She said that a hush just came down on the room so she stopped. It was just past midnight and someone started to sing *Auld Lang Syne*.

Should auld acquaintance be forgot

And never brought to mind,
Should auld acqaintance be forgot
And auld lang syne?
For auld lang, my dear
For auld lang syne
We'll take a cup o' kindness yet
For auld lang syne...

'And that was my first ever public venture,' said Nancy, but she can be assured that many an experienced Burns orator would have been proud to create such a hush in the room. And we remember that Burns himself said:

My Muse, tho hamely in attire,
May touch the heart..

A further reminder that 'guid gear' can gang in 'sma buik' came in a letter from France. In the audience for *The Robert Burns Story* at the Bellisle Hotel in Ayr was Mary Wigley who was celebrating her 50th birthday by touring all the Burns places in the south-west of Scotland before attending a summer school at Auchencairnie. The difference was that she came from France to do so. She now lives in Lyon with her husband Mike and together they run the only Burns club in the mainland of Europe. Numbered 1120 on the Federation Roll, its membership includes no less than four nationalities. In 1996 it was only two years old, but growing. A very small bud, it deserves to flower. Coincidentally, it was another Lyon that featured in the next Burns excerpt. This time, not the place but the person. no less than the President of a far older Burns Club, Kilmarnock No 0, R.Stuart Lyon.

Towards the end of 1997, the Balvenie Distillery in Banff, one of the last traditional whisky-makers in Scotland, growing its own barley and boasting its own coopers and coppersmiths, sponsored a competition organised by the Burns Federation. Club members were asked to submit an Immortal Memory lasting no longer that 7.5 minutes on tape for adjudication by judges from the Speakers' Panel of Glasgow to determine who would be the first Balvenie Master of Burns. The presentation was held in the Burns Room of the Mitchell Library in Glasgow on 22 January 1998 and from more than 70 entrants the winner was declared to be R. Stuart Lyon of Newmilns in Ayrshire, who received a cash prize for his club, a magnificent quaich – and a bottle of Balvenie's finest Single Barrel Whisky – which he assures me is still unopened at the time of this writing. This is part of his winning entry:

> Today, ladies and gentlemen, mankind is very much aware and indeed concerned about the environment we live in. Our generation is aware more than any other that this planet earth holds the memories of our past history, that it struggles with the present demands of an ambitious and often uncaring society and yet it continues to nurture and caress our dreams and our desires for a brighter and a happier future. Such were the desires of Robert Burns over 200 years ago. A burning desire to enrich and dignify the life of the common man, the merry friendly country folk, the poor oppressed honest man, the toil worn cotter, all the ordinary every day folk upon whose toils obscure that a man's a man for a that.
>
> He wrote in the Doric the language of the common folks of Scotland but he wrote for all mankind irrespective of race or creed and he delighted in putting down those who thought themselves to be high and mighty. He hated long faces, smug professions and pious posturing – people like Holy Willie who claimed the whole breadth of life's highway and the whole harvest of life's fields.
>
> He used nature to highlight the concerns he held for his fellow man and wrote *The Twa Dogs* to show man's inhumanity to man. Two dogs from very different backgrounds but who cherished their commonality of spirit and their friendship. The first was called Caesar –
>
> His locked, letter'd braw brass collar
> Shewd him a gentleman and scholar,
> But though he wis o high degree
> The fient a pride, nae pride had he
> But wad hae spent an hour caressin
> Ev'n wae a tinkler-gypsy's messin –'
> The second dog was his bosum buddy Luath –
> 'He was a gash an faithfu tyke
> As ever lapt a sheugh or dyke,
> His honest sonsie baws'nt face
> Ay gat him friends in ilka place
> Nae doubt but they were fain o ither
> And unco pack an thick the gither –
>
> The dogs discuss their respective masters and the societies

they lived in. They decry mans materialistic ways, his life of drunkenness and debauchery and their lady's backstabbing tittle tattle. Burns sweeps us along in this humorous and thought-provoking work then brings us down to earth when the dogs are parting:

> And up they gat and shook their lugs
> Rejoiced they were na men but dogs.

In *To A Louse* Burns criticises that loathsome creature but again at the end of the poem he stops us in our tracks – he ask us to stand back and take a good look at ourselves – to look behind the painted faces and the fancy clothes:

> O wad some power the giftie gie us
> To see oursels as ithers see us;
> It wad frae monie a blunder free us
> And foolish notion...

How Burns must have loved writing... His works are full of humour – sometimes light hearted, some times base, and often satirical – how sad it is that such humour was written during brief fitful joys snatched from a life of poverty and ill health.

He also used nature as a backdrop to some of the most beautiful love songs ever written – 'How can ye chant ye little birds and I sae weary fu o care' – *My love is like a red, red rose.* And where in all of literature can we find words more likely to tear at the heart strings of even the most hardened of men than –

> Had we never loved sae kindly,
> had we never loved sae blindly
> never met or never parted
> we had ne'er been broken hearted.'

Some of his most poignant lines however were reserved as thanks to Jessie Lewars for nursing him during his final illness–

> O were I monarch o the globe
> Wi' thee to reign wi thee to reign
> The brightest jewel in my crown
> Would be my queen, would be my queen.

Words like these are not conjured from the conscious mind of a literary genius but are straight from the heart. The fact that as a poet he has been hailed as one of the greatest by all the great poets who came after him – is not enough. Greater and more everlasting and meaningful than that, he has been hailed by the common man as the poet of humanity...

Ladies and gentleman I would ask you to charge your glasses,

> be upstanding and drink with me a toast to the immortal memory of Robert Burns.

Since the Balvenie Distillers have not seen fit to sponsor a second Burns Master competition, Mr Stuart Lyon retains his undisputed title.

Professor R.J.S.Grant is Professor Emeritus of Theology in the Department of English at the University of Alberta in Edmonton, Canada. Raymond Grant is not your usual 'gentleman in black' as Burns described men of the cloth, nor is he your usual academic. Now retired, he travels extensively, and, at the time of writing, holds the position of Literary Advisor to the *Burns Chronicle*. His book on Burns in 1986 was appropriately entitled *The Laughter of Love*. He also spent some time in Prague during his career and will frequently open his peroration in Czech as he did at the University of Alberta's Faculty Club on 26 January 1998.

> Vazeni hoste, Damy a Panove, dobry vecer!
> Honoured guests, Ladies and Gentlemen, good evening!
>
> It is again my pleasure and privilege to bid you welcome to Burns Night at the Faculty Club as we carry out our pleasant duty of honouring the immortal memory of the great poet of the human heart, Robert Burns!

The following is an edited extract:

> There are those who for prurience' sake concentrate on the legend of Robert Burns the fervent nationalist, the hard drinker, the ardent wencher, the rabid revolutionary, and set him along side our patron saint Andrew to be Scotland's patron sinner. But Burns himself gives the lie to such exaggeration of the laughter of love as he smiles down on us in benediction in the east room of the Burns Museum at Alloway from the two stained glass windows made by Cottier & Co. of London. No, the key to Burns is his combination of laughter and love. How Burns would like to be of our number this evening to share our laughter–
>
> In Scotland, I heard a variant of the sheep's head joke. It concerned the English lady who insisted that everything English was superior to every Scottish equivalent. Entering an Edinburgh butcher's shop, she said, 'Give me a sheep's head – and be sure it's from an English sheep.' The butcher shouted to his assistant, 'Jock, bring ben a sheep's heid, but first tak oot the brains!' Then he confided to his

astonished customer 'We'll leave in the eyes, so that'll see you through the week.' Any Scottish housewife would have appreciated that.

An expatriate couple had just celebrated their silver wedding anniversary. A friend asked the husband, 'What did you do to celebrate?' 'Oh, I took the wife to Scotland.' 'What will you do to celebrate your golden wedding, then?' 'I'll maybe go and fetch her back!'

Grampian television sent a reporter to interview the oldest inhabitant of a Donside village. 'Have you lived here all your life?' 'Weel, nae yet.'

'How far back can you remember?' 'I canna min' bein' born, but ah div min' the dogs barkin' as the midwife gaed awa!'

The owner of an Aberdeen pub reported that the glass coin jar for charitable donations had been stolen from the end of the bar. Police say that they are confident of making an early arrest, as both coins had been clearly marked.

While I was in the North-East, I saw a fellow on one back of the River Dee call to a chap on the opposite bank, 'How do I get to the other side?' 'You're on the other side!' he shouted back. Come to think of it, he was right enough.

When I was in London, I met a fellow Scot, who complained that the natives are not very friendly 'At three o' clock every morning,' he told me, 'they hammer on my bedroom door, on the walls, even on the ceiling. Sometimes they hammer so loudly I canna hear myself playing the pipes.'

I overheard three wee boys talking about their fathers. The first one said, 'My Dad's an awful coward – when he sees a fight going on, he hides in the kitchen.' The second said, 'My Dad's a worse coward – when it's thunder and lightning, he hides in the basement.' And the third said, 'My Dad's even worse – when my Mum was in the hospital having her appendix out, he had to sleep with the woman next door!'

I read in the paper about three Irishmen counting – one could count and the other couldn't.

An Irishman, a Welshman, an Englishman and a Scot were sharing the same compartment on a train. After a while, the Irishman started to pull potatoes from his bag and began to throw them out the window. The Welshman turned to him and asked, 'What are you doing?' The Irishman said, 'We have so many potatoes in Ireland – I'm sick and tired of looking at them!' Shortly after, the Welshman began pulling leeks from his bag and throwing them out the window. The Irishman asked, 'And what are you doing then?' The Welshman replied, 'We have so many of these damned things in Wales – I'm sick and tired of looking at them!' Inspired by the others, the Scotsman opened the train compartment door and pushed out the Englishman.

Finally, a Scottish bus driver was giving a tour of Scotland to a group of tourists. As the tour went through the countryside and the driver would point out sights of interest. He drove by one area and said, 'Over there is where the Scottish PULVERISED the English.' They drove on a little further and the driver pointed to another site by the roadway and said, 'This is the place where the Scottish MASSACRED the English.' Not much further down the road the driver told his passengers that on the right was the great battlefield where the Scottish again WHIPPED the English. At this a stiff English accent protested 'My good man, didn't the English ever win?' 'Not when I'm driving,' was the response.

If the purpose of tonight's festivities is to share jokes old and new be to enjoy haggis, neeps, tatties, and whisky, and to throw our essential Scottishness in the teeth of the world, it is also to celebrate the Immortal Memory of the Ploughman poet who is at one and the same time quintessentially Scottish and, at the same time, of universal appeal. It is the heavy responsibility of the Burns Night orator to attempt to resolve this enigma, and it is to honour this unique poet of the human heart that we gather together tonight. In him is that that mixture of love and laughter that now, as always, is the vital antidote to oppression, terrorism, uncharity, hypocrisy, pomposity, the slings and arrows of outrageous Fortune. Burns's poetry puts down the mighty from their seats and exalts those of low degree as he sings the great anthems of the infinite worth of the individual human spirit:

He'll hae misfortunes great and sma',
But ay a heart aboon them a';
He'll be a credit 'till us a',
We'll a' be proud o' Robin

We will always have Burns with us to teach us common humanity, charity, pride and worth, in poetry whose appeal is not just Scottish but also universal. It is almost two and a half centuries since the birth of Burns, and over two centuries since his passing. We do not have the man, we no longer have the life, but we do have the poetry without which the world and the hearts of its people would be immeasurably the poorer, the poetry of the human heart and its essential liberty.

For the future be prepar'd,
Guard, wherever thou canst guard,
But thy utmost duly done,
Welcome what thou can'st not shun:-
Follies past, give thou to air;
Make their consequence thy care:
Keep the name of MAN in mind,
And dishonour not thy kind.-
Reverence with lowly heart
Him whose wondrous work thou art;
Keep his goodness still in view,
Thy trust – and thy example too.
Who made the heart,'tis He alone
Decidedly can try us:
He knows each chord, its various tone,
Each spring, its various bias:

Then at the balance let's be mute,
We never can adjust it;
What's done we partly may compute,
But know not what's resisted.

In the heart that is true, there is no room for man's inhumanity to man, only room for love, love for the ladies, one's friends, one's fellow human beings, a wee, homeless field mouse, an auld mare, a crushed daisy, a wounded hare, the disadvantaged in this life, liberty, dignity, love for the eternal and infinite value of every human spirit. And we will continue to turn to Burns for the laughter of love:

We've faults and failins – granted clearly!
We're frail, backsliding mortals merely;
Eve's bonie squad, priests wyte them sheerly
For our grand fa';
But still, but still, I like them dearly –
God bless them a'!
O wad some Power the giftie gie us
To see oursels as ithers see us!
It wad frae monie a blunder free us,
An foolish notion:
What airs in dress an gait wad lea'e us,
An ev'n devotion!

The laughter of love is Burns's independent guess at the secrets of the universe. Learn first to laugh at yourself, then to laugh at life, and the corollary love will fill the heart and ward off the world's blows and buffets from the invincible spirit which is within. Given this impregnable laughter of love, Burns could survive onslaughts that would have broken a lesser man, could survive poverty, could withstand ingratitude and envy while he sang as the lark in the clear Ayrshire sky of the dignity and destiny of mice and men.

When I insisted so strongly upon returning from Prague to Edmonton in time for January 25th, my colleagues in the Protestant Theological Faculty thought immediately of the Feast of the Conversion of St. Paul, and could not quite understand why I was so fixated on the Conversion of Svati Pavel. Bringing light to these gentiles, I told them of the true significance of January 25th, the celebration of the 239th anniversary of the birth of Robert Burns. 'Ah! Robert Burns,' they said reverently, and asked their inevitable question, 'Was Robert Burns a Christian?' To which I gave them a direct, authoritative and unequivocal answer 'Yes – and no. Burns had a firm faith in the divine creator whose love pervades and permeates the universe, but his expression of that faith was not so much Christian as Pauline.' And they did question me further, saying unto me, 'Is Robert Burns, then, Scotland's patron saint?' To which I did make reply, saying unto them, 'No – much more important than that, he is the whole world's patron sinner.'

The title of Bozena Köllnová's translation, *Darebné Verse Roberta Burnse* turned out to mean 'Wicked or Scurrilous Verses of Robert Burns,' a somewhat strange title, as the volume contained alongside *Holy Willie's Prayer* and *Tam o Shanter* translations of such poems as *Auld Lang Syne* and *Is there for honest poverty*, that great anthem to independence of spirit and the indomitable courage of those who resist oppression. I shall try to get my tongue round the final stanza in Czech:

Toz modli se, at skonci se
Odvcka nase pre,
Then let us pray that come it may,
As come it will for a' that,
At poctivost a moudra ctnost
Jsou postaveny vse!

That Sense and Worth, o'er a' the earth
Shall bear the gree, and a' that.
Tak je to psano od veku
Pres tovse a pres to vse
For a' that, and a' that,
Its comin yet for a' that,
Stane se clovck clovku
Na zemi bratrem pres to vse.
That Man to Man the warld o'er
Shall brothers be for a' that.

I realise now that we Scots and Scots-Canadians must share our national bard with other nations when they are in dire need of the great poet of the human heart. In his verse he has bequeathed to all nations on the earth a resource of love and strength from which both individuals and peoples draw what they need to go on living, to hold their heads high as part of the brotherhood and sisterhood of mankind. Robert Burns was not just the national poet of Scotland; he was also the patron sinner of all people, everywhere and everywhen.

Wherever Deity hath set
Her signet on our human clay;
Wherever honour, truth, and love
Shall hold united sway:
Wherever Independence stern
The spangled minion spurns,
There find embalmed in every breast
The name of ROBERT BURNS!

With these words of James Macfarlan I come to the end of my contribution to the evening. I say again that it is a pleasure and my privilege to be here with you at the Faculty Club and to join with you in your celebration of the great poet of the human heart. Let us therefore honour his memory after our usual manner. Please charge your glasses, be upstanding, and join me in a toast to the Immortal Memory of ROBERT BURNS!

Dr Ian D.Duncan is a respected consultant and Reader at Ninewells Hospital and Medical School, Dundee, and lives in a thatched replica (circa 1745) of Burns Cottage in Glamis not too far from the Queen Mother's Scottish Castle. I had the chance to see this charming dwelling for myself when I was touring in Scotland during 2001. It is indeed like the Alloway Cottage, only richer. I couldn't resist knocking at the door and asking Mrs Duncan if her husband were at home. Unfortunately, he wasn't. Dr Duncan is also a 'Colonel' in the 2nd Battalion of the Crochallan Fencibles, in which he outranks his good friend and fellow-physician, David Purdie, who features in the following chapter. It is not known whether Ian speaks as a doctor or a colonel – or both – but he is a noted Burnsian, as was shown when he was invited to propose the final toast of the 20th-century to the Immortal Memory at the Globe Inn, Dumfries. However, he prefers to offer this compilation the version he gave of this same speech at the Burns Club of Atlanta and the Heather and Thistle Society of Houston in the following year – 'it's slightly different with its American twist'.

> Mr Chairman, Chieftain, Ladies and Gentlemen, thank you very much indeed for your most generous invitation to join you in your homeland, America, in celebrating your connections with my homeland, Scotland and the life and works of Robert Burns.
>
> Our story begins in the Mearns in North East Scotland in the middle of the 18th-century when two brothers set out from Clochnahill to make their fortunes. At the end of the farm road they shook hands wishing one another well. Robert turned North and William headed in the opposite direction perhaps passing my recently erected cottage en route to Edinburgh where he helped lay out The Meadows, a public park. The advice has always been 'Go West, young man', so when the work ran out that is exactly what he did and found employment as head gardener to the wealthy Dr William Ferguson, a retired London-Scottish doctor and Provost of Ayr. Driven on by ambition he leased 7 acres for a market garden in Alloway where he married a local lass. With his own two hands he built a simple cottage of clay and thatch and there on 25th January 1759 Agnes Burnes nee Broun gave birth to her first child, Robert. He was only just over a week old when the gable end of the cottage was blown in by a storm.
>
> Twas then a blast o Janwar win'
> Blew hansel in on Robin...
>
> That was the first but not the last time that his world crashed around him and after only 37 short years full of sound and fury Robert Burns died of rheumatic heart disease.

He'll hae misfortunes great and sma
But ay a heart aboon them a',
He'll be a credit till us a':
We'll a' be proud o Robin!

He said it, but he was absolutely right, and a credit not only to his native Ayrshire, not only to Scotland, but to the world in general where, at this time of year, millions of men and women are meeting like us to celebrate his immortal memory. What is so memorable, so immortal about this self-styled simple, ploughman poet? A POET – most certainly – a PLOUGHMAN – temporarily – but SIMPLE – NEVER.

Though the family were poor, William Burnes set a great store by a sound education. Robert was gifted with innate intelligence and a retentive memory. He had no distractions. – no radio, no television, no surfing the net. He loved books and read assiduously about geography, theology, biblical history, philosophy, political economy. He studied a wide range of subjects as different as surveying and botany, anthropology and physics, heraldry and music. Above all he loved contemporary novels and volumes of poetry. No, this was no simple heaven taught ploughman but a polymath in the best Renaissance tradition more than capable of holding his own in any company. A winner without doubt had he appeared on the television quiz game, 'Who wants to be a millionaire?' He was convivial, interesting, witty, amusing. He would never bore the pants off you, although in the case of the ladies he might well charm them off!

He became reasonably fluent in French and had a smattering of Latin. He could and did write in formal English – Anglicisation had been progressing since the Union of Parliaments in 1707 – Burns reacted by writing in the guid Scots tongue. Reading *The Life of Wallace* had an even more profound effect on the young poet than seeing the film *Braveheart* has had on today's youth. In his own words 'the story of Wallace poured a Scottish prejudice into my veins which will boil along there until the flood-gates of life shut in eternal rest.' Bonnie Prince Charlie's '45 rising had ended in rout and disarray on Culloden's bloody field a mere 13 years before the poet's birth and he liked to believe that his paternal grandfather had been out in the '15 in support of the Old Pretender. He collected, revised and reworked Jacobite songs. Romantically, sentimentally, Burns was a supporter of the

Stuarts and no great lover of the Hanoverians who occupied the throne.

'Is it not remarkable,' he wrote to his friend Mrs Dunlop in 1788, 'odiously remarkable that – in this very reign of heavenly Hanoverianism – an empire beyond the Atlantic has had its Revolution too, and for the same maladministration and legislative misdemeanors in the illustrious and sapienipotent Family of Hanover as was complained of in the "tyrannical and bloody house of Stuart"?' The last phrase is in inverted commas and I rather think his tongue was very firmly in his cheek when he wrote that. He was certainly being careful but his sentimental Jacobitism, and guarded support for the American Revolution led to fervent Jacobinism and expressed support for the French Revolutionaries which almost cost him his job as an Exciseman. What is revealed is his strongly held belief in basic human rights, liberty, equality and the importance of fraternity.

It's hardly in a body's pow'r,
To keep, at times, frae being sour,
To see how things are shar'd;
How best o' chiels are whyles in want,
While Coofs on countless thousands rant,
And ken na how to wair't.

Writing in the guid Scots tongue, he was following in the footsteps of his role models, Allan Ramsay and Robert Fergusson, especially the latter, who sadly died in impoverished circumstances in Edinburgh at an even earlier age than Burns. He was only 24.

O Fergusson, thy glorious parts
Ill suited law's dry, musty arts!
My curse upon your whunstane hearts,
Ye En'brugh Gentry!
The tythe o' what ye waste at cartes
Wad stow'd his pantry.

While Fergusson wrote about city matters, Burns wrote about country matters. On turning up a mouse's nest with his plough he observed:

Thy wee bit housie, too, in ruin!
Its silly wa's the win's are strewin!
An naething, now, to big a new ane,
O foggage green!
An bleak December's win's ensuin,

Baith snell an keen.
But Mousie, thou art no thy lane,
In proving foresight may be vain:
The best-laid schemes o mice and men
Gang aft agley,
An lea'e us nought but grief and pain,
For promis'd joy!

That last was from the heart. It was November 1785. He had become a father for the first time six months earlier and he had not planned that.

Welcome my bonie, sweet, wee dochter!
Tho ye come here a wee unsought for...

Burns tells his friend, John Rankine how the 'poacher-court' got to hear of the 'paitrick hen' he had brought down with his 'gun', so he had to 'thole the blethers' and pay the fee but promises that as soon as the 'clockin-time is by' and the child is born, he plans to go 'sportin by and by' to get value for his guinea. He was as good as his word but it was not the same 'paitrick hen' that he brought down this time. This time it was one of the Belles of Mauchline, Bonnie Jean Armour.

As far as the lasses went Burns had a 'tinder heart' and although Jean eventually married him and bore him nine children further amorous adventures produced even more 'fruit o' monie a merry dint'. 'Our Rab should have had twa wives,' was Jean's comment when she found that Anna Park, Anna of the gowden locks, was expecting Rabbie's child at the same time as she was. The children were born nine days apart and Jean looked after both.

All professions employ their own technical vocabulary, their jargon which leaves outsiders bewildered and mine is no exception. However, his many encounters with the midwives of the day afforded Robert Burns an unusual familiarity with obstetric and gynaecological terminology.

First you, John Brown, there's witness borne,
And affidavit made and sworn
That ye ae bred a hurly-burly
'Bout Jeany Mitchell's tirlie-whirlie,
And blooster'd at her regulator,
Till a' her wheels gang clitter-clatter.

Next, Sandy Dow, you're here indicted
To have, as publickly you're wyted,

Been clandestinely upward whirlin
The petticoats o Maggie Borelan,
And giein her canister a rattle,
That months to come it winna settle.

As I went round the wards in Ninewells Hospital, Dundee shortly before my departure I saw one girl suffering from the effects of severe canister rattling and another whose regulator was irrevocably blooster'd!

Robert Burns' love for women spawned more than children. Coupled with sensitivity it gave birth to a whole generation of love songs whose beauty and pathos still bring a tear to the e'e, a tingle to the spine and a lump to the throat more than 200 years later.

Yestreen, when to the trembling string
The dance gaed thro' the lighted ha',
To thee my fancy took its wing,
I sat, but neither heard nor saw:
Tho this was fair, and that was braw,
And yon the toast of a' the town,
I sigh'd, and said amang them a'-
'Ye are na Mary Morison!'

Burns described this as one of his juvenile works and we are not sure which lass he had in mind. We do know, however, that while he was building his farm house at Ellisland in preparation for his wife joining him he penned this one for her:-

Of a' the airts the wind can blaw
I dearly like the west,
For there the bonie lassie lives,
The lassie I lo'e best.
There wild woods grow, and rivers row
And mony a hill between,
But day and night my fancy's flight
Is ever wi' my Jean.
I see her in the dewy flowers –
I see her sweet and fair.
I hear her in the tunefu birds –
I hear her charm the air.
There's not a bonie flower that springs
By fountain, shaw, or green,
There's not a bonie bird that sings,
But minds me o my Jean.

This softness, this gentleness, this affection for womankind lasted until the bitter end and as he lay dying in his house in the Mill Vennel in Dumfries that summer of 1796, he penned these words for Jessie Lewars the lassie across the road who was helping Jean to nurse him.

O, wert thou in the cauld blast
on yonder lea, on yonder lea,
My plaidie to the angry airt
I'd shelter thee, I'd shelter thee.

I find it very moving that on the 25th of July 1796 as the body of Robert Burns was being laid to rest in the nearby St. Michael's churchyard his widow, Jean was giving birth to Maxwell. And so in a very tangible way his memory lived on.

Rabbie was no transcendental poet. He did not have to look beyond his surroundings for inspiration. He wrote about what he saw, what he experienced, people he knew, people he met, people at work, at play, at home, in the country, in love, in the grip of passion. He has painted a picture of the times so clearly it is almost as if we have seen it for ourselves.

He has left us a treasury of Scottish literature, of Scottish songs but the sentiments and the appeal are universal.

After his death, monuments and statues were erected all over the world to commemorate Robert Burns but the greatest monument is the fact that we are here this evening...

Ladies and Gentlemen, will you please charge your glasses and rise with me and toast THE IMMORTAL MEMORY OF ROBERT BURNS.

It was also time to toast the new Millennium.

Who would wish for many years?
(Letter to Mrs Dunlop)

12
The Millennium Burns

Burns wrote like an angel and lived like a man.
(Ogden Nash)

Let the speeches roll...

Major-Adjutant David W. Purdie of the 2nd Battalion of the Crochallan Fencibles was not in the least over-awed when he rose to address the exalted company assembled in the National Museum of Scotland at the invitation of the Burns Federation for the first Burns Night of the Millenium. This 'boy from Prestwick' who was taught Burns, Boswell and Johnson by his father, studied medicine when his heart was really in the classics, but that heart is seen in the Immortal Memory which follows. Dr. Purdie, as he is otherwise known, had delivered the same toast at the last West Sound Burns Supper of the old century, so he saw no reason why he should not carry on where he left off.

Mr. Chairman, First Minister, Ladies & Gentlemen

I thought that, tonight, I would tell you a story. And should the telling of a story seem to you surprising and, indeed, rather unfit for the great Toast of the Immortal Memory, let me remind you that the telling of tales has a long and ancient tradition in the Kingdom of Scotland. From the modern after-dinner speech back through the time of the Makars in the Middle Ages, right back to the time of the seannachies round the hearth fires of our ancestors at home – and round their campfires on active service in the field – the Scots have always called for the great stories from their speakers and bards. Such is the story I would tell you tonight – indeed the only story I may tell you tonight.

It is the story of how on earth it came about that an infant born in a two-roomed cottage which sat – and still sits – by a roadside in rural western Ayrshire became the man now universally accepted by modern critical scholarship as one of the greatest lyric poets ever produced in all of Europe. A man whose work sits in the lyric tradition going back through Catullus and Horace (whom he so resembled) to Alcaeus, Pindar and the poetess Sappho in Ancient Greece. A man whose poetry earned the warm praise of the great poets of the Romantic Movement who came immediately after him: Wordsworth, John Keats, Lord Byron, Walter Scott; A man whose ability to interweave words and music into song earned him the praise of the great German composers Joseph Haydn, Felix Mendelssohn and Ludwig Van Beethoven who were later to orchestrate so many of his songs for the piano. A man whose political positions, whose radical proposals for reform, whose championship of the dignity and the primacy of the Common Man, was to earn him the approval of statesmen of the stamp of Gladstone, Wilberforce and Abraham Lincoln.

The story opens on Braes of Bervie between Laurencekirk and Stonehaven in that part of north eastern Scotland – the Howe of the Mearns – later to be made famous by Lewis Grassic Gibbon in Cloud Howe and Sunset Song. It opens with a scene familiar among farming families to this very day – the departure from the family farm –in this case Clochnahill in the parish of Dunottor – of one of the sons. The year is probably 1748 and Scotland is in turmoil in the aftermath of our last great civil war, the Jacobite rising of the '45 in which, some 18 months previously, the Jacobite cause of the House of Stuart had perished for ever on the field of Culloden.

Our story opens with the 26 year old William Burns – one of the great unsung heroes of this story – leaving Clochnahill in the company of his brother Robert and going south seeking work in the trade of landscape gardener. William Burns epitomised those very virtues which the Scots have always admired in men and women of whatever race or nation. He was hardy of body, he was independent of mind, he revered education in its broad sense and he feared neither man or beast, save only his Maker. And south to Edinburgh he went and found work in the laying out of the great park just south of the Old Town, then known as Hope Park and which we know today as The Meadows. And so if we may imagine Williams Burns pausing in his labours and looking up at the great castle of Edinburgh upon its rock, he may well have already known that his wanderings in Scotland were not finished. He may possbily have already known that he would one day settle in the West. What he could never know – or even remotely imagine – was that the cottage that he was to build with his own hands in far off Alloway would one day take its place alongside that very castle of Edinburgh as one of the most famous structures which grace the soil of Scotland, visited each year by tens of thousands from all over the world. For move to Ayrshire Williams Burns did. He worked briefly for the great family of the Fairlies at Dundonald and then he feued land from Provost Ferguson of Ayr by the banks of the River Doon – and there, his wanderings past, he came to rest.

In November 1757, the Rev. James McKnight DD arose in his pulpit in the old Kirk of Maybole and, unknown to himself or his congregation, spoke the opening lines of a drama the direct result of which is our happy conjunction, this great occasion tonight in Edinburgh. For the Rev. James, a great scholar by the way, and later to be Moderator of the General Assembly, intimated in the old style of the Kirk of Scotland which many of us remember so well from childhood that there was; a purpose of marriage between Agnes Brown, spinster, residing at Maybole in the parish of Maybole – and William Burns, bachelor, residing at Alloway in the parish of Ayr – of which proclamation was thereby made. The marriage was to be happy, it was to last for 27 years until they were parted by death and ,on a wild winter's night in January 1759, Agnes Burns, nee Brown, was safely delivered of a live male infant, the first fruit of that union. The child was vigorous and strong and, in the old Scots tradition, he was named for his paternal grandfather – hence Robert. He was to be the poet Burns. He was to die, 37 years, later of the cardiac complications of untreated chronic rheumatic fever in Dumfries, leaving behind him a desolate widow, six children under the age of 10, and a body of poetry and song which will ever remain one of the brightest jewels in the crown of our literature.

So what manner of man was this Burns, this Ayrshire farmer and, latterly, this Dumfries-shire officer of the Excise, that here tonight in the National Museum in Edinburgh and at literally thousands of locations throughout the known world this week, men and women like us are sitting down together, people with surnames the same as ours, to listen to the songs, hear the poetry and rise in salute to what has indeed proved, so far, to be an Immortal Memory. What manner of man?

Physically, the poet was 5'9" tall, stockily built, and possessed of great physical strength in his prime. His handsome features are familiar to us from the great portrait by his friend Alexander Nasmyth, which hangs to this day in our National Portrait Gallery – having been gifted by the poet's soldier son Colonel William Burns with the simple and splendid stipulation – that it become the property of the People of Scotland forever. His complexion was dark, his forehead broad and his hair black, but the most arresting feature of his physical presence, clear from the Nasmyth portrait and attested repeatedly by those who knew him in the flesh, was – the eyes. For example, when John Gibson Lockhart was writing the first scholarly biography of Burns in 1828, he wrote for information to his father-in-law. Now Lockhart was married to Sophia Scott, daughter of the author of *Waverley* and in his letter of reply to his son-in-law, Walter Scott cast his mind back 40 years to his one and only meeting with Burns in Prof Adam Fergusson's drawing room at Sciennes Hill House – now Braid Place – in Edinburgh.

Sir Walter wrote 'I would have taken him, had I not known who he was, for a very sagacious Scottish farmer of the old school. Only the eye betrayed the poetic character and temperament – and it glowed, I say literally glowed when he spoke of something with feeling or interest. I have not seen such an eye in a human head.' Those of you familiar with the biography of Walter Scott will recall that he was personally acquainted with two Kings and with all the leaders of the literary, academic and intellectual spheres of his day – yet never in all that vast acquaintance had he seen anything like the black glowing eyes of the poet.

Similarly, Josiah Walker, later to be Professor of Classics at Glasgow University and who knew Burns well, wrote that it was in his great black eyes that lay the truest index of his genius. Remarkable eyes, he said – full of mind. And, indeed, the eye is but the mirror of the mind and there is little doubt that the mind of the poet was one of remarkable depth. John Ramsay of Ochtertyre, gentleman farmer, literary critic and author of Scotland and Scotsmen of the 18th Century' wrote, 'I have been in the company of many men of Genius – and some of them poets, but I never met with such flashes of intellectual brightness as came from him – the very impulse of the moment, the very spark of celestial fire.'

As to his depth of mind, consider this. Dugald Stewart liked to discuss moral and ethical topics with Burns on the walks they took together to the Braid Hills outside Edinburgh. A simple statement. But if you consider that Dugald Stewart did not suffer fools at all, let alone gladly, and if you further consider that Stewart was the Professor of Moral Philosophy at the University of Edinburgh, a man whose speculations in epistemology and metaphysics moved in the very stratosphere of human thought, a man who was our leading philosopher following the death of the great David Hume ten years earlier – when you consider that this man enjoyed moral and ethical debate with Burns then you have a clear marker for the poet's sheer capacity for thought and argument.

But what of his literary development? When William Burns died of tuberculosis in the spring of 1784, Robert and his brother Gilbert took their widowed mother and their sisters to the farm of Mossgiel which sits on the high road between the village of Mauchline and the town of Kilmarnock in Ayrshire – and here the story really gets going, for it was here at Mossgiel that, in some way, all the influences of his young life – he was then 25 – came together and provided the genesis of the great poetry. These influences were; his own native intelligence; his eye for the human and agricultural landscape around him; the broad education in classical and literary history which his father, despite straitened circumstances, had provided for him; his store of folk song and tradition and mythology acquired from the singing of his mother and her servant Betty Davidson at Mount Oliphant and Lochlie; his resonance with the ceaseless ebb and surge of the seasons upon his farm; and, finally, his profound affection for the geography and the history of his native land. Ability to marry the two central ingredients of breadth of vision and depth of language is the genesis of all great poetry and it was Burns' absolute command of the great resonant Doric tongue of our forefathers with its tremendous graphic imagery and verbal firepower which allowed all of the above influences to come together in that one remarkable mind – and the poetry began to come.

This was also the time of the development of his radical politics which were to cause him such difficulties later in his life as we shall see. They stemmed as always from his championship of the social worth of the common man and the freedoms which must be accorded by society and the State in order to preserve that worth and dignity. Thus we find him writing in the great *Epistle to Davy*, his friend David Sillar, that neither title, nor rank nor worldly wealth could produce true happiness which could only be generated from within the heart and mind, just as Plato, quoting Socrates, had said two millenia before in Ancient Athens. As Burns has it;

the heart's aye the part, aye, that maks us richt – or wrang.

Nothing seemed to be too small to escape his notice. As is well known, one morning, ploughing for his winter barley in the parks of Mossgiel, he drove the ploughshare – the coulter – through the nest of a fieldmouse. His gaudsman, John Blane, driving the horses went after the mouse with a pattle – the tool for resharpening the ploughshare and a fearful weapon. Sixty years later, an old man in Kilmarnock, Blane was to recall that morning for Robert Chambers, Burns' biographer. The poet had checked him, made him stop. 'Leave it, John', he said 'let it live'. For the rest of the morning the poet had been silent and withdrawn and Blane, who guessed what was going on, knew not to interupt – for composition was afoot.

That day Burns went back at noon, as he habitually did, to the farmhouse of Mossgiel with his men for the midday meal, and then climbed up to the tiny room below the eaves which he shared with his brother Gilbert and in which was a plain deal table with a drawer. From the drawer he would take out a sheet of paper and his goose quill pen – and the verses would come. We know this from his younger sister Isabella who later was to recount that when the poet went back out into the afternoon, back to the fields, she would steal up to the little room beneath the eaves, open the drawer, take out the paper and read, for the first time the verses, new that very morning.

Wee sleekit cow'rin tim'rous beastie...

So runs the famous opening. He then flicks a switch and suddenly, from the glorious Doric of the first verse we are immediately into standard, pure, Augustan English. Burns wrote easily in both tongues and, at his best, we can barely see the join.

I'm truly sorry man's dominion
Has broken nature's social union
And justifies that ill opinion

Which makes thee startle
At me, thy poor earth born companion –
And fellow mortal.

It is absolutely remarkable to see the concept of the ecosystem – nature's social union – set out in verse 200 hundred years before it became a natural science. And then, of course, comes what philosophers term induction, the inductive leap from the concrete to the abstract, from the specific to the general which carries the poet's concept of the relevance of his observations to the wider world;

But moosie, thou art no' thy lane
In proving foresight may be vain
The best laid schemes of mice and men
Gang aft a'gley
And leave us nocht but grief and pain
For promised joy

And even smaller yet, in the kirk of Mauchline one Sunday, he sat joyously watching the young lady in the pew in front of him, There she sat in all her Sunday finery, including large new Lunardi bonnet, all unaware, as she attentively listenied to the sermon, that a splendid *pediculus capitis vulgaris* – or common headlouse, was marching majestically across the rim of her finery.

O Jennie, dinna loss your heid,
And set your beauty a' aspread
Ye little ken what cursed speed
The blastie's makin...

This wonderful description is followed, again, by an inductive leap to the general;

Oh, wad some pow'r the Giftie gie us
To see ourselves as others see us
It would from many a blunder free us
And foolish notion...

The foolish notions were almost certainly those of the Orthodox Calvinist wing of the Kirk which held sway under the Rev. Auld in Mauchline. The central notion being that by confessing adherence to the theological tenets of the Calvinistic Faith one could enrol onself among the Elect of God, secure a guaranteed place in Paradise and aquit oneself of irregularities in one's dealing with one's fellow men.

'Nonsense', said Burns in Ayrshire.

'Nonsense', said the great David Hume in Edinburgh. A man's

principles and behaviour should anticipate judgement during life and by his fellow men , not in some metaphysical hereafter at a tribunal convened by a Deity.

He thus turned his firepower onto his natural and most immediate target, the canting hypocrisy of certain human elements of the Kirk. Burns took careful aim and opened fire on the Rev Alexander Moodie, Minister of Riccarton at Kilmarnock, one of the most feared hellfire preachers of the 18th Century. In the great satire, the *Holy Tulzie* – a Tulzie is a fullscale scrap – Burns invisages Moodie's flock as real sheep with Moodie, their Shepherd directing from which stank – or pool of water – they must drink, thirsting as they do, after righteousness...

What flock wi' Moodie's flock could rank
Sa hale and hearty every shank
Nae poisoned, sour Ariminian stank
He let them taste
But Calvin's well – aye clear – they drank
Oh – sic a Feast!

Note the superb and crushing irony of the very word 'feast'. He then shifted aim to a bigger target, and went for Mr William Fisher. His friend and landlord, Gavin Hamilton, a Solicitor in Mauchline, had been persecuted by the Kirk for, among other crimes, setting a beggar to work in his garden upon the Sabbath. The persecution was led by the Minister, the Rev William 'Daddy' Auld and his chief henchman among the Kirk Session, William Fisher, the farmer of Montgarswood. With the poem, *Holy Willie's Prayer*, Burns opened fire on Fisher in what my own father, correctly, once described as the greatest example of poetical character assassination in the language. Into the bedroom at Montgarswood we go, where Burns' Muse overhears the Holy Will at his devotions;

Lord I am here, a chosen sample
to prove thy Grace is great
and ample...

Responsibility for this miserable carnal sinner's crimes and misdemeanours are resolutely placed at the Lord's door for, were it not His will, surely his Will would not! The hypocrisy rises to Olympian heights as this dawns on Willie;

...e'en so, thy haun' must e'en be borne –
until thou lift it !

Thus Burns' broadsides raked the worthies of the Session fore and aft. The Kirk, was, however not without its own spiritual artillery and Burns, being Burns, was not slow at furnishing ammunition for the reply. The Kirk Session minutes for 4th April 1786 are extant and I have seen them. They record:

> The Session, having been informed that Jean Armour – an unmarried woman – is said to be with child, appoint James Lambie and William Fisher to speak to the parents.

We will assume, ladies and gentlemen, after this effluxion of time, that James Lambie performed this delicate and sensitive task with diplomacy and skill. We may be utterly assured, however, that his partner did so with vengeful glee – for did you notice the name? It was William Fisher on the Armour doorstep, the very same Holy Willie, still red raw from the lash of the poet's pen. Jean Armour, daughter of James Armour, master mason, was in serious trouble. Her father, a pillar of the Kirk, was apparently not aware of the liaison between his daughter and Burns, whom he regarded as a dangerous freethinking rake. Told of her daughter's condition, Armour fainted clean away. He was revived with a stiff cordial and got up demanding to know the name of the father. He was told – and down he went again.

Jean was packed off to to house of her Uncle's, John Purdie – no relation – in Paisley to hide her shame while the poet, after consideration of his position, decided it might be better to create a new life in the West Indies since old Armour had had destroyed the marriage certificate between the pair. He tells us that his trunk was already on the road to Greenock and to the brig, Nancy, which was to take him to Kingston, Jamaica – where he had secured a position of overseer on a plantation owned by the brother of his friend Dr James Douglas in Ayr. He was stopped from this disastrous course of action by the roar of applause which greeted the publication in July 1786 of *Poems chiefly in the Scottish dialect* – John Wilson, Kilmarnock, printer. He was advised, rightly, that he should capitalise on the resounding success of the book by seeking the publication of a second edition in Scotland's literary and capital city. In other words, his course lay not to the West – and the North Atlantic – but East, and Edinburgh.

This was a time towards the final culmination of the

Scottish Enlightenment, that remarkable flowering of our intelligentsia with whole new sciences coming to birth; geology by Hutton, organic chemistry by Black, political economy by Adam Smith and empirical philosophy by David Hume, some literally within the confines of the city of Edinburgh. It was a time when Benjamin Franklin, Ambassador to the Court of St James's, of the infant United States, could write home to his wife in Pennsylvania 'It is truly a remarkable thing that a man might stand, as I did but yesterday, at the cross of Edinburgh and, within the space of one hour, take the hand of a dozen men of genius.'

In Edinburgh he was lionised. He was the star of the social season of 1786-87. There were society breakfasts, literary lunches, evening receptions, dinners, balls. Alison Cockburn wrote to a friend that the whole town was agog with the ploughman bard who was the very image of his profession, wonderously handsome, strong and coorse! It did not turn his head however and, sharing a flat in the old town with his friend John Richmond, he set about producing an enlarged and improved second edition of the poems which were printed by a man who became his great friend. This was William Smellie, first editor of the *Encyclopaedia Britannica* and founder of the great convivial dining club the Crochallan Fencibles which met in Dawney Douglas' Tavern in the Anchor Close off the Canongate. His publisher, William Creech, brought out the second edition in the spring of the following year, 1787 and armed with the proceeds, the poet set off on the second phase of his literary life – for this was to be the era of the Songs.

Poetry was in fact largely behind him and, although he continued to write verse for the rest of his life, his principle function henceforward was to be song collecting and song writing. This he prosecuted throughout the three tours which he took in the spring summer and autumn of 1787; first to the Borders – and indeed over the Border briefly – with Robert Ainslie, his young lawyer friend from Edinburgh; to the West Highlands on his own and, lastly, on the great northern tour in a chaise and pair with another friend, Willie Nicol, Classics Master of the High School of Edinburgh – a brilliant classical scholar and as wild, irascible and hard drinking a companion as could be found . Travelling with Nicol, Burns wrote, was like travelling with a loaded Blunderbuss at half cock. Off they set across West Lothian, up through Stirlingshire, Perthshire and Inverness-shire, across to Aberdeen and down through the Mearns and Angus and thus back to Edinburgh, a round trip of over 500 miles.

Throughout these tours the poet took down, from the singing of the people, from fish wives and farmers wives and spey wives and from men of all conditions and backgrounds, the vernacular folk songs of the country. This was a tradition which was in danger of being lost for want of being transcribed, set to music and published. The rescue, for such it was, of the Scottish vernacular folk song, was largely due to the poet, something for which he has been given nothing like the credit which is his due. From then to the end of his life he saw published through his Edinburgh collaborators James Johnson and James Thomson, some 400 of our songs appearing as they did in the Johnson's *Scots Musical Museum* and in Thomson's *Select Scottish Aires*. All human life was, and is, in these songs; songs of farming, songs of fighting, songs of meeting, songs of loving, songs of parting. And just as the great Raeburn captured in his paintings the faces of that remarkable generation of Scotland in the late 18th century, so Burns captured their music and their songs and, in them, their aspirations and their history – in short, their very nature. Of all the songs, the most famous are the love songs.

My luve is like a red, red rose...

Ae fond kiss, and then we sever...

And these he brought back to Edinburgh, some in fragmentary form, some fully finished – to the parlour of the house in St James's Square in the new town in which he stayed over the winter of 1787-88. This was the home of his great friend William Cruickshank, where the daughter of the house, Jenny Cruickshank aged 12, would play a chosen air over and over and over again on the harpsichord as the poet sat beside her drafting and redrafting and crafting the words until they fitted the air like a hand in a silken glove. This description we have from Professor Josiah Walker, who visited the family in January 1788, and was not allowed by William Cruickshank into the room where the poet and young Jenny were working, because it would be a disturbance to them. And to Jenny, herself, went a book, an inscribed 2nd edition of his poems, and a dedication of one of the Songs. The poet always paid his dues. No man, or woman either, ever did him a favour and lived to regret the day. The song he dedicated to her was one of his finest:

A rosebud by my early walk
Adown a corn enclos-ed bawk
Say gently bent its thorny stalk
All on a dewy morning.
Ere twice the shades of dawn were fled
In all its crimson glory spread,
And drooping rich the dewy head
Its scents the early morning.

It sounds like a pastoral. A flower blooms in a Scottish meadow, but it is not a pastoral. It is an allegory. An allegory of youth, beauty, its advance to maturity and ultimate decay – always a favourite subject with poets. And in a later verse he foresees her future:

Thou sweet rosebud, young and gay
Shalt beauteous blaze upon the day
And bless the parents evening ray,
That watched thy early morning.

The published song carried only the simple epigraph – *To a very young Lady*. And the world wondered with a smile – who was the rosebud? He did not live to see it, but he was right. She did 'beauteous blaze upon the day'. The rosebud, indeed, became the rose. Jenny Cruickshank married James Henderson, solicitor, in the town of Jedburgh in the Borders and together they raised a large and successful family. And after her death 1845, her eldest son recounted that, in her last moments, his mother as she failed had recalled her own happy childhood in her father's house in Edinburgh – and, with great and quiet pride, the fact that it was she – who had been the rosebud.

The greatest of the historical Songs is, of course, the song which Burns put into the mouth of our hero King on that midsummer morning, long ago – on the Carse of Stirling – on the day that our forefathers fought for and won their freedom. We know that on his journeys throughout Scotland the poet had been first intrigued and then electrified to discover, wherever he went – from the Border Marches to Aberdeenshire – that the march tune Hey Tuttie Taitie was firmly believed by the people to have been the very march which was played – on the instruments of the time – as the Scots army advanced on to the field of Bannockburn. We know also that he spent many months drafting and redrafting and crafting words which would not only fit the air but would give an accurate account of the engagement and the sheer scale of the national achievement of our forefathers under King Robert .I'm certain that he went to Barbour. He went to John Barbour's great work and our earliest surviving long poem *The Bruce*, written by a man born in 1320 just six years after the battle and who had talked to men who had themselves been present and had taken part in the battle

And Burns, following Barbour, begins with the King firmly telling the troops that this was to the last battle – the final engagement of a war which had lasted twenty-eight terrible years. They were going to conclusions with our mighty neighbour and, come the day's end – they would either stand masters of that field or lie beneath it –on a bed of blood – forever. There was no alternative. Welcome, sings Burns, Welcome to your gory bed – or to victory. And Barbour describes how the men of the army's four divisions then knelt in their ranks and every man was shriven, that is, confessed and absolved of his sins – in the expectation of his imminent death. And Barbour describes how at that moment, far across the field, Edward Plantagenet, King of England, saw them kneel. And he turned to Sir Ingram de Umfraville a brave English knight and Crusader and said 'They kneel! These men ask for Mercy'. And De Umfraville, veteran solider that he was said, 'They do, Sire. They ask for Mercy – but not from you. These men are asking Mercy of a higher Power.'

And Barbour then describes how the King rode down the ranks calling out that if there was any man present who was not committed to the cause, any man whose heart had failed him, any man who had not stomach for what was about to happen, then that man might freely depart and leave the field and return to his home – for he, Robert, did not choose to die in that man's company. And, as Barbour says, The ranks stood fast.

Wha wad be a traitour knave
Wha could fill a coward's grave
Wha sae base – as be a *slave*
Let him turn – and flee.

And the climax comes, as so often with Burns, in the fourth verse when, with the tension at breaking point – at the very moment of the assault – the King, about to bring his vizor down – turns to the troops one last time – and through Burns eyes we can see him astride his nervous charger – as he levels the great broadsword at them, saying:

Wha for Scotland's King and Law,
Freedom's sword will *strongly* draw,
Free men stand – and *free* men fa'
(And he swings round towards the English line)
Let him – follow me.

And the advance was on. And, as was to be said centuries later, they fought like Scotsmen – and they won their freedom.

But the poet could not tour the country and collect songs for a living. He had to return to work and he took a farm. He took Ellisland in Nithsdale, 7 miles above the city of Dumfries. His tenancy of the farm lasted but 3 years – for it was stony ground. Indeed, the poet wrote to a friend that a verse was missing from the Book of Genesis and that verse was:

And the Lord riddled all creation –
And the riddlings he threw on Ellisland.

Ellisland, however, produced *Tam o Shanter*, that incomparable narrative poem of ghosts, bogles and witchcraft but little else. Indeed, Tam has galloped further than his original ride, as it were, along the Nith bank at Ellisland down the farm road to the road end and on into literary history. He has turned up in numerous languages around the world. I have in my possession a splendid book, *Robert Burns in Other Tongues* by William Jacks, MP for Stirlingshire at the turn of the century. And in this we find a remarkable translation of *Tam o Shanter* by Professor Erich Reute of the University of Heidelberg. *Tam o Shanter* in German. Now, in my view only two languages in Europe are ideal, nay supreme, vehicles for personal abuse and these are the Scots Doric and the German. For example, here is Kate in the Doric giving Tam hell for his social delinquencies:

Oh Tam had thou but be sae wise
As ta'en they ain wife Kate's advice etc

That was Kate. Now in Reute's translation is 'Kathe' 'O, Tam das war nicht wohlgethan etc' was

nahmst du guten rat nicht an
oft spracht dein weib du zeist zu locker,
ein schwatzer, tagdieb, kneipenhocker
und nah beim Gottshaus am Sonntag,
trankst du im bierhaus bis zum Montag!

If you read this out loud in your very best German accent with increasing volume and you will get a flavour of the venom. We are talking serious abuse here!

In 1791 the poet moved to Dumfries and here his last 5 years were to be spent as a gauger, in the Excise – forerunner of the Inland Revenue. His misfortunes began to crowd upon him at this time. His health began materially to fail. He was subject to repeated attacks of what we now suspect to have been endocarditis, inflammation of the lining of the heart, a condition which follows on from rheumatic fever, and which was eventually to kill him. In 1791 his great friend and patron, his Maecenas – the Earl of Glencairn – died and was the subject of the great '*Lament for James, Earl of Glencairn* with its powerful concluding stanza:

The bridegroom may forget the bride
Was made his wedded wife yestreen
The monarch may forget the crown
That on his head an hour has been –
The mother may forget the child
That smiles so sweetly at her knee –
But I'll remember you, Glencairn
And all that thou has done for me.

He was also in trouble for his political opinions which he never cared to hide. The poet was not a revolutionary, he was a radical and a reformer. What he wished to see were changes in the Constitution which seem second nature to us now, a secret ballot, a broad adult suffrage and fixed-term parliaments. When, in 1999, the people of Scotland elected and then summoned our restored Parliament to Edinburgh, it was by universal suffrage, and secret ballot, and for a fixed term. But these were dangerous views in the Britain of 1792 where the Government of Pitt's first administration – with Henry Dundas of Arniston as Home Secretary, was extremely edgy in the aftermath of the loss of our American Colonies and with the French Revolution now in full swing across the Channel. Burns was carpeted by his ultimate superior, Robert Graham of Fintry, fortunately a friend and admirer of the poet, and formally reminded that he was a civil servant, a government officer and that he was paid to act not think. He was told, in effect, 'Burns, watch your tongue and for God's sake watch your pen.

His contract could be terminated without compensation

and, having already sold the copyright of his poems to Creech, his Edinburgh publisher, his Excise salary was all that stood between him and his family and destitution. However, it is my view that he did not truly seek subversion of the State. He wanted the State to reform , not revolt, in order to avoid the horrors now clearly visible across the Channel. He wished to see reform based on the willing adherence of a free people to the three great pillars of our unwritten constitution which are to this day the Monarchy, the Parliament and the Law.

But by this time he had begun to die – and death came for him slowly. The diagnosis of endocarditis superimposed on chronic rheumatic fever is in the opinion of Sir James Crichton-Brown of the Royal Infirmary of Edinburgh the true diagnosis – and I think the evidence proves him right.

We would have treated him with pencillin today but it was to be 80 years before another boy would be born in Ayrshire, another Ayrshireman of genius called Alexander Fleming who would later make that most momentous of medical discoveries. Burns's physician, Maxwell, sent him to sea bathing at Brow Well on the Solway near where the river Nith having flowed past Ellisland and through Dumfries town eventually reaches the Solway – and its journey's end. But without effective treatment the poet literally died by inches until death mercifully released him on 21st July 1796.

Four days later his coffin was taken on a gun carriage before thousands of silent mourners from the Town House of Dumfries to his burial in St Michael's Kirkyard. There then followed the short midsummer night. We know that the day after the funeral was a glorious cloudless day of high Summer and, as Professor Hans Hecht reflected in his great literary biography of Burns – 'the Sun which rose so early on the morrow over the sleeping town ,casting his beams on the fresh earth of that new grave was surely the sun of Immortality'.

Yes, he lives on. He lives on for many reasons. Principal among them is that wherever our people are, be they at home in Scotland or wherever they have gone throughout the known world, as settlers, farmers, soldiers, administrators, Governors of the old empire and the later Commonwealth, they simply took the poet with them. Throughout the great emigrations of the 18th, 19th and the present century, the poet's works would be packed – together with the household effects of the people, into the family kist, and taken to the seaports and down into the holds of the awful emigrant ships and away. Across the North Atlantic they went, to the St Lawrence in Canada or to the Carolinas and Georgia in the US, or on the longer journey to the Cape of Storms and the veldt of Southern Africa and on the even longer journey, taken by tens of thousands of our people, across the wild southern ocean to the very shores of Australia and New Zealand.

This we know from their diaries and the traditions of their descendants. And the people took Burns with them, not just because he spoke to them in the language and in the accents of home. That would not have been sufficient. They took him with them because Burns has always something to say; to the struggling farmer, to the uncertain lover, to the young soldier facing his first action. And the message, delivered in a score of different ways, is simple in essence and always the same; it is, 'Courage, brother, do not falter'. And in the poems and the songs he also called them, and us, to our duties as the inheritors of a fine tradition. The tradition of plain dealing and the plain speaking of our minds. Our passion for the education of the children, our innate contempt for displays of wealth, for bombast and empty show.And above all he prompts us never to neglect defence of the five great freedoms which our fiery ancestors bought for us sometimes at a terrible price: our freedom to think, to assemble, to vote, to worship, and to act, limited only by our own Common and Statute Law.

But most of all the poet lives on because of his timeless personal and moral philosophy. I could dilate upon it in abstract terms but in a sense it is easier and more acceptable to do so by referring to the poetry itself. The philosophy is in the poetry and it is perhaps clearest in one of the greatest of all the songs, the one which we know as *A Man's A Man for a' that*.

It's a poor title, simply taken from within the song itself. A better would be *Anthem for the Common Man* for, above all, this poem epitomises the essential creed of this brave singer, the essential brotherhood of all the creatures we know as Man, with the preservation of the rights of universal mankind, being the central goal of men who know their duty. That a democratic sense was apparent among the Scots was something of which the poet was clearly proud, as was the fact that our ancestors would always seek to protect the freedom of the nation by diplomacy and force of argument if possible but, if necessary, at the very point of the sword. It is a matter of quiet pride that if you take away all our achievements in the physical and natural sciences, in engineering and in medicine and had we only given the poetry and songs of Burns to the world, we could hold up our heads among the Nations. But remember, said Ralph Waldo Emerson, the great American writer, the Songs of Burns do not belong to Scotland and the Scots. They are the property – and the solace – of Mankind.

And in this year which has seen the new Millennium as well as the 50th anniversary of the great UN Declaration of Human Rights, it is remarkable that one of the greatest political statements in this field should have come not from one of the sages of antiquity, nor from one of the luminaries of the Renaissance, but from the pen of an Ayrshire Farmer...

> Then let us pray, that come it may
> As come it will, for a' that...
> That sense and worth ,o'er a' the Earth
> Shall bear the gree an' a' that
> For a' that an' a' that, it's comin' yet, for a' that...
> That man to man – the world o'er
> Shall brothers be – for a' that.

And, for an epitaph ?

Those of you like myself and Mr Chairman who are devotees of the great game which Scotland gave to the world , if you ever have occasion to play at Prestwick St Nicholas, I charge you to pause before a great plaque in the Clubhouse. Upon this you will see listed the names of 66 Members and sons of Members who failed to return to the Clubhouse after the two great wars. Below their names is their epitaph, one which I have never seen on any other monument or tombstone or cenotaph. The words are by Pericles, the great Athenian general and statesman, the man who had the Parthenon built to crown the Acropolis and under whom Athens came to the apogee of her imperial power in the 5th Century BC. In a speech at the public funeral of the Athenian dead at the conclusion of the first year of the great war with Sparta, which was to prove fatal to imperial Athens, Pericles spoke an epitaph of the dead in terms which, if transposed to the singular, made a and fitting epitaph for Burns, another young man who also took up arms and who also made war – not in

> his case against the historical foes of the nation but against that other dark Axis of powers which beset all mankind – ignorance, allied to hyprocrisy allied to intolerance and oppression – and the words are these;
>
> > And so he gave his life unto the Common Wealth
> > – and achieved thereby for his memory, praise
> > that will not die. And with that came the greatest
> > of the resting places – not the grave in which his
> > bones are laid – but rather a home, a home in the
> > minds of men.
>
> And Pericles concludes with the tremendous line
>
> > ανδρον γαρ επιφανον πασα γε ταφος
> > For great men have the whole earth as their
> > Immortal Memory.
>
> And with that, Mr Chairman, I put to you the incontestable proposition that the Memory of the Poet is worthy of a Toast. Mr. Chairman, First Minister, Ladies & Gentlemen, pray charge your glasses and rise for the Toast – The Immortal Memory of Robert Burns.

After such a titanic oration one wants to pause. One needs to. Only silence can follow such supreme and comprehensive statement. It has been left uncut because it harks back to the great Rosebery tradition of generous public speaking in that when the audience has enjoyed its banquet for the body, it is offered a feast for the mind and when it works at this level it is solace for the soul. One has to hear it on the night to savour it fully but even on the page such speeches serve as a monumental memory and, in this instance, one well worthy of Burns in the new millennium.

And if Dr Purdie is the Rosebery for our day then that irrespressible lawyer from Glasgow, Mr Len Murray, is the Sheriff Smith. Mr Murray is also a considerable orator but diffidently hides his learning under a deliberate cloak of frivolity. What he can't hide, however, is his knowledge and understanding of Burns. He is in constant demand as a proposer of the Immortal Memory, and one can understand why. After his usual jocular preliminaries, which are always effective, Mr Murray began in earnest with an anecdote.

> Ranjit Singh was a student with me at Glasgow University. One Burns day he asked me, 'Why do the Scots make such a fuss of Robert Burns?' I said, 'Probably because he was a good poet.' But Rajit was not convinced by such an answer and had

another question for me. In his native Delhi there is a famous Burns Supper every year. And he asked me – 'What did Robert Burns have to do with India?' And I'm sorry to say that I couldn't tell him. But I started then to wonder why Robert Burns is so important to so many, both here and abroad. We have had other poets, and other heroes, yet we do not afford them the veneration that we afford to Robert Burns. Why? And perhaps more importantly, why should other nations celebrate the birth of Burns?

Every year since 1801, a chain of universal friendship and fellowship makes its way around the world at this time. And wherever friends meet and friends eat the name of Robert Burns is revered. When the Burns Supper is finishing in Dunedin they have already sat down in Perth in Western Australia. And when they are rising from the tables in Perth they are already seated in Singapore. And the chain of friendship follows the setting sun and makes its way westwards to India, to the middle east, to Africa and to Europe, to this country, and then over the Atlantic and across that great continent of America to its Western seaboard and beyond. And so on right around the world and right around the clock.

And on 25 January of each year and for many days before and after, there is not an hour of the day or night when a Burns Supper is not taking place somewhere on this earth. And there is no other institution of man of which that can be said. The English have Shakespeare; the Americans have Longfellow; the Italians have Dante and the Germans have Goethe. Every one of them an internationally known and respected figure. But to none of them is paid the type of homage that is paid to Burns, even in their own country let alone abroad... There is no international acclaim of any one of them yet Robert Burns is universally revered.

His works have been translated into at least 56 languages and published in more than two thousand editions. There are more statues of Robert Burns throughout the world than of any other figure in literature.

No other writer of any nationality has ever been afforded such universal acceptance. And why should this be? It cannot be just for the quality of his poetry and writings. Scotland has produced other world ranking poets and writers in Robert Fergusson, (my elder brother in misfortune Burns called him),

James Hogg the Ettrick Shepherd, Walter Scott and the incomparable Robert Louis Stevenson. Yet we do not venerate them as we do Burns.

And something else to make us wonder.

Robert Burns was a product of the great Scottish Enlightenment.

That Golden Age in the late eighteenth century when Scotland produced more men of letters, more men of science and more men of learning than did any other nation on God's earth. In just about every discipline known to man a Scot led the way. But why is it that in spite of all the great Scots of that time (and there were many) it is the *star o' Rabbie Burns that rose abun' them a'*?

Part of the answer must lie in what he did to preserve the language and the heritage of this country at a time when it was in mortal danger.

And let us look at that time in which he lived.

First of all, a wave of anglicisation had been sweeping this country. It had begun as a trickle with the Union of the Crowns in 1603; and it became a flood with the Union of the Parliaments in 1707. Let me not be political but it turned out not to be a Union at all. It was an absorption of the old Scots Parliament into the Parliament of England. The rules and customs and practices of the Parliament in Edinburgh were swept aside and within but a handful of years it had been forgotten. Throughout the 18th century the flood tide of anglicisation continued. And it was against that tide that Robert Burns wrote.

Secondly, these were the post-Culloden years In July 1745 seven men landed at Moidart. (One of them was a Murray, incidentally.) A month later they raised a standard at Glenfinnan, the standard of the Royal House of Stewart, ancient Kings of Scotland. A torch was thrown on the smouldering embers of the Jacobite movement. The flame that resulted would burn for only eight short months till it was crushed out by the Hanoverian Army at Culloden on the 16th of April the following year. That army was led by William Augustus, Duke of Cumberland, the 25-year old third son of His Britannic Majesty, the German, George II. The Scots people gave Cumberland a soubriquet and seldom could any soubriquet have been more appropriate – they called him the Butcher. The pillage and the carnage perpetrated in the King's name in the Highlands of Scotland (aye and in the Lowlands too) spoke adequate testimony to that.

Shortly after the slaughter of Culloden, the Heritable Jurisdictions Act and the Disarming Acts were passed. The bagpipe was declared an instrument of war and was proscribed; the carrying of arms was forbidden under penalty of death and the wearing of the tartan under pain of transportation. And the prohibitions would endure for 36 long and horrible years. Lord President Forbes (Scotland's most senior judge and a staunch Hanoverian) protested to London at the new legislation. The protests were to no avail. London ignored him. So what's new? Parliament, that institution so close to the Scottish people, debated what to do. Some suggested clearing the country and recolonising it with 'decent God-fearing people from the South.' Others suggested sterilising all Jacobite women. But Cumberland, he knew what to do, for he wrote home to his father: 'This generation must be stamped out.'

The policy of repression throughout Scotland was inexorable; accused were often tried in England lest Scottish judges or juries were too soft. The axeman at Tower Hill was busy and John Prebble, that adopted Scot and brilliant historian, tells us how the hangman's rope sang at Carlisle and at York. The English named a flower after the Duke of Cumberland – the Sweet William. The Scots people have always known it as the stinkin' wullie and that perhaps says it all. He was given a hero's welcome when eventually he went back to London. His father increased his Civil List allowance from £15,000 per annum to £40,000. £40,000 a year in 1746. Not bad, for a butcher. That other German who lived in London, George Frederick Handel, composed a piece of music in his honour: *See the Conquering Hero Comes.* Remember its origin the next time you hear it.

Meanwhile all things English were being embraced. Even the ladies on the streets of the old town of Edinburgh, members of a profession even older than mine, advertised their wares, however few, in the newly arrived English tongue. And schools teaching that language were springing up all over the country. And James Beattie, Professor of Moral Philosophy at Marischal College Aberdeen, would write: 'Poetry is not poetry unless it is written in English.' The tide of Anglophilia reached its high water mark in 1782 when the sycophantic James Craig, architect of Edinburgh's New Town, created a perpetual memory to that family who had presided over the greatest carnage known in this country when he called the streets of his new town after them. And so we have George Street, and Hanover Street, and Frederick Street and the rest. This wave of anglicisation did irreparable harm not just to the language, but also to the culture and the heritage of Scotland.

But Robert Burns believed that these were things worth preserving so he set about to preserve them. 'The poetic genius of my country,' he wrote, 'bade me sing the loves, the joys, the rural scenes and rural pleasures of my natal soil in my native tongue.' And so he wrote his songs and his poetry in that tongue. And he wrote with a simple beauty that no other, whether before him or after, has ever achieved.

Till a' the seas gang dry my dear
And the rocks melt wi' the sun
And I will luve thee still my dear
While the sands o' life shall run.

Thirty, simple words. And everyone a monosyllable. No one else has ever written with such simplicity across the whole spectrum of man's experience and emotion, from zenith to nadir. And in his works mankind are born and beget their kind and die. But throughout, his work is always supreme. There is no greater tale in any language than *Tam o Shanter*, nor any satire better than *Holy Willie's Prayer*. There is nothing more mournful than *Ye Banks and Braes;* And what love song is there to excel *Ae Fond Kiss* written to Agnes McElhose when they parted in December 1791? And she would write in her diary on 6 December 1831 'This day I shall never forget. Parted with Burns in the year 1791 never more to meet in this world. Oh may we meet in heaven!' Nor is there anything more poignant than O *Wert Thou in the Cauld Blast*, one of the last poems he ever wrote and dedicated to young Jessie Lewars who nursed him and who cared for him until his untimely end.

But whatever his other achievements, Burns thought his most important and his most compelling duty was to preserve the traditional folk songs and folk music of Scotland. And in this his efforts were Herculean. For he collected them, then he patched and he cobbled and he mended them, till he had produced things of beauty and all of this he did without reward and he constantly refused any payment for his efforts. About 380 songs, each one a priceless gem. One cannot imagine Scots song without the contributions of Burns. And were it not for him, you and I would belong to a nation almost bereft of traditional music and song. As a people we have a culture, and a heritage of which we should be incredibly proud. They are equalled by few and surpassed by none. And we owe so much of that to Robert Burns. All of these things perhaps explain the immortality of Robert Burns to us, the Scots. But what of his universality?

Why is he so universally honoured and why is he so relevant to Delhi and to peoples all over the world in a way that no other writer can ever be?

Remember that the world in which he lived was a world of opulence and oppression. By accident of birth all were born either with privilege or in poverty. With privilege there was wealth and position – with poverty, there was despair and destitution. Inequality and injustice were everywhere. And it was that world of privilege and position, poverty and injustice that Burns constantly condemned. And so his pen became the voice of the people; and he expressed the thoughts and the hopes of the people. And thus the message of Robert Burns became a universal message for all people; for all nations; and for all times.

It is a message of friendship, a message of fellowship; but above all it is a message of love. And it is just as vibrant and just as relevant today as when it was written over two hundred years ago. No figure in world literature had ever written with such compassion for his fellow man.

> Whatever mitigates the woes or increases the happiness of others,this is my criterion of goodness; but whatever injures society at large or any individual in it, then this is my measure of iniquity.

And elsewhere he wrote:

> God knows I'm no saint, but if I could, and I believe that I do it as far as I can, I would wipe all tears from all eyes.

He died at the age of only 37. We can but marvel at what he achieved and wonder what he might have achieved had he lived his full biblical span.

The twenty-first of July 1796, the day of his death, must

surely rank as yet another of the darker days in the history of Scotland. And at his funeral on the 25th of July when the procession was wending its way through the crowded streets of Dumfries to St Michael's Kirkyard, an auld buddy was heard to call out 'An wha will be oor poet noo?' – a question still unanswered two hundred and five years later.

The Memory of Robert Burns will be immortal, not just for Scots people everywhere; but for people of every nation and every race and every colour whose lives have been touched by this unique genius. Tell your children, aye, and your children's children about him and tell them just how wonderful is the legacy which he left; they will never have one that is more beautiful. This is what his Immortal Memory means to me and these are the thoughts which I want to share with you; thoughts which I want you to take away with you tonight; And perhaps, occasionally, you will recall them, so that if ever you are asked, as I once was, why do we make a fuss about Robert Burns, you will be able to tell them. Tell them if you will that he did more than any other to preserve the language, the culture, the heritage, aye the very soul of Scotland. And he did it all when Scotland faced the greatest threat to its survival as a nation that it has ever known.

I am always honoured, Chairman, when I am asked to propose the Toast to the Immortal Memory at any Burns Supper. But being invited here to propose the Toast on this magnificent occasion and amongst the largest Burns Suppers in the world, is one of the greatest honours that can ever be conferred on any Scottish speaker. I am very conscious of that honour and I shall always be proud of it. For this is certainly the proudest toast for any Scot to propose and for any Scot to drink, recalling as it does surely the greatest Scot of all time.

Ladies and gentlemen, fill your glasses now if you will. Aye, fill them to the very brim, for this is a toast we shall drink with joy and with pride. Joy at his memory and pride in that wonderful legacy which he left for us.

Join me now if you will. Take your glasses in your hands, and raise them high with me as I give you the greatest, the proudest Scottish toast of them all, the Immortal Memory of Robert Burns.

That really says it all. But not quite. If, as the Bible says, those that are last shall be first then it seems appropriate that the last Memory in this collection should be from what many consider to be the first Burns club – Paisley. This club, situated as it now is in the refurbished cottage home of its founder, Robert Tannahill is unique in that it draws its speakers each year from its own members, limited each year to 40. From this quorum an astonishing standard of oration and Burns scholarship has been maintained by 133 Presidents since the initial Memory proposed by Mr McLaren in 1805. In 2001, it was the turn of President T. Lennie Herd, and he was called on by the Croupier, Ken Walton, to rise after what was described as a 'typically dreich January day' to propose the toast – To the Memory of Our Immortal Bard.

Mr Lennie Herd's main worry was that of many Burns speakers. How he could possibly make it different from all that had gone before? Then he had the idea of discussing how other Great Scots viewed the Greatest Scot of them all. This is an edited version of his speech based on this topic given in the Alexander Wilson Suite of the George A. Clark Town Hall, Paisley on 25 January 2001. After a modest preamble, the speaker got on to the theme of his address – Great Scots.

> In searching out Great Scots I found... [there was] only one attempt to rank them in order of greatness... This was issued by the publishers of *Who's Who in Scotland* after surveying some 1500 of Scotland's movers and shakers, the great and good, who make up the subscription list and entries... This audience will not be surprised that the runaway winner was our very own Robert Burns but most of the Top Twenty were pre-18th-century figures – people like Wallace, Bruce, Knoox, King James VI etc – I've looked at the remainder, a mere handful, and found five who achieved international recognition as great men and who were happy to document their love of Burns's works.
>
> The first of these is Andrew Carnegie, born in Dunfermline in 1835. Aged twelve, he emigrated to the USA with his parents. He went on to create a massive business empire in railways, rolling stock and steel production, but his greatness as a man is attributed mostly to the astonishing scale of his philanthropy. He amassed a fortune of $500,000,000 in '1900' money – the richest man in the world some said – before he undertook the massive task of giving it all away... and the very first penny he earned of that fortune was from

his primary schoolteacher in Dunfermline for reciting – not reading – all eleven stanzas of Burns's *Man was Made to Mourn* before the whole school... There are a number of themes in this poem which might have influenced the young man. [Such as]
Of youth:

O Man, while in they early years
How prodigal of time
Mis-spending all thy precious hours
Thy glorious, youthful prime...

Of brotherhood

And Man, whose heaven-erected face
The smiles of love adorn,
Man's inhumanity to man
Makes countless thousands mourn.

Of joblessness

See yonder poor, o'erlabour'd wight
Subject, mean and vile
Who begs a brother of the earth
To give him leave to toil...

Of independence

If I'm designed yon lordling's slave –
By Nature's law designed –
Why was an independent wish
E'er planted in my mind?

An early Carnegie biographer wrote:

It is impossible to exaggerate the influence of the national poet on this particular worshipper. Burns remained Carnegie's favourite – and not just as a poet but as a philosopher, guide and mentor – all his life...' Carnegie himself wrote, 'I gloated over the gems of Burns like a Prince of India over his jewels.' He also said – 'The day is not far distant when the man who dies leaing behind him millions of available wealth, which was free to administer during life, will pass away *unwept, unhonoured and unsung*. The man who dies rich, dies disgraced'... Carnegie susequently finanaced the building of almost 3,000 libraries throughout the world, specifying only three main conditions .

1) Use of the libraries must be free of charge

2) The local authority must undertake to maintain book stocks

3) A bust of Burns must be displayed in a prominent position

Interestingly, there was no stipulation that the name of Carnegie should be in the library name.

The next Great Scot in the poll was Sir Walter Scott, born in 1771 in Edinburgh, inventor of the historical novel... [and] said to be an equally significant figure to Burns in renewing the sense of Scottish nationhood. They met in Professor Ferguson's house in Edinburgh during 1787 and Scott descibed Burns as 'The boast of Scotland' and 'one of the most singular men by whose appearance our age has been distinguished'. He also said, 'I had sense and feeling enough to be much interested in his poetry and would have given the world to know him.' He wrote of Burns in 1809,

> In the society of men of taste... he was eloquent, impressive and instructing. But it was in female circles that his powers of expression displayed their utmost fascination... his conversation lost all its hardness, and often became so energetic and impressive, as to dissolve the whole company into tears. The traits of sensibility which, told of another, would sound like instances of gross affectation, were so native to the soul of this extraordinary man, and burst from him so involuntarily, that they not only obtained full credence as to the genuine feelings of his own heart, but melted into unthought of sympathy all who witnessed them.

In his Journal of 1826, he wrote, 'I have always reckoned Burns and Byron the most genuine poetic geniuses of my time and half a century before me. We have however many men of high poetical talent but of that ever-gushing and perpetual fountain of natural water... Long life to thy fame and peace to thy soul, Rob Burns! When I want to express a sentiment I feel strongly, I find a phrase in Shakespeare – or in thee.' Scott was clearly much impressed by Burns.

A further Great Scot was was James Clerk Maxwell, the physicist, who was born in Edinburgh in 1831... of whom Albert Enstein himself said – 'His work was the most profound and the most fruitful that physics has experienced since the time of Newton'. His biographer and life-long friend, Lewis Campbell, wrote of Maxwell. 'I well remember with what feeling he once repeated to me the lines of Burns,

> The Muse, nae poet ever fand her,

Till by himself he learned to wander,
Adown some trottin' burn's meander
An no think lang;
O sweet to stray, and pensive ponder
A heary-felt sang.'

Maxwell was voracious reader as a child and developed a love for poetry which emerged throughoout his academic life. His poetic works were published in an 1882 edition of his biography... and he went on to combine his poetic and academic interests to a point where presented complex mathematical problemes, and their solutions, in verse. But there was no doubt where his poetic inspiration lay.

Gin a body meet a body
Flyin' through the air.
Gin a body hit a body,
Will it fly? And where?
Ilka impact has its measure,
Ne'er a ane hae I,
Yet a' the lads they measure me
Or, at least, they try.

Lewis Campbell attributed the genius of Clerk Maxwell in equal part to scientiific industry, philosophic insight and poetic feeling – a feeling engendered by an early love of Burns.

Since Sir Alexander Fleming, the great pioneer of antibiotics and the discoverer of penicillin, was born in Darvel, Ayrshire and educated at Kilmarnock Academy there is no doubt that the works of Burns would feature on the curriculum [but] there is no record of Fleming's interest in Burns in his earlier life. This is not surprising since he had the reputation of being very dour and taciturn... One colleague said that trying to converse with Fleming was 'like playing tennis with a man who, when he receives a service, puts the ball in his pocket.' Yet this same man, in later life, said while lecturing on the theme of 'Success in Life',

> Burns, who never earned more than fifty pounds a year, has gained immortality while millionaired and rulers of nations are quite forgotten.
> It seems rather a pity that some politicians are not disciples of Robert Burns. Some of them have had worldly success... but Burns lives on and they will be forgotten.

Robert Burns has been the man who, perhaps more than any other, has helped to bind Scotsmen together.'

[Finally] to one of my own heroes, that great American Scot and pioneer conservationist , John Muir, who created the idea of the national park and has some two hundred parks, trails, forests and lakes named after him in the United States. He even his his own day in the US calendar. Yet he was in fact a Scotsman born in Dunbar in 1838 and emigrated to Wisconsin at the age of eleven. He became the world's first ecologist before the word was invented, uniquely combining, for the first time, knowledge of geology, botany and biology. Yet he was steeped in the poems and songs of Robert Burns and throughout his life he acknowledged the effect that Burns's words and thoughts had on him... Burns in particular gave Muir a profound respect for the democratic intellect and an utter disregard for matters of class, political power or social position... his conservation campaign was pitched against the flood-tide of rampant capitalism in the form of timber, mining, oil and railroad interests. He even persuaded the then President of the United States, Teddy Roosevelt to join him for a week's walking and camping in Yosemite in order to gain protected status for some some of the country's finest scenery. [Muir] walked thousands of miles through the US wilderness armed only with two books – *The New Testament* and *The Poems and Songs of Robert Burns*.

In February 1969, he wrote of his visit to the Californian Sierra:

> I was singing bits of Highland Mary, oft repeating the lines.
>
> There simmer first unfaulds her robes
> And there they longer tarry...

[And] from his journal on 25 January 1906:

> It is surely a fine thing to stop now and then in the throng of our everyday tasks to contemplate the works and ways of God's great men, sent down from time to time to guide and bless mankind. And it is glorious to know that one of the greatest men who appeared in the 18th-century was a Scotsman, Robert Burns. His lessons of divine love and sympathy to humanity which he preached in his poems and sent forth white-hot from his heart have gone ringing and singing around the globe, stirring the heart of every nation and race...
>
> What is the secret of it all? It is his inspiring genius

> derived from heaven, glowing with all-embracing sympathy. The man of science, the naturalist too often loses sight of the essential oneness of all living things... while the eye of the Poet, the Seer, never closes on the kinship of all God's creatures, and his heart ever beats in sympathy with great and small alike as 'earth-born companions and fellow-mortals' equally dependent on heaven's love. He extended pity and sympathy even to the deil...
>
> Hear me, Auld Hangie, for a wee
> An let poor damned bodies be;
> I'm sure sma' pleasure it cann gie,
> E'en to a deil,
> To skelp an scaud poor dogs like me
> An hear us sqeal...
> But fare-ye--weel, Auld Nickie-Ben!
> O wad ye tak a thought an men'!
> Ye aiblins might – I dinna ken
> Still hae a stake:
> I'm wae tae think upo' yon den,
> Ev'n for your sake.

Muir continued:

> On my lonely walks I often thought how fine it would be to have the company of Burns. Indeed he was always with me for I had him in my heart. On my first long walk from Indiana to the Gulf of Mexico I sang his songs all the way. The whole country and the people, beasts and birds seem to like them.
>
> Throughout these last hundred and ten years thousands of good men have been telling God's love; but the man who has done most to warm human hearts and bring to light the kinship of the world is Burns, Robert Burns the Scotsman.

It's impressive that such a high proportion of Scotland's greatest have been influenced by Burns... and while they might not have him as their sole influence, he was the one influence these five greatest of Great Scots had in common. But what's more impressive is the probability that, with this high degree of influence at the tip, the iceberg of not-quite-so-great Scots all the way down to ordinary Scots is likely to contain many whose lives have been influenced for the better by Burns's work. Why just Scots? With more than two thousand editions of his work, in more than fifty languages, produced since his death, this pattern will surely be reflected beyond Scotland.

And there is more than a past tense to this story... with world-wide communications opening up possibilities even Burns could never have imagined... the opportunities for Burns to be a very positive force for Mankind will continue to grow...

Gentlemen – please join me in the toast –

The Immortal Memory of Robert Burns.

A well-deserved standing ovation from the company was followed by a rousing chorus of *There Was A Lad* led with authority by Robbie Menzies.

At 9.28pm the President called for an interval.

And, as we prepare to retire from these pages, we must now let these words from Paisley, and all the fine words that have gone before down the years from a' the airts, sink in and find their place at the back of our minds, where everything of importance seems to lie. But we are left with a thought.

For all his avowed patriotism, Burns headed no nationalist revival, nor established a Scottish cause yet, on the whole, he is undoubtedly loved by the great majority of the Scottish people. Apart from William Wallace, and to a lesser extent, Robert Bruce, he is their only local hero. Even today, behind the industrialisation, and commercialisation of Burns as an icon, there is a genuinely warm feeling towards the man throughout the country. It is only another aspect of the Burns cult that is unique to Scotland. The nearest one might get to this national feeling for one man was America's attitude to Mark Twain or Will Rogers, France to Balzac or Victor Hugo, Russia to Pushkin or Tolstoy, India to Tagore, China to Lao Tsu. Japan to Basho. They get near but they don't quite make the deeply personal relationship Burns has with all Scots. He is still appropriate to the common dream, still apt to our own time, still alive in the aspirations of ordinary people who live on in the belief and hope that the best of their days are coming.

Burns knew he would make his mark, he knew he would be remembered. He was well aware of his own posterity, as most geniuses are. Even in his last frustrated years he still knew the stuff that went in to the life-mix – the love, hate, joy, misery and mirth we all know, one way or another – and he set these feelings and emotions in words and to songs that have lasted imperishably. We can read Burns today and feel something of what he felt then. We become a part of him as he remains from year to year a part of us.

Yes, Robert Burns, you are indeed immortal.

Thanks for the memory.

A last request permit me here
When yearly ye assemble a',
One round, I ask it with a tear
Which none but craftsmen ever saw!
To him, the Bard, that's far awa.
(The Farewell)

APPENDIX

To Prepare the Supper

J.F.T Thomson

(As given in the *Burns Chronicle* 1979)

As the years go on Burns Suppers are becoming more and more popular. For every Supper organised by an official Burns Club, there are scores run by all sorts of groups and associations. Whilst it is good to know that the memory of Burns is thus respected and whilst these occasions are run as fundraisers, it is clear that some guild lines are necessary for hardworking but innocent secretaries of Women's Guilds and bowling clubs and, in some instanced, for Burns Club committees. This subject concerned the Executive of the Burns Federation and, as a result of the pooling of long experience, the following outline was compiled and made available to organisations seeking advice on how to run a Burns Supper. As a means of comparison it might prove useful to readers of the *Chronicle.*

The duties of the Chairman are to keep the various items of the evening flowing and it must be stressed that, the function being a tribute to Robert Burns, it lies within his authority to ensure that the 'Immortal Memory' and its prelude are conducted in a manner suiting the dignity of the occasion. On the other hand, there is a measure of humour and light-heartedness about the toast 'To The Lassies' and its response. There is no need for the Chairman to act as the 'funny' story teller but rather to link the various toasts and readings in a manner appropriate to the occasion.

His first duty, after the 'top table' has been led into the assembly, is to welcome the company and to have grace said. If the Chairman or any official does this duty, a 'grace before meal' as composed by Burns would be suitable.

Soup, or an equivalent first course may be served and, immediately upon its conclusion, the Chairman awaits the piping in of the haggis. For this, a piper precedes the chef (or his nominee) bearing aloft the haggis. The company may stand and clap in time to the music. On reaching the appointed place at the top table, these two are joined by the reader who recites Burns' address *To A Haggis*. In order that the assembled company view the occasion, all should resume their seats. At the end of the recitation, the Chairman then offers the piper, the chef and the reader a 'guid dram' of whisky (lemonade or orange juice, if appropriate). Following the libation, the audience usually rises once more to applaud out the piper and the chef.

Dinner then resumes and the Chairman can relax until the appropriate time for his proposing the 'Loyal Toast'. At the conclusion of the meal, there is usually granted a short interval for the clearing of tables. Before, during or immediately after this break, the opportunity might be taken to sell copies of the *Burns Chronicle*, the organ of the Federation, or to make a collection for the Jean Armour Burns Houses – a monument dear to the heart of Burns where twelve wonderful old ladies are housed at Mauchline.

Following upon the meal, the Chairman introduces a singer to perform a couple of Burns songs, as a preliminary to the main toast of the evening, the 'Immortal Memory' of Robert Burns. This toast should normally be in a serious vein, paying tribute to the poet. There are circumstances in which a humorous toast could be made but such occasions are so rare and difficult that the 'sermon' type tribute is the rule. The ideal length of the principal toast is 25 minutes – a briefer time is considered sketchy and only the most gifted speakers can command the interest of a company beyond the half hour. It goes without saying that, when the 'Immortal Memory' is pledged, the entire company rises to drink the toast.

Following upon a mixture of songs and readings from the works of Burns, the subsidiary toasts and their replies are given. Such toasts are:

The Toast to the Lassies: usually a most happy and humorous toast in which the ladies are taken to task for their shortcomings, either from illustrations from Burns's works or from local knowledge. The reply can be equally funny with man and his (drinking) mates being slated by the poorer, patient and suffering wives.

As an alternative, a toast may be drunk to 'Bonnie Jean', Burns's spouse, with her fine qualities reflecting the superiority of womanhood over the socially-inclined male. On balance, this toast and its reply allow a measure of humour between the sexes but it is usual to conclude on a complimentary note to the opposite sex. Neither toast nor reply should exceed ten minutes and ideally should be timed at six minutes.

Another subsidiary toast might be that of the town in which the function is being held, especially if the Provost or Mayor is in attendance. Or, the toast may be to the association organising the Supper. This complimentary/critical speech should not exceed the ideal six minutes and the civic or other dignitary should reply suitable to the context of the toast and again within the ideal six minutes.

The speeches and replies, together with the songs and readings completed, it remains for the Chairman to tie up the proceedings. Some official might give a speech or expression of thanks to the speakers and artistes or, again, a comprehensive vote of thanks to the Chairman and Artistes but care should be taken to thank the hardworking secretary who organises the function but who is often missed out in the vote of thanks. The evening, however, would not be complete without the singing of *Auld Lang Syne* and it is expressly desired that the correct version be sung. A good move is to print the words on the back of the toast/menu card so that we get 'syne' and not the BBC 'Zyne' and the foreign words, 'for the sake of' are completely omitted.

Whether or not a dance follows the formal part of the evening is up to the make up of the particular society organising the function but it is the Chairman's duty to keep going the Scottish flavour of the evening and to ensure that there is a balance of dignity and humour to meet the needs of the occasion.

From scenes like these, auld Scotia's grandeur springs
That make her lov'd at home, rever'd abroad...
(The Cottar's Saturday Night)

Notes for the Speaker

John Cairney

The notes on the form of the Supper given above are the views of a good man, a good friend and a good Burnsian. His intentions as such, should be regarded, respected and retained, but the ritual of the Supper is by no means Holy Writ, no matter the estimable source. There were no rules at the beginning. Over the years the thing just grew. It had, as has been mentioned, Masonic roots, so the rites have their basis in Masonic ritual, but today, as with most things, anything goes. The only thing to remember is that ultimately the intention is to honour Burns and he must be at the heart of proceedings, whether in the telling of his story or in the recitation or singing of his works.

As an actor, my bias was toward the spoken word and this was no disadvantage when dealing with Burns. He provides such words that often one only has to say them and they work for themselves. The only trouble is that some speakers consider that their own words are superior, their own views more apposite, their own conclusions the only correct ones. Yet, as one finds in discovering Burns, there are layers within layers of meaning and things are not often what they seem. He had the artist's gift of irony and the subtleties are often only revealed at a second look. We all know that he was a great poet (in his best work) but he was also a fantastic prose stylist in most of what he wrote, and this is what makes him a gift to the performer. Any letter will show his mastery of words, and there is little need to improve on this by paraphrase or re-interpretation.

A good toast is like a good sermon – it is based on a text and it follows it through to a conclusion. It is better not to merely recite the life. That has been done so often that the path hacked out by pedestrian speakers over the years is now a gully that can attract only the unimaginative. The good speaker is nearly always an explorer, that is, he makes his own way. The trouble is that there are so many ways one can go. The best way is to take an aspect and develop it. What that aspect of Burns is is a matter of taste. Often it is a case of following your instinct. If you do you are halfway to being original. You then work it out in relation to your own strengths as a speaker and to your assessment of the kind of audience to whom you are going to speak.

As with anything in communication, it is horses for courses. The whole science of cybernetics is based on educated cunning. You give an audience what it wants but try to surprise them in how you give it. It's like giving a present. A lot of the pleasure for the receiver is in the wrapping, as long as you remember that the wrapping isn't the present. Only please don't make it a mere rag-bag of jokes. That is buying your Memory from the Supermarket. You can do much better if you shop around and anyway, you would be amazed what you can do for yourself if you only take time to think about it.

The length of the Memory is a piece of string. You only use the amount you need. It is often a matter of stamina. If you are tired standing, be assured your audience will be even more tired sitting. It's all a matter of good manners: never outstay your welcome. The first cough is a signal, the second is a warning. Shuffling feet and whispers are a threat and when all of these things happen at once – sit down. As the speaker of the Immortal Memory you are on your own, but if you lean on Burns he will see you through. After all, he is the whole reason and purpose of your all being there. Everything is there already in his work, you only have to look for it, but try not to overburden your text with quotes. The audience read their Burns at home, they want to know who your Burns is.

Whatever you say, always know before you start how you are going to end because that is what people remember, that is what they take home with them. As has been said, any fool can start a speech, it takes a wise man to finish one. You can take all the time you like at the start but you need to be firm and controlled by the end. You must know what you want to leave with the audience and everything must be geared to that. The best start is a slow one. This is when the audience is most on your side. Don't panic, take your time. You have everyone on your side at the start, it's up to you to lose them. There was one famous incident at a Burns Supper in Bridgeton when one particularly pompous speaker, remarked that he seemed to have lost his audience. 'You have,' came the immediate and concerted response.

For the most part, the audience is on your side, everyone there wants you to do well. They don't want to feel embarrassed or made uncomfortable by your uncertainty or undue nervousness. Nerves and stage fright go with the game. Whatever happens, you have to do it, so you might as well do it well. That way, you'll earn your standing ovation. Oddly enough, the best applause from any audience is silence. At least a kind of silence that is the result of a lot of breaths being held, and then released in an explosion of applause. I have known it only a few times in a long career but one can never forget it. It happened to me in Canada, on a cruise ship, in Perthshire, in Geneva and at a West Sound Burns Supper. You see, I can count the occasions on the fingers of one hand, yet I've been standing on my feet before an audience for fifty years. Yes, silence is golden.

The thing is to get your lines laid out so that they make the best effect. Or you can use someone's lines. Jack Whyte, a well-known Canadian Scot, told me honestly that he begans his Burns career by trying to remember what he had seen me do in Scotland when he was a schoolboy in Paisley. Anything can spark one off. It is to recognise the starting that is the tricky thing. It can be a complicated operation arriving at a speaking script. Words are not to be wasted. If they come in an avalanche the audience is drowned in sound, if they come too sparingly, the audience is denied continuity and, therefore, starved of any meaning. Bear in mind that a speech is meant to be spoken, not read. Otherwise you might as well distribute a pamphlet. Ideally, if you know what you want to say they will hear what you want them to hear.. The only thing an audience resents is being taken for granted and talked down to.

Finally, as a speaker, the only thing you have to keep in mind is that you are there for their sake, they are not there for yours. If you know your Burns and you know yourself, you will know you have nothing to fear. There are so many more important things in life than making the toast to the Immortal Memory but at the time it doesn't seem like that. But if it comes from the heart, it will go to the heart.

Good luck, and may Burns go with you.

In ploughman phrase, 'God send you speed'
The daily to grow wiser
And may you better reck the rede
Than ever did the advisor
(Advice to a Young Friend)

Select Bibliography

It's no' in books, it's no in lear,
To make us truly blest...

(Epistle to Davie)

Atkinson, Edward	(Editor) *Printed Orations and Other Burns Speeches from around the World.*
Bell, Maureen	*Tae the Lassies* – Sleepytown Books, Ellon, 2001. also *The Burns Calendar* 2001.
Bold, Alan	*A Burns Companion* (1991). Robert Burns – a pictorial profile (1992). *Rhymer Rab*, an *Anthology of the Prose and Poetry of Burns* (1993).
Burns Chronicle	Index of Articles 1892/1925 and 1926/45 by J.C.Ewing.
Burnsiana	Alloway Publishing 1988 (Compiler: James A.Mackay).
Butler, Montague C	*Robert Burns in Esperanto* 1926.
Cairney, John	*A Moment White*, Glasgow 1986. *The Man Who Played Robert Burns*, Edinburgh 1987. *On the Trail of Robert Burns*, Edinburgh 2000. (Editor) *The Luath Burns Companion*, Edinburgh 2001.
Campbell, John Ross	*Burns the Democrat*, Glasgow 1945.
Connor, Dr J. and Elma (Editors)	*Chronicle of the 200th Anniversary of the Death of Robert Burns*, London, Ontario, Canada 1997.
Crawford, Thomas	*Burns*, Edinburgh 1960. *Boswell, Burns and the French Revolution. The Saltire Society*, Edinburgh 1990
Corbett, William	*Robert Burns in English*, 1892.
Douglas, Hugh	*Burns Supper Companion*, Ayr 1981.
Dolan, Sir Patrick	*Songs of Liberty*, Glasgow 1943.
Esslemont, Peter	*Brithers A' – A Miscellany in 3 parts*, Aberdeen 1933.

Ewing, James C — *The First Burns Nicht*, Chambers Journal, 1947.

Ferguson, John deLancey — *Pride and Passion*, New York 1939. Also *The Letters of Robert Burns* (1953).

Hecht, Hans — Heidleberg 1919 (Translated Jane Lymburn 1936).

Hunter, Clark — *Let Burns Speak – An Edited Autobiography*, Paisley 1961.

Jacks, William — *Robert Burns in Other Tongues*, Glasgow 1896.

Kinsley, James — *Burns Poems and Songs*, Oxford University Press, 1971.

Lindsay, Maurice — *Robert Burns – The Man, the Work and the Legend*, 1954.
(Editor) *The Burns Encyclopaedia*, London 1959.

Low, Donald A. — *Critical Essays on Robert Burns*, London 1975.

Mackay, James A. — *The Burns Federation 1885-1985*, Kilmarnock 1985. *The Complete Works of Robert Burns*, Alloway 1986. *The Complete Letters of Robert Burns*, Alloway 1987. *Burns A-Z, The Complete Word Finder*, Dumfries1990.

Mattick, Irvin — (Editor) *There was A Lad* – Burns Anniversary Addreses compiled from the records of the Burns Club of St Louis, Missouri, USA 1955-64.

Montgomerie, William — (Editor) *New Judgements – Essays on Robert Burns* William Maclellan, Glasgow 1947.

McNaught, Duncan — *The Truth About Robert Burns*, Glasgow 1921.

Ross, John D. — (Editor) *The Memory of Burns* – Brief Addresses commemorating the genius of Scotland's Illustrious Bard, Edinburgh 1899.

Seymour, W.K. — *Robert Burns in English*, 1954.

Sprott, Gavin — *Robert Burns, Farmer*, National Museums of Scotland 1990.
Robert Burns: Pride and Passion, National Museum and National Library of Scotland, 1996.

Stevenson, R.L. — *Some Aspects of Robert Burns* in *Familiar Studies of Men and Books*, Tusitala Edition, London 1928.

Stirling, James Hutchison — (Editor) *Burns in Drama* (1878), Murison Collection.

Walker, Marshall — *His Power Survives*, Waikato University, New Zealand.

Wallace, William — *Poetical Works of Robert Burns*, Edinburgh 1958.

Wright, Clarissa Dickson — *The Haggis – A little history* , Belfast 1996.

Young, John — Robert Burns, *A Man for All Seasons*, Aberdeen 1996.

Some other books published by **LUATH** PRESS

The Luath Burns Companion

John Cairney

ISBN 1 84282 000 1 PBK £10.00

'Robert Burns was born in a thunderstorm and lived his brief life by flashes of lightning.'

So says John Cairney in his introduction. In those flashes his genius revealed itself.

This collection is not another 'complete works' but a personal selection from 'The Man Who Played Robert Burns'. This is very much John's book. His favourites are reproduced here and he talks about them with an obvious love of the man and his work. His depth of knowledge and understanding has been garnered over forty years of study, writing and performance. The collection includes sixty poems, songs and other works; and an essay that explores Burns's life and influences, his triumphs and tragedies. This informed introduction provides the reader with an insight into Burns's world.

Burns's work has drama, passion, pathos and humour. His careful workmanship is concealed by the spontaneity of his verse. He was always a forward thinking man and remains a writer for the future.

ON THE TRAIL OF

On the Trail of Robert Burns

John Cairney

ISBN 0 946487 51 0 PBK £7.99

Is there anything new to say about Robert Burns?

John Cairney says it's time to trash Burns the Brand and come on the trail of the real Robert Burns. He is the best of travelling companions on this convivial, entertaining journey to the heart of the Burns story.

Internationally known as 'the face of Robert Burns', John Cairney believes that the traditional Burns tourist trail urgently needs to find a new direction. In an acting career spanning forty years he has often lived and breathed Robert Burns on stage. *On the Trail of Robert Burns* shows just how well he can get under the skin of a character. This fascinating journey around Scotland is a rediscovery of Scotland's national bard as a flesh and blood genius.

On the Trail of Robert Burns outlines five tours, mainly in Scotland. Key sites include:

Alloway - Burns' birthplace. 'Tam O' Shanter' draws on the witch-stories about Alloway Kirk first heard by Burns in his childhood.
Mossgiel - between 1784 and 1786 in a phenomenal burst of creativity Burns wrote some of his most memorable poems including 'Holy Willie's Prayer' and 'To a Mouse.'
Kilmarnock - the famous Kilmarnock edition of *Poems Chiefly in the Scottish Dialect* published in 1786.
Edinburgh - fame and Clarinda (among others) embraced him.
Dumfries - Burns died at the age of 37. The trail ends at the Burns mausoleum in St Michael's churchyard.

'For me an aim I never fash
I rhyme for fun'.
ROBERT BURNS

'My love affair on stage with Burns started in London in 1959. It was consumated on stage at the Traverse Theatre in Edinburgh in 1965 and has continued happily ever since'.

JOHN CAIRNEY

'The trail is expertly, touchingly and amusingly followed'. THE HERALD

On the Trail of Robert Service

GW Lockhart

ISBN 0 946487 24 3 PBK £7.99

Robert Service is famed world-wide for his eye-witness verse-pictures of the Klondike goldrush. As a war poet, his work outsold Owen and Sassoon, and he went on to become the world's first million selling poet. In search of adventure and new experiences, he emigrated from Scotland to Canada in 1890 where he was caught up in the aftermath of the raging gold fever. His vivid dramatic verse bring to life the wild, larger than life characters of the gold rush Yukon, their bar-room brawls, their lust for gold, their trigger-happy gambles with life and love. 'The Shooting of Dan McGrew' is perhaps his most famous poem:

A bunch of the boys were whooping it up in the Malamute saloon;
The kid that handles the music box was hitting a ragtime tune;
Back of the bar in a solo game, sat Dangerous Dan McGrew,
And watching his luck was his light o'love, the lady that's known as Lou.

His storytelling powers have brought Robert Service enduring fame, particularly in North America and Scotland where he is something of a cult figure.

Starting in Scotland, *On the Trail of Robert Service* follows Service as he wanders through British Columbia, Oregon, California, Mexico, Cuba, Tahiti, Russia, Turkey and the Balkans, finally 'settling' in France.

This revised edition includes an expanded selection of illustrations of scenes from the Klondike as well as several photographs from the family of Robert Service on his travels around the world.

Wallace Lockhart, an expert on Scottish traditional folk music and dance, is the author of *Highland Balls & Village Halls* and *Fiddles & Folk*. His relish for a well-told tale in popular vernacular led him to fall in love with the verse of Robert Service and write his biography.

'A fitting tribute to a remarkable man - a bank clerk who wanted to become a cowboy. It is hard to imagine a bank clerk writing such lines as:
A bunch of boys were whooping it up...
The income from his writing actually exceeded his bank salary by a factor of five and he resigned to pursue a full time writing career.' Charles Munn, THE SCOTTISH BANKER

'Robert Service claimed he wrote for those who wouldn't be seen dead reading poetry. His was an almost unbelievably mobile life... Lockhart hangs on breathlessly, enthusiastically unearthing clues to the poet's life.' Ruth Thomas, SCOTTISH BOOK COLLECTOR

'This enthralling biography will delight Service lovers in both the Old World and the New.' Marilyn Wright, SCOTS INDEPENDENT

Kate o Shanter's Tale and other poems

Matthew Fitt

ISBN 1 84282 028 1 PB £6.99

After a wild night-oot up at Kirk Alloway, Tam o Shanter has got some explaining to do.

How does Kate take the news o his hell-raising ceilidh wi the witches?

Why is the family cuddie wrapped aroond a lamp post?

Does Tam get his tea or has he had his chips?

Read and recited at Burns Suppers all over the world, Kate o Shanter's Tale is a classic of modern Scots poetry. Complemented by more rants and whigmaleeries by Scots writer Matthew Fitt, this vibrant first collection engages as much as it entertains.

'Only the most stony-hearted of readers could fail to be exhilarated by the wit, speed and passion of Matthew Fitt's Scots poems.' DON PATERSON

'a literary cosmonaut' TOM HUBBARD

'Matthew Fitt's poetry jooks aboot with all the verve and vivacity of his lauded Chic Charnley, and at least as much cheek. He raises heroes, coups icons, gives voice to nag, radge, gossip and drunk then, soon as you have him sussed, he stops, considers Scotland, Prague, a miner, an old aunt, with insight and intensity that leaves you breathless. A rich, exciting collection crammed with pithy, vigorous Scots.' JANET PAISLEY

The Whisky Muse
Scotch Whisky in Poem and Song

Collected and introduced by ROBIN LAING
Illustrated by BOB DEWAR

ISBN 0 946487 95 2 PBK £12.99

Whisky – the water of life, perhaps Scotland's best known contribution to the world
Muse – goddess of creative endeavour

Poems to be read aloud

Collected and with an introduction by Tom Atkinson

ISBN 0 946487 00 6 PBK £5.00

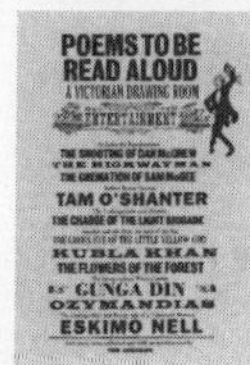

This personal collection of doggerel and verse ranging from the tear-jerking *Green Eye of the Yellow God* to the rarely printed, bawdy *Eskimo Nell* has a lively cult following. Much borrowed and rarely returned, this is a book for reading aloud in very good company, preferably after a dram or twa. You are guaranteed a warm welcome if you arrive at a gathering with this little volume in your pocket.

Scots Poems to be Read Aloud

Collectit an wi an innin by
Stuart McHardy

ISBN 0 946487 81 2 PBK £5.00

This personal collection of well-known and not-so-well-known Scots poems to read aloud includes great works of art and simple pieces of questionable 'literary merit'.

'Scots Poems to be Read Aloud is pure entertainment – at home, on a stag or a hen night, Hogmanay, Burns Night, in fact any party night.'
SUNDAY POST

Scottish Roots

From gravestone to website: The step-by-step guide to tracing your Scottish ancestors

Alwyn James

ISBN 1 84282 007 9 PB £9.99

New revised and updated edition

Now incorporates both on-line and off-line sources of information

Genealogy made interesting, easy and fun

Whether you are descended from sheep-stealers or landed gentry this is the way to find out

Robert Redford may to be descended from Mary Queen of Scots - are you?

Who? When? Where? Alwyn James's revised guide to genealogy provides the answers

- Clear step-by-step instructions and useful advice for tracing your family tree
- The ideal starting point even for those who knew little more than a grandparent
- No need to be on the spot - includes a chapter on distance research
- How to start, all the preparations required, starting at home

For anyone interested in researching their family history, *Scottish Roots* provides an excellent, comprehensible step-by-step guide to tracing your Scottish ancestry. Using the example two Scots trying to discover their roots, Alwyn James illustrates how easy it is to commence the research process and gradually compile a worthwhile family tree. He navigates the reader through the first steps of sourcing family details, making contact with distant relatives and preparing to collate any new information.

Few countries can compare with Scottish record keeping in the past 250 years and the author explains in detail, but in simple terms, how to go about searching for family records in New Register House, the Scottish Record Office, local libraries and folk museums. Details of costs associated with record searching are provided along with advice on maintaining realistic expectations during your research.

This new and updated edition of the guide includes information on how to access family data utilising electronic resources and the Internet – a must if conducting research from an overseas base – and is a very welcome addition to the family library.

'Indispensable' CALEDONIA MAGAZINE

THE QUEST FOR

The Quest for the Celtic Key

Karen Ralls-MacLeod and
Ian Robertson

ISBN 0 946487 73 1 HB £18.99

The Quest for Arthur

Stuart McHardy

ISBN 1 842820 12 5 HB £16.99

POLITICS & CURRENT ISSUES

Scotlands of the Mind

Angus Calder

ISBN 1 84282 008 7 PB £9.99

Trident on Trial: the case for people's disarmament

Angie Zelter

ISBN 1 84282 004 4 PB £9.99

Uncomfortably Numb: A Prison Requiem

Maureen Maguire

ISBN 1 84282 001 X PB £8.99

Scotland: Land & Power – Agenda for Land Reform

Andy Wightman

ISBN 0 946487 70 7 PB £5.00

Old Scotland New Scotland
Jeff Fallow
ISBN 0 946487 40 5 PB £6.99

Some Assembly Required: Scottish Parliament
David Shepherd
ISBN 0 946487 84 7 PB £7.99

Notes from the North
Emma Wood
ISBN 0 946487 46 4 PB £8.99

NATURAL WORLD

The Hydro Boys: pioneers of renewable energy
Emma Wood
ISBN 1 84282 016 8 HB £16.99

Wild Scotland
James McCarthy
ISBN 0 946487 37 5 PB £7.50

Wild Lives: Otters – On the Swirl of the Tide
Bridget MacCaskill
ISBN 0 946487 67 7 PB £9.99

Wild Lives: Foxes – The Blood is Wild
Bridget MacCaskill
ISBN 0 946487 71 5 PB £9.99

Scotland – Land & People: An Inhabited Solitude
James McCarthy
ISBN 0 946487 57 X PB £7.99

The Highland Geology Trail
John L Roberts
ISBN 0 946487 36 7 PB £4.99

'Nothing but Heather!'
Gerry Cambridge
ISBN 0 946487 49 9 PB £15.00

Red Sky at Night
John Barrington
ISBN 0 946487 60 X PB £8.99

Listen to the Trees
Don MacCaskill
ISBN 0 946487 65 0 PB £9.99

ISLANDS

The Islands that Roofed the World: Easdale, Belnahua, Luing & Seil:
Mary Withall
ISBN 0 946487 76 6 PB £4.99

Rum: Nature's Island
Magnus Magnusson
ISBN 0 946487 32 4 PB £7.95

LUATH GUIDES TO SCOTLAND

The North West Highlands: Roads to the Isles
Tom Atkinson
ISBN 0 946487 54 5 PB £4.95

Mull and Iona: Highways and Byways
Peter Macnab
ISBN 0 946487 58 8 PB £4.95

The Northern Highlands: The Empty Lands
Tom Atkinson
ISBN 0 946487 55 3 PB £4.95

The West Highlands: The Lonely Lands
Tom Atkinson
ISBN 0 946487 56 1 PB £4.95

South West Scotland
Tom Atkinson
ISBN 0 946487 04 9 PB £4.95

TRAVEL & LEISURE

Die Kleine Schottlandfibel [Scotland Guide in German]
Hans-Walter Arends
ISBN 0 946487 89 8 PB £8.99

Let's Explore Edinburgh Old Town
Anne Bruce English
ISBN 0 946487 98 7 PB £4.99

Edinburgh's Historic Mile
Duncan Priddle
ISBN 0 946487 97 9 PB £2.99

Pilgrims in the Rough: St Andrews beyond the 19th hole
Michael Tobert
ISBN 0 946487 74 X PB £7.99

FOOD & DRINK

The Whisky Muse: Scotch whisky in poem & song
various, ed. Robin Laing
ISBN 0 946487 95 2 PB £12.99

First Foods Fast: good simple baby meals
Lara Boyd
ISBN 1 84282 002 8 PB £4.99

Edinburgh and Leith Pub Guide
Stuart McHardy
ISBN 0 946487 80 4 PB £4.95

WALK WITH LUATH

Skye 360: walking the coastline of Skye
Andrew Dempster
ISBN 0 946487 85 5 PB £8.99

Walks in the Cairngorms
Ernest Cross
ISBN 0 946487 09 X PB £4.95

Short Walks in the Cairngorms
Ernest Cross
ISBN 0 946487 23 5 PB £4.95

The Joy of Hillwalking
Ralph Storer
ISBN 0 946487 28 6 PB £7.50

Scotland's Mountains before the Mountaineers
Ian R Mitchell
ISBN 0 946487 39 1 PB £9.99

Mountain Days and Bothy Nights
Dave Brown and Ian R Mitchell
ISBN 0 946487 15 4 PB £7.50

SPORT

Ski & Snowboard Scotland
Hilary Parke
ISBN 0 946487 35 9 PB £6.99

Over the Top with the Tartan Army
Andy McArthur
ISBN 0 946487 45 6 PB £7.99

BIOGRAPHY

The Last Lighthouse
Sharma Krauskopf
ISBN 0 946487 96 0 PB £7.99

Tobermory Teuchter
Peter Macnab
ISBN 0 946487 41 3 PB £7.99

Bare Feet and Tackety Boots
Archie Cameron
ISBN 0 946487 17 0 PB £7.95

Come Dungeons Dark
John Taylor Caldwell
ISBN 0 946487 19 7 PB £6.95

HISTORY

Civil Warrior
Robin Bell
ISBN 1 84282 013 3 HB £10.99

A Passion for Scotland
David R Ross
ISBN 1 84282 019 2 PB £5.99

Reportage Scotland
Louise Yeoman
ISBN 0 946487 61 8 PB £9.99

Blind Harry's Wallace
Hamilton of Gilbert-
ISBN 0 946487 33 2 PB £8.99

Blind Harry's Wallace
field [intro/ed Elspeth King]
ISBN 0 946487 43 X HB £15.00

SOCIAL HISTORY

Pumpherston: the story of a shale oil village
Sybil Cavanagh
ISBN 1 84282 011 7 HB £17.99

Pumpherston: the story of a shale oil village
Sybil Cavanagh
ISBN 1 84282 015 X PB £7.99

Shale Voices
Alistair Findlay
ISBN 0 946487 78 2 HB £17.99

Shale Voices
Alistair Findlay
ISBN 0 946487 63 4 PB £10.99

A Word for Scotland
Jack Campbell
ISBN 0 946487 48 0 PB £12.99

ON THE TRAIL OF

On the Trail of William Wallace
David R Ross
ISBN 0 946487 47 2 PB £7.99

On the Trail of Robert the Bruce
David R Ross
ISBN 0 946487 52 9 PB £7.99

On the Trail of Mary Queen of Scots
J Keith Cheetham
ISBN 0 946487 50 2 PB £7.99

On the Trail of Bonnie Prince Charlie
David R Ross
ISBN 0 946487 68 5 PB £7.99

On the Trail of John Muir
Cherry Good
ISBN 0 946487 62 6 PB £7.99

On the Trail of Queen Victoria in the Highlands
Ian R Mitchell
ISBN 0 946487 79 0 PB £7.99

On the Trail of the Pilgrim Fathers
J Keith Cheetham
ISBN 0 946487 83 9 PB £7.99

FOLKLORE

Scotland: Myth, Legend & Folklore
Stuart McHardy
ISBN 0 946487 69 3 PB £7.99

Luath Storyteller: Highland Myths & Legends
George W Macpherson
ISBN 1 84282 003 6 PB £5.00

Tales of the North Coast
Alan Temperley
ISBN 0 946487 18 9 PB £8.99

Tall Tales from an Island
Peter Macnab
ISBN 0 946487 07 3 PB £8.99

The Supernatural Highlands
Francis Thompson
ISBN 0 946487 31 6 PB £8.99

DANCE

The Scottish Wedding Book
G Wallace Lockhart
ISBN 1 94282 010 9 PB £12.99

Fiddles and Folk
G Wallace Lockhart
ISBN 0 946487 38 3 PB £7.95

Highland Balls and Village Halls
G Wallace Lockhart
ISBN 0 946487 12 X PB £6.95

POETRY

Bad Ass Raindrop
Kokumo Rocks
ISBN 1 84282 018 4 PB £6.99

Caledonian Cramboclink: the Poetry of
William Neill
ISBN 0 946487 53 7 PB £8.99

Men and Beasts: wild men & tame animals
Val Gillies & Rebecca Marr
ISBN 0 946487 92 8 PB £15.00

CARTOONS

Broomie Law
Cinders McLeod
ISBN 0 946487 99 5 PB £4.00

FICTION

The Road Dance
John MacKay
ISBN 1 84282 024 9 PB £9.99

Milk Treading
Nick Smith
ISBN 0 946487 75 8 PB £9.99

The Strange Case of RL Stevenson
Richard Woodhead
ISBN 0 946487 86 3 HB £16.99

But n Ben A-Go-Go
Matthew Fitt
ISBN 1 84282 014 1 PB £6.99

But n Ben A-Go-Go
Matthew Fitt
ISBN 0 946487 82 0 HB £10.99

Grave Robbers
Robin Mitchell
ISBN 0 946487 72 3 PB £7.99

The Bannockburn Years
William Scott
ISBN 0 946487 34 0 PB £7.95

The Great Melnikov
Hugh MacLachlan
ISBN 0 946487 42 1 PB £7.95

LANGUAGE

Luath Scots Language Learner [Book]
L Colin Wilson
ISBN 0 946487 91 X PB £9.99

Luath Scots Language Learner [Double Audio CD Set]
L Colin Wilson
ISBN 1 84282 026 5 CD £16.99

Luath Press Limited

committed to publishing well written books worth reading

LUATH PRESS takes its name from Robert Burns, whose little collie Luath (*Gael.*, swift or nimble) tripped up Jean Armour at a wedding and gave him the chance to speak to the woman who was to be his wife and the abiding love of his life. Burns called one of *The Twa Dogs* Luath after Cuchullin's hunting dog in *Ossian's Fingal*. Luath Press grew up in the heart of Burns country, and now resides a few steps up the road from Burns' first lodgings in Edinburgh's Royal Mile.

Luath offers you distinctive writing with a hint of unexpected pleasures.

Most UK and US bookshops either carry our books in stock or can order them for you. To order direct from us, please send a £sterling cheque, postal order, international money order or your credit card details (number, address of cardholder and expiry date) to us at the address below. Please add post and packing as follows: UK – £1.00 per delivery address; overseas surface mail – £2.50 per delivery address; overseas airmail – £3.50 for the first book to each delivery address, plus £1.00 for each additional book by airmail to the same address. If your order is a gift, we will happily enclose your card or message at no extra charge.

ILLUSTRATION: IAN KELLAS

Luath Press Limited
543/2 Castlehill
The Royal Mile
Edinburgh EH1 2ND
Scotland
Telephone: 0131 225 4326 (24 hours)
Fax: 0131 225 4324
email: gavin.macdougall@luath.co.uk
Website: www.luath.co.uk